MUSEUMS FOR THE 1980s

MUSEUMS
for the 1980s

A SURVEY OF WORLD TRENDS

by

Kenneth Hudson

with a foreword by

Georges Henri Rivière
Permanent Adviser to the
International Council of Museums (ICOM)

HM

Holmes & Meier Publishers New York

unesco

First published in the United States of America 1977 by
Holmes & Meier Publishers, Inc.
New York, New York 10003

Library of Congress Cataloging in Publication Data
Hudson, Kenneth.
   Museums for the 1980s

   Bibliography: p.
   Includes index.
   1. Museums.   I. Title.
AM5.H8   1977   069   77–24930
ISBN 0–8419–0327–1

PRINTED IN GREAT BRITAIN

Contents

Foreword

Kenneth Hudson has to his credit several works in a field to which he brings an acutely observing eye and in which he has earned for himself not only listeners and friends but, I might even add accomplices – and, for all that, without in any way suppressing those flashes of wit and that humour that no one would dream of holding against an Englishman.

The book he is presenting here is by no means that definitive treatise on modern museology that has been and must continue to be envisaged in the highest international circles concerned – that is to say, that thorough, interdisciplinary, collective work which is called for and which must inevitably be undertaken one day.

Nevertheless, Kenneth Hudson's book is a critical perspective on the museum of our time and as it is likely to be in the near future. He has approached his task by means of a questionnaire which was addressed to museums in the old and new worlds and has guided an exchange of views with their staff, with the people who frequent their galleries and with the authorities who ultimately control their functioning.

The result is a composite and variegated array of impressions and reactions, yet presented with a logic governed by a regard turned to the past as well as a view towards the future.

I look forward to this work achieving the success that we heartily wish it, one that will advance the cause of the institution we serve. And, who knows, it may well succeed in attracting new devotees who, as Montaigne said of Paris, will come to love the museum 'so tenderly that even its spottes, its blemishes and its wartes' shall become dear unto them.

Georges Henri Rivière
Permanent Adviser to the International
Council of Museums (ICOM)

Acknowledgements

UNESCO and the publishers would like to thank the many people throughout the world who have helped in the preparation of this work, by providing information, personally, by correspondence or by completing questionnaires; suggesting lines of enquiry; or commenting on the draft of the text. Particular gratitude is due to the following:

Mr S. K. Andhare
Prince of Wales Museum of Western
India, Bombay

Mr Frank Atkinson
Director, Open-Air Museum of the
North-East, Beamish

Mrs Smita J. Baxi
Director, Crafts Museum, New Delhi

Mr A. K. Bhattacharyya
Director, Indian Museum, Calcutta

Miss Jacqueline Boël
International Friends of Museums,
Brussels

Mr William A. Bostick
Administrator and Secretary, The
Detroit Institute of Arts

Mr D. M. Boston
Director, The Horniman Museum,
London

Mr Jeffrey Boswall
BBC Natural History Unit, Bristol

Mr M. O. Bulma
Ministry of Culture and Community
Development, Kampala

Mrs Fernanda de Camargo e Almeida
Chairman, ICOM National
Committee, Brazil

Mrs Maria Elisa Carrazzoni
Director, Museum of Fine Art, Rio
de Janeiro

Mr Nathaniel arap Chumo
Wildlife Clubs of Kenya Association,
Nairobi

Father David Clement
Sukuma Museum, Mwanza

Mr Neil Cossons
Director, Ironbridge Gorge Museum
Trust, Telford

Mr Orazio Curti
Director, National Museum of
Science and Technology 'Leonardo
da Vinci', Milan

Dr V. P. Dwivedi
National Museum, New Delhi

Mr Marcel Evrard
Director, Museum of Man and
Industry, Le Creusot

Mr A. Frischknecht
Swiss Technorama Foundation,
Winterthur

Mrs Coral Ordóñez García
National Museum of Anthropology,
Mexico City

Dr Günther Gottman
Deutsches Museum, Munich

Mr Jerzy Jasiuk
Director, National Technical
Museum, Warsaw

Dr Jan Jelinek
Director, Moravian Museum, Brno

Dr A. K. Nazmul Karim
Professor of Sociology, Dacca
University

Dr Pieter Ketner
UNESCO Regional Office of Science
and Technology for Africa, Nairobi

Mr John R. Kinard
Director, Anacostia Neighborhood
Museum, Washington, DC

Dr Josef Kuba
Director, National Technical
Museum, Prague

Mr Lourenço Luis Lacombe
Director, Imperial Museum,
Petropolis

Dr Mackay
National Museum, Nairobi

Dr Jiri Majer
National Technical Museum, Prague

Mr Brian McWilliams
Norwich Castle Museum

Mr Mahmoud Mesallam
formerly Director, Museum of
Science and Technology, Cairo

Mr Biswanath Mukerji
Principal, College of Art, New Delhi

Mr Kwesi Myles
Ghana Museums and Monuments,
Accra

Mr Justice Feroze Nana
Karachi

Mr Samuel Oliver
Director, National Museum of Fine
Art, Buenos Aires

Mrs Ulla Keding Olofsson
Riksutställningar, Stockholm

Mr Paz
National Museum of Fine Arts,
Buenos Aires

Mr Paul Perrot
Assistant Secretary for Museum
Programs, Smithsonian Institution,
Washington, DC

Mr Andrew Pierssené
Norfolk Carnegie Project

Dr Gunnar Pipping
National Technical Museum,
Stockholm

Mr Gerardo Butto Raposo de
Camona
Director, National Historical
Museum, Rio de Janeiro

Mr José de Santiago
Sub-Director, National Museum of
History, Mexico City

Mr Hamo Sassoon
Director, Fort Jesus Museum,
Mombasa

Mr Gunnar Sillén
State Restoration Architect,
Stockholm

Mr Sigvard Strandh
Director, National Technical
Museum, Stockholm

Mrs Nalini Haridas Swali
Secretary, Museum Society of
Bombay

Professor M. Vasquez
Deputy Director, National Museum
of Anthropology, Mexico City

Dr L Vlcskó
Director-General, Hungarian
Agricultural Museum, Budapest

Dr Otfried Wagenbreth
Technical University of Weimar

Mr Alfred Waldis
Director, Swiss Transport Museum,
Lucerne

Miss Elizabeth Wangari
Nairobi National Park

Mr J. A. R. Wembah-Rashid
Director, National Museum of
Tanzania

Dr A. E. Werner
formerly Keeper of Research
Laboratory, British Museum, and
now Director, Pacific Regional
Conservation Centre, Honolulu

The assistance and encouragement given throughout the period of planning and research by the staff of ICOM have been invaluable and greatly appreciated. Without the facilities of the ICOM Documentation Centre and the expert and kindly advice of Georges Henri Rivière, Hugues de Varine-Bohan, Luis Monreal and their colleagues, nothing would have been possible. My particular thanks are due to Raj Isar, of UNESCO, whose advice and suggestions have been invaluable, in a field full of potential international problems and incidents, and to Ann Nicholls, who has supervised the preparation of the manuscript and selection of the photographs through their many stages.

The author would also like to express his gratitude to those officials and friends in many countries who, by providing hospitality and transport on a most generous scale, have made possible the first-hand contacts and gathering of information without which serious errors of judgement would have been inevitable.

The information throughout refers to the situation at the time of writing. Museums, however, like any other type of organisation, are in a constant and highly desirable state of flux and transformation. Staff come and go, deaths regrettably occur and policies are modified. The author feels no obligation to apologise for what is no more than a fact of life, editorially inconvenient as it may be, but he would be grateful if news of any recent changes could be communicated to him.

Introduction

ATTEMPTS TO DEFINE 'MUSEUM'

At the 10th General Conference of the International Council of Museums, held in Copenhagen in 1974, it was made clear that museums throughout the world are coming to regard themselves less and less as self-contained professional units and more and more as cultural centres for the communities within which they operate. One could summarise the change by saying that museums are no longer considered to be merely storehouses or agents for the preservation of a country's cultural and natural heritage, but powerful instruments of education in the broadest sense. What a museum is attempting to achieve has become more important than what it is. This trend, which is unmistakable, makes the definition of a museum increasingly difficult and perhaps increasingly pointless. The rapid increase in new types of museum – technical, scientific, agricultural, ecological, ethnographical – throughout the world has strained the traditional definitions to breaking point. For many years ICOM has tried hard and progressively to define a museum in a way which might be found reasonably satisfactory from Canada to the Congo. It is an unenviable task and, inevitably, the definition has had to be modified from time to time, with a diplomatic phrase added here and an explosive word removed there.

The 1971 version embodies the wisdom developed over many years of argument, conferences and international battles. 'The museum', ICOM suggested, 'is an institution which serves the community. It acquires, preserves, makes intelligible and, as an essential part of its function, presents to the public the material evidence concerning man and nature. It does this in such a way as to provide opportunities for study, education and enjoyment.'

But who, one may reasonably ask, is to decide whether a museum is serving the community or not? What proportion of the community does it have to serve in order to justify its existence? What limits are to be set to such a vague concept as 'the community'? What level of intelligence and education is assumed when the museum attempts to make its collections intelligible?

The museum, as Richard Grove has pointed out, 'is a nearly unique peculiarity. A hospital is a hospital. A library is a library. A rose is a rose. But a museum is Colonial Williamsburg, Mrs. Wilkerson's Figure Bottle Museum, the Museum of Modern Art, the Sea Lion Caves, the American Museum of Natural History, the Barton Museum of Whiskey History, the Cloisters, and Noell's Ark Chimpanzee Farm and Gorilla Show.'[1]

If the word 'museum' is required to cover both the American Museum of Natural History and Mrs Wilkerson's Figure Bottle Museum, it could conceivably have outlived its usefulness. Both institutions might well claim that they were providing 'opportunities for study, education and enjoyment', yet a discriminating observer would almost certainly sense some essential difference between the two. Pressed to say what this difference was, he would probably answer that the American Museum of Natural History was not primarily aiming to make money from the public, whereas Mrs Wilkerson certainly was. He might also add that in the case of Mrs Wilkerson the balance between study, education and enjoyment was unsatisfactory. But who is to say where enjoyment ends and education begins? How can one possibly judge what is going through a museum visitor's mind as he stands gazing at a Giotto or a giraffe?

By 1974 the ICOM definition had been completely overhauled and rebuilt and a number of previous ambiguities removed. According to the Statutes adopted at the 10th General Assembly in that year, a museum is 'a non-profit-making, permanent institution in the service of society and of its development, and open to the public, which acquires, conserves, researches, communicates, and exhibits, for purposes of study, education and enjoyment, material evidence of man and his environment'.

The following are considered to comply with this definition, in addition to museums designated as such:

(a) Conservation institutes and exhibition galleries permanently maintained by libraries and archive centres.

(b) Natural, archaeological, and ethnographic monuments and sites and historical monuments and sites of a museum nature, for their acquisition, conservation and communication activities.

(c) Institutions displaying live specimens, such as botanical and zoological gardens, aquaria, vivaria, etc.

(d) Nature reserves.

(e) Science centres and planetaria.

It is clear from this that a much greater range of institutions now has the right to the name 'museum' than was the case only twenty years ago, but not every museum appears to have the same liberal views as ICOM itself. In 1974–

5, while this very wide definition was in the process of being absorbed and accepted by the museum profession as a whole, the author of the present work invited people throughout the world who were professionally involved in museum work to write down their own brief definition of the word 'museum'. A few avoided the problem by saying that they found the ICOM definition perfectly satisfactory[2] and that they had no modifications to suggest, and others[3] were able to content themselves with their countries' legal definition of a museum. 'In Japan,' we were informed, 'the definition given in Article 2 of Museum Law (Law No. 285 of 1951, revised several times) is used most widely. Some museologists prefer a somewhat different wording, but the import is substantially the same. Therefore, you can safely judge that the word "museum" is defined in Japan according to the above-mentioned Law, as cited below:

'"Museums" as used in this Law shall mean such organs (excluding citizens' public halls under the Social Education Law and the libraries under the Library Law), which have the purpose of collecting, keeping in custody inclusive of fostering, and exhibiting materials concerning history, fine art, ethnic customs, industries, natural science, etc., so that they are offered for public use under educational care, and of conducting necessary business to serve for people's cultural attainments, research, survey, recreation, etc., and of making research and survey pertaining to such materials.'

A number of respondents put the instructional function of the museum first. According to the Director of the Museum of Archaeology in Barcelona, a museum is 'a didactic institution which carries out its task of cultural dissemination by audio-visual techniques which are employed in display areas of various kinds'. The Museum of Folklore and Ethnology at Thessaloniki, Greece, considered a museum to be 'a place where one displays, scientifically and didactically, objects of works of art which produce for the visitor conditions in which he is likely to add to his knowledge'. In Cologne, the Römisch-Germanisches Museum saw its function as 'providing material with which our citizens can educate themselves', and in Nicosia the Cyprus Museum believed its duty was 'to give the museum an educational aspect and make it a research centre'.

The words 'culture' and 'cultural' are much used outside the English-speaking countries in connection with museums and very little within them. The Institution of Conservation and Methodology of Museums in Budapest believes that 'a museum is a cultural institution, performing tasks of collection, research and education'. The Executive of the Association of Museum Curators in Madrid saw a museum as having 'purely cultural aims', and the Bardo National Museum in Tunisia regards itself as 'a cultural and educational centre, reflecting civilisations which have existed in Tunisia'.

The developing countries of the world frequently stress the importance of museums as a means of spreading and reinforcing the national conscious-

Museum of Oxford. A room-setting showing how the room of a Gentleman Commoner at the University might have looked in the late 1770s. The fine panelling is taken from a house in the High Street and is typical of the kind a rich undergraduate bought for his room. The Oxford colleges encouraged students to have their rooms panelled, and refunded two-thirds of the cost. The young gentlemen borrowed furniture from home to furnish their rooms, or bought it from their predecessors for two-thirds of the original price.

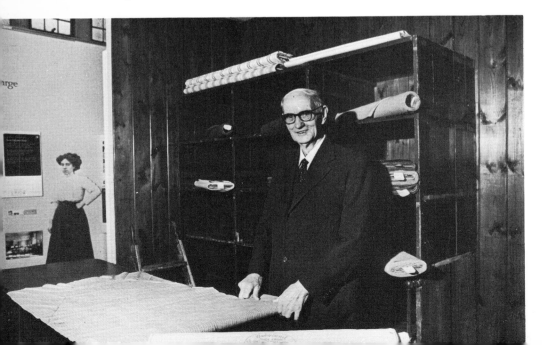

Museum of Oxford, England. A corner of Cape's store, Oxford. The photograph shows 82-year-old Mr Charles Francis behind a counter which was taken from the shop in 1972, shortly before the building was demolished. The fabrics on the shelves are similar to those sold by Mr Francis, who worked at Cape's for 54 years.

Sukuma Museum, Mwanza, Tanzania. The Boo 'Isolo' game. Many visitors come to the Museum in order to learn to play this traditional African game.

Sukuma Museum, Mwanza. A Mqanza (healer) demonstrates to visitors his method of killing a hen in order to consult the entrails.

ness or, as they often express it, the national culture. In such new states as Ghana or Tanzania, the word 'culture' has a powerful emotive force. To be independent is to assert the vigour and autonomy of one's own culture and it is unthinkable that museums, schools, newspapers or any other means of public enlightenment would think or act differently. 'Culture', in such a context, is both the accumulated traditions of the national territory and the basis of all Government policy and planning.

The Anglo-Saxon countries tend to avoid the word 'culture', except in a scientific or ethnological sense, and to be somewhat embarrassed by it. Most of the rest of the world, however, uses the term easily and naturally enough, although not always with a great deal of precision. 'Culture' undoubtedly varies in meaning from country to country and for that reason it is a word to be used with great caution. ICOM has

acted prudently in omitting it from its current definition of a museum. It was, however, still in use in 1951, when the Executive Committee decided that ICOM would recognise as a museum 'any permanent institution which conserves and displays, for purposes of study, education and enjoyment, collections of objects of cultural or scientific significance'. Nowadays, the definition very wisely plays down 'culture' which can and often does have élitist, political-theological and nationalistic overtones, and emphasises instead 'community'.

The aim of 'serving the community' brings problems of its own. Any institution which consciously and deliberately sets out to do this will necessarily find itself compelled to find some means of measuring its success. It will have to discover, as a continuous process, what its customers think about the goods being offered to them. The community museum is unavoidably involved in market research. The old-style autocratic museum, of which many still survive, was under no such obligation. But merely to monitor the results of what one has already done is inadequate and uncreative. The true skill of any form of market research, and that practised in museums is no exception, lies first in asking the right questions and second in using one's findings to produce something which is closer to what the customer really wants. Monitoring by itself is of no great value.

During the past twenty-five years especially, the museum-going public has changed a great deal, and it is still changing. Its range of interests has widened, it is far less reverent and respectful in its attitudes, it expects to find electronic and other modern technical facilities adequately used, it distinguishes less and less between a museum and an exhibition, it considers the intellect to be no more prestigious or respectable than the emotions, and it sees no reason to pay attention to the subject-division and specialisms which are so dear to academics. This is a reflection of a fundamental change in thought and behaviour throughout the world, and in all fields of activity. People are no longer content to have their lives run for them dictatorially by a few powerful and privileged people. They are increasingly demanding a say in the planning and the organisation.

It remains true, however, that a museum is essentially an institution in which objects – a better phrase, perhaps, is 'real things' – are the principal means of communication. Dr Alma S. Wittlin uses this fact in order to arrive at what one might call a negative definition of museums.[4]

Establishments [she says] in which objects are not used at all, or are not used as main carriers of messages, are not museums, whatever their qualities may be otherwise. A place in which people are exposed to changing lights or to a galaxy of light and sound unrelated to objects may offer a new kind of symphony or a carnival, according to its quality, but it is not a museum. If a few objects provided by a museum or by any source are used in a club or a recreation centre among other items on the programme, such as dancing or discussions of current problems and of vocational opportunities, the place still retains its identity. The term museum is neither better nor worse than the term club or centre. We dim the outlook on our goals if we instil terms with connotations of borrowed status. . . .

There is considerable scope for a combination of objects with other media, with brief motion pictures illustrating a single concept or with appropriately designed (and not overdesigned) suitably sized and placed graphics, but objects have to remain the stars of the cast.

Few museologists would disagree with this, but in order to accept Dr Wittlin's theory completely one has to define 'object' in a wider sense than many people feel to be reasonable. Can a living plant or fish or animal be reasonably termed an object, without straining the ordinary use of language? Is it carrying empire-building too far to call a botanical garden, a zoo or an aquarium or, for that matter, a library a museum? A library certainly contains objects and it might well be described as a museum of books, but it somehow seems more sensible to continue to call it a library.

Zoos and aquaria are, perhaps, borderline cases, but ICOM and Dr Wittlin might find themselves in greater difficulties with the San Francisco Museum of Conceptual Art, which describes itself as functioning on two levels, 'as a storehouse and library for documentation of events and happenings and conceptual projects from all over the world, but primarily as a place where these may take place and be witnessed'. There are, either fortunately or

Visitors learning how to handle a snake at the Snake Park, National Museum, Nairobi, Kenya.

regrettably, no patent rights attached to the world 'museum'. The most unworthy and incongruous institution is free to describe itself as a museum, despite the attempts made in many countries to establish some kind of official criterion. In the United States, for instance, the American Museums Association has set up a system of accreditation. In order to be approved in this way a museum has to meet three requirements – it must have a permanent collection, it must have a professional staff and it must take proper pains to display its material to the public. Yet, ironically, it is perfectly possible for a dull museum to receive accreditation and a lively one to be denied it.

In a period of rapid and fundamental social change it is natural and highly desirable that those in charge of museums should ask themselves with some frequency such questions as 'Why does this museum exist? How relevant is it to the needs and conditions of the society in which it exists? What, things being as they are, is its main task? How do I measure its success?' The public answers to these questions are not, of course, always the same as the private answers and many of the statements made by museologists in published articles and at international conferences need to be interpreted with some skill, and with considerable knowledge of the countries in which these experts operate.

There is some pressure within American society and increasingly elsewhere, too, which makes it difficult to make a public statement in simple,

straightforward language. Museologists are all too likely to produce such unhelpful sentences as: 'The affectable changes in attitude and involvement by museum visitors, as a result of integrated museum experience, is observable within the museum environment' The urge to grade-up one's utterances by weaving in sociological jargon is difficult to resist, and the result is often a totally misleading impression of the person or institution concerned. No museum could be less pompous or academic than the Brooklyn Children's Museum in New York, yet a member of its staff found it possible to define a museum as 'a facility devoted to the preservation and promotion of the cultural arts and sciences through the use of specific resources that generally are not maintained in the course of daily events or used within the context of daily routine', phrases which do not suggest the lively, original Brooklyn Children's Museum at all.

Many museums see their prime function as that of preserving the relics of the past. The National Museum of Denmark, for instance, considers itself to be 'an institution for assembling material evidence of the past for display to the present and conservation in the future'. The Vatican Museums believe that a museum is 'a place intended for the preservation and display of unwritten testimonies of the past'. Few museums nowadays would find it either possible or politic to place such a strong emphasis on preserving the achievements of the past. In India, on the other hand, there is a widespread feeling that the museums of that country are far too concerned with ancient history and that the generation which has grown up since Independence is much more anxious to be informed about what has been happening in more recent years. The Ministry of Education has devoted much money and thought to producing well-written school textbooks on social studies and modern history and it would like to see this new kind of teaching, which has started in the classrooms, reflected and continued in museums. In its campaign to divert attention from the past, the Ministry is giving all the support it can to the teaching of science and technology, and it considers that museums have an important part to play in this.

Brooklyn Children's Museum, New York. Dance class for children.

The official Chinese attitude to history, whether inside or outside museums, has not always been easy to understand. At one point there was a strongly marked tendency to decry and even to reject the traditional culture, and Western visitors were surprised by such experiences as being taken round a pottery which had been operating for more than six hundred years and being told that it had produced nothing of any value or interest before 1949. This appeared particularly strange to one visitor, who felt that the current output of the pottery was in no way to be compared with what had been made there previously.

It is not easy for a developing country, which must always be conscious that time is not on its side, to show the regard for history and tradition which, ideally, one might hope to see. If, for political reasons, the past is viewed in a selective fashion or if certain features in the country's history are exaggerated to an unjustified extent, the task of some museum curators may become difficult or even impossible. The problem is a complicated one, especially in the case of museums which are concerned with history and ethnography. There may, for instance, be no agreed or acceptable guidelines as to the history of the country as a whole, but there can, within the same country, be a strong consensus of opinion on the history of a particular region or a particular period.

The National Museum in Ghana

takes a view which one hopes will work out satisfactorily in practice. 'A museum', it says, 'is an institution which acquires, preserves and presents material to the public, not for profit, but for their information and enjoyment. The museum should take the interest of all sections of its community into consideration; it should highlight some of the current topical subjects in the community, such as agriculture, health and politics. It should not acquire everything, but should encourage the community to cherish its culture.'

'Current topical subjects' are not easy to handle within a museum context, often because of philosophical and political disagreements within the local or national community. In many, perhaps most, countries there is no problem. Certain subjects are known to be of public importance and there is general acceptance of the broad lines of presentation. Elsewhere, however – and this is true of most Western countries – highly topical and socially important matters can be so controversial that museum directors can be excused from fighting shy of them. This can show itself in curious ways. In East Berlin, for instance, there is the excellent Museum of German History. Such a museum is possible, because the German Democratic Republic has an agreed philosophy of history. Contemporary events can therefore be reflected in temporary exhibitions, in the sure knowledge that the past and the present will not find themselves in conflict. There is, however, no really comparable national Museum of German History in the Federal Republic, or for that matter in France, England or the United States, because in these countries there is no common agreement on the interpretation of the nation's history.

National Museum, Peking, People's Republic of China. Modern horizontal design overlaid with reproductions of historically significant forms.

Yeh S'ing Village, near Juichin, Kiangsi Province, People's Republic of China. An early guerrilla centre; the entire village is preserved as a national memorial. The house in the picture was lived in by Mao Tse-tung.

Museum of German History, Berlin, GDR. Reconstruction of hut interior at concentration camp.

A Chinese museum finds no difficulty whatever in arranging a special exhibition on the necessity and methods of birth control. An American or Belgium museum would almost certainly find itself unable to do so. On the other hand, the Museum of the City of New York experienced no serious problems in devoting part of its space, in the spring of 1974, to an exhibition illustrating the dangers and treatment of venereal disease, since no citizens and taxpayers in New York would be likely to come forward to state that venereal disease was a desirable feature of society, which should be officially encouraged.

One can sense throughout the world, however, two developments of great importance to museums. One is a growing feeling that the past and the present shade off into one another and that a sensitivity to the achievements of the past can be a great help towards understanding the present. The second notable change, compared with twenty or thirty years ago, is a willingness to accept the fact that museums can be appreciated emotionally and sensually as well as intellectually. This is, as yet, best understood, perhaps, in art museums. 'Today's museum', says the Museum of Fine Art in Rio de Janeiro, 'is a place in which visitors acquire experiences and receive impressions which stimulate their powers of thought and their creative ability.' The Royal Scottish Museum, in Edinburgh, speaks of 'using objects made by man or produced by nature' to 'enrich the human experience'. 'Experience', nevertheless, is a word that should be used with considerable care. It can easily degenerate into a jargon term, behind which it is all too easy for the lazy or woolly-minded curator to shelter.

Museum of the City of New York. Special exhibition on the history, extent and effects of venereal disease. The photograph shows Betty Maingot, one of the Museum's guides, with some of the exhibits.

Ironbridge Gorge Museum, Shropshire, England. The driver of the steam colliery winding engine demonstrates its operation to a school party.

Old Sturbridge Village, Massachusetts, USA. A young visitor tries his hand at threshing corn with a flail.

THE CHANGING CONCEPT OF A MUSEUM'S FUNCTION

To emphasise 'experience' can, however, lead a museum a very long way from traditional methods of display, and force it to realise, however unwillingly, that it is in the communication business. It is dangerous and ridiculous, even so, to become enthusiastic about 'communication' without having a clear idea as to what one is trying to communicate or why or to whom. Merely to 'communicate' is as absurd a concept as to 'love' or to 'believe'. Another fashionable museum word, 'participation', is often used in the same loose and largely meaningless way.

There were examples of this regrettable modern tendency to allow the heart to conquer the head at a seminar held in 1967 at the Museum of the City of New York. In the course of the proceedings, Dr Marshall McLuhan expressed a characteristically exaggerated and provocative view, when he attacked what he described as 'the story-line approach' – using artifacts to illustrate a story or theme. He praised Expo 67 on the grounds that it was the first world's fair to have no story-line whatever. It was, he said, 'just a mosaic of discontinuous items in which people took an immense satisfaction precisely *because* they weren't being told anything about the overall pattern or shape of it, but they were free to discover and participate and involve themselves in the total overall thing. The result was that they never got fatigued.'[5]

During the seminar, the general outline of the 'participating' museum emerged. It would ask the visitor questions, rather than give him answers. It would encourage visitors to touch objects. It would give equal value to understanding through the ear and understanding through the eye. It would assume that communication was both complex and untidy, that the person 'who lives in an oral world, that is, where the primary method of communication is by mouth to ear, lives at the centre of a sphere where communication comes into him simultaneously from all sides, banging at him'.

Dr McLuhan's ideas of what a museum can and should do are clearly very different from those current in the museum world thirty or forty years ago. They are possible only as a result of new electronic tools and they illustrate how museums need to be continually redefined, within the context of new technical resources and new social demands.

Museums were a product of the Renaissance, a product of an aristocratic and hierarchical society which believed that art and scholarship were for a closed circle. In Europe and in most colonial territories, museums and art galleries began at a time when the people who controlled them had a contempt for the masses. Collections were formed by men who wished to display them to others with the same tastes and the same level of knowledge as themselves, to connoisseurs and scholars. Any idea that there might be a duty to make this material interesting or intelligible to a wider range of visitors would have seemed ludicrous.

In the seventeenth century only distinguished travellers and foreign scholars were, as a rule, permitted to see the collections belong to the European princes, which were often housed in the palaces themselves. A similar attitude controlled visits to the botanical gardens. After 1700 the general public was admitted to the Imperial Gallery in Vienna on payment of a fee and there were similar opportunities in Rome, at the Quirinal Palace, and in Madrid, at the Escorial. On the other hand, the pictures belonging to the French monarchy remained inaccessible to the public until half-way through the eighteenth century when, as a result of petitions, about a hundred paintings were hung in the Luxembourg Palace, where the public could see them on two days a week. At one time England had a particularly bad name for the secrecy and possessiveness of her collectors. The wealthy English, who bought widely in Italy and other continental countries throughout the seventeenth and eighteenth centuries, had little feeling that their collections might, as cultural assets, belong to the nation or to Europe as a whole and that it was irresponsible to prevent other people from enjoying them. Some, at least, of the German courts took a more generous and progressive view. The gallery at Dresden, for example, could be viewed without difficulty from 1746 onwards.

When public museums, such as the British Museum, were established in Europe at the end of the century, they carried on the traditions of the private collections. They might belong to the state, or to a body of trustees, but they were as exclusive and élitist as their predecessors. They were run by autocrats, who asked for nobody's advice as to how the collections should be presented or organised. Visitors were admitted as a privilege, not as a right, and consequently gratitude and admiration, not criticism, was required of them.

But, in any case, the language in which criticism could be expressed took a long time to develop. To bring together into, say, Arundel House in London works of art from Italy, Germany, the Netherlands, Greece and the Middle East was to transform them into something artificial and different. The museum, an entirely European development, removes the picture or sculpture from its original, meaningful context and compels the visitor to see it as an isolated abstraction, a work of art. To analyse and describe it in terms of this new concept demanded a fresh attitude, a different kind of expertise and a specialised phraseology.

The point has been well made by André Malraux. 'A Romanesque crucifix', he reminds us, 'was not regarded by its contemporaries as a work of sculpture, nor Cimabue's "Madonna" as a picture. Even Pheidias' "Pallas Athene" was not, primarily, a statue.'[6] Similarly, African cult objects and tribal regalia lose one dimension and gain another when they are transferred to a museum, although this can be avoided if the museologist and designer are sensitive to the culture of the country in question and are determined to create a museum context which reflects it. In its original functional setting, a painting or a piece of sculpture contributes to a mood of relaxation and reflection, which makes contemplation possible. Put into a gallery, it has to compete with other works, in an atmosphere which is neutral, if not actually hostile to it. An art gallery, as Malraux rightly points out, 'is as preposterous as would be a concert in which one listened to a programme of ill-assorted pieces following in unbroken succession'. In such a situation, our approach to art has grown steadily more intellectualised. Deprived of the opportunity to exercise what were once relevant emotions, we can interpret only through our brains.

This is true of all types of museum. A machine becomes a dead artifact once it is torn from its natural habitat and put on show in a building which neither looks nor smells like a factory or workshop. A stuffed tiger in a museum is a stuffed tiger in a museum, not a tiger. An illuminated codex loses most

Brooklyn Children's Museum, New York. Children playing on the aerial bridge. The bridge, 52 feet high, is one of several ways in which children can reach the rooftop park of the Museum.

of its significance once it is removed from the monastery where it belonged. It is no accident that museums have become temples of scholarship. The scholar responds with his brain, not with his feelings. But the majority of visitors to museums are not scholars or intellectuals, a fact which the museum world has taken a remarkably long time to realise.

The growth of connoisseurship during the eighteenth and nineteenth centuries inevitably made ordinary people feel inferior when faced with what had now become works of art. So long as a religious picture or statue or monstrance remained in a church it belonged to everyone and had meaning for everyone. Once it was moved into a museum, a different set of values began to operate. Museums, unlike churches, have a remarkable power of making the uneducated feel inferior.

Not all art is meant to be regarded in a spirit of reverence, a truth which often escapes art-historians and art-critics. To stand near the display of Picassos in New York's Museum of Modern Art and to eavesdrop on the earnest conversations which surround even the painter's most frolicsome and light-hearted canvases is to become aware of the leaden feet on which scholarship can make its way.

By the end of the eighteenth century, art, like literature, formed part of the pattern of life, the sub-culture, which most of those strolling round a gallery or reading a poem shared, and which a clerk, a washerwoman or a mechanic did not share. Museums devoted to things other than the arts were in a different situation. There was no agreed taste relating to stuffed birds, no connoisseurship of Pacific island weapons or costumes. Potentially, at least, the non-art museums were more democratic, a fact which is of great importance in understanding the traditions of the American museum. The pattern of museum growth in America has been exactly the opposite of what occurred in Europe. In France, Germany, England and the other European countries private collections came first and public museums developed from them. In America, on the other hand, public

museums were in existence long before the great private collections began to be formed. During the present century many private American collections have been bequeathed to museums or transformed into public institutions, so reproducing a process which had been noticeable in Europe more than a century earlier. By this time, however, the American idea of a museum established for the benefit of the whole community had struck deep roots.

The pioneering museums, Charleston (1793), the Peale Museum (1782) and Salem (1799), grew up, as most early museums did, in a completely disorderly, unplanned way. Yet, as the reminiscences of visitors make clear, this old-fashioned chaos had, and still has a strong appeal for children and unsophisticated adults, for whom a museum was essentially a chamber of wonders, a romantic place which scientific arrangement could only spoil. It is a debatable point which kind of museum the visitor finds most frustrating and exhausting – the small, crowded, poorly lit museum in which he has to do very little walking but a great deal of peering, adjustment and identification, or the large, orderly museum, where everything is scientifically regimented and clearly labelled, but where room passes into room in an apparently endless sequence, an impossible challenge both to the mind and the feet.

THE POPULARISATION OF MUSEUMS

What changed the relationship between museums and the public in a fundamental way was not the insight of museologists or the enterprise of curators, but a long succession of international exhibitions,[7] begun by the Great Exhibition in London in 1851. These exhibitions benefited museums by giving them a social importance and a political power that they never had before. They attracted very large numbers of visitors of all classes, and they compelled governments to realise that the sciences and the useful arts were the proper concern of the community as a whole. Formal learning – scholarship – and social needs were brought closer together and the definition of culture was considerably, if belatedly and inadequately, broadened. The international exhibitions were, of course, commercial enterprises, but their importance extended far beyond mere business success. As T. R. Adams has said, 'they opened the way for the renaissance of the modern museum in terms of dramatic displays relevant to the social life of the community'.[8] Not that all museums followed this example. Many of them remained as stiff and dull as if these immensely popular exhibitions had never existed. But the climate within which museums operated had changed.

North of England Open-Air Museum, Beamish. (above) The Visible Stores, which visitors can see through a glass-panelled wall. This makes a virtue of necessity. A museum has to have storage and there is no reason to conceal it. To be allowed to look inside anyone's store-cupboard is exciting. A secret door has been opened.

(below) A group of blind people learning about the Museum's collections by touch.

method of lighting, and the death-like stillness that reigns'.[9]

'The primary purpose and function of a museum and its exhibits is to educate', wrote Lothar P. Witteborg of the American Museum of Natural History in 1958[10] The task of the curator and designer was to achieve 'a meaningful presentation which tells a story'. By no means everyone today would agree with these assumptions. Is 'telling a story' the best way of achieving 'meaningful presentation'? Are people who have become accustomed to the impressionistic methods of television and the cinema willing to accept the established learning tradition of moving in an orderly and logical sequence from one piece of information to the next? Why should a museum put such an enormous emphasis on acquiring information? Is 'education' totally unconnected with attitudes and emotions? Are the only reputable thoughts those which are based on 'scientific research'? Is it right, or possible, for museums to attempt to control visitors' responses? There is a certain touching arrogance in the belief that one can select, arrange and present objects in a museum in such a way that everyone who sees them should and will respond in a prescribed and guaranteed manner. Fortunately for humanity, they will not.

One can, of course, hope to condition visitors' emotions without wishing to determine which facts they absorb or in what pattern. In 1815 Ludwig I of Bavaria engaged the fashionable, if misguided, architect Wittelsbach to design him a new sculpture gallery in which there should be a calculated splendour, 'which could communicate to the observer the concept of reverence which should be paid to the masterpieces of antiquity'. This was not to be a didactic museum. Atmosphere was more important than facts.

MUSEUMS AND 'EDUCATION'

It is only comparatively recently, however, that it has become generally respectable to regard education and pleasure as closely linked, both for children and for adults. This change in attitude will be discussed later – it is of immense importance to museological thinking – and here one may perhaps content oneself with the observation that puritanism has had a long run for its money in museums. The educational mission of most of the men who founded and directed museums during the second half of the nineteenth century had a sternly disciplined and almost religious flavour to it. Their museums were temples of self-improvement, which made few concessions to human weakness and which were 'places so cold and repelling in their nature that, if a person have the hardihood to enter them, he cannot fail to be struck by the chilling nature of their contents, the unsatisfactory

In both France and Germany, nineteenth-century museums were often founded in order to encourage patriotic feelings. It is easy to smile at the seriousness with which the Germans in particular took their museums last century. Museums were a spearhead of nationalism, display points of glorious tradition, opportunities to condition the minds of the public. At an exhibition held in the Zeughaus, Berlin, in 1844 visitors were guided along a predetermined route through its galleries, so that they should see everything in the correct order and miss nothing. The design of the building made it difficult to achieve this by means of notices, doors and corridors, so that movement in the correct direction was ensured by spoken or shouted commands, in orthodox Prussian military fashion.

The idea that museum visitors can be trusted to educate themselves and all a public body can do is to provide opportunities for this process to take place was, in general, more typical of America than of Europe during the nineteenth and early twentieth centuries, but in recent years American museums have shown signs of abandoning their faith in 'open' education and of relying increasingly on more formal programmes, either independently or in collaboration with schools and colleges.

It is evident that, in all countries, there are two distinct breeds of people. One is driven on by a desire to teach, to instruct, to improve, and the other by a need to entertain, to please. Each type of motivation can become a self-defeating obsession. The teacher who believes that education is a serious, even grim business, characterised by unceasing toil and an indifference to pleasure or social comfort, is as dangerous a person as the public entertainer who sees the emotions as all-important. Museums, like schools, swing backwards and forwards between these two extremes. Before 1914, the educators were almost certainly in a majority among museum curators and directors, but since then the distinction between education and entertainment has become much less sharply marked.

The change has not been to everyone's taste and its pace has varied considerably from country to country. The Victorians had a remarkable capacity for feeling guilty about enjoying themselves. For their peace of mind and eventual salvation they needed to discover a serious purpose behind what might otherwise be considered mere amusement or self-indulgence. The new countries are almost equally puritanical and a similar attitude is to be found within the Socialist countries, where the State museums are, at least in theory, totally integrated into the educational system. In practice, however, the visitor is likely to discover a number of surprises, especially away from the major cities. But, whether in Poland, Cuba, China or Libya, the notion that museums are places in which to while away a wet afternoon not unpleasantly would not be very common.

In the Socialist countries it is accepted that culture is an entity, in which every citizen has a share. Culture includes everything that human beings do, make and think. It cannot be fragmented and it is not a veneer laid on the top of everyday existence. Since, by definition, a museum is a cultural institution, it cannot be irrelevant or unimportant within a Socialist society. Many people who work in Western countries are envious of this situation. They would like to feel that their museum had an agreed, definite function. Nowadays, and whatever the position may have been fifty or a hundred years ago, they are not content for their museum to exist, to be well stocked and well arranged, and to provide them with an adequate living. They want it to be for something, and from this point of view the integrated, purposeful Socialist museum can be seen as very attractive. 'On the whole,' Alma Wittlin has said,[11] 'the European museum is an ill-adjusted and in many cases a functionless institution. This fact is revealed both by the attitude to museums of the public, which is in fact supposed to benefit from them, and by the views of experts. The public is indifferent to museums.'

Museums, like other goods and services, have been sold very hard in America and, if the number of visitors is the only yardstick of success, with excellent results. In America and elsewhere, too, one can be permitted, perhaps, the suspicion that the purposeful visitor has a higher prestige and makes the staff feel happier than the person who simply strolls around. A more tolerant view is that of that very great curator, Molly Harrison, the creator of the Geffrye Museum in London, who was not burdened with the frenetic and puritanical qualities which have become sadly common within the museum field. 'Museums', she believed, 'are meeting places, not only for dating on a wet Sunday afternoon, but in more subtle ways. Here values meet; those of the specialist are rubbed against those of the public, children's interests compete with those of adults, the protection of rare objects vies with their display, the individual visitor's concern may be the very opposite of that of the group, whether adult or child.'[12]

In 1888 Mr G. Brown Goode told the American Historical Association that 'an efficient educational museum may be described as a collection of instructive labels, each illustrated by a well-selected specimen'. Such a museum would have exceedingly little appeal for the general public. It would be a filing-cabinet for specialists. Most people do not divide their interests into subject-compartments and they do not regard their lives as a period of preparation for an unknown examination. 'Education' means quite different things to scholars and professionals and to the general public, and, before one can decide how well or how badly a museum is carrying out its 'educational function', one must ask 'whose education'? Many museologists and educationists fail to do this. They assume that there is an absolute concept called 'education', and the results of their criticism can be both sterile and ridiculous.

THE MUSEUM-GOING PUBLIC

The public, as a homogeneous unit, does not exist, and it is a waste of time to search for it or to attempt to cater for its needs. For museums, as for libraries, concerts and airlines, there are many publics, each made up of individuals with approximately similar interests, abilities, backgrounds and temperaments. To meet the precise requirements of every member of every group is clearly impossible. What is more reasonable is to try to identify a few important motives for visiting a museum and then to do one's best to arrange the museum in such a way as to satisfy these motives.

The Director of the National Museum of Ethnology at Leiden, in the Netherlands, has distinguished three motives,[13] each of which makes particular demands on the way in which the museum displays its material. The aesthetic approach 'requires a well-thought out presentation, which uses a quiet but neutral background to do justice to a limited number of objects of

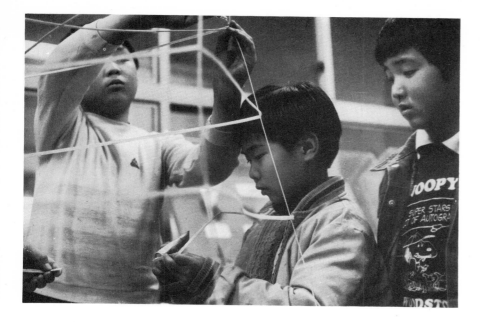

National Science Museum, Tokyo. Children working in one of the Museum's workshop groups, where scientific principles are absorbed through practical experiments.

artistic value, arranged in the most effective way possible'. The romantic or escapist approach 'requires that a series of pieces that are interesting for purely human reasons be presented in such a way that they, as it were, invite participation or identification with the society that they represent. In such a setting the human figure should be present, and it should be portrayed as realistically as possible'. The intellectual approach, 'the wish to satisfy a certain thirst for knowledge', demands 'a schematic arrangement which almost literally takes the visitor by the hand and leads him step by step from one suggestion or conclusion to another'.

Most museum directors are aware, at least in a vague way, that their visitors fall into something like these three categories and realise the great difficulty of pleasing and satisfying all three at the same time. In the course of preparing the present work, it has been valuable to study the replies given by a wide range of museums to three questions:

1. Which types of museum do you feel to be particularly valuable for your country at the present time?
2. What do you see as your most important tasks at the present time?
3. By what techniques are you endeavouring to make your museum more attractive, more accessible?

From this, and other evidence, it is clear that, within the museum field, fundamental and creative thinking is more widespread, and probably more

encouraged, in some countries than in others. The practical results of thinking and planning will be discussed in detail in subsequent chapters, but at this stage it seems useful to draw attention to certain broad tendencies.

NEW DEVELOPMENTS IN MUSEUM ORGANISATION

The first is a growing interest in 'museums without walls', community museums and eco-museums. The National Science Museum in Tokyo belives that museums of this kind are urgently needed in Japan, for two reasons:

(a) The previous concept of museum collections, as objects cut away from their natural environment, is completely inadequate in to-day's society.

(b) Preservation of the human environment is a global problem. Unless this is thought about internationally and apart from the conditions of particular countries, human existence may become impossible in the future. On the other hand, this is also a problem of individual citizens, and each individual must construct his own idea of the human environment through personal experience. A museum devoted to the preservation of the environment must be directly linked with the local community and managed by the local community.

The implication here is that the days of the museum as a self-contained institution, as a storehouse of wonders or as a temple of the arts are numbered. The museum of the future, or perhaps one should say one kind of museum of the future, will be a means of helping people to become aware of the past, present and future of the area in which they live. The emphasis will be on residents, rather than visitors, and the distinction between what people have in their homes and what happens at that time to be in the museum will be very fluid. A museum of this type – Anacostia, in Washington, is an indication of how it might be organised – might well have no permanent collections in the conventional sense, yet it would be something more than an exhibition. The right word to describe it has probably still to be found, but, if it could be rid of the élitist associations with which it is cursed in the Anglo-Saxon world, 'cultural centre' might do quite well. Suppose, for instance, that what is now known as the Sukuma Museum, near Mwanza, in Tanzania, were to be called the Sukuma Cultural Centre instead? Established over the past twenty years by the Catholic Society of St Cecilia, under the leadership and inspiration of a Canadian priest, Father David Clement, the Museum has devoted itself to preserving and encouraging the traditional culture of the Sukuma tribe, the largest in Tanzania. This task has been accomplished – or, perhaps it would be more accurate to say, is being accomplished – in three ways: by setting up a permanent body, a Cultural Research Committee; by arranging an exhibition of traditional artifacts in four pavilions; and by organising a school of Tanzanian handicrafts and a group of dancers who perform the Sukuma dances to a very high standard. The whole project, and indeed all the work of the St Cecilia Society, is seen as an integrated unit, the aim being to help the Sukuma people to adapt their old skills, customs

Sukuma Museum. Museum office, built in the traditional local style.

and traditions to the modern world. No purely static museum, no collection of objects could achieve this on its own, no matter how brilliant the methods of presentation might be. To be effective, the Museum must be a place where activities take place, as well as somewhere where artifacts are preserved. For such a concept, 'museum' seems an inadequate description. 'Cultural Centre' seems more satisfactory.

In Ghana this particular nettle has been firmly grasped. The National Cultural Centre, covering an area of about 120 acres, in the centre of Kumasi, has been designed as a national park, 'to provide for rest and recreation and to reflect and promote the cultural heritage of Ghana'.[14] Its complex includes a folk museum, built to the pattern of a chief's palace; an exhibition gallery for works by contemporary artists; an open-air theatre and dance arena; a gallery and shop for displaying and selling handicrafts; a reconstructed village, with a shrine, cocoa farm, poultry farm, zoo, children's adventure playground; and a restaurant where local dishes can be eaten.

'The Centre', says its 1972 Report, 'already bustles, apart from visiting artistes and guests, with the practices and performances of its own cultural clubs and societies – a choir, drama group, modern dancing club, and not less than twenty traditional dance groups, representing the various ethnic areas of Ghana.' At Kumasi, as at Mwanza, the object has been to interest and involve the people as a whole, to show that the national heritage is a company in which everyone holds shares. It is not easy to decide to what extent the National Museums in their respective countries approve of what is being achieved at these outspokenly popular institutions, and one suspects a certain amount of unease at the ratio of showmanship to scholarship. This suspicion and perhaps fear is not peculiar to the developing countries of the world. It is very much a reality in, for example, France, the Soviet Union and the United States, where the firmly-established, scholarly breed of museum director and curator has shown itself quick to criticise forms of popularisation which could be regarded as threats to the *status quo*.

'Today', reported a 1970 article in *Museum*,[15]

some museums, many of them regional and especially in the United States, are calling themselves art centres. They possess few, if any, permanent collections and do little scholarly research. Instead they arrange travelling or especially organised loan exhibitions and frequently offer concerts, films, plays, dance programmes and other performing arts activities. Thoughtful critics have wondered whether these museums, in ceasing to be 'the attics of civilization', go too far in exhibiting masterpieces of painting for charity drives or balls and in popularizing capsule displays such as *Isn't Science Fun?* or *Five Minutes of American History*. If a museum thus abdicates its educational function and instead merely entertains, it will not last for long. The converse is equally true. The museum which tries to educate without entertaining has little future either.

Sukuma Museum. Dance troupe in Copenhagen on an overseas tour (1973). This particular dance shows how the Sukuma sift their grain, while singing and dancing.

But, as we have already indicated, the dividing line between entertainment and education is very thin and increasingly unreal. The same article in *Museum* points out, quite rightly, that 'the cultural activity of a community suffers when the performing arts and arts centres are considered "living" and the already established museums and galleries "dead"'. It notes with approval that museum adult education programmes in Africa and South-East Asia 'are made highly palatable by association with performances of traditional music, drama and dance The Sunday gamelan concerts in the Djakarta Museum, for example, lure throngs of delighted Indonesians into the museum.'

Using artistic performances in order to 'lure throngs of delighted Indonesians', Ghanaians, Tanzanians and other peoples into museums seems now to be a well-accepted practice, although there are still those, especially in the major national museums, who believe strongly that museums are essentially serious-minded places for serious-minded people, and that all this new-fangled enjoyment amounts almost to singing drunken songs in church.

Another rapidly developing trend is to take museum activities to the people, rather than to bring the people to the museum. This can be done physically, by means of trailers fitted out as mobile museums, or electronically, by using television. Either method demands a staff of considerable adaptability and resourcefulness, anxious to establish contact with ordinary people and to use museum material to arouse an interest in science, archaeology, natural history or whatever the theme of the exhibition or programme may be. But, as we shall show later, the important aspect of what we term 'taking the museum to the people' is not the mechanical achievement, considerable as that may be, but the revolution in museological and social attitude which it represents. To project the museum in this way is to put one's emphasis on using objects and collections, instead of merely possessing and preserving them, to be concerned with the public reaction to them. A mobile museum or a television presentation is a symbol of a new concept of what the relationship between the museum and the world outside it should be.

At the end of July 1975, India began a year-long experiment to use a communications satellite made available by the Americans to beam television programmes directly into 2400 remote villages. This project, the first in the world to broadcast television programmes regularly from space, was given the name of SITE (Satellite Instructional Television Experiment). A centre at Ahmedabad sends programmes to the satellite for re-transmission all over the Indian continent. The signals are caught by cheap aerial dishes made of wire netting – chicken-wire – placed on the rooftop of a central building in the village, usually a school-house or a community centre. A converter feeds the signals into Indian-built 24-inch television receivers – made especially rugged, to withstand heat, dust and vandalism – around which the villagers sit in the evening in order to view and to learn. The programmes carry information on matters of vital importance to rural India – agricultural techniques, nutrition and birth control – as well as local and national news and entertainment. The total cost of equipping each village has been only £250.

The organisation has been on a scale previously believed to be impossible in India. In each village one person has been appointed to be responsible for the

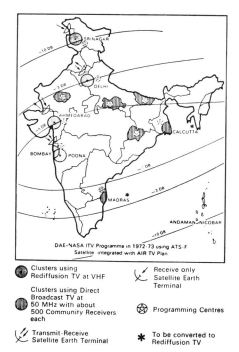

Clusters using Rediffusion TV at VHF

Clusters using Direct Broadcast TV at 50 MHz with about 500 Community Receivers each

Transmit-Receive Satellite Earth Terminal

Receive only Satellite Earth Terminal

Programming Centres

To be converted to Rediffusion TV

Distribution and reception system for the SITE experiment.

receiving set, with a substitute on hand in case he should die, become ill or move elsewhere. If the set stops working, the custodian puts a tick in the appropriate box on a pre-addressed, pre-stamped postcard and sends it to the local maintenance centre, which is never more than sixty miles away and is equipped with a stock of spare parts, a jeep and a crew of trained engineers.

India is the first country in the world to set up such a system, but many others are certain to follow within the next ten years and the effect on all forms of information and education, including those provided by museums, is incalculable. For the first time, people in the rural areas are receiving a service comparable to what is provided in the cities, and without any need to move from the place where they live. They are no longer compelled to remain in cultural darkness, third-class citizens. The success of a scheme like SITE depends partly on good technical planning and organisation, but even more on the imagination and adventurous spirit of the people who create the programmes. The day SITE began, the museums on India were, whether they liked it or not, operating in a different world.

'In a developing country such as ours', says the Ghana Museums Service,

one cannot build museums in all the administrative regions of the country. So we operate from the main centres, taking selected exhibits into the rural areas and showing them to schools and to the adult population. We explain our activities in this way, and the exhibits and the information they provide are shown to the local people and vividly discussed with them. Exhibitions which in the past were mounted on the basis of their aesthetics are being changed to reflect more of the functions of objects. The public are reacting favourably, especially those who have had no formal education.

The techniques needed by the staff of a mobile museum are entirely different from those used by their colleagues at a city centre, but museums, such as the Indian Museum in Calcutta and the Ghana Museum in Accra, which have been experimenting in this way, have learned a great deal about museum presentation and public relations as a result. The men and women who go out into the villages with travelling exhibi-

National Science Museum, Tokyo, Japan. Members of the botanical training course engaged on microscopic observations of moss and lichens.

tions educate themselves a great deal in the process. They have escaped from the closed world of their country's intelligentsia.

A different way of involving the outside world in a museum's work is to make sure that a wide range of public activities is centred on the museum – workshops, clubs, discussion groups, concerts and demonstrations are a few of the possibilities. One of the most interesting and original ventures in this direction is the Study Room at the National Science Museum, Tokyo. Opened in 1974, this is a self-teaching laboratory for people who want to study and carry out research experiments on their own initiative. This is closely linked with the Museum's programme of graded exhibitions, carefully planned to allow visitors to walk before they run and to discover specialised interests after they have first been given an opportunity to understand the broad range of scientific concepts and methods.

Throughout the world, museums complain that funds are inadequate to allow them to make the improvements which they know to be necessary, if they are to attract a more satisfactory cross-section of visitors. One is bound to wonder if this shortage of money may not be permanent and if it will ever be possible to build and maintain the traditional type of museum with publicly-provided finance alone. Elaborate lighting, generous use of space, and electronically-controlled displays

and effects are extremely expensive. So too are air-conditioned exhibition buildings, modern workshops and offices and properly-equipped stores for reserve collections. It may well be that the next ten years will demonstrate the truth of the prophecy made recently by the Director of the Swiss Transport Museum in Lucerne. By the end of the 1980s, he forecasts, there will be only two kinds of museum – a very few large and prestigious institutions, such as the Louvre, the British Museum and the Smithsonian, which will continue to be maintained out of public funds, come what may, and a much larger number of places which will have to pay their own way, by means of donations and grants from industry and from private individuals, income from entrance fees and from sales of publications, models, slides, films, tapes and surplus objects. The director of the second kind of museum will have to be an essentially entrepreneurial rather than a scholarly person. If he is successful, the museum will survive; if he is unsuccessful, it will wither and die.

In the broad sense, Mr Waldis' prophesy may come true, at least in the non-socialist countries of the world, but small museums, like small farms, have a remarkable capacity for survival, against all the economic odds. Museums are, in any case, a spectrum, not two groups of extremes. They come in all sizes, not merely large and small, and their sources of finance are equally varied. What a museum has to fear most

is not death, but a miserable, long-drawn-out decline. It is not difficult to find a number of museums in any country which are already in this unenviable situation. Quite a number of them are in the Socialist countries, which illustrates the fact that the entrepreneurial temperament exists independently of political systems. The fact that a museum serves a Socialist society does not automatically provide it with all the funds it needs or would like. East or West, the exceptionally able, energetic, well-connected and enterprising director will find ways of ensuring that his particular museum does rather better and if possible a good deal better than the average; and there seems no reason to believe that such an unequal state of affairs will not persist into the 1980s and far beyond.

One should not, in any case, continue to think of museums as institutions which can be fed only from the resources of the countries in which they happen to be located. A particular nation's cultural heritage belongs both to itself and to the world, and an important part of UNESCO's activity within the museum field has been to discover ways of putting this concept into practice. There is now growing support for what was at one time a revolutionary idea, that museum collections and museum personnel should be in continual movement around the world, partly in order to do away with the wastefulness and sterility of large 'reserve' collections – which can be translated to mean 'material which the museum does not know what to do with' – and partly to provide a way in which large museums can help small museums and rich countries poorer countries. As this aim gradually becomes implemented – there are great psychological difficulties to be overcome – the nature of the investment which has to be made by individual museums will change and so, too, one hopes, will the notion of 'rich' museums and 'poor' museums, since all museums will be drawing their resources from the same huge international bank of material and expertise.

Such a fundamental change in attitudes will not, of course, be achieved overnight, even in the most favourable circumstances, and, in the short run, only time will show how well founded Mr Waldis' intuition is likely to be and, in particular, how far one will be able to go in raising money directly from the visitors to museums. Meanwhile, one observes that there is a worldwide controversy over the practice of charging for admission to museums. Those who advocate charges do so on the grounds that there is no essential difference between paying to go into a museum and paying for a seat in a theatre. The opponents of this view say that the contents of museums form part of the national heritage and are therefore public property. Why, then, they ask, should the public have to find money for the privilege of seeing and using what belongs to it already? In this situation of financial stringency two things seem certain. The first is that the most-visited museums will, on the whole, be those which have learned how to adapt themselves to changing social conditions. The second is that far too many museums have been attempting the impossible for years and are steadily making themselves more frustrated and, if one dares to say so, more ridiculous. 'The impossible' includes maintaining, heating and ventilating a hopelessly grand and out-of-date building, dreaming of a large specialist staff, buying items in an increasingly competitive and costly international commercial market, and issuing a steady stream of well-illustrated, beautifully printed and expensive publications. Museums, like other institutions, are everywhere moving into an age of tight budgets and reduced spending, which seems likely to make efficiency and ingenuity the prime virtues. It is very possible that the museum of ten and twenty years ahead will find it easier to employ the all-rounder than the specialist and that museology courses and training schemes will reflect this.

The future historian of museums and museology may well decide that 1971 was the year in which it became obvious beyond all reasonable doubt that there would have to be fundamental changes in the philosophy and aims of museums, and that the traditional attitudes were leading to disaster. In 1971 ICOM met in Grenoble and during the proceedings of the General Council an African delegate, from Benin, made four points with considerable heat and vigour. Museums, he said, were not integrated into the contemporary world

and formed no real part of it; they were élitist, and of no use whatever to the majority of people, in all countries; they were obsolete; and they ought to disappear, so that the public money could be spent to better purpose.

A group of museum experts from Latin American countries, who were at Grenoble, asked themselves two questions when they had had time to digest this vigorous and passionate contribution to the discussion. First, were the statements true, and if they were, was it inevitable and certain that museums could not be changed before disaster finally overwhelmed them? To come to a decision on these matters and to try to work out a policy for the future, they organised in 1972, at Santiago, Chile, what was described as 'a round table on the function of Latin American museums in the contemporary world'.[16] The conclusions reached at this meeting are relevant to every country in the world, not merely to Latin America.

First, they stated, with all possible firmness and conviction, that 'the social, economic and cultural changes occurring in the world, and particularly in many underdeveloped areas, constitute a challenge to museology'. Museology, one should remember, had been redefined by ICOM in the key year, 1971, as 'the science of museums'. Its business, according to ICOM, is to study the history of museums, their role in society, methods of research, conservation, education and organisation, relations with the physical environment and typology. Armed with a definition as comprehensive as this, the Latin American Round Table could say, with perfect justice, that the great changes which were shaking and transforming world society were indeed 'a challenge to museology'.

The members then went on to say that 'most of the problems revealed by contemporary society have their roots in situations of injustice and cannot be solved until those injustices are rectified' and that a solution of these problems 'is not confined to a single science or discipline any more than the decision concerning the best solutions and the way of implementing them belongs to a single social group, but rather requires the full, conscious and committed participation of all sections of society'.

The museum, it was felt, must be part of this process. It helps to 'mould the consciousness of the communities it serves', it 'presents contemporary

problems', it 'links together past and present', and 'identifies itself with indispensable structural changes'. There was no suggestion that existing specialised museums should be closed down or abandoned, but, in order to meet current social needs, there had to be 'a gradual change in the outlook of curators and administrators and in the institutional structures for which they are responsible', so that a steady progress towards 'the integrated museum' might be ensured.

THE INTEGRATED MUSEUM

This phrase, 'the integrated museum', is the key to the new approach. The integration refers to the museum's public activity, to a realisation that it exists to meet the needs of people, not merely to preserve what the French call the *patrimoine*, the national cultural heritage. In order to achieve this, certain time-honoured practices will have to go. As a former Director-General of ICOM, Mr Hugues de Varine-Bohan, has recently said, 'It is necessary to break down old-established barriers between museums and research institutes, break down the psychological and hierarchical barriers between museums themselves. What has to be done is to organise systematically, and on all levels, co-operation.'

What integration and co-operation mean, in museum terms, has been admirably illustrated by one of the greatest and most flexible-minded of all museologists, the ever-young Georges Henri Rivière, in his plan for the Museum of Negro Civilisation at Dakar, a museum which is planned, it should be noted, to include nothing later than the eve of the colonial period. It is to be, one might say, not only a Museum of Negro Civilisation, but a Museum of Negro Civilisation undefiled, which is something rather different. To create the kind of museum which would justify the enormous investment of money and talent that is envisaged, Mr Rivière envisages a fusion of seven disciplines or, as he prefers to call them, approaches – anthropological, ecological, techno-economical, sociological, ideological, aesthetic and historical. Museology worthy of the name must, he believes, now embrace and show itself capable of absorbing all these different ways of looking at human activity. This is what the much-misused, but still useful word 'inter-disciplinarity' means, and there can be no doubt that now, in 1977, museology which does not draw its nourishment from as wide a range of disciplines as possible will quickly wither and die away. Whether sufficient of today's museologists can be trusted to bring themselves up to date in this way is another matter.

Less optimistic people than Mr Rivière might take the view that museums are far too important to be entrusted to museologists and that other kinds of people, such as sociologists and psychologists, will need to be brought in to help, either on contract from time to time or as permanent members of the museum staff. More hopefully and more probably, it means that museographic techniques will have to be brought up to date and that a new generation of museum employees will learn to ask themselves, almost instictively, 'What is this exhibit going to mean to the people who see it? What will it do for them? How will it help them to understand the world and their place in it a little better?' This is what the integrated interdisciplinary museum is about. It will use every device, every technique, every kind of feedback and research to make sure that its collections are not thrown into a cultural vacuum, that they really do speak in an intelligible way to the people who see them, whether in the museum building, on television or through the medium of a mobile unit which travels around taking the exhibits to the customer. It will plan for real people and real interests. At present, many, perhaps most, of the world's large museums start too far forward and make totally unjustified assumptions about how much people know already before they visit the museum. As evidence of this, one observes that the Children's Departments of a number of American museums are full of adults, busy acquiring the basic information that the main museum has failed to give them.

It is probable that most museums of the new type will be fairly small and not in capital cities. One might, perhaps, go further and forecast that within the next ten or twenty years the most adventurous, exciting and socially relevant work will be taking place in provincial centres, or in what would previously have been considered extremely unpromising areas of large cities. Countries such as Iran, Jordan and Algeria, which are not already

encumbered with large, old-established museums of the traditional type, may also find it relatively easy to set up new museums which are geared to the needs and mental habits of today, rather than yesterday. What has been happening recently in Mexico may well be establishing a pattern which is about to be repeated in many other parts of the world.

There are few more prestigious or more widely publicised museums anywhere than the National Museum of Anthropology in Mexico City. Its superb building, the quality of its collections and its generous annual budget have combined to make it one of the wonders of the museum world. No expense was spared to ensure its success and most visitors from other countries have returned home in a slightly dazed condition, hardly able to believe that expenditure on such a scale was still possible.

At the end of 1972, however, after the Santiago Round Table, a careful research study was carried out to find out just who was coming to the Museum. November and December were chosen for the survey, because each year November has the lowest attendance figure and December the highest. Among the many interesting facts revealed by this investigation was that working-class people, of any age, were almost completely unrepresented among the visitors to the Museum. Every known publicity device and form of enticement had failed to attract them to what was evidently regarded as a place designed by highly educated people for other highly educated people. The only answer seemed to be to create what would be, in effect, a museum mission.

The area they chose for their first experiment was Tacubaya, a slum area on the outskirts of Mexico City, of the type known in Mexico as a 'lost city'. This kind of slum-settlement is found all over the world and it is very common in Latin America. In 1973, when the decision was taken to establish an outpost, a mission, of the National Museum of Anthropology at Tacubaya, it contained 6860 familes, with just over 43,000 inhabitants – about 0.6 per cent of the whole population of Mexico City. A very high proportion of the people who lived there were totally illiterate and many were unemployed. Few of the children attended any kind of school. It was hardly surprising that the Tacubayans were not accustomed to make a

journey across town to the National Museum of Anthropology. They were, for the most part, completely unaware of its existence and, even if they had been put into buses and taken there, the marble splendours, the fountains and the well-dressed visitors would have terrified them.

Before the Museum took any real action at Tacubaya, it carried out what it described in its reports as a multidisciplinary research project, which is a way of saying that a mixed team of museologists and social scientists took a detailed look at the area, first to find out as much as possible about the attitudes, habits and potential of the families who lived there, and then to get their co-operation in setting up a special kind of museum which was to be designed and run specifically for them.

A piece of waste ground was cleared and levelled, and on it was put a complex of small hexagonal pavilions. Four of them fitted together, to make up the museum proper, and a fifth was put on its own, rather like a small bandstand. It was to be used, among other things, as a projection booth for throwing films and slides on to a big open-air screen. These little portable buildings were, like the shacks the people lived in, made of steel, but whereas the museum used new sheets of metal, the local inhabitants had to content themselves with old petrol cans, beaten flat.

The purpose of the museum is to take objects from the main museum, and to use them for special displays, which remain on the site for four or five months. All the resources and talents of the mother-museum are available and the full range of display techniques is used – models, slides, films, animation of all kinds, tapes – in order to create a museum which is lively and which can communicate with non-readers. There is a uniformed attendant, who was brought up in Tacubaya and understands the people, but rules and regulations are minimal. Smoking and games are permitted within the museum area, dogs and other pet animals may be brought in and any object on display may be touched. The atmosphere is delightfully informal and many boys and girls spend several hours a day at the museum, using it as a kind of club. Vandalism and damage have been insignificant. Members of the staff of the mother-museum pay frequent visits to Tacubaya, to maintain contact and to talk to local people about a great many more things than museums. Without it

La Casa del Museo, Mexico City: an experimental museum-centre in an urban slum. The exterior of the Museum.

(centre) *Part of the Museum interior, showing method of construction and style of display.*

having been planned this way, this little neighbourhood museum now functions as a general advice bureau, dealing with health problems, with educational opportunities and with marital disputes. It would be no exaggeration to say that it has become the local cultural centre, and once that stage has been reached any museum is entitled to say that it is fully integrated with its community. The fact that it has become a cultural centre by accident, rather than design, does not detract in any way from the value of the achievement.

Scattered over the five continents, there are many museums which are breaking new ground, in an effort to prove that the museum is not necessarily an obsolete, élitist institution and that it has an essential part to play in the world of today and tomorrow. A wide range of experiment and innovation is in progress, to discover the best ways of making contact with the public, of using museum collections to the maximum advantage, of recruiting and training suitable staff, and of making sure that the budget is managed, not merely spent. Museum professionals find it increasingly difficult – it is unfortunately too early to say impossible – to adopt an authoritarian position. To achieve the impact they are anxious to achieve, they are coming to realise that they must involve the community in what the museum is trying to do. Methods which are highly successful in one country may not distinguish themselves in another, but, given the will to adapt, there are very few experiments which are interesting and useful only within one set of national boundaries. In the following chapters we set out and discuss a series of what appear to us to be significant examples of what might be described as modern museum thinking in action, in the hope that such an approach will stimulate and encourage both those who plan and run museums and those who benefit from them.

Dalby Forest Park, north-east England. Wildlife exhibit in the Visitor Centre.

Living History Farm, Polk County, Iowa, USA. Log-cabin and its builder, in period dress. This museum-farm recreates pioneer life in the 1840s, when much of Iowa was settled.

(below) *Threshing in progress, with steam-driven thresher.*

Old Sturbridge Village, Massachusetts, USA. 'Dairymaid', in period dress, churning butter in the farm kitchen.

(below) *Ironbridge Gorge Museum, Shropshire, England. Preparing vehicles for a special event, 'Horses in Harness'.*

1 The Museum's Resources

THE PRINCIPLES OF COLLECTION

Every museum, as Mr Georges Henri Rivière has pointed out in his plan for one of the most enterprising and important museums to be conceived during the past century, the Museum of Negro Civilisation at Dakar, Senegal, has two kinds of resources at its disposal, those which are fixed and, short of an earthquake or a fire, immovable, and those which can be moved about and rearranged at will. The immovable resources are considered here in a later section, and our present concern is with what might be termed the museum's stock of objects and with its acquisition. From this point of view, museums fall into two categories:

1. Those which are brand-new and which are being established from nothing, from the ground up.
2. Those which have been in existence for some time and which have the task of building up their collections year by year, of obtaining additional material to fill gaps and to replace inferior specimens.

Certain principles and needs are common to both types of museum, in whatever parts of the world they may be situated, but it is easier to explain and justify the procedure to be followed if one concentrates to begin with on the problems of the completely new museum.

Mr Rivière has produced,[1] if not a recipe for success, at least a basic plan of operations which appears difficult to improve on. Thinking particularly of the Dakar Museum, he divides a museum's resources into what he calls direct and indirect documentation of the story which one is trying to tell.

The direct documentation consists of objects of all types, 'direct evidence of the technology, the economy, the social organisation and, above all, of the cultural expression of the different negro civilisations and of their diffusion beyond black Africa itself'. Such objects would include paintings, carvings, sculpture and artifacts of every kind. To make proper sense of them, it would also be necessary to have what might be described as environmental specimens as well, to illustrate the natural features, the plants and the living creatures of the areas where black people are to be found now and which they have inhabited in the past.

The indirect documentation is to be achieved by means of records which tell one more about the objects. These records would include books and other printed and written material, music, photographs, films, video-tapes and sound recordings.

A hundred years ago, before museology began to have any claim to be a science, a museum acquired its collections, for the most part, in a haphazard manner. It accepted many unwanted and useless gifts, largely because it could think of no convincing reason for refusing them, it bought items which appeared to be bargains and which fell approximately within its field of activity and it usually thought of exhibits as individual objects, to be owned and displayed without the supporting material which would make them meaningful. A modern museum, of the kind proposed for Dakar, has to proceed in quite a different way. In the words of Mr Rivière, it must 'base its collecting policy on the principle of systemisation and selection. Its acquisitions and its exchanges must be programmed.'

This is certainly correct. Any new museum should 'programme' the methods by which it proposes to build up its resources, in the sense that it should set out what it would ideally like to have and reject everything else. In practice, however, some degree of compromise is inevitable. To have a museum at all during the early years it may be necessary to make do for a while with certain objects which one realises are not the best of their kind, but which, with luck, will be replaced later by superior examples.

In any case, museum curators are usually only too well aware that they are working against the clock and that much material has to be obtained before it disappears for ever or, in some instances, before the agents of foreign collectors spirit it out of the country. In such circumstances the only sensible policy is to acquire first and select afterwards.

COLLECTION AND FIELDWORK IN DEVELOPING COUNTRIES

Geneviève Dournon-Taurelle has described[2] how the Barthelémy Boganda Museum, at Bangui, in the Central African Republic, set about the task, during the late 1960s, of making a museum out of nothing. The first phase of the new museum, the Department of Popular Arts and Traditions, was inaugurated in 1966. The museum had to serve two purposes, 'to preserve a cultural heritage threatened by extinction in a more or less distant future and to reawaken public appreciation, particularly in the towns, of past and surviving material cultures'. The newly-appointed staff had to cover the whole field of museographical work, from finding and documenting objects to displaying them in the museum, and to a considerable extent they had to learn as they went along. So far as possible, fieldwork was confined to the dry season, when roads were passable and living conditions easier, and cataloguing, conservation and other work which had to be done on the museum premises was reserved for the rainy season.

The first of the long series of collecting missions, which eventually covered the whole country, took place in January 1965. Accompanied by an ethnologist who knew the local people and was respected by them, the two very inexperienced but enthusiastic fieldworkers made their first professional appearance late one afternoon in a village which consisted of four huts. They came away with a piece of beaten bark which served as a kind of cloth, the first of 1200 items which made up the museum's collection when it opened early in 1967.

The two fieldworkers operated by trial and error. They always sent advance notice of their arrival in a village and they made a point of staying in the same base camp for several weeks, which gave them an opportunity to understand the lives and customs of the people in the district and to stimulate an interest in the museum's work.

'In the early morning', Mrs Dournon-Taurelle recalls,

the collectors set off, accompanied by a local guide, along a stretch 10 to 20 km. long and stopped in every village. At each halt they met the tribal chief or a leader and explained to him the reasons for their search, the kind of objects they were seeking and their purpose, which was to bring together in a communal dwelling, an 'ancestral home', strong, weather-proof and protected against termites and bad weather, the objects belonging to their ancestral culture – this, in order to serve as a testimony for the future generations and for the young people as well as for the detribalised townfolk, the reality and consistency of ways of life which were being changed or were disappearing through contact with modern life and the introduction of foreign customs.

Having, as they hoped, made their aims clear, the collectors told the local people they would be coming back later to see what kind of objects could be offered to them for the new museum. If all went well and good relations had been established, a pile of odds and ends would have been got together for inspection in the meeting hut. These would normally include both domestic items and hunting trophies – the items traditionally bought by Europeans, but not wanted by the new type of national museum, which was not concerned with the tastes and requirements of Europeans at all.

The collectors had, as one of their prime duties, to find out as much as they could about the social and cultural associations of each object they accepted. This demanded a great deal of time and patience, as well as a well-developed sense of curiosity. A wooden spoon, for instance, was the beginning of a fruitful enquiry into cooking traditions, food taboos, hunting techniques and the use of fire. A piece of antelope horn led to a discussion of the treatment of diseases and of the instruments used by medicine men, and finally, a great and unexpected triumph, to the production and purchase of the medicine man's large skin bag, with its strange assortment of contents. One piece of information led to another, often in a disconnected and illogical way. A question about a glass-bead necklace, which had been used as a barter object in the slave trade, caused an old man to show the collectors three pairs of double bells which had formerly served as part of a bride's dowry. The fieldworkers made full use of their time at each stopping-point. While objects were being inspected and assessed by one member of the team, another was using his tape-recorder to collect examples of traditional music for the museum's sound archives.

A similar system has been established, with considerable success, in a number of African, Asian and Latin American countries. In Ghana, conditions have been exceptionally favourable, in that it has not been difficult to recruit and train the right kind of people and to find the money to finance their work. The Director of the National Museum, Mr Richard B. Nunoo, lays down[3] four basic requirements for this type of fieldworker.

1. He must be 'friendly, tactful, trustworthy and have a flair for collecting'.

2. He 'should have lived long enough in the district or area to be familiar with the local traditions and customs'.

3. He 'must be fluent in the local language or dialect'.

4. His education must have been such as to enable him 'to write full particulars of every object collected, and, where possible, to add sketches'.

Once recruited, the fieldworkers are given an initial training course at the Museum's headquarters in Accra.

They are taught how to write up information, how to store objects properly as an interim measure, how to run a small office, and what to do about surface finds. The course is usually given by a trained ethnologist or archaeologist, who also has a particular interest in technology. On being posted, collectors are formally introduced to the local people, either by the Secretary to the Traditional Council or by the chief's spokesman. The new collector is also taken to see any important persons who, for one reason or another, were not present at the meeting just mentioned. He is also introduced to the local police, who help in tracking down illegal collectors.

To distinguish him from illegal collectors, the official representative carries an identity card, personally signed by the Director of the National Museum.

In each village or township of any size, an exhibition is then arranged in a school, community centre or some other suitable building, to show local people, including schoolchildren, the kinds of objects they might usefully contribute to the national collections. The collector then starts work, by going from house to house asking people what items they would be prepared to offer. Repeat-visits are often made, until it is evident that everything that is likely to be forthcoming on this particular occasion has been handed over. The Ghana method obviously demands remarkable qualities of patience, persistence and persuasiveness on the part of its collectors, together with outstanding physical stamina, since they often have to drive long distances over very bad roads in order to reach people in the remote parts of their area.

Not infrequently, the bulk of the donations come from the chief of the district himself. Sometimes the chief will call a carefully-chosen group of his people together, particularly those who he has reason to believe have interesting objects in their possession, and, in Mr Nunoo's diplomatic words, 'persuades them to give generously to help a good cause'. Occasionally, the museum is able to enrol sub-chiefs as their collectors. This allows a very helpful network to be created, with the sub-chief's relatives collecting under his supervision and writing up notes on the specimens collected if it should happen that the sub-chief himself cannot read or write.

At this point one has to state as firmly as possible that the results the collectors achieve must depend on what the museum sees its function to be. If, for example, the museum's interests are centred wholly on the pre-colonial past, the collector is unlikely to be encouraged to collect early twentieth-century material. If the emphasis is overwhelmingly on reflecting the indigenous culture, European items, however significant they may be, are likely to be disregarded.

This problem is particularly acute in Africa. Until independence, the 'natives' were officially disallowed a history. The white ruling class had history, which was taught at school and college, and their black subjects had customs and traditions. In recent years, the wise policy has been adopted in most of these countries of referring to something known as 'African studies', a blanket-term which includes history, archaeology, anthropology and ethnology. From all the information contributed by these special disciplines, the history of each country will one day be written in a way which will satisfy national con-

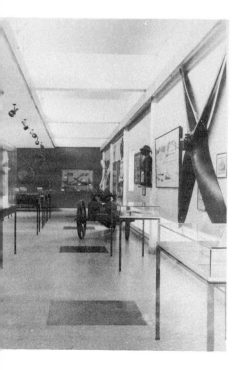

sciousness and aspirations, and which will allow past and present to mingle and to shade off into one another without feelings of inferiority and embarrassment.[4] Meanwhile, however, one fears that valuable material is being allowed to disappear because it does not correspond with the national mood, which may well be different in ten years' time. There are notable exceptions to this. The National Museum in Dar-es-Salaam, for instance, has a most interesting section devoted to the period of German colonial occupation. The impact of this is all the stronger from having this strangely incongruous European material side by side, in the same building, with collections illustrating the indigenous Tanzanian culture.

COLLECTING POLICY AND THE INTEGRATED MUSEUM

But the problems of presenting the evidence of former colonisation and present nationalism within the same museum, objectively and constructively, are very great and, in practice, rarely overcome. Collecting policy, in most cases, reflects this. Even the most imaginative and forward-looking museum director or curator can resist the tide only to a limited extent, although he may well keep items in store which, under present conditions, it would be impolitic or even dangerous to display. In twenty or thirty years' time, however, a new generation of museologists may find it possible to bring these objects from their temporary retirement and to display them to a new public which will be glad to have the opportunity of seeing them.

This problem is by no means peculiar to Africa, although, for sound historical reasons, it is particularly strongly in evidence there. There are a number of most interesting reflections of the same type of dilemma in Latin America. The National Historical Museum in Buenos Aires might be more appropriately and

National Museum, Dar-es-Salaam, Tanzania. Section of History Gallery devoted to relics of the period of German rule. The picture also shows the ventilation louvres at ground level.

honestly called the National Museum of Military History or the Museum of Nationalist History. Excellently arranged on the best modern principles, it is concerned entirely with generals, admirals, revolutions and struggles for independence. Given the circumstances of Argentina during the nineteenth and early twentieth centuries, this is not in itself altogether unreasonable, but what is nowadays so surprising and unsatisfactory is that the story is told entirely in terms of Great Men. Every conceivable item relating to San Martin and the other national heroes has been preserved, but there is nothing whatever to show what effects several generations of upheavals had on the lives and aspirations of the ordinary citizens of the country. To have, in the 1970s, a museum calling itself the National Historical Museum from which the collections and displays of the common people are almost totally absent is surely an absurdity. Within a few years, the policy will no doubt change, but when that happens one wonders how difficult it is going to be to collect the material needed to reflect the activities of this hitherto ignored section of the population and, even more necessary and difficult, to give a balanced picture of the last forty years in the history of Argentina, a formidable challenge to any museologist.

The National Museum of History in Mexico City is, to its great credit, already beginning to grapple with this fundamental problem. Hitherto it has been, like its counterpart in Buenos Aires, a museum which has presented the lives, tastes and achievements of the rich and powerful. A former palace, superbly situated on the top of a wooded hill overlooking the city, it is visited by very large numbers of Mexicans each year – by a great many more, in fact, than the internationally famous National Museum of Anthropology – but, up to the present, it has reflected as narrow a view of history as Argentina's National Historical Museum – swords, guns, princes, generals and archbishops. A fresh, young and vigorous management, with a different view of what history is about, is now, with the full support of the Government, setting about the task of remodelling the museum to present a picture of the social, industrial and technological development of Mexico, a reorientation which will demand a completely different policy of both acquisition and display.

It is worth noting that in 1973, when the new team took over, the museum had no catalogue or register whatever of its enormous collections, whether the items were on display or in store. Not surprisingly, many objects had been appropriated surreptitiously over the years by the directors of provincial museums who felt, with some justice, that it was better that they should use this apparently unwanted and forgotten material for the benefit of the public than that it should moulder away in the palace vaults. One should add, as a matter of justice, that between 1973 and 1975 the whole of the museum's collection was catalogued for the first time, so that the riches of the available resources are now apparent.

UNESCO's Santiago Round Table of 1972, to which reference has already been made above, aimed deliberately at forcing museums to look critically at what they were doing and, by bringing museologists and specialists in quite different fields together, to cut through the inbred, not to say incestuous, pattern of traditional thinking which had been rightly criticised at ICOM's General Conference in Grenoble in 1971 and which ICOM itself has been making strenuous and continous efforts to change. At the Round Table, museums were accused of 'doing very little, and sometimes virtually nothing, on behalf of the underprivileged' and of

being unwilling or unable to meet the demands of a developing society. The argument that museums were not the proper bodies to deal with such matters as the reduction of illiteracy or malnutrition, or the more effective use of natural resources, was rejected. Museums, it was eventually agreed, were in the front line of any attack on social evils. They had been originally conceived in terms of the past, to 'assemble, catalogue, conserve and exhibit the works of previous cultures', and they were now being compelled, by the pressure of events, to become involved with what was happening in their own time, to become 'a vector which starts in the present and whose far end is in the past'.

It is interesting to speculate what effect this new policy of the 'integrated' or 'integral' museum (one hears both terms used) is likely to have on the principles by which museums of various types and sizes collect and present material for display. Three very different museums, all in Latin America, will make the point.

In Rio de Janeiro, a small Museum of the Indian was established in 1953, long before integrated museums were being talked about. It had very little money then and it has very little now. Its task was to tell the public about Brazilian Indians, a section of the national community which had remained at

little more than a Stone Age level of technology. The message of the Museum to its visitors was that the Indian was their friend, to be cared for and protected, not exterminated or exploited, and that, like any other category of human being, he was an interesting person in his own right. The Museum's collections were made in order to explain, within the limits of the available resources, the Indians' traditional way of life and to illustrate the objects they were capable of making at their best. These, it is emphasised, are fellow-citizens of whom we can be proud, but whose culture, if we are not sufficiently watchful, will become debilitated to a point at which no recovery is possible. And, to prove this last point, there is a display of debased Indian handicrafts, produced to meet a tourist demand.

This is a museum with a very clear and straightforward collecting policy. 'We will obtain', the staff have said in effect, 'examples of what the Indians have made in the past and what they are making today and we will use these objects to create a better understanding of the Indians and of the social predicament in which they find themselves today. We will do all we can to send our visitors away determined to do what they can to improve the situation.' This in its aims and its methods, is a microcosm of the socially integrated museum. The Museum of the Indian would like to have a rather larger and less out-of-the-way building and it is a little tired of being so chronically short of funds, but there would be no point in having a collection of, say, twice the present size. Doubling the number of exhibits would not allow the job to be done twice as successfully as it is being done at the present time. On the other hand, it would be satisfying to be able to know that every exhibit was the best of its kind, and a larger budget would make it possible to replace second-quality by first-quality objects. The second-quality objects could then be assembled as loan collections to schools and colleges or put into a separate section for visitors to touch and handle. More money and more space would also ease the present congestion, which at

Museum of the Indian, Rio de Janeiro, Brazil. Guided tour for schoolchildren.

the moment is inevitable when a couple of large school parties arrive together, and provide the funds to engage one or two more technicians or guides or to build better display cases. To go beyond these objectives, however, would make no sense.

To go first to the Museum of the Indian and then to the National Museum in the same city is an illuminating, if depressing experience. It would be difficult to imagine a less integrated museum anywhere in the world than the National Museum in Rio de Janeiro. Housed since 1892 in the old Imperial Palace, a soul-killing three-storeyed building, this huge and completely antiquated museum, with forty-eight rooms and precisely one museologist, has practically no points of contact at all with contemporary life. From the public's point of view, the major attractions are the park which it is fortunate enough to have retained and which is a favourite picnicking place for families with small children, the cloakroom, where bags and other belongings can be left until lunchtime, and the lavatories, conveniently situated near the main entrance. The museum as a whole is no more than a gigantic filing cabinet of archaeological, ethnographical and natural history specimens, an annexe to an almost equally large

library. There is nothing to suggest that visitors are considered to be of any importance or relevance. This is, in its conception and its philosophy, a kind of mini-university, a situation which will probably become even more obvious if and when the Museum is transferred to its splendid new building on the University campus, a soil in which the policy adopted at Santiago is unlikely to strike deep roots for some time to come. The collections here are essentially for scholars and students, and they have been built up much as a library would be. They are for reference, study and comparison, not for inspiration, encouragement or enlightenment.

The Museum of the Unconscious, on the other hand, also in Rio de Janeiro, achieves what the National Museum would evidently regard as impossible: it is immensely interesting to the general public and at the same time of great scientific value. If any museum in Latin America is entitled to be called integrated, this one certainly is. Its collections have arisen in a way which makes their social purpose and value inevitable. The Museum forms part of a mental hospital, which for more than twenty years has encouraged its patients to paint and to sculpt as a form of therapy. This activity is entirely voluntary, but everything that is produced is carefully filed away, with the date and the patient's name, so that it can be used as a form of clinical note and comparisons made between the work the same person is producing today and, say, six months or two years ago. This is not, of course, to assess progress in craftsmanship, but as evidence of changes in the patient's state of mind. It so happens, however, that this hospital is in a fairly densely-populated urban area and, as is the case everywhere, a mental hospital causes apprehension and, to some extent, hostility among people living in the district. The hospital has taken a number of steps to allay these fears and to persuade the public at large to take a sympathetic and informed interest in the nature of mental illness and in the various methods of treatment.

A museum of examples of the work done in the hospital's art department seemed a sensible form of public rela-

Museum of the Unconscious, Rio de Janeiro, Brazil. Painting by psychiatric patient in the hospital to which the Museum is attached.

tions and it has, in fact, proved a highly successful experiment. Advice on the selection and arrangement of the exhibits – there were many thousands to choose from – was given by experienced museologists and the resulting museum has proved of great interest, both to patients and their families and to visitors from the surrounding district. From a medical and scientific point of view, what is to be seen in the Museum is no more than the tip of the iceberg, the iceberg itself being the great quantity of material on shelves in the store-room, a wonderful quarry for research workers and an encouraging justification for many years of effort and confidence on the part of the hospital staff.

Nothing in the Museum of the Unconscious has needed to be bought. The collection has grown naturally and it is rooted in the place where it is displayed. The museological expertise in this case is of two kinds: first, to see and understand the need and to identify oneself with it; and, second, to make suggestions as to the choice and display of the objects. The collection itself existed before the Museum was thought of and continues to grow steadily without any outside assistance.

Another kind of 'natural' museum is to be found in Kenya, and to a lesser extent in Uganda and Tanzania. These museums are an offshoot of Kenya's extremely successful Wildlife Clubs, which were started in 1968 at Togomo College, near Mount Kenya, where an American teacher introduced the idea to a nineteen-year-old student, Nathaniel Chumo, who is now National Organiser of the movement, with a base at the National Museum in Nairobi. There are now Wildlife Clubs in universities as well as schools, the former tending, of course, to be more sophisticated.

As part of its activities, each Club is encouraged to set up its own museum, which in many cases is the only museum in the area, and a centre of interest to local people in general, not only to members of the Club. The exhibits relate for the most part to the archaeology, palaeontology, birds, animals, reptiles and plants of the Club's immediate district, and members are given practical help with the techniques of classification, labelling and arrangement. In the rural areas some Clubs have been able to build their own museum rooms with natural materials – wood, mud and fibres. This is not possible in the town Clubs and many of them have to content themselves with the corner of a laboratory or classroom, or with a full display of their collection once or twice a year.

THE CURSE OF THE INTERNATIONAL MARKET IN ART

The gulf between the Wildlife Club Museum of the Park Road Secondary School, Nairobi, which has practically no budget a year, and the American Museum of Natural History in New York, which has a budget of several million dollars, is much narrower than that which exists between the National Gallery in London and the Crafts Museum in New Delhi. The reason for this is partly economic and partly psychological. Neither the Nairobi nor the New York museum is involved in the international collectors' market, which means that there is little, if any, inclination to consider the objects of display in money terms. Big and important as it is, the American Museum of Natural History is unlikely to be found represented at an auction, bidding against someone from the Moscow State University Zoological Museum for a stuffed elephant, and the Park Road Secondary School, Nairobi, like the

Crafts Museum in Delhi, is in no position to bid or outbid at any auction at all. The National Gallery, on the other hand, like major art galleries throughout the world, is always attempting to buy what it feels to be a very desirable painting and to discover funds for what is certain to be an exceedingly expensive business, since, although there are many elephants, feather head-dresses and boomerangs in the world, every painting by Rembrandt and Dali is unique. It is, in fact, this uniqueness which makes it so desirable and its cost so high, as museums compete with one another and with wealthy private collectors to secure works of art, no matter what the price, which will improve the 'quality' – that is, the market value – of their collections. The criminal world thrives on such commercial cupidity, and many collections, both private and public, contain stolen material which they treasure, but which, for the time being, they dare not display.

There is a certain irony and even justice in this apparently idiotic situation, since in many countries valuable private collections fall into the lap of museums every year, either, as in the United States, as gifts which a rich person can set against his tax liabilities, or, as in Britain, as material acquired by the Treasury in lieu of death duties or

Cyprus Museum, Nicosia. Terracotta figurine, 1400–1200 BC, from an official Cyprus Government excavation.

Capital Gains Tax and passed on to what is felt to be a suitable or deserving museum. Meanwhile, other rich people are building up collections by buying, through agents and dealers, objects from the poorer countries, which these countries need in order to create and strengthen their own museums. Such transactions are often completely illegal and are only made possible by the existence of a widespread and well-organised international system of theft and smuggling. This will be discussed in more detail later, but meanwhile it is important to note than the fundamental reason why this illegal trade flourishes to the extent that it does is that a highly rewarding public and private market exists and that, despite the continuous efforts of UNESCO and ICOM, governments have so far shown themselves largely powerless to stamp it out.

EXCHANGES AND THE CONCEPT OF CULTURAL PROPERTY

In August 1975, UNESCO prepared a very important report, 'the exchange of original objects and specimens among institutions in different countries', to

Kajeido Secondary School, Kenya. Wildlife Club Museum.

help draw up a draft international recommendation on this subject. This was, more precisely, a preliminary report, for discussion and adoption at the General Conference of the organisation in 1976. It followed the *Convention concerning the Protection, at National Level, of the Cultural and National Heritage* (1972) and the *Convention on the Means of Prohibiting and Preventing the Illicit Export, Import and Transfer of Ownership of Cultural Property* (1970).

The 1975 report defined cultural property as 'property designated by each state as being of importance for archaeology, prehistory, history, literature, art and science'. The phrase 'designated by each state' is significant. Only the country which owns an object has the right to say whether it is important or not. In practice, it is unlikely that an expert in, say, the United States will argue with an expert from Nigeria over the degree of importance of a Benin bronze, but the right to differ is explicitly allowed in the definition of cultural property and it is not inconceivable that an important legal issue might be made of it.

'Cultural property', observed the report, 'belongs both to the national community holding it and to mankind as a whole.' To emphasise this, it proposed the concept of co-ownership, by which an object would be legally owned by two countries at the same time and moved between them as required. There would undoubtedly be both legal and psychological problems, but they could be overcome, given the will to do so. A system of co-ownership would have two advantages. In the words of the report:

1. It would reduce competition between major cultural institutions, which is one of the factors that contribute to the regrettable rise in the price of the items in a collection, by inducing such institutions to make joint acquisitions instead of competing with one another.

2. It is an initial attempt to formulate in legal terms a basic ethical idea, namely that cultural property is part of the heritage of the whole international community.

Co-ownership is a revolutionary idea, which would confer immense benefits on museums throughout the world, and one can only hope that it succeeds quickly, partly for financial reasons and partly to temper and liberalise some of the more extreme forms of cultural nationalism. Meanwhile, a good deal can be achieved by the sensible use of the traditional kind of international exchange between museums.

The price-difference between what might be termed the object-producing countries and the object-consuming countries can, in certain circumstances, be overcome by the international exchange of material between museums. As the Indian museologist, Vinod Dwivedi, has pointed out[5] it is impossible for an Indian museum to buy European paintings in the open market, because sufficient funds are simply not available. But, he says, with understandable pleasure and relief, Indian art is steadily gaining in popularity abroad and this has 'created a very favourable atmosphere' for exchanges between India and other countries. As an example of what can be achieved in this way, the National Museum in New Delhi has exchanged two South Indian stone sculptures with the Philadelphia Museum of Art, which has provided four medieval European sculptures in return.

Exchanges are, of course, not necessarily or most frequently on an international basis. As Dr Dwivedi and others have pointed out, every museum of any size possesses quantities, sometimes great quantities, of material which it cannot hope to display and which may well contain duplicates of items already on exhibition. The museum at Hanley, in England, has, for example, more than two hundred eighteenth-century pottery milk-jugs, in the form of a cow. They are ranged side by side on a shelf in the store, like some huge herd on a farm, doing nothing but appreciate in value as the years go by. This is investment-banking, not museology, and hundreds of museums throughout the world are guilty of the same unhelpful, unsocial practice.

Exchanges between museums in the same country not only enrich collections, but help to break down parochialism, which is as stultifying in the museum field as in any other. In India, for example, most museums are regional in character. 'The result', as Dr Dwivedi notes,

is that a south Indian visiting a southern museum sees only south Indian objects and his counterpart from the north sees only northern objects in museums of his region. This he may not find very attractive. But if two such institutions exchange objects, there will be so much new to look at and to appreciate. When a visitor finds that people in other parts of India also worship deities similar to his own gods and goddesses, there is bound to be a feeling of greater affinity and thus the museums can play an active part in national integration.

It is clear that regionalism is more highly regarded in some countries than in others. In Ghana, for example, the National Museum, which has established branch museums in provincial centres, has taken great pains to ensure that each museum reflects the national culture and is not merely a mirror of the life and traditions of its own district. In France and Britain, on the other hand, where the national identity has been firmly established for centuries, the pressure is in the opposite direction and regional museums are valued for their regionalism, and for the variety and difference this represents in a civilisation in which standardisation and uniformity are increasingly becoming the norm.

'Regionalism' implies depth as well as comprehensiveness, and the new type of regional museum is not satisfied with the mere collecting of objects which was acceptable even twenty-five years ago. Today's regional museum is attempting to discover the essence and flavour of its own particular part of the country and to collect material which will reflect these special characteristics in every possible way.

One of the most interesting attempts to do this is being made in the English county of Norfolk. The project, called Norfolk Heritage, now forms part of the Norfolk Museums Service, after a pioneering period financed by the Carnegie Trust. The aim has been nothing less than to find 'possible ways of interpreting the total heritage of the county of Norfolk to the public',[6] to encourage the understanding of the county as a whole and to 'treat the total heritage of the region as a collection, the region itself being a kind of museum to be drawn upon to illustrate the region's story, and the story of the life and work of a people'. This is basically the same policy as the Museum of Man and Industry is following for a much smaller area, around Le Creusot in France. It involves the total absorption of the museum into the district in which it is located, or rather, considering the museum building as no more than a single part of a much larger museum, the district itself.

'The characteristics of a region and its people', says the Norfolk survey,

> may be explained by the inter-relationship between many aspects of the geological, natural, historical, social and cultural, among others. A typical South Norfolk farmhouse, for instance, may be the product of the local geology (in its building materials), local social history (in its scale and design), local agricultural practice (in its plan and relationship to fields and farm buildings) and local economic history (in its survival in its present form). If it is moated, then questions of local soil texture and drainage, and local custom are involved. If it incorporates brick, then local transport systems – and so on. Looked at in this way, a host of features in the landscape, objects in local museums, and even non-material things, such as customs or dialect, may take on a new significance and a new value, and the heritage of a region brought alive to the visitor.

And not only to the visitor, one is tempted to interject. The heritage of a region is of greatest importance to the people who live in it. Visitors are, so to speak, a bonus.

In Wales, the Welsh Folk Museum has defined its task as one of recording and interpreting 'the ingrained traditions of a region or locality from the point of view of material and non-material culture'.[7] The Museum's former director, Dr J. Geraint Jenkins, has set out his conviction that it is the duty of the ethnologist 'to record details of a community's life in the past as well as the living traditions of that community in the present, for in our work we can never ignore present day phenomena', and goes on to quote with approval two sentences from a British report written twenty years earlier. In this we are reminded that

> history never ceases to be made. We are never at the end of time, but always in the middle of it. With every economic, social or industrial change, there goes an atmosphere, a whole world of habit, incident, thought and terminology, the memory and savour of which can be preserved only if recovered from the

lips of those who lived in it and through it.[8]

This is, of course, precisely what Mr Rivière has advocated in his plan for the Museum of Negro Civilisation at Dakar. He and Dr Jenkins talk the same museum language, although one is writing about Senegal and the other about Wales, two countries which could hardly be more different. The similarity of their thought and their conclusions point to the wisdom of the inscription over the first, introductory, room at the National Museum of Anthropology in Mexico City. In translation it reads: 'All men meet the same needs with different resources and in different ways. All cultures are equally valid.'

We can never be reminded often enough that

> the mere collection and study of material objects, the mere recording of details of a building or workshop is not enough. One has to go further and discover the social organisation, the economic conditions, language, lore, customs and the whole culture associated with those objects. Collection is not an end in itself, but merely the means of reaching those people to whom those material objects had the meaning of everyday things.[9]

Museum of the Institute of Ethiopian Studies, Addis Ababa, Ethiopia. Grave markers from Konso.

The Martyr's Cottage, East Bilney, Norfolk, England. The reputed dwelling, now semi-derelict, of Thomas Bilney, martyred at Norwich in 1530. The cottage, which forms part of the Carnegie Project, is to be restored as a museum. It presents a conservation problem: how should such a building be conserved, interpreted and made accessible to the public?

RECORDING AND CATALOGUING

Collection should not, indeed, be an end in itself, but if it is to take place at all it should be systematic and recorded in a way which provides the kind of information which future generations are likely to find helpful. One cannot be completely confident about this, since there is no way of knowing what questions the students or the museum visitors of the year 2000 or 2050 will want to ask. Any recording system must necessarily be based on those aspects of the subject which are felt to be relevant and important today. The needs and interests of the future are another matter, but one cannot wait for the future to arrive before taking action.

After many years' pioneering experience of classification and cataloguing at the Museum of Popular Arts and Traditions in Paris, Miss Oddon, now of the ICOM Training Unit, went to the Centre for the Training of African Museum Technicians at Jos, in Nigeria, and, in the course of her work there, drew up what she called a *Guide for the Cataloguing and Analysis of Collections in General Museums*. This is a remarkable document of thirty-two pages, which explains in considerable detail how the standardised ICOM Catalogue Card is to be completed. It is intended, she says, to be 'a teaching document for museographers responsible for documenting collections', and it was written with the intention of making it possible for students to present information in a form which was suitable for automatic data selection systems, which are being installed now in those countries able to afford them.

The card contains twenty-three items. They are listed as Appendix 1.1 at the end of this chapter, and fully explained by Miss Oddon in the *Guide*. If this procedure is followed, the museum will have a full and, one would hope, foolproof description of every object in its collection, with its origins, condition, appearance and purpose meticulously and concisely described.

The method used and recommended by the National Museum in Delhi[10] is considerably simpler than Miss Oddon's, but, for this reason, provides a good deal less information. Eleven categories of detail are required, covering much the same ground as the ICOM list, but in a much shorter space. The list is reproduced here as Appendix 1.2. In the Delhi system, the catalogue card has a small photograph of the object on the back, together with the negative number.

COMPUTER INDEXING OF MUSEUM OBJECTS

Cataloguing and indexing is a necessary but tedious and time-consuming task, involving, if traditional methods are followed, a great deal of hand-labour. In certain countries, where clerical workers are abundant and can still be hired cheaply, there may be no particular reason to depart from the old system, but elsewhere every possible opportunity to save costs has to be seized as soon as it becomes available. Computer indexing has for a long time been regarded by the museum profession, if not exactly with eagerness and longing, at least with hope, and it now seems to have reached a point of development at which it has become a practical proposition. The United States, the German Federal Republic, France and Britain have all been experimenting with similar systems. The British so far appears to be the simplest and the cheapest.

It has been developed and tested by the Information Retrieval Group of the Museums Association, known professionally as IRGMA. It was clear from the beginning that the information required from any system would vary considerably according to the type of service required. A specialist museum existing primarily for research would

```
               RECORDING INFORMATION


     Introduction

     The following section describes how to record information in
     a way suitable for use in both a catalogue and an index.

     Details of the practical methods to be used when recording
     information in a box on a card are given in the separate
     subject instructions.


     Natural and Controlled language

     When producing a CATALOGUE you may wish to record within a
     box on a card any relevant terms in natural language. In
     this way the subtle distinctions between words and the
     different connotations placed on them may be fully
     exploited. The record is a valuable source of information in
     its own right, and should not be distorted.

     In contrast, for indexing purposes it is desirable to define
     strictly both the form and the type of words allowed in a
     given box. The efficiency of an INDEX is increased by
     careful control of terms.

     Consider, for example, the result of one curator stating
     that an object was bought, and another that a similar object
     was purchased. These imply the same concept, but the two
     words would appear separately in an index. Restriction to
     bought improves the index with no loss of information. In
     contrast, auctioned is a subdivision of sold. Restriction to
     sold simplifies the index but loses information.

     In general, major loss of information due to such
     restrictions is not acceptable in a primary record. A
     balance has to be found between the conflicting demands of
     primary recording and index construction.

     IRGMA achieves this balance in two ways. We put few
     restrictions on the words and phrases you can use, but do
     propose the adoption of a particular type of analysis
     (keyword and detail analysis) and a set of standard
     procedures (conventions) when recording these words and
     phrases.

     The aim of this approach is to aid the recording of accurate
     unambiguous information, and to make the information easier
     to manipulate and process. It greatly improves the value of
     the information for index construction.
```

Page from booklet, 'Introduction to the IRGMA Documentation System', 1976.

probably need what IRGMA calls 'deep indexing facilities', while a general museum, concerned mainly with presenting the collections to the public, would be more likely to want information on a wide variety of themes. To meet this situation, IRGMA has developed 'a flexible interdisciplinary system'. This, when used with a computer, does not limit the quantity of information which can be stored and the curator or research worker writes normal, not computer, language in order to record his data and receives it back in the same form.

It was found that museum information could be expressed in terms of a few recurring concepts or elements, such as time; place; person. The description of an item is built up within the structure provided by the record card by using the appropriate basic elements and placing them in their context. For example, a date will be added to the card relating to acquisition, manufacture, modification or discovery, and to the person who may be the user, manufacturer, donor collector. In this way, the basically simple structure can be repeated in as many contexts as required in order to accommodate all the necessary information, but in a manner which is the same for all disciplines. The setting out of the information within the structure is controlled by a set of rules, known as the Museum Documentation Standard.

The instructions to make sure that the information goes to the correct place in the computer store can be pre-printed on the necessary form or card, and, provided they are associated with the element to be recorded, the position of the information on the form is of no consequence. If certain elements are not required for a particular purpose, they can be omitted altogether. A particular recording specification is known as a data standard.

The method has been tested in a wide range of subject areas. One, carried out in 1973, involved the deep indexing of electrostatic apparatus, and another, undertaken with the assistance of more than a hundred curators in British museums, involved the use of forms designed specially for general museum objects, archaeology, botany, geology, history artifacts, natural history, paintings and drawings, photography and scientific instruments.

The analysis of the results proved invaluable in making revisions to the cards, and the instructions which went with them, before making them generally available. In January 1976, record cards and instructions were available in the following subject areas: museum objects (general applications), archaeology, fine art, geology, history artifacts, mineral specimens, natural history and scientific instruments. This is the first time that different recording cards, designed to meet museum requirements in a variety of disciplines and using a common interdisciplinary structure, have become available anywhere in the world. As the information is recorded in ordinary language, the cards can also be used as index cards, for use with traditional retrieval methods. An example of one of the record cards is reproduced at the end of this chapter as Appendix 1.3. This card has been designed with the cataloguing requirements of the small general museum in mind. The left-hand margin contains a series of terms which represent the major divisions of the IRGMA standards and into which the information about the item can be placed.

IDENTITY: the unique identity number (e.g. accession number)
IDENTIFICATION: the name of the item and any class to which it belongs
PRODUCTION: the circumstances and processes involved
COLLECTION: the circumstances of collection
ASSOCIATION: its historical associations
ACQUISITION: the circumstances of acquisition.
DESCRIPTION: the description including physical form, iconography of pictures, etc.
PROCESS: any processes involving the item, particularly reproduction and conservation
DOCUMENTATION: details of any documentation
NOTES: other information

Each of these major units of data are subdivided into the body of the card to accommodate the concepts of:

person	part
place	reference
time	cross-reference
description	

The record of a single item is made up of one or more cards depending on the amount of information available and additional information may be added to the record simply by completing further cards.

The use of recording and information systems of this kind is certain to increase during the next ten years, but, at the present time, two very important questions remain to be answered – is computer-based registration more efficient than the traditional method and does it save money?

Natural History Museum, Bern, Switzerland. Diorama display of Swiss birds.

The computer system can be and, one hopes, will be a great deal quicker and more efficient if sufficient museums are in a position to use it. Ideally, one would like to see an international system which at least all the major museums in the world could use, in much the same way as doctors and hospitals now have access to a worldwide computer bank of data for information and diagnosis. Apart from the obvious value of such a system to museologists and research workers, the existence of an international computer store of this kind could cause difficulties for the traffickers in objects stolen from museums, rather as the ability to move fingerprint and blood group details rapidly from country to country helps the police to identify criminals in general.

What this means, in effect, is that the extra efficiency lies mainly on the information retrieval, the output side of the system, rather than on the processing or input side. The documentation process can be divided into two parts. The input stage is a skilled operation which involves museological expertise in identifying and recording all the significant information about the item. There is no mechanical or electronic substitute for this and the costs are the same, whether the information is to be used manually or by machine. The information can, of course, be handwritten straight on to a card, but if a catalogue card is typed for a card-index, then again the manpower or, more probably, womanpower costs are about the same, whether the card is for manual use or the typing operation is generating computer input. At the Sedgwick Museum, Cambridge, an experiment carried out in 1972 showed that cataloguing for existing retrieval methods cost 66.6p for each item and 65.5p for computer use. The Cambridge tests had another value. It is recognised that the retrieval of information by computer to meet every possible requirement would be expensive, although much of the extra cost would be justified by the fact that many more people would use the retrieval system. At present, the difficulties of finding out what objects a museum, especially in another country, has or has not got are frequently so great that the seeker after information is too discouraged even to begin. IRGMA believes, however, that most museum information retrieval requirements can be met through the use of differently ordered indexes arranged, for example, by name, date or location. It was found in the Cambridge experiments that such indexes can be produced by machine at about 1 per cent of the cost of achieving the same results by hand.

THEFT: ITS ENCOURAGEMENT AND PREVENTION

No one pretends that a record of an object, however carefully that record is prepared, is the equivalent of the object itself, but it is clear that, if something is destroyed, damaged or stolen, the existence of a good record is a welcome substitute for what has been lost. Apart from the activities of criminals, which are becoming more widespread and better planned each year, wars, revolutions, vandalism and sabotage seem to have become an almost normal feature of world society, and the resulting destruction of museums, works of art and historical material of all kinds is on a terrifying scale. In circumstances such as these – and there is no reason to suppose that they will not continue throughout the 1980s – a modern, worldwide system of information storage becomes extremely urgent and one can only regret that both UNESCO and individual governments have so far not been in a position to finance computer-based storage and retrieval systems on the scale required.

We have said that an international computer system should make life more difficult for thieves and for those who deal in stolen museum material. This assumes two things which do not yet appear to have been publicly stated: that museums should be under a legal obligation to register the details of their collections and accessions in this way; and that the system should be programmed to add the details of thefts to the master-tape. It would then be a hazardous, if not impossible, undertaking for a public museum to add to its collection any item which had been acquired illegally. The same safeguard would not, unfortunately, apply to private collections, where a high proportion of stolen objects find a home.

As William A. Bostick, of the Detroit Institute of Arts, has pointed out, there is a long tradition of pillage and theft of works of art. It is not a modern phenomenon.

The illegal acquisition of one country's cultural property by a foreign, culturally thirsty state or art collection [he reminds us] has been

Natural History Museum, Bern. Method of displaying African mammals: Oryx.

going on since the dawn of history with no significant interruption. Art was generally considered one of the spoils of armed invasion, and when this brutal method stopped, art was acquired with money – a less bloody means but in many cases hardly less rapacious. Scarcely any category of art conqueror can be considered without guilt in this sad, long history – national governments, heads of State, museums, museum directors, eminent art historians, curators, dealers and art collectors.[11]

It has been, in Mr Bostick's phrase, 'a long and bloody war', and, as in all wars, the protests have come from the economically or militarily weak countries, not from the strong.

Napoleon's art acquisition programme [he recalls], especially in Italy, enriched French museums. A number of masterpieces returned home after Waterloo but a *buona parte* remained in France. Twentieth-century rumblings from Greece about the Elgin marbles being in Britain echo nineteenth-century grumblings from the British public and press criticizing Lord Elgin for bringing all those stones to England. German archaeologists invaded the Near East equipped with scientific knowledge and methods. No protective national laws kept many of the treasures from going to Germany. American millionaires sent their art *avant-garde* to Europe with the

Termessos, Turkey. Sarcophagus looted by thieves, a not uncommon occurrence, especially where the site is in a remote rural area.

powerful arsenal of dollars, some of dubious ethical origin when judged from a sociological standpoint. With no defensive laws to protect their national heritage, the Italians, French, English, Dutch, Belgians, Spaniards, Greeks, and even the Russians were easy prey. Some art historians might call it brilliant connoisseurship. Others may prefer to label it *The Rape of Europa*.

A survey carried out during 1972 and 1973 by the General Secretariat of INTERPOL[12] showed that twenty-six countries were particularly concerned about the theft of cultural property. Thirteen were in Europe, two in Africa, one in North America, five in South America and five in Asia. The countries involved could be divided, it was reported to INTERPOL's General Assembly in Ottawa in 1973, into two main categories, 'those countries which possess art objects in places to which the public have access (for example, museums, churches, galleries, etc.), and those countries which have considerable archaeological treasures and are the victims of illegal digs and thefts from excavations'.

Some of the countries circularised gave details of the types of places where thefts had occurred. Belgium reported 164 thefts from churches and chapels between 1970 and 1973, 117 from private premises and 40 from museums and galleries. In Finland, there were 45 thefts from museums, 4 from churches, and 8 from private premises. Thieves did very well in France, where 212 thefts were reported from churches, 131 from castles and 67 from museums. The United Kingdom gave details of large-scale robberies at country houses.

Very few of the thefts occurred at places which had security systems, but the United States pointed out, 'while the risk of theft was rather less in premises equipped with highly modern anti-theft equipment, the art thief with a particular work of art in mind tended to improve his techniques'.

The consensus of opinion seemed to be that very valuable objects were generally found, apparently because it was difficult to dispose of them, but that objects of lesser value were only rarely recovered. Where they did reappear, they were usually in the hands of

dealers, but the United States also mentioned the private collections of professional thieves who had acquired a taste for valuable art treasures.

The problem is serious, growing and worldwide. In 1972 UNESCO convened a meeting, held in Brussels, of international organisations which are concerned with the security of cultural property; in 1973 another conference, also sponsored by UNESCO, dealt with the theft and illegal transfer of ownership of works of art; and, again in 1973, the French National Committee of ICOM held a seminar, at St Maximin, on the security of museum objects.

But the thieves, it has to be remembered, are not the only guilty parties. Museums themselves, abetted by story-hunting journalists, carry a share of the responsibility by habitually referring to their 'treasures' and by emphasising the 'priceless' nature of items in their collections. This is, of course, the continuation of a very old tradition, which was established long before public museums were thought of. The private collections and treasure chambers of kings and princes were, in most cases, the result of greed, and, however beautiful the items in them may have been, the fact that they were valuable and a proof of riches was never lost sight of.

One of the most encouraging features of the situation now is that the prices fetched by works of art at auctions have shown strong signs of levelling out and, in some instances, of declining. If this tendency continues, as one very much hopes it will, these items will begin to lose much of their attraction as investments. With the sale value increasing steadily year by year, as it has for half a century and more, it has been worth a collector's while to buy a painting or a carving, which in some cases might well be stolen, and to hide it away, if necessary for many years, before finally releasing it back on to the market, in the hope that the theft would meanwhile have been forgotten.

It is not always easy to check the origins of something one is thinking of buying. An honest dealer, trusted by a museum or private collector, may himself have been deceived, and a dishonest or semi-honest dealer may prefer, on behalf of his client, to forget facts he may suspect or know. There is often a considerable delay between an object being stolen and dealers hearing about it. This is unlikely to happen in the case of famous works – if a Rembrandt were to be stolen from the Rijksmuseum in Amsterdam today every major art dealer in the world would know within a matter of hours. The difficulty arises mainly with items of secondary importance, especially if they happen to be anonymous – a Chinese jade or an Inca carving – and if they have never passed through a saleroom.

Once INTERPOL is informed and given a full description of the stolen article, details are sent to national police authorities throughout the world, who in turn are supposed to pass on the information to dealers, museums and any other kinds of people who might be asked to buy the item. This is normally a fairly slow process, partly because INTERPOL's headquarters in Paris tends to distribute its descriptions in batches at regular intervals, rather than immediately it has the news that a particular object has been stolen, and partly because the people who should be able to describe the object are not always able to do so quickly or accurately. Given a week or two's start before the information gets round the world, a thief's task is a great deal easier.

INTERPOL's notices are sent out in both French and English and, wherever possible, with photographs. The English text of a 'good' notice, that is, one which has been drawn up on the basis of full information, reads like this:

During the night of 12th/13th April, 1973, unidentified offenders gained entry to the church in St. Ouen l'Aumône (Val d'Oise) and stole a statue of the Virgin and Child, known as the 'Vierge ouvrante', dating from the 14th century, in polychrome wood, and listed in the 'Répertoire des Monuments Historiques français' since 1897.

The statue is 140 cm. in height, carved from a single walnut stock by an unknown artist.

The Virgin is seated in a stiff pose, on a throne with a heavy base decorated with quadrilobate gothic ornamentation.

The statue is in two equal sections, having been sawn from the top of the head to the base (see photo 1). The sections are hinged to the column of the base and when opened form a triptych, the third panel being constituted by the back of the statue.

Inside, twelve niches have been carved out and one of the upper niches shows Christ on the Cross at Calvary, with the Virgin and St. John the Evangelist kneeling at the foot of the Cross.

The other niches contain statues of Christ, standing, with a halo and wearing a tunic, and the twelve apostles (see photo 2).

To provide INTERPOL with this amount of detail of the 'Vierge ouvrante' may not have been particularly difficult – the statue had, after all, been officially listed as an historic monument since 1897 and it was not exactly unknown to art historians – but museum curators might find it useful to test themselves and their colleagues by imagining that an item had been stolen from their own museum and then attempting to describe it, for INTERPOL purposes, in similar detail. If the collection has been catalogued in the ways indicated above, the task should not present any great problem. It is, in fact, no bad thing, when cataloguing a newly-acquired item, to ask oneself if what one has written on the form, together with an attached photograph, would serve as the basis of an adequate INTERPOL description.

The General Conference of UNESCO adopted, in November 1964, a series of recommendations to its member states on the means of prohibiting and preventing the illegal export, import and transfer of ownership of cultural property. Six years later, in 1970, ICOM made ten recommendations for ethical rules governing museum acquisitions and ten suggestions for putting this code into effect. This code has subsequently been adopted by a number of national associations of museums, including the American Association of Museums, and by many individual museums, but it is not easy to persuade museums which, like those in the United States, have their own board of trustees and are anxious to preserve their independence, to agree to follow the policy laid down by some outside authority.

The ICOM Code parallels a measure agreed to by UNESCO in the same year, the *Convention on the Means of Prohibiting and Preventing the Illicit Import, Export and Transfer of Ownership of Cultural Property*. By October 1975 only twenty-five member states had ratified the Convention. The USSR, USA, France and Britain have not so far done so, but one hopes that their decision will not be long delayed. The twenty-five agreed:

1. to prohibit the import of cultural property stolen from a museum or a religious or secular public monument or similar institution in another State party to the Convention ... provided that such property is documented as appertaining to the inventory of that institution;
2. at the request of the State Party of origin, to take appropriate steps to recover and return any such cultural property imported after the entry into force of this convention in both States concerned, provided, however, that the requesting State shall pay just compensation to an innocent purchaser or to a person who has valid title to that property;
3. to oblige antique dealers, subject to penal or administrative sanctions, to maintain a register recording the origins of each item of cultural property, names and addresses of the supplier, etc.

It will be noticed that the UNESCO Convention only applies if both countries involved in an illegal transaction have ratified the Convention. At the present time, for example, Turkey and Egypt – two countries which are a frequent source of stolen material – have ratified it, but the United States – probably the major recipient of such goods – has not. In such circumstances, Turkey cannot request the support of UNESCO within the terms of the Convention.

The point regarding adequate documentation is of great importance. If an object is not registered in the inventory of any institution, it will almost certainly be exceedingly difficult to recover it, even when both countries are parties to the Convention. This means that material stolen from tombs or other archaeological sites and from many churches is extremely vulnerable. The law of, say, Greece or Turkey may forbid the export of such articles, but if they have never been positively identified, and recorded, to get them back may be almost impossible.

In any case, as William A. Bostick has very sensibly pointed out,[13]

the real policing of any acquisition ethics policy rests with a museum's professional staff, particularly the director. No board of trustees possesses the art expertise to enforce a policy that it has solemnly adopted. Even the national or regional direction of a museum is limited in controlling the director of a public museum who may place the reputation-enhancing aspects of the acquisition of a masterpiece above the ethics of that acquisition. And the censorship of such a director will have to come from his colleagues in other museums who have adopted ethical acquisition policies and are conscientiously trying to abide by them.

The only permanent and reliable safeguard against theft from museums and other places in which cultural property is kept is a fundamental change in the concept of 'value'. So long as 'value' is equated with 'market value', there will be thefts, no matter how much is spent on security measures. Critics of the capitalist system point out that it has encouraged people at all levels of society to rate objects and services, almost instinctively, in terms of what they are likely to fetch in the market. By this standard, something which sells at $10,000 is automatically and beyond question superior to something priced at a mere $1000. That the lower-priced article may be more beautiful or of greater historical or social significance is of no consequence. This philosophy is the thieves' charter and it is essential

to undermine it, attack it and ridicule it at every possible opportunity. So long as museums continue to regard themselves as treasure-houses, thefts will continue.

The two counter-tendencies which need to be encouraged are, first, the establishment and popularisation of museums and collections in which the market value of the exhibits is low, and, second, the exchanges of objects between museums on a far greater scale than we have become accustomed to seeing so far. Both, in their different ways, can function as an antidote to the 'we have more Picassos than you have' poison.

An obvious example of the low-value, high-interest collection is the neighbourhood or community museum, now found in many different forms around the world. In such museums as Anacostia, in Washington, and Le Creusot, in Burgundy, the 'value' of the collection lies in the fact that it exists and in its totality. The individual objects in the museum are not such as to attract international gangs of criminals. They are significant and interesting only because the creative ability of the organisers, designers and curators have made them so. Disperse the collections and scatter them around the world's salerooms and the items would fetch very little, if anything at all. The Anacostia Museum in Washington can create a very effective display to show the cultural importance of rats in a slum neighbourhood, but the market value of the central feature of such a display, a dead rat lying on the ground, is nil.

It is true that, by creating fashions, museums may create or help to create market value. A successful exhibition of, for example, nineteenth-century heating-stoves or clothes and furniture of the 1920s may arouse so much interest that the objects begin to have what they did not have before, status, prestige and official recognition. Junk then becomes desirable and saleable, as one has noticed very clearly in the case of Victoriana, and previously disregarded folk art and peasant handicrafts move into the yearned for and expensive category. One must, however, keep a sense of proportion in these matters. Robberies of Bulgarian peasant blouses and

Victorian washstand jugs are not yet sufficiently important or widespread to make the headlines or to cause INTERPOL serious worries, and even museums with very little money to spend can, for the most part, still get hold of these things if they feel they need them.

One curious feature of the collecting habit is worth mentioning. People rarely collect what their own kind of person used or made in the past. They collect what are to them exotics. Farmers do not build up collections of old agricultural implements, locomotive drivers are rarely found to have homes crammed with railway bygones and it is not the furniture makers who buy old furniture. This can lead to curious results in the museum field, where much of the impetus and motivation come from a wish to show how other people lived and worked. The curator or director who lives in a pleasant suburban house does not, for the most part, wish to put all other tasks aside in order to create the world's finest collection of suburbiana. He goes for Georgian silver, the life of the American Indian or the Australian aborigine, the ecology of the Arizona desert or the history of coalmining. Mr William Bostick has remarked[14] that in Detroit, as elsewhere in the United

Museum of German History, Berlin, GDR. Side-by-side reconstructions of a worker's kitchen-cum-living room and a middle-class sitting room, c. 1900.

States, art museums are under great pressure from the black community to develop their collections of African art. But, strangely, there are in America few black people, however well-to-do, who collect African art. They expect the white man to do that for them. One could observe, in the same connection, that in Britain resistance to demolishing old churches or to their conversion to new purposes tends to be strongest among people who never go to church.

The more the field covered by museum collections widens and the more 'ordinary' objects it embraces, the more confused thieves, and also, one must add, dealers, are going to become, and that, to any rational and public-spirited person, can only be a very good thing. Much the best way of defeating an opponent is to confuse him. But a broadening of taste and interest is to be encouraged for many reasons other than mere prudence, the chief being that it protects museums against charges, often justified, of élitism. Medieval European painting and Chinese porcelain rest on a cushion of several generations of expert knowledge and of innumerable scholarly books and articles. Collections of such objects are extremely likely to make the ordinary, non-expert person feel small, to convince him that he has come to the wrong

Netherlands Museum of Distillation and Spirits, Schiedam. Still.

place. Local history, however, wildlife collections, industrial and technical archaeology and the life of the past fifty years have a much wider appeal and are more calculated to give the museum visitor a feeling of security and of being among friends.

It is regrettable, for this reason, that such a high proportion of the international exchanges of material which take place between museums are of what must be frankly described as connoisseur material. The West German Museum of Toys, the Swiss Museum of Clockmaking and the Netherlands Museum of Distillation and Spirits do not send parts of their fascinating, easily intelligible collections abroad from time to time. Nor does the Nantucket Whaling Museum, the Farmers Museum at Cooperstown, New York, or the Museum of Walloon Life at Liège. What moves around the world is eighteenth-century French painting, Egyptian and Chinese art, and Benin bronzes. As Mr Bostick rightly said, 'art-historians, that great international freemasonry, have had things their own way for much too long'.[15] Apart from conservatism and tradition, there are a number of well-established reasons for this:

1. There is the kind of exhibition which always has a well-prepared, scholarly catalogue, which helps the international reputation of its author and of the exhibition organisers long after the exhibition itself has closed.
2. Provided the exhibition takes place in a very large city, usually the capital, and continues for several weeks, a large number of visitors can be stimulated without too much difficulty, by the skilful use of superlatives in one's publicity. The exhibition is the first, the biggest; enormous difficulties have had to be overcome in order to make it possible at all; such an opportunity may never occur again.
3. The market value of the exhibits is known to be prodigious and is advertised accordingly. Press and television coverage are therefore assured.

4. Exhibitions of yesterday's art are politically safe, or can be made to appear so. The art of the day before yesterday is even safer.

But this near-monopoly of exchanges by the archaeologists and art historians is being increasingly challenged by the more adventurous and public-spirited museum directors, who see it as both socially and culturally irresponsible and professionally indefensible. It conflicts with the multi-disciplinary approach, which is receiving more and more support each year, and, most serious criticism of all, it achieves its successes by ignoring the questions that a large proportion of visitors and potential visitors want to ask. To make sure of the next exhibition, the international organisers play politically very safe. When they do not, as in the case of the 1972 London exhibition of early Soviet architecture, they know there will be political controversy and political difficulties which interfere with scholarly work and, for the sake of future peace and achievement, these things are best avoided.

There is a great hunger in all countries for information, real information, about the way in which the rest of the world lives and the films and exhibitions which show this are both very popular and very difficult to arrange, because most of the world's governments are sensitive and frightened about international comparisons. But who can doubt the phenomenal success of a travelling exhibition which showed the complete interior of say, six Russian, Swedish or Canadian homes, with plans, photographs and actual objects? Or of the household budgets and feeding habits of these same six households? Many other possibilities suggest themselves: twenty-four hours in the life of a military conscript; ways of spending a holiday; the career, personality and taste of contemporary political leaders; the form that corruption takes in different countries; newspaper and magazine production; and so on. One knows from conversations with both museologists and members of the public in many countries that there is a great wish for such international exchanges of museum material and, at the same time, a realisation that nothing but tightly controlled propaganda exercises are likely to be tolerated or financed.

What is clearly required, and what is equally clearly in the process of developing, is a much broader view of what UNESCO has termed[16] 'licit and supervised circulation of cultural property between States'. 'Cultural property' includes both the 'Mona Lisa' and a photograph of the living-room of a French steelworker, a fact which may be politically awkward but which has to be realised and insisted on, in the interests of honesty, genuine international understanding and, not least, museology.

It is absolutely correct, as UNESCO stated in its 1973 Report, that international travelling exhibitions can 'allow a broad foreign public to get better knowledge of the culture of the country of origin', and that 'long-term exchanges or gifts of cultural property constitute a valuable instrument for the communication of cultures'. The Report gives the impression, however, that the experts responsible for it were thinking wholly in terms of art and archaeology, although natural history and ethnography must have been referred to in the course of discussion at the conference. To this extent, the document, with its valuable recommendations, needs to be brought up to date, in order to meet the present-day demands of museums and their public and, indeed, to make a new kind of public possible.

Such a development is implied, although not specifically mentioned, in the Report on international museum exchanges submitted to UNESCO in 1975 by Mr Goy and Mr de Varine-Bohan.[17] One cannot, as a matter of either professional integrity or common sense, accept that certain items reflecting a national culture, at any point in history, are for export and exchange and others are not. Culture is a whole or it is nothing.

Until recently, the concept of exchanges between museums has been a very narrow one. London will have its grand exhibition of paintings by Turner, Paris will do the same for Picasso, the National Museum in Cairo will send its Tutankhamun treasures around the world and China will put its ancient art on tour. Private and public collections will be approached to lend items to make the exhibition larger and more comprehensive, and the well-publicised attendance figures will be taken as sufficient proof of the exhibition's success. International exchanges, in other words, have been overwhelmingly within the fields of archaeology and fine art, and for the most part between what are, in world terms, rich countries.

So far, very little attention has been given to the enormous and far-reaching possibilities of exchanges between developing countries, although the value of this is now becoming much more widely realised. The past and present of Ghana should and could be a matter of great interest to people in Tanzania and Botswana. The construction of the Tanzania–Zambia railway by the Chinese, a remarkable technical achievement, carried out quickly and efficiently and with a minimum of international friction, deserves what it has so far not had, a first-class travelling exhibition which could be shown throughout Africa and China. The National Museums in Dar-es-Salaam, Peking and Lusaka might well have considered using the opportunity to mount special exhibitions to show something of the life and traditions of the three countries involved, but nothing of the kind was in fact done.

It is a curious and sad fact that although European and North American museums are full of works of art and ethnographical material from all the countries of Asia, South America and Africa, it is comparatively rare for a museum in, for example, Brazil to have much to say about Argentina, or for a museum in Uganda to show much interest in the culture of the Sudan or Ethiopia. This is partly the result of conventional thinking and partly of a lack of confidence – some African countries, for instance, do not yet appear to believe, for all their public display of national strength, that their traditions, history or artifacts are of interest to their neighbours. Museum-

exchanges within Africa, which are very likely to grow within the next ten years, will be impressive evidence that national confidence has risen above its base-line.

One can also hope and expect to see a considerable increase in the exchange of both individual objects and complete displays between the different regions of the same country, especially where these regions are ethnic as well as geographical. As yet, few of the developing countries have shown signs of imitating the model provided by Ghana in this respect, and of deliberately making sure that every regional museum devotes much of its space to material from other regions. The present situation contains many ironies and examples of a lack of courage and imagination. In Montreal, for instance, it is no doubt admirable that there should be a superb museum collection of objects made by Eskimos, as a way of showing people in this part of Canada something of the skills and artistic talent of their fellow-citizens in remote parts of the country. But it is equally necessary that Eskimos living in these same remote territories should be introduced, through museums and exhibitions, to the other sub-cultures which exist within Canadian territory. One could say much the same of the Museum of the Indian in Rio de Janeiro. Why, one wonders, is there no Museum of the Indian in the areas where the Brazilian Indians actually live? Why is there no kind of museum or collection illustrating American life in Ireland, which provided America with so many of its citizens, or no Museum of Irish Culture in New York or Boston? Why, above all, have museums in politically divided and mutually hostile regions of the world so far given their citizens so little opportunity to learn something about the 'enemy's' traditions and way of living, in the hope that differences and misunderstandings may one day cease to be the burden and the handicap that they are today?

APPENDIX 1.1

ICOM Catalogue Card

1. *Number of the object* or of the specimen in the Museum.
2. *Name of the Museum,* and, in some cases, name of the collection to which the object at present belongs in the Museum.
3. *Name of the administrative body or department* responsible for the Museum in which the item is housed (Province, City, Ministry, University, and so on).
4. *Classification,* i.e. general field of collection to which the item belongs (Art, Ethnography, Natural History, etc.).
   Sub-classifications can be added here, to follow the practice of a particular museum and the character of the object indicated, if it should happen to be a reproduction, reconstruction, forgery, sample, model, interpretation or translation.
5. *Location* in the Museum.
6. *Geographical origins of the item.*
7. *Nomenclature of designation of the object.* This may be the 'name in the Museum's usual language', the 'scientific name, if one exists', the 'common or vernacular name', or all three.

8. *Name of the author, artist or craftsman,* or, in the case of natural objects, the *Name of the Class, Order, Family or Genus.*
9. *Materials of which the item is made.*
10. *Manufacturing and transformation.* This includes the technique and place (in a house, in a workshop, etc.); the kind of worker involved; the measurement and weight of the object; how long it took to make; a description of any decoration, with a note on the significance of the decoration. Where applicable, it also includes a description of the smell of the object and of the sound it makes.
11. *Date, method, source and place of acquisition.* 'Source', in this context, includes the local ecological conditions, where such information is relevant.
12. *Price paid or estimated value,* at a stated date.
13. *Name of collector and of expedition.*
14. *Cultural or ethnic group* to which the object belonged.
15. *Function or use of the object.*
16. *Character, traditional value or significance attached to the item.* This includes an assessment of the item as rare, commonplace or archaic.

17. *Ownership at the time of acquisition.*
18. *Chronological data,* i.e. when or approximately when the object was made and used.
19. *Style, school or influences represented.*
20. *Historical background of the item.* This includes the record of ownership, exhibition and previous sale.
21. *Condition and preservation of the item.* This means the condition when it was acquired and any conservation treatment, possibly of a first-aid nature, which it has subsequently been given.
22. *Museographical notes.* These include dates of identification and cataloguing, references to photographs, films or reproductions, and recordings, and to any exhibitions or catalogues in which the object may have appeared.
23. *Bibliographical references.*

Miss Oddon's card and explanatory notes may be usefully compared with other attempts to carry out the same essential task of registration and cataloguing.

APPENDIX 1.2

New Delhi Catalogue Card

1. Accession Number
   (e.g. 66.682)
2. Subject or title
   (e.g. 'Reconciliation of Lovers')
3. Provenance
   (e.g. Pahari, Kangra School)
4. Period
   (e.g. E. 19th Cent. AD)
5. Medium
   (e.g. painting on paper)
6. Negative Number
   (e.g. 357–66)
7. Mode of acquisition
   (e.g. gift of such-and-such)

8. Description
   (e.g. Radha leans on her elbow on her bed, lifts her veil and looks at her Sakhi (*confidante*) standing at the foot of the bed, while Krishna kneels at Radha's feet. Lamps on either side of the bed. Beyond the terrace are an ewer and bowl on a low table and another light (lamp). Trees in the background and a crescent moon in the sky. Colours used: red, green, blue, yellow, brown, gold and black. Perhaps illustration to Rasikapriya of Keshav)

9. Published
   (e.g. A. K. Coomaraswamy, *Rajput Painting,* Oxford, 1916, describes this painting, which was then in his collection)
10. Location
    (e.g. storage, almirah no. 10, shelf no. 6)
11. Exhibition
    (e.g. Alger House, Detroit Institute of Arts, 1952)

APPENDIX 1.3

IRGMA Catalogue Card

Card of	File	Institution : identity number :	Part

IDENTIFICATION

| Simple name | D | title/serial number | D | Number of items |

| C | full name | D pattern date | D identifier : date | D | D |

PRODUCTION

| Method | person's role | name : date | D place | D | D |

| C |

ASSOCIATION

| Keyword | person | D date |
| service/unit | | D |

| C | place | D event | D | D |

| Keyword | person | D date |
| service/unit | | D |

| C | place | D event | D | D |
| C | Related items | D |

ACQUISITION

| Method | acquired from : date |

| C | | D price | D | Conditions Yes/No | Copyright Yes/No | D | D | Valuation : date | D |

MILITARY ARTEFACT   © Museums Association 1977   April 1977
Published by the MDAU, Duxford Airfield, Duxford, Cambridgeshire, U.K.

MUSEUM LOCATION
RECORDER
DESCRIPTION

Location : date	Recorder : date
Component parts	
Condition	Completeness
Part : materials	part : materials
Dimension measured value and units	Inscription	method	position
	Mark	
	transcription	note
	description	
	transcription	note	D
	description	
Part : aspect : description	part : aspect : description	D

PROCESS

| Conservation Reproduction | other | method : operator : date : note | cross-reference | D |
| Conservation Reproduction | other | method : operator : date : note | cross-reference | D |

DOCUMENTATION

| L | class | author : date : title : journal or publisher : volume : note | Drawing or photo |

NOTES

| Notes |

IRGMA cataloguing system. Front and back of one of the series of record cards.

2 Conservation

During the past thirty years, there has been a notable shift in museum priorities, as a consequence of the growing realisation that mere acquisition is a sterile activity and that there is no point in the broadest sense usable. Collections which are falling to pieces or which nobody is allowed to see or study are not really worth having. On the other hand, once a museum is committed to a policy of making its possessions available either to students or to the general public, it cannot escape the duty of conservation. The national heritage is not, even so, to be seen as an assembly of perfectly embalmed corpses. It exists, and is helped to survive, in order to stimulate the imagination and shape the thinking of successive generations. It is cared for in order to build bridges between past and present members of the national and international community. Without such bridges, life becomes unnecessary, shallow, pointless and unreal. Viewed in this way, conservation is both a prime duty and a highly creative activity, and within recent years a wide range of technical discoveries has placed it on a far more solid and scientific basis.

THE 'WASA' AS A SYMBOL OF MODERN CONSERVATION METHODS

The treatment of the woodwork of the great seventeenth-century warship, *Wasa*, a task which has been going on since 1961 and has cost a very large amount of money, symbolises the enormous advances which have taken place in conservation techniques during the past fifty years, and, as the largest and most ambitious piece of museum conservation ever attempted, it has brought a group of skills from the background workshops, where they normally hide themselves away, into the full light of publicity and attention. By deciding to admit the public to watch the work being carried out, the organisers of this prodigious feat have not only created a widespread interest in the techniques involved, but have contrived at the same time to cover a remarkably large proportion of the cost.

Wasa has been, in fact, a microcosm of the problems, both scientific and financial, which modern conservationists have to face. A brief account of these problems and of the way in which they have been solved forms a very good introduction to this highly important aspect of museology.

When the *Wasa* was brought to the surface on 24 April 1961, after spending 333 years on the bed of Stockholm harbour, very little detailed consideration had been given to what might be called the museum side of the ship's future. Opinions ranged from saying that no treatment of any kind would be necessary, because she had been built of heart of oak, to the other extreme, stated with equal confidence, that to attempt to preserve the ship would be a ludicrous failure and a total waste of money. Once exposed to the air, she would disintegrate almost before the

The 'Wasa' conservation project, Stockholm, Sweden. The ship in her special concrete dock, before erection of the building to protect and display her.

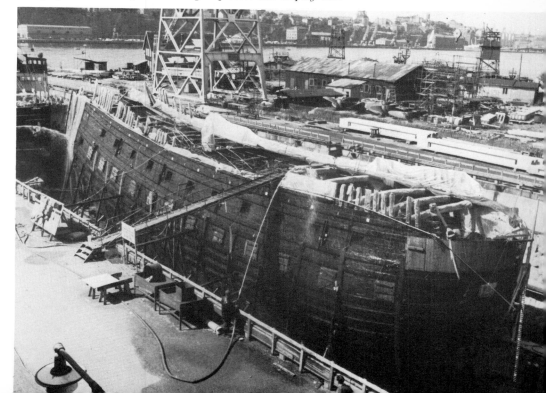

The 'Wasa'. Spraying of the hull in operation.   *The 'Wasa'. Wooden sculptures in conservation vat.*

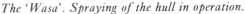

eyes of the people who were trying to save her for posterity. To make an objective and properly informed decision about this a special committee was set up, called to begin with the Wasa Preservation Committee and then, from 1964, reorganised as the National Maritime Museum Preservation Committee. It consisted of experts on all the types of material which were likely to be found in the *Wasa*, and a preservation section made up of people who would eventually have to organise the work. The Committee had, and still has, regular meetings, to discuss progress and to make recommendations.

The wood, mainly oak, but with some birch, had been affected in various ways, depending on its position in the ship and on the kind of wood. In general, the surfaces which had not been covered with clay had decayed most, to a depth of up to one centimetre. The main cause of decay was a type of mould-producing fungus, 'soft-rot', which can live under water. Before studies were made of the *Wasa*, it was not reckoned that this type of fungus affected wood to any considerable extent. It was also noticed, and this again was a pioneering observation, that 'soft-rot' had done less damage where timbers had had iron fastenings at the joints, even though the iron had long since rusted away.

The moisture content of the wood varied enormously, depending largely on the severity of the fungus attack. There was no evidence of shipworm, which is, in fact, not a worm but a mussel, which destroys wood by boring. The absence of this mussel in the water surrounding the *Wasa* was attributed to the low temperature, the lack of oxygen and the low salt content.

Protection against further rotting and against insects was not thought to be a serious problem, providing the water content of the wood was kept within safe limits. Shrinkage was, however, a considerable worry. To estimate the shrinkage which could have been expected if the wood had been permitted to dry naturally, tests were made with wood taken from the *Wasa* at room temperature and humidity, but without exposure to direct sunlight or other forms of accelerated drying. The results made it clear that preservation was absolutely essential. Contractions of 15 per cent and more were measured on test pieces, so that if the hull had not been given preservative treatment there would have been such a high degree of shrinkage that the entire ship would have had to be taken to pieces and later restored, an impossibly expensive and long-drawn-out process.

The obvious conclusion was that the wood must not be allowed to dry and shrink. For several months after the ship was raised to the surface, the inside of the hull was kept constantly sprayed with fresh water and the outside with sea-water. By the end of the autumn, a shelter had been built over the *Wasa* and the air-conditioning plant could be set in operation before the cold Stockholm winter began. If this timetable had not been kept to, the water in the wood and between the joints would have frozen and the hull would have been subjected to dangerous stresses and strains.

Meanwhile, laboratory work had been proceeding to discover how the wood could be satisfactorily preserved, since obviously one could not go on spraying it with water for ever. There was no previous experience which could be drawn on. An organic find of such dimensions – the hull alone has a total surface area of more than four acres – had never been preserved before.

It soon became evident that no existing chemical composition could solve the two main problems, rot protection and stabilisation of dimension. Something new had to be invented, and, since speed was essential, the necessary research work was carried out by Government research establishments, by public institutions and private companies, and by the preservation section itself. Eventually two products emerged as suitable, one a new composition of fungicides with polyethylene glycol (PEG) containing borax and boric acid, for treating single objects – there were about 25,000 in tanks – and the other

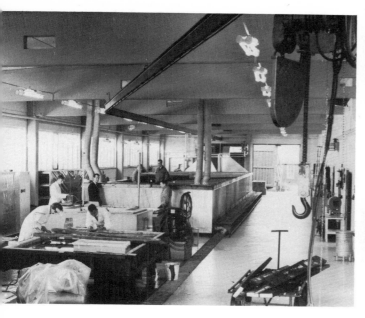

The 'Wasa'. Preservation hall for loose finds.

The 'Wasa'. Oven for conservation of iron objects by reduction with hydrogen.

the same composition together with methylpolysiloxane, for the treatment of the hull by means of an automatic spraying system.

'Visitors are surprised', says Lars Barkman, the Head of the *Wasa* Preservation Department, 'that the preservation of the *Wasa* takes place quite openly, so that everyone interested can follow the work. Since the beginning it has been natural for the staff concerned to avoid any mystery-making and we hope that the experiences, together with the development of the methods and the technique of preservation, will be useful to other preservation centres of archaeological finds and also to modern inpregnation industries.'

This is certainly the case. *Wasa* has been a gigantic conservation laboratory, not only for wood, but for all the other materials found on board, including textiles; ceramics; glass; alloys of copper, lead or tin; iron. One of the most interesting technical installations is a special furnace for treating iron finds. By this method, dry hydrogen gas is used to reduce the rust back to iron and, in other cases, to dry the objects in nitrogen in order to protect them.

If *Wasa* had been raised fifty or even twenty-five years earlier, there is little doubt that she would now be in very poor condition and might well have needed to be almost rebuilt, had that been financially possible. What has

been done in Stockholm since 1961 emphasises the completely different technical and scientific basis on which the conservation of museum material now rests. The change has been not only in the actual methods of treatment but also in the theoretical approach to the subject. This has been brought about by the establishment on an ever-increasing scale of museum laboratories. In these laboratories, the scientist has the opportunity of applying his specialised knowledge to a fundamental understanding of the various problems that can arise in the preservative treatment of museum material. He can then carry out planned research in close collaboration with museum curators. This scientific co-operative approach has led to the concept of what is now termed conservation, which embraces much more than the empirical approach of restorers, who in the past were mainly concerned with mere repair and restoration of museum objects and used materials largely of natural origin such as animal and vegetable glues and natural waxes and resins. Conservation involves a two-stage approach, first an understanding of the causes of the deterioration of museum objects which may occur when they are exposed to unsuitable environmental conditions in the museum or, in the case of archaeological material, may result from burial in the ground or immersion

in water. Then, secondly, there is the task of developing new, reliable methods of treatment based on theoretical considerations and tested by practical experimentation.

THE DEVELOPMENT OF MUSEUM LABORATORIES

The history of conservation, in the broad sense, goes back as far as the beginnings of museums and art galleries, but for many years – until the beginning of the present century, in fact – it was undertaken on a very amateur basis and in many instances, owing to a lack of understanding of the nature and behaviour of materials, it piled up even worse conservation problems for the future. What was done lacked any scientific background. It was based on the efforts, often very devoted and painstaking, of craftsmen who used all that existed for them to use, experience and standard craft techniques. The Victoria and Albert Museum has one of the oldest traditions of restoration work in what it used to call its 'art workroom', but this did not become a full department of conservation, with a scientific background, until 1960.

The first museum laboratories were established in about 1900 at the Staatliches Museum in Berlin and at the Nationalmuseet in Copenhagen, where

British Museum, London. A corner of the Conservation and Research Laboratories, showing the scale of investment required by a major museum.

scientific methods for the treatment of museum objects were carried out by Rathgen, who produced the first text-book on the subject, and by Rosenberg, who wrote a book devoted to the treatment of iron objects. After the First World War, the idea of museum laboratories was extended to other countries, some of the most notable examples being the British Museum Research Laboratory, established in 1921, dealing mainly with antiquities; the Chemical Laboratory of Antiquities in the Egyptian Museum, Cairo, established in 1923; the Laboratory for the Scientific Study of Paintings and Works of Art in the Louvre, Paris, and the Technical Laboratory of the Metropolitan Museum of Art, New York, both established in 1931; the Central Laboratory of Belgian Museums (now known as the Royal Institute of the Artistic Heritage) established in 1934; and in Germany, the Laboratory for Scientific Research relating to Paintings at the Doerner-Institut, established in 1938. In 1936 a laboratory was set up in the newly-formed Institute of Archaeology in the University of London, to train archaeologists in the techniques of conservation.

In Britain, the Courtauld Institute of Art established a conservation laboratory for fine art in 1946 and this was followed by one at the National Gallery in 1947, although both had had scientists on their staff since before the war. After the Second World War the establishment of museum laboratories spread on an increasing scale throughout the world. In a list of laboratory museums and restoration studios attached to museums and art galleries published in 1960 by the International Centre for the Study of the Conservation and Restoration of Cultural Property 133 such institutions are noted in 38 countries. The geographical distribution was:

	Countries	*Institutions*
Africa	2	3
Americas	3	30
Asia	8	13
Europe	24	85
Oceania	1	2

Among these institutions there were upwards of thirty museum laboratories in which scientific personnel were engaged on research in conservation. Since 1960 a number of important museum laboratories have been estab-

lished in other museums and art galleries, so that it can be said that the development of scientific conservation has proceeded steadily, if not as rapidly as one might have wished.

The present position is far from satisfactory, however. 'During recent years', said a recent report,[1] 'there has been an increasing feeling of unease in the museum world about the inadequacy of the conservation services which are available for the collections.' This, in plain terms, means that museums cannot look after their collections properly. The authors of this report came to the conclusion that more than half the material in the museums of the United Kingdom was in need of conservation, and there is no reason to suppose that the situation is any better elsewhere. 'In all except archaeological departments and units,' they believed, 'the backlog of material awaiting conservation is increasing and this is most serious in private and local museums.' The situation was worst, they felt, in fine art, ethnography and natural history collections, mainly because this type of material demanded specialist treatment. Items connected with industrial archaeology, science and technology, folklore and bygones, on the other hand, appeared to be reasonably well provided for, since this kind of material is often cared for by members of the curatorial staff, or by volunteers.

The shortage of money and trained conservation staff is, in Britain as in other countries, causing some types of museum to restrict their collections. 'The main categories of material being turned down', the Report tells us,

are industrial archaeology, science and technology (mainly due to lack of trained conservators and space to store acquisitions); natural history (as no training is available in this country in mounting large specimens and it is expensive and unsatisfactory to use foreign-based facilities); textiles; and archaeology, especially waterlogged wood, as the facilities for treating large objects do not exist.

About 450 people describing themselves as conservators have been traced in the United Kingdom. They work in 202 museums and galleries, but this certainly does not mean that each conservation unit has 2.2 conservators, since many of the people concerned are employed in the large institutions, especially the national museums, which may employ four or five of this kind of specialist. Another way of making the same point is to say that, for work requiring a skilled, trained conservator, the majority of museums, in Britain as elsewhere, have either to employ some-one working privately or get help from a larger and better equipped museum. In a number of countries it is assumed that conservation will have to be to a large extent centralised, in order to make the maximum use of scarce facilities and to provide proper opportunities for training. Thailand, for example, has a Central Conservation Laboratory in Bangkok, as part of the Department of Fine Arts. It has well-trained conservators and scientists on its staff, several of whom have studied at specialist institutions abroad – paper and textiles in Japan, Chinese ceramics at Taipei, mural painting in Rome. Its laboratory began in a very modest way, in two huts, but today it has a building of its own, with special rooms devoted to

Bavarian National Museum, Munich, GFR. Textile restoration workshops.

Sixteenth-century embroidery from Hardwick Hall, after conservation work by the Textile Conservation Centre, Hampton Court Palace, London.

The Textile Conservation Centre. Part of a model of the facilities the Centre would like to have.

metals, ceramics, textiles, stone and wall-painting. Much of its equipment was provided by UNESCO and the laboratory is gradually being equipped for more advanced work.

Looking ahead ten or twenty years, it seems most unlikely that any country, however wealthy, will find it either possible or desirable to provide more than a small proportion of its museums with the kind of conservation facilities and staff which will allow every item in a museum's collection to be efficiently looked after on the premises, with no outside assistance. To do so would indeed be as wasteful as for each small museum to employ a full-time professional designer. On the other hand, a great deal is lost if there is no one on the staff who is able to carry out the more elementary conservation work efficiently and who enjoys doing so. Any museological course which fails to give its students a chance to obtain adequate practical experience of this kind is a poor course and a number have rightly come under criticism recently for this reason.

The saddest situation a museum can find itself in, and one which is unfortunately by no means uncommon in the developing countries, is to have a skilled conservator on its staff, who knows exactly what has to be done and has the ability to do it, but who cannot use his talents because the museum lacks the necessary funds. At least one major Indian museum, the Prince of Wales Museum in Bombay, is in precisely this position. The soil in Bombay contains a great deal of salt, which seeps into, up and through porous walls. Assisted by wind and rain, salt has percolated through the walls of the Museum's picture gallery, damaging, in some instances seriously, the collection of European paintings. The conservator, who is a specialist in picture restoration and has studied in Italy, would like to restore the pictures and the Director would like to treat the walls in order to stop the salt-damage from continuing, but since there is no money for the necessary building work or for another full-time administrator, the conservator has to spend most of his time on general duties and the paintings decay a little more each year. This is a somewhat unusual variant of the situation commented on by the International Institute of Conservation's United Kingdom Group. 'Conservation carried out by curators', the Group declared, in the Report to which reference has already been made, 'causes us concern. It is a waste of their time and museum training if they have to carry out their own conservation.' It is presumably equally true that it is a waste of a conservator's time if he has to carry out curatorial or administrative duties.

INTERNATIONAL CO-OPERATION IN CONSERVATION

With the increasing awareness of the need for scientific conservation and a world shortage of the money needed to carry out research, it has long been realised that some form of international collaboration between curators, scientists and restorers working in the various museums and art galleries is essential, if properly planned research into new methods of conservation is to be carried out. This international co-operation was naturally fostered at an early date by the International Council of Museums under the guidance of Georges Henri Rivière, at that time Director of ICOM. The first step was taken in 1948 when a Committee on the Care of Paintings, representing experts from twelve countries, was set up by ICOM and met for the first time in London in 1948 and in succeeding years in Rome and Paris. In 1950 the International Committee of Museum Research Laboratories was set up, also under the aegis of ICOM, and held joint meetings with the above Committee at regular three-yearly intervals until, in 1967, they were combined as the ICOM Committee for Conservation. Another significant step was taken in 1959, when the International Centre for the Study of the Preservation and

London Bridge, moved to the United States at great expense and reconstructed at Lake Havasu City, Arizona.

Restoration of Cultural Property was established in Rome by UNESCO as an independent inter-governmental organisation to encourage international co-operation in the study and dissemination of information concerned with the scientific and technical problems of the conservation of cultural property. This centre derives its income from a payment of 1 per cent of the contribution that a Member State makes to UNESCO.

A contribution of a rather different kind towards international co-operation was the formation in 1950 of a professional body, the International Institute for Conservation of Historic and Artistic Works. The Institute has its headquarters in London, at 608 Grand Buildings, Trafalgar Square, WC2. Personal members of the Institute are of two grades – fellows and associates. Fellowship is a professional qualification conferred on persons who, through their knowledge, skill and experience, are regarded as specialists of outstanding ability concerned with conservation. The grade of associateship is intended to provide for those persons who may not possess the necessary professional qualifications, but who are interested in the aims of the Institute and wish to take part in its activities. In addition, there is institutional membership, open to any corporate body (such as a museum, library, university) which is interested in the work of the Institute and wishes to receive its publications. The Institute publishes the quarterly journal *Studies in Conservation*, and *Art and Archaeology Technical Abstracts*, which appears twice yearly. The aims of the Institute are also fostered by the organisation of international conferences to focus attention on selected aspects of conservation. These have included: Recent Advances in Conservation (Rome, 1961), Textile Conservation (Delft, 1964), Museum Climatology (London, 1967), Conservation of Stone and Wooden Objects (New York, 1970), and Conservation of Paintings and Graphic Arts (Lisbon, 1972). The twenty-fifth anniversary of the Institute was celebrated by a sixth international conference in Stockholm, with the theme of Conservation in Archaeology and the Applied Arts. The Institute has now over 2000 members drawn from fifty-five countries.

Two frequently heard criticisms of the Institute, and of its journal, *Studies in Conservation*, are that they display too much interest in paintings and textiles and too little in other branches of museum work, and that they are over-concerned with science and scientific examination and under-concerned with the applications of science, that is, with conservation. An analysis of *Studies in Conservation* for the ten-year period 1964–73 supports this to some extent. Of a total of 169 articles, 69 were devoted to conservation and the remainder to scientific examination. Of the 169, 55 articles related to oil paintings, watercolours and miniatures; 42 to antiquities and mural paintings; 15 to textiles; 7 to ethnography; 14 to sculpture; 10 to climatology and the environment; and 26 to miscellaneous subjects. There is an almost complete absence of papers on science and technology, furniture and woodwork, geology and, most regrettably of all, natural history.

The *Bulletin of the American Institute for Conservation of Historic and Artistic Works* shows a not dissimilar proportion of subjects and of scientific and practical papers, but the American publication is superior in two respects – it includes regular comments on treatments which have failed, as well as on those which have succeeded, and it provides a forum of information, usually in the form of brief notes, on new materials and techniques in all branches of conservation.

A good deal of information about various aspects of conservation is to be found in technical and scientific journals, and in general museum publications. What is notably lacking, however, is a worldwide system of summarising current literature dealing with the conservation field as a whole. *Art and Archaeology Technical Abstracts* covers only part of what is required and one hopes very much that the next ten years will produce something more comprehensive, so that duplication in research can be avoided and new ideas brought quickly to the people who need to know about them.

It should be pointed out, perhaps, that, in the matter of conservation, the wishes of museologists on the one hand and of connoisseurs and dealers on the other are not always the same. The museum conservator is concerned only with what will benefit the object and permit it to last longer; the connoisseur's requirements, on the other hand, may be more subjective and emotional.

An excellent example of this divergence of views is given by Dr O. P.

Agrawal, Chief Chemist and Head of the Central Conservation Laboratory at the National Museum, New Delhi. Writing about the conservation of museum objects in Thailand,[2] Dr Agrawal records that many of the bronze sculptures and images he has examined there have been suffering from a form of corrosion known as 'bronze disease', which appears as green waxy spots. This green chloride patina is harmful to the bronze, because its formation is a continuous process, generating hydrochloric acid which eats away the copper in the bronze, and it has to be removed by chemical means if the object is not to decay. Most art connoisseurs and dealers, for psychological rather than technical reasons, prefer bronze objects to have a green patina and see the removal of the patina as a form of damage. This strange attitude, as Dr Agrawal points out, will only change with time and as a result of a determined and sustained educational campaign.

CONTROL OF MUSEUM ENVIRONMENT

The survival of museum collections, in both temperate and tropical countries, depends on the creation of a satisfactory micro-climate within the museum area. If museum objects are left to fend for themselves and to fight off the destructive attacks of atmospheric pollution, damp, heat, strong sunshine and insects, their future is gloomy at best. The task of the museum curator is to look after the material in his charge better than nature would. How much better depends entirely on the amount of money he has at his disposal and on the relative importance he gives to conservation and display, which are traditional and inevitable enemies.

In the belief that prevention is better and usually cheaper than cure, one of the most important tasks undertaken by the scientist working in a museum laboratory is to study the effect of different environmental conditions on museum objects – whether on exhibition or in storage. In this way it is possible to determine the environmental factors which are likely to lead to progressive deterioration and then to discover methods of controlling the ambient conditions so as to ensure the preservation of the collections in museums. This has in fact become a special aspect of conservation, now

National Museum, New Delhi, India. Central Conservation Laboratory. The Laboratory, the largest and best equipped in India and South-East Asia, undertakes the conservation of works of art belonging both to the National Museum and to the smaller Indian museums which are without conservation facilities of their own. The Laboratory also provides a nine-month training course for young conservators.

Fitzwilliam Museum, Cambridge, England. Modern arrangement and lighting in a Victorian gallery.

referred to as museum climatology. The museum objects likely to suffer damage if exposed to unfavourable atmospheric conditions are those made of organic materials such as wood, ivory, textiles and paper, and the possible agencies causing damage are pollutants, undesirable variations in relative humidity, and biological attack by insects and mould growth.

The common atmospheric pollutants are sulphur dioxide and hydrogen sulphide derived from the combustion of coal and oil, ozone and nitrogen dioxide and what scientists call particulate matter and the layman knows as dust.

Sulphur dioxide can be the cause of extensive damage to museum objects and library and archival material; it is readily converted into sulphuric acid, which causes the progressive degradation of a wide variety of materials. Paper becomes weak and brittle; textiles are 'tendered', due to loss of mechanical strength, and eventually disintegrate; leather suffers a breakdown of its structure to a powdery and decayed condition (so called 'red rot'); and limestone, marble and frescoes decay because the calcium carbonate is converted into calcium sulphate with a doubling of volume, so that the surface expands, flakes and powders. Hydrogen sulphide reacts with all the metals of antiquity, except gold, to form dark-coloured sulphides – the tarnishing of silver being the commonest museum problem. Also, it will react with paint films containing white lead, causing darkening.

Clean air legislation is now decreasing the amount of dirt in the air of many cities and industrial areas, but the level of sulphur dioxide is unfortunately rising with the growth of industry. There is a strong case, therefore, for removing sulphur dioxide from the atmosphere of all urban museums in industrialised countries. This can be achieved by passing the circulating air through either an activated charcoal filter or through a water spray incorporated in the air-conditioning system. No special precautions need to be taken to remove hydrogen sulphide; instead, it has become common practice to apply a lacquer to silver objects to protect them against tarnishing.

Ozone and nitrogen dioxide have recently become a serious menace in certain towns in the United States: they arise from the exhaust gases of automobiles in the winter smog of cities such as Los Angeles which are blessed with a great deal of sunshine. Owing to their powerful oxidising action these gases cause damage to organic materials and they are consequently a potential hazard in museums. They can be removed by the use of suitable filters.

All the particulate matter which can settle on museum objects is airborne and much of it, particularly in cities, is tarry and adheres tenaciously to sculptures, tapestries and textiles. To prevent this, high priority must be given in urban museums to filtering the air. Salt in the air is a problem for museums near the sea, and for museums in arid zones wind-borne sand and dust constitute a hazard that can be completely cured only by filtering.

The problem of environmental control has to be seen in proportion. Air-conditioning is an expensive affair and its results are by no means always good, a fact that is only slowly becoming recognised. In a wealthy city with an unpleasant summer climate, like Washington DC, air-conditioning has become almost universal during the past fifty years, in homes, offices and public buildings. Pollutants can be trapped and collected in the air-conditioning plant, but the heat removed from buildings has to go somewhere and the only possible place is the atmosphere. One unwanted but unavoidable effect of air-conditioning in Washington and other cities in America and Australia is therefore to make the streets much hotter, a situation that is made worse by the huge areas of paved surface which modern civilisation involves. A tolerable temperature inside a building is consequently achieved only at the expense of an intolerable temperate outside, and the shock of passing from one to another is unpleasant and occasionally dangerous.

It is inconceivable that during the next twenty years Calcutta or Cairo or Lagos will install air-conditioning systems on the scale that Washington has done. The money and the incentive will simply not be there. In these and many other cases throughout the world, the country needs and the people want a great many things more urgently than air-conditioning. One can imagine, however, that in each of the major cities of the developing countries a few outstandingly important public buildings – hotels, government offices, conference centres – will be equipped with this expensive modern luxury and that the people who sit, sleep and walk in them will feel highly privileged as a result. How many museums will share this privilege is a matter of speculation. The answer, probably, is very few and those that do achieve it will in most instances have to forgo other amenities and facilities in exchange. Faced with a choice of this kind, how many museum directors are going to opt for air-conditioning and postpone indefinitely their hopes of more storage space, better workshops or a larger exhibition area? One can say, with complete truth, that a museum needs air-conditioning, but one is also entitled to ask, 'At the price of what?' It is fair to point out, too, that not all large cities are equally industrialised or have an equally polluted atmosphere. What applies to Tokyo or Frankfurt or Paris, with their great armies of motorcars and central-heating plants, does not apply with anything like the same force to New Delhi, Alexandria or Nairobi.

All that can safely be said is that nowadays efficient methods for the control of air pollution in museums are available and, where the money exists, desirable. It is also self-evident, or should be, that expenditure on practical conservation is a waste of resources if an object that has deteriorated as a result of its environment is replaced in the same environment after treatment, since it is certain to deteriorate again. If, on the other hand, an exhibit that has received proper conservative treatment is housed in an atmosphere in which the level of atmospheric pollution, the relative humidity, and the lighting are maintained with the standards recommended by the International Institute for Conservation,[3] it will probably not need further treatment for many years. Air-conditioning by itself is only half the story, however. It becomes a virtually useless luxury unless adequate monitoring of the pollutants is carried out; this need not be continuous and can be manual or automatic, but it should be carried out regularly and the information passed on to a responsible authority in the museum.

By world standards, the technical facilities available to museum staff in Britain can be reckoned good, and museums in many other countries would consider themselves extremely fortunate if they were equipped to a level which British museologists consider quite inadequate and which is certainly inferior to what the Americans have become used to. If the provision of monitoring equipment in British museums can be taken to represent the average provision which is now made in the more fortunate countries, it will be seen that there is still a very long way to go before the position can be felt to be satisfactory.

A recent survey[4] in Britain showed that in 1973 – the figure may, of course, have improved since – 71 per cent of the museums investigated had equipment for measuring relative humidity, 35 per cent had light meters and 24 per cent ultra-violet monitors. The monitoring of atmospheric pollutants which cause both chemical and physical damage to exhibits was undertaken in only 10 per cent of the museums with conservation staff. Since the detailed and systematic monitoring of atmospheric pollutants requires expensive equipment and a laboratory to analyse the results, it is not surprising that the figure is so low.

What is a more disturbing revelation in the survey is the small proportion of museums which have ever sought outside professional advice on environmental control, since even if one cannot afford to buy monitoring equipment for oneself, it is always possible to obtain at least some of the information one needs by having the necessary scientific work done on contract. Of all the museums in the sample, only 64 per cent had sought such advice. When these museums were examined in relation to their size, as reflected in the total number of staff, they fell into three distinct groups. In those employing a total staff of less than 10, about half had sought advice. Of those with over 11 and under 200 employees, just over 90 per cent had had advice, and in the last group, those with more than 200 employees, all have had advice. It is clear, therefore, that it is the small museums which are in greatest need of help and in which the collections are most at risk. Corresponding figures are so far not available for other countries, but it seems very probable that a similar pattern would be observed elsewhere.

Organic materials are susceptible to damage arising from shrinkage and expansion due to absorption of moisture when the relative humidity is too high and loss of moisture when the relative humidity is too low. To avoid these dimensional changes in moisture-sensitive materials, a reasonable balance has to be maintained between the normal moisture content of the material composing museum objects and that of the ambient air. In practice, this means that the relative humidity in museums should not be allowed to rise above 60 per cent or fall below about 45 per cent, and that whenever possible it should be maintained at some set value between these limits. In art galleries in which panel paintings are exhibited the relative humidity should be stabilised at 55 ± 5 per cent. The temperature is dictated by human comfort at about 20°C.

The needs for controlling the museum environment are now well recognised and the main problem is, on the whole, not the lack of knowledge but the difficulty of applying knowledge. Air-conditioning systems have been installed in many established museums – the cost of doing this in old buildings is always high, even in countries where labour is cheap – and in the construction of new museums air-conditioning is looked upon as essential and forms an integral part of the design. Alternatively, particularly in museums being built in tropical countries, where the maintenance of air-conditioning can be prohibitively expensive, owing to the high natural humidity, the cost of electricity and the amount of heat to be removed from the building, architects are concerned to design the museums so that fluctuations in relative humidity can be naturally reduced as far as possible. If for any particular reason the installation of air-condition-

ing is impracticable, the requisite control of relative humidity can be achieved in those areas of a museum where moisture-sensitive material is exposed by installing humidifiers and/or dehumidifiers, in restricted areas or in showcases. Portable equipment for controlling humidity is not expensive and does not necessarily have to be bought abroad. Manufacturing it is now a considerable industry in a number of tropical and near-tropical countries and this tendency is certain to increase as the range and size of its market grows. One well-known Indian manufacturer, Tropical Refrigeration Industries, of Bombay, counts among its customers laboratories, research establishments, printers and lithographers, the data-processing industry, communication centres and libraries. Museums are merely one sales outlet among many, but they benefit, both in price and reliability, from the total size of the market. And, in any case, portable dehumidifers constitute only part of the production of a company which is concerned with helping people to live more comfortably in a hot climate. In India, as elsewhere in the tropics, keeping cool has become big business.

Large ceiling-mounted fans, of the type normally found in hotels, restaurants and other public buildings in tropical countries, are a cheap and invaluable means of keeping the air moving round a room and of bringing the temperature down a welcome few degrees. They are certainly not to be disdained, even in these days of air-conditioning, and in many museums they represent the possible, whereas air-con-

National Museum, Dar-es-Salaam, Tanzania. Exterior, showing general design with double row of ventilation louvres.

ditioning is a near-impossible dream. It is interesting to notice in this connection that two modern and well-run African museums, the National Museum in Accra and the National Museum in Dar-es-Salaam, have very little air-conditioning and pin their faith to fans, louvres, blinds and to a well-thought-out architectural design which encourages the free movement of air throughout the building. The resulting temperature is perfectly tolerable and pleasant and makes leaving the museum building and re-entering the outside world much less of a shock. At Dar-es-Salaam, air-conditioning is confined to the museum's library, which is also used as the boardroom, the argument presumably being not that the books need an air-conditioned atmosphere, but that those engaged in research or meetings are likely to spend long periods sitting down in a restricted area and at close quarters with a number of other people, who are all breathing, sweating and making both themselves and the room steadily hotter and more difficult to work in.

Museum objects composed of organic materials are susceptible to biological damage due either to insect attack or mould growth.[5] This problem is one that is particularly prevalent in museums in tropical countries. Insect attack can be countered by the periodic fumigation of the collections or by the use of suitable insecticidal preparations, and these precautions have now become almost a routine procedure in many museums throughout the world. Textiles and works of art on paper or parchment are particularly liable to suffer damage on account of mould growth; they provide a nutrient medium for fungi, which will grow rapidly if the relative humidity is high, i.e. above 65 per cent, and if there is an inadequate air circulation. Such a moist, stagnant environment is a particular problem in humid tropical countries, and special precautions involving the extensive use of fungicidal preparations must be taken in museums in these countries.

Paper and other materials used to write on suffer from more afflictions than attacks by insects or mould. In a number of tropical countries palm-leaves have been extensively used for writing purposes and in South-East Asia many religious texts are still written on palm-leaves, either with a pointed stylus or with pen and ink. In the course of time, palm-leaves become brittle and start to break. Their flexibility can be restored by soaking them in a suitable oil, like citronella or camphor. If they have already become very weak, either through age or as a result of insect damage, they can be laminated between cellulose acetate sheets. Palm-leaves, like paper, can be damaged by acidity in ink or paint. This, if treatment is too long delayed, causes the leaf or sheet to disintegrate. The only remedy is de-acidification, a difficult process to control, because it tends to change the tonal value of the colours.

CONTROL OF LIGHTING IN MUSEUMS

Even when precautions are taken to protect museum objects from atmospheric pollution, adverse climatic conditions and biological attack, there still remain the very real hazards arising from exposure to light, because many materials are susceptible to photochemical degradation. Such light-sensitive materials are to be found in the following categories:

Pigments and dyestuffs (including inks)
Textile fibres – cotton, linen, wool and silk
Paper, wood
Paint media, varnishes

Exposure to uncontrolled illumination will cause the fading of certain pigments and dyestuffs.[6] This occurs most noticeably in watercolours and illuminated manuscripts. Textile fibres themselves are colourless and are not rapidly affected by light, but in a fabric where the fibres are associated with dyes, mordants and pigments, complex reactions occur under the influence of light, causing the fibres to weaken or, in the technical phrase, 'tender'. This tendering is particularly apparent in tapestries where the silk threads used in the 'high lights' may be badly decayed. Silk flags and banners also deteriorate to a serious extent.

Exposure of paper to light causes embrittlement and discoloration and some furniture woods become bleached. Similarly, light slowly erodes paint media and varnishes, causing discoloration and physical breakdown.

The extent of the damage to these sensitive materials depends on three factors: the actual level of illumination,

New England Conservation Center, North Andover, Massachusetts, USA. Part of the paper restoration laboratory. A co-operative venture by the six New England states to allow public libraries and other non-profit-making bodies to have documentary material restored and repaired at cost, using the most up-to-date methods. The machine in the background moulds new paper directly on to a damaged document, from pulp.

the total time of exposure and the quality (i.e. the spectral composition) of the light source. The ultra-violet component in the light source is most potent in causing photochemical degradation and this should be eliminated as far as possible. This can be done by interposing an ultra-violet absorbing filter between the light source and the museum object. Such filters are now available as varnishes or plastic sheets and films. Their efficiency can be evaluated by measuring the proportion of ultra-violet radiation with a special monitor. The best-known and most used monitor, the ELSEC UV, Type 678, is made in England and cost, in 1975, about £200. It is simple to use and, by pointing it towards each source of light, one can obtain an immediate reading of the total amount of ultra-violet radiation from this course.

In considering the question of the level of illumination a balance has to be struck between the level needed to give adequate viewing conditions of the museum object and that demanded by conservation. The situation most satisfactory to conservationists is one in which nothing is ever displayed, a point of view which is unlikely to commend itself to most museum directors and curators. Experience has led to the following recommended maximum values of illumination: 300 lux for objects insensitive to light – metal, stone, glass and ceramics; 150 lux for objects of medium sensitivity – oil and tempera

paintings, undyed leather, wood, horn and ivory; and 50 lux for objects particularly sensitive to light – watercolours, prints and drawings, textiles and costumes, manuscripts and miniatures, dyed leather and many natural history specimens. The lux is the international unit of illumination value and is equal to one lumen per square metre (an alternative unit used in Great Britain and the USA is the foot-candle, which is expressed as one lumen per square foot and is approximately equal to 10 lux). To check that the conditions of lighting are being controlled correctly it is necessary to measure the illumination value with a light-meter.

Once the dangers inherent in museum lighting are realised, much can be done to mitigate, if not eliminate, them without involving oneself in great expense. The following principles should always be kept in mind when planning new exhibitions and modifying old ones.

(i) Storage rooms and galleries should be kept unlighted when not open to the public.
(ii) Direct sunlight should always be rigorously excluded by the use of blinds, louvres or curtains.
(iii) Light-sensitive material should not be kept on permanent exhibition unless conditions can be strictly controlled.
(iv) Ultra-violet absorbing filters

should be used where appropriate. This can be effected by using special slightly-tinted glass in the cases or by covering each fluorescent tube with a wrapping of Uvecran or other suitable vinyl plastic. Inside the cases, it is helpful to make use of what are called 'cold mirrors', which cut off most of the infra-red from spotlights.

It is evident that considerable progress has been made in recent years on the problems of lighting and conservation in museums, and there appears to be general agreement on the basic principles involved and the practical methods to be adopted so as to reduce the potential hazards. It seems worth while, even so, to emphasise certain points on which misunderstanding still occurs.

The first is that although incandescent lamps produce very little ultra-violet light and consequently a negligible amount of photo-chemical activity, their infra-red radiation is a source of heat, especially when the object exposed to it is of deep colour. This danger is not serious in a normally ventilated room, but it has to be carefully considered when spotlights are used or when the lighting source is a closed case.

A second often overlooked point is that the same degree of infra-red radiation from a lamp can produce quite different degrees of absorption on different parts of a picture or other vulnerable object. The maximum absorption, and therefore heat, occurs on the darkest colours which absorb the maximum and reflect back the minimum. The reflecting power of varnish, too, varies a great deal, according to whether it is matt or shiny.

An ingenious and, from a visitor's point of view, very impressive and exciting form of lighting has been devised for the paintings, all by Rubens, at the Art Gallery in Vaduz, Liechtenstein. There is no natural lighting and by arranging spotlights to play only on the highlights of the pictures – those least affected by infra-red light – a dramatic effect is obtained

National Postal Museum, London, England. Method of storage and display, showing how stamps are protected by low-intensity lighting.

and the minimum damage is caused to the pictures.

CONSERVATION AND DISPLAY

After considering the needs of conservation as regards control of the environment and lighting, the question now arises as to how these requirements can be correlated with the demands of display which are to communicate and to create an exhibit which is aesthetically pleasing. A 'design' for conservation is concerned with preventing deliberate display decisions that may prove unacceptable because they may cause damage to the museum objects and works of art on exhibition by exposing them to adverse atmospheric conditions and unsuitable lighting. With free-standing objects practical problems

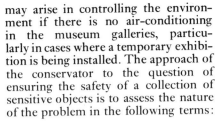

may arise in controlling the environment if there is no air-conditioning in the museum galleries, particularly in cases where a temporary exhibition is being installed. The approach of the conservator to the question of ensuring the safety of a collection of sensitive objects is to assess the nature of the problem in the following terms:

(*a*) To specify the characteristics of an acceptable environment.

(*b*) To investigate the normal climatic conditions inside the museum with a view to making a forecast of the relative humidity and temperature during the exhibition if no controls are exercised.

(*c*) To test and install equipment capable of modifying the gallery conditions so as to produce the required acceptable environment.

In addition to this problem of general control of the ambient atmosphere there is the question of the design of showcases to be considered from the conservation point of view. The closed showcase has become standard in museums because it is supposed to be the only practical way of preventing vandalism, although a hammer can make short work of a showcase, but it is not so widely recognised that it also make short work of a showcase, but it is not so widely recognised that it also makes it possible to create stable environmental conditions, a microcase backed with moisture-containing material such as wood or cloth is preferable from the conservation point of view to a bare showcase made of nonabsorbent material, because a more equable climate can be maintained inside the showcase in the desired range of 50 to 60 per cent relative humidity, if the temperature inside the case

Detroit Institute of Arts, USA. Method of displaying and lighting paintings.

(below) *North Kimbell Museum, Fort Worth, Texas, USA. Use of natural light in a new museum building (1974). The light-slits run the length of the cycloidal concrete vaults and the natural light is diffused evenly across the galleries through specially designed filters. Supplementary illumination is available from groups of spotlights, which can be angled and directed as required.*

remains fairly constant. This latter criterion may raise an awkward question from the display point of view. If showcases are internally lit the heat output from the light source must be kept as low as possible, and if spotlights which can generate heat are used as an external source of lighting, every precaution must be taken to ensure that they do not cause an undesirable rise of temperature inside the showcase. One often used method of achieving this is to mount the lights outside not inside the case.

As well as controlling the relative humidity in showcases, attention also has to be given to the exclusion of atmospheric pollutants. This means that showcases should be made as airtight as possible – any case made more than thirty years ago is almost certainly not airtight – and in special circumstances it may be necessary to devise a technique whereby the intake of air is filtered. Another possible source of pollution in showcases can be the materials used in their construction; certain materials may give off volatile sulphur compounds that will cause tarnishing, and others may evolve organic acid vapours that will attack certain metals, in particular alloys containing lead and zinc.

The problems that arise in connection with conservation and display can therefore be summarised as follows:

(*a*) The maintenance of correct conditions of relative humidity and temperature for the objects on display.
(*b*) The avoidance of light sources that generate an unnecessary amount of heat.
(*c*) The designing of showcases to ensure maximum protection against intake of atmospheric pollutants.
(*d*) The testing of materials used in constructing showcases to make sure that they do not evolve pollutants.

One related topic in the context of conservation and display is the possible damage to museum objects and works of art by thermal radiation from the very powerful light sources used for filming and television. It is essential that filters should be used on these lights to eliminate the heat (i.e. infrared) radiation, and this should be made clear in advance, and in writing.

The needs of conservation and display need not be opposed; the practical problems can be resolved by co-operation between the designer, who seeks to realise the exhibition on an aesthetic level, and the conservator, who advises upon the necessary conditions to ensure the safety of the objects on display.

CONSERVATION AND THE OPEN-AIR SITE MUSEUM

But, as we have indicated earlier, museums are exploding beyond their walls, a fact which causes conservationists serious anxieties, but to which they will somehow have to accommodate themselves. It is quite impossible to think of 'conserving' material in an open-air museum, or a house-museum, or a site-museum, in the same terms as in a conventional kind of museum-within-a-building, and it may well be that in twenty years' time half the world's museums will be of the new type. This will involve – it is already doing so – a complete new set of techniques and priorities among museologists in general and conservation experts in particular and a change in emphasis within the whole field of conservation, so that the care of paintings and fine art in general ceases to dominate the thinking of the profession in the way that it has for so long.

If one visits the oldest of the open-air museums, at Skansen, it is evident that these wooden buildings and their contents have 'suffered', if that is the correct word for a natural process, from the harsh Swedish climate and from the fact that most of the buildings are unheated during the winter. A certain lack of ventilation is also apparent, and if one visits Skansen in the spring the interiors feel rather damp and mouldy. The situation improves during the summer, but there is a general and inevitable process of decay going on throughout the museum, just as there is in any wooden buildings anywhere, in or out of a museum. Consequently, the structures, fittings and, to a lesser extent, the furniture are in constant need of repair and refurbishing. Timbers have to be replaced, roofs reshingled or rethatched, repainting carried out, insects dealt with. There is nothing shameful, backward or unprofessional about this. If these old

mills and arms and workshops were not at Skansen, most of them would have been pulled down or burnt down years ago. The Museum has prolonged their life by probably several generations and this, in Skansen's terms, is what conservation means, and must mean. At a well-organised open-air museum, such as Skansen, or the Gamle By at Bergen, or the Netherlands Open-Air Museum at Arnhem, or the Village Museum in Bucharest, or the Weald and Downland Museum near Chichester in England, it is possible to keep skilled craftsmen fully employed throughout the year on the repair and maintenance of these old buildings, something which would have been much more difficult had they remained on their original sites.

Open-air museums are, of course, benefiting like all others from new techniques and materials and they take full advantage of, for example, up-to-date methods of dealing with insects and fungus. But they realise, in most cases, that their exhibits are necessarily in a process of renewal all the time. A controlled environment is impossible to contemplate. All one can do is to say, in effect, 'We are looking after these objects to the best of our ability, so that you can see how our ancestors used to live.' Even if, in a hundred years' time, a house contained not a single original timber, the curators would be fully entitled to say that the museum had followed a consistent and effective conservation policy.

Temple in Central Gabon, reconstructed with the use of traditional materials.

Monterey, California, USA. California's first theatre, before restoration.

(below) *The theatre after restoration.*

now, in the late twentieth century, is to communicate, and that, in such a situation, the views of a puritanical conservator may need to be disciplined, although they should, of course, always be listened to with respect. Museums exist primarily to serve human needs, not to keep conservators in a state of permanent bliss, and some degree of expendability among museum objects is inevitable.

CONSERVATION TECHNIQUES IN THE MUSEUM

In the past the materials used by the repairer/craftsman were very largely of natural origin – animal and vegetable glues, natural waxes and resins – and the technical processes were dictated by the properties of whatever natural material seemed most suitable for the particular job in hand. As a result, progress in developing new methods of conservation were severely limited. However, during the past few decades advances in high polymer organic chemistry have resulted in the production of a wide range of new synthetic materials (commonly referred to as plastics), certain of which are of great value in conservation. These synthetic materials are not to be regarded as mere substitutes for the natural materials that were previously used. Many of them are in fact distinctive substances in their own right, possessing a combination of physical and chemical properties which is not to be found in any natural material. One thinks, for example, of the wide range of synthetic waxes and the non-solvent epoxy and polyester resins. For this reason, synthetic materials can provide the opportunity to develop improved and more reliable methods of conservation. At the same time it must be emphasised that no synthetic material should be used in conservation unless its properties are reasonably well known. This implies that the composition of a synthetic material must be known in all essential details and its permanence and properties assessed experimentally. It is one of the functions of the scientist working in

In at least one instance, at Bodie, California, the aim has been to maintain the buildings in what is called 'a state of arrested decay'. This ghost-town left behind by the nineteenth-century gold boom is very popular with tourists, who visit it for what it is, a ghost-town. It is consequently as proper to maintain it in its present form – a skilled task, since maintenance must always go far enough, but not too far – as it is to perform a similar act of kindness and reverence for the Forum in Rome.

This amounts to saying three things:

(*a*) that one must recognise the limits of conservation in any particular case;

(*b*) that some degree of decay is inevitable, and one might as well accept the fact. In certain instances, such as the grass and pole huts of an African village museum, decay can be very rapid, and extensive repairs, if not rebuilding, may be needed every ten years. In others, such as stone houses or churches, the process can be slow enough to be dealt with by normal annual maintenance.

(*c*) that the prime aim of a museum

Fitzwilliam Museum, Cambridge, England. New gallery (1966) for twentieth-century paintings.

(below) *Ulster Museum, Belfast, Northern Ireland. Part of bird display.*

a museum laboratory to carry out the evaluation of synthetic materials and also to provide a basic vocabulary to enable the conservator to choose the material he needs from the bewilderingly large number of trade names used to describe materials of essentially the same type. Such information has been incorporated in the publication, *Synthetic Materials used in the Conservation of Cultural Property*, issued by the International Centre for Conservation in Rome.

As examples of the use of synthetic materials in conservation one may cite:

(*a*) the use of epoxy resins and polyester resins as adhesives and consolidants for the reinforcement of disintegrated museum objects; they have the special advantage of good penetration and of setting *in situ* at room temperature without appreciable shrinkage;

(*b*) the use of the water-soluble polyethylene glycol waxes for the treatment of objects of wood and leather excavated in a waterlogged condition;

(*c*) the use of 'soluble' nylon (i.e. N-methoxy-methyl nylon soluble in methyl or ethyl alcohol) for the consolidation of friable or fragile surfaces – the film formed is remarkably flexible and matt;

(*d*) the use of polyvinyl acetate and polyacrylate resins as adhesives and consolidants;

(*e*) the use of polycyclohexanone resins as picture varnishes; they are similar in character to the natural resins mastic and dammar as regards varnishing quality but are more resistant to yellowing.

These modern materials, which are all produced commercially, have contributed greatly to the development of new techniques in conservation. As well as assessing the potential value of new materials in conservation the museum scientist also applies his specialised knowledge to developing chemical techniques for the treatment of a wide range of antiquities that have suffered

corrosion in the ground. Sound methods have been worked out for treating corroded bronze, silver, lead and iron objects, and the methods used can be adapted to the special conditions of the objects. Similarly successful techniques have been evolved for the treatment of decayed stone and for the desalting of ceramic objects which have absorbed soluble salts that constitute a latest source of deterioration. There are also effective techniques of consolidative reduction which is used for the treatment of corroded silver and lead objects.

Conservations with museologists in different types of museum in a number of countries, some rich and some poor, suggest that solutions to the following problems would be particularly welcome:

1. Delaying the decay and disintegration of straw and grass thatch.
2. De-rusting large items of machinery and protecting them against further rusting.
3. Longer-lasting paints for external use – a most important factor in

the maintenance budget of open-air museums.

4. New, cheap and strong materials for making picture frames quickly in the museum's own workshop. What is apparently wanted here is some form of plastic moulding process which allows the frame and the 'glass' needed to protect and hang, say, a poster, to be made in one and the same operation.

5. Anti-fading substances which can be sprayed on textiles or paper, or into which they can be dipped.

6. Synthetic substitutes for feathers, hair and shell, so that convincing replicas of animals, birds and shells can be made. The days when wild creatures had to be killed and nests robbed in order to provide specimens for museums must surely be drawing to an end, especially since the natural objects are so difficult and expensive to preserve. Superb fibre-glass elephants, with the original hairs inserted in the fibre-glass, which have been made for museum purposes in Africa, illustrate the opportunities which new materials have made available.

It seems probable that, during the next decade, more and more museums are going to be demanding this-is-guaranteed-to-work material for conservation purposes. Knowing that the number of highly-trained specialists and the amount of money required to pay them are both certain to be very limited, realistic museum directors are turning their attention towards compromises. Whatever the ideal situation might be, the facts of the world situation suggest that the museum profession needs, more than anything else, a series of extremely practical and up-to-date do-it-yourself manuals, aimed at the present needs of museums in the developing countries and of small museums everywhere.

CONSERVATION TECHNIQUES IN THE FIELD

This means, essentially, first-aid, giving an object just sufficient practical attention to make sure that it reaches the end of its journey in no worse condition than it started. It may be, of course, that 'the field' is where the object is destined to remain, that the museum is to be, so to speak, built around it, but we are thinking at the moment more especially of archaeological objects, plants, dead animals, birds and reptiles which have to be moved, possibly several hundred miles, to the point at which they are to receive professional conservation treatment. One can usefully concentrate on archaeology since, in all countries, a high proportion of museum accessions fall into this category, and since those who collect natural history specimens are usually adept at taking off the skins and keeping them reasonably fresh, or at bringing plants in the condition required by the museum for either display or research.

The facilities available for the immediate treatment of excavated material are usually rather primitive. This means that any on-site treatment must be limited to what is essential to lift the object or to temporarily consolidate it. The work carried out at this stage must be reversible, as it will probably be necessary to remove the consolidant when full-scale treatment is undertaken in the laboratory. The field conservator should therefore have the ability to visualise the complete treatment of excavated material, the initial stages in the field and the later stages which will be carried out in the laboratory. Some archaeologists carry out fieldwork without giving due thought to possible conservation problems and without the necessary basic equipment and expertise to deal with those that may arise.

If an object is flaking or structurally weak, it will be necessary to strengthen it by impregnation with a suitable consolidant, applied in a dilute solution either by brush or by spray to the object in the ground or by immersion when it has been removed from the ground. When an object is in such a fragile or fragmentary state that it cannot be strengthened for lifting with a consolidant alone, some form of rigid support will have to be inserted under the object. In some cases it may be considered desirable to take impressions or casts of archaeological features that emerge during an excavation, e.g. the moulding of the impression of the ship in the Sutton Hoo ship burial.

Another general principle of conservation in the field is to ensure that excavated material does not suffer an abrupt change in its environment. This means, for example, that organic material such as waterlogged leather, ivory or wood should be kept damp, and that porous ceramic objects which may have absorbed soluble salts should not be allowed to dry out quickly. It should go without saying, but no harm is done by emphasising the point, that first-aid treatment is to be avoided which may destroy evidence of archaeological significance. Eager as he may be to safeguard the object, neither the field-worker nor the conservator has any right to do this at the expense of destroying archaeological evidence. One is thinking, of course, of legal archaeology. The prime task of illegal archaeologists and dealers is to get the material out of the country and into the hands of a purchaser as soon as possible. All that these people require of an object is that it shall be in saleable condition.

SCIENTIFIC PREPARATION FOR CONSERVATION

An important feature of modern conservation is the use of scientific aids to obtain information about the actual condition of an object so that the precise nature of the problem involved can be diagnosed and the correct treatment worked out. The principal aids are: radiography, X-ray diffraction analysis, metallography, spectrographic analysis and microscopy.

Radiography is used, for example, to detect any decorative inlay that may be hidden underneath corrosion, or to ascertain the internal structure of an object. The information obtained may have an important bearing upon the subsequent method of treatment; if inlay is found to be present, in the case of a corroded iron object, the structure of the iron will dictate the extent to which mechanical cleaning can be attempted. Radiography can also be used as a guide in any subsequent mechanical cleaning for the removal of the overlying layer of corrosion.

Metallography is carried out to examine corroded objects in order to obtain information about the actual physical condition of the metal and the extent of the corrosion. This technique has proved valuable in dealing with the restoration of ancient silver objects, which are usually in a brittle condition and require to be annealed to make the silver ductile, so that the object can be repaired or re-shaped. The process of annealing can be controlled by metallographic examination in cases where the embrittlement does not respond to normal annealing. Similarly, the extent of corrosion can readily be determined by metallographic examination, to discover to what extent removal of the corrosion products may be feasible.

X-ray diffraction analysis is used to identify corrosion products and to determine the nature of any inlays which may be present. This information is important in connection with subsequent treatment when it may be necessary to remove corrosion and to choose for the purpose chemical reagents that will not attack the inlay. In a similar way qualitative spectrographic analysis is used to determine the precise nature of the material of which the object is made.

Microscopic examination of objects is of importance to conservation work – in many cases mechanical cleaning of small, delicate objects is carried out under the microscope. Recently the scanning electron microscope has been introduced for studying the extent to which consolidants penetrate. This has been used to monitor the treatment of decayed stone and waterlogged wooden objects.

DESIGN OF WORKSHOPS FOR CONSERVATION

To be fully effective, a conservation department should be associated with a museum or art gallery and not sited in isolation. This principle has been admirably followed in the new Hamilton-Kerr Institute for the restoration of paintings. Equipped and staffed to the highest standards, the Institute forms part of the Fitzwilliam Museum, Cambridge, although its rural site a few miles outside the city, at Whittlesford, allows it to develop an identity and existence of its own. The first essential in the process of design is to recognise the particular functions to be served by the department. They will include the following:

(i) Documentation of an object accepted for treatment, including photography and preliminary examination to assess its chemical and physical condition.
(ii) Facilities for carrying out the necessary methods of treatment.
(iii) Giving advice upon environmental conditions suitable for the display and storage of specific objects.
(iv) Making of replicas and the preparation and maintenance of displays in the galleries.

The extent to which these functions can

be carried out will be related to the size of the workshop, the number of staff and their professional qualifications.

A practical design for a conservation workshop will be related to the nature of the work to be carried out. Documentation, coupled with preliminary examination, will necessitate provision for clerical work and the storage of written records, photography and storage of photographic records, and an examination area with microscopes and possibly X-ray equipment. The preparation of replicas and displays in galleries will require equipment for casting and moulding and facilities for metalwork, woodwork and working in perspex. The remaining and most important function concerns the actual methods of treatment, the variety of which will depend upon the types of museum objects to be dealt with. Here certain general guidelines may be given from the point of view of the materials involved.

Organic materials, e.g. objects of wood, leather, ivory and textiles, will need ample bench space, and trays, containers, conditioning chambers, ovens and sinks will be needed for the treatments involved. The treatment of metal objects introduces a need for more elaborate equipment such as tools for mechanical cleaning and apparatus for carrying out electrolytic reduction. The processes involved in the treatment of ceramics and stone usually call for extensive bench space for washing, desalting and repair, but do not necessitate the use of complex equipment.

In the actual design of the workshops special attention will have to be given to fixed features which may be classified as follows: structural; services, i.e. ventilation, electricity and plumbing; and furniture.

DOCUMENTATION

The importance of keeping proper records of treatments done on museum objects cannot be over-emphasised. The reasons for keeping such records are briefly as follows:

1. A treatment may significantly alter the appearance, or even the structure, of an object.
2. The reasons for the success or failure of a given treatment cannot be assessed, if an adequate record is not available for consultation.

3. It may be necessary to carry out further work, or possibly a new treatment in the light of advances in conservation.

The record should contain information describing:

(i) the appearance of the object before treatment, supplemented with photographs (both general and detailed of any particular features) and radiographs where applicable;
(ii) the aims of the proposed treatment, including a diagnosis of the condition of the object;
(iii) a detailed record of the treatment, stage by stage, supported, where necessary, with photographs.

The actual recording can be made using either notebooks or simple card files (item cards). Notebooks should be of the duplicate type, from which one copy can be removed for storage in a central file. The use of card files is convenient and has the advantage that it is self-indexing, if the cards can be duplicated to cover key-words or provided they can be adequately cross-referenced or colour-coded along the top of the card. For information retrieval of the documentation the systems available are:

1. Edge-punched cards which are self-indexing but are limited in the number of cards that can be conveniently sorted, the upper limit being about 2000.
2. Feature cards which can be used for indexing up to 10,000 items. These cannot be used for the storage of actual information, but are intended for retrieval of information from an existing system of files, in which the dossiers are numbered from 1 upwards and stored in numerical order. The system is extremely versatile, since a large number of features can be employed.

No document can be quite as descriptive as a photograph, and it will therefore be essential for a conservation department to have its own photographic facilities, or ready access to such facilities. The photography of museum objects for record purposes is a specialised subject, and requires special training and appropriate equipment.

TRAINING IN CONSERVATION

Conservators are, or should be, essential members of a curator–conservator–scientist team, each with a special part to play in understanding and preserving the object. The conservator must be in a position to conduct a useful dialogue with both the curator and the scientist, and for any collaboration to be successful it must take place on equal terms. This is only possible if the conservator is an educated person, not a mere technician, with a considerable knowledge of science, technology, history and art. Training in conservation is of the first importance in museum work, and formal training courses have been established in a number of countries. The basic aim of these courses is to produce conservators with not only a theoretical knowledge of the materials and methods used in modern conservation, but with the necessary manual skills to carry out the work. Ideally, the formal course of training should lead to the award of a qualification (diploma or degree) which will confer professional status and give due recognition to the status of the conservator in the museum. The present position in Britain, which is probably neither much better nor worse than that to be found in most museologically advanced countries, is that a third of all full-time conservators have no professional qualifications whatever, a situation which can hardly be regarded as a satisfactory one.

There would appear to be in general three approaches to the manner in which training in conservation can be carried out. These are:

1. Apprenticeship 'in service' training.
2. Training at some form of technical institution.
3. Training schemes attached to university departments.

Apprenticeship has for long been the traditional type of training. It was primarily designed to teach practical skills in conservation at the hands of an experienced practitioner, but there is a growing tendency to combine this with formal theoretical training by permitting conservators working in museums to have time off to attend lectures at an academic or technical institution in order to obtain a certificate in conservation such as that awarded by the Museums Association in Britain. It is interesting to observe that the Canadian Conservation Institute has recently introduced a three-year 'in-service' scheme of training for graduates in art, archaeology or science; this might be considered as a hybrid of 'in-service' training and university training.

The second approach to training involves a full-time formal course in a technical institution for the aspiring conservator who has acquired from school the qualifications necessary for entry to the institution. Examples of such courses are those run by the Institute of Archaeology of London University, the Central Römisch-Germanisches Museum in Mainz, the Central Institute for the Conservation and Restoration of Works of Art in Madrid; the Institute for the Technology of Painting, in the State Academy for the Study of Fine Art in Vienna; the Central Institute for Restoration, Rome; the Faculty of Conservation in the Academy of Fine Art, Warsaw; the Department of Technology and Restoration in the Academy of Fine Art in Prague, and the Central State Workshops for the Restoration of Works of Art in Moscow. In addition, UNESCO has assisted in the establishment of centres for primary training in Jos, Nigeria, in Mexico City and in New Delhi. In these, regional considerations are influential in the choice of candidates and in the curriculum at each centre.

The training schemes attached to university departments are essentially postgraduate courses, in that the students have a first degree in an appropriate arts or science discipline. Such training schemes are run by the Fine Arts Department of New York University, the Winterthur Program in the Conservation of Artistic and Historic Objects at the University of Delaware, and the Cooperstown Graduate Program organised by the State University of New York, in co-operation with the New York State Historical Association.

In addition to these basic training courses, mention should also be made of courses in advanced training, i.e. refresher courses for qualified personnel. One such course is run by the Royal Institute of the Artistic Heritage in Brussels, who accept ten qualified conservators for a formal one-year advanced course, and a similar type of training is organised jointly by the Institute of Archaeology and the British Museum Research Laboratory, and by the International Centre for Conservation, in Rome.

The extent to which conservation has become a science-based study is indicated by the syllabuses of two short courses held in 1975 at the Courtauld Institute of Art in London.

The first, 'Macroscopy in Art and Archaeological Conservation', was 'a comprehensive course for conservators who wish to acquire or improve their knowledge of various scientific methods used in the conservation and examination of historic and artistic works'. The sessions covered macrophotography, in both black and white and colour; low-power surface microscopy and photomicroscopy; technique and interpretation in the use of X-radiography, infra-red photography and infra-red Vidicon equipment; the sampling and study of paint cross-sections; X-ray diffraction; colorimetry.

The second course, 'Microscopy in Art and Archaeological Conservation', was introduced by the statement, 'Polarised light microscopy has been found a most useful approach to the characterisation of pigments, surface coatings and fibres.' It was concerned with basic optical microscopy; illumination; resolution; micrometry; crystal properties of pigments; and the technique of taking samples invisible to the naked eye.

Such courses make it clear that the museum conservator has progressed a long way from his traditional craftsman status, but it is important to notice that they were planned for conservators whose work was with the fine arts and archaeology, and that they took place in London. These two weaknesses in training are to be observed all over the world. Courses in archaeology and fine art are, from a conservation point of view, relatively over-provided and courses for those specialising in ethnography, industry and technology, the decorative arts and natural history, seriously under-provided. Strenuous efforts are being made, especially by ICOM, to redress the balance.

A more fundamental object to most existing courses is that they are appropriate only to technologically advanced countries. What a large part of the world needs is a range of conservation techniques which are based on intermediate not advanced technology. Given suitable instruction and encouragement, men and women in the developing countries are capable of carrying out remarkable feats of conservation with the help of very simple tools, equipment and materials. It is possible that their work is not always of the high standard which is expected and obtained in the museum workshops and laboratories of Rome and Washington, but to wait until the whole world has the facilities of Rome and Washington is to condemn a large part of the cultural heritage of the countries in the third world to disastrous decay and eventual disappearance.

Conservation, like most other activities, suffers greatly from being thought about only in single-state terms, and by an obsession with what has been achieved in prosperous Western countries. At the present time, the ideal – and realisable – organisation for a country such as France, Poland or the United States would be something like this:

At the national level
Large, well-equipped laboratories, carrying out research on materials and techniques, and including a number of highly specialised centres, such as that at Fort Jean, Marseilles, which is concerned entirely with the restoration and conservation of material found under the sea.

At the regional level
Laboratories and workshops, carrying out some research, but concerned mainly with carrying out conservation work which demands a special degree of skill and equipment beyond the scope of the smaller local museum.

At the local level
Laboratories and workshops with trained personnel using fairly basic equipment to deal with the routine conservation and maintenance of the museum's collections.

One would assume constant and close liaison and co-operation between all three levels, with problems which cannot be solved at C being passed up to B and then, in some instances, further up to A. In a rough and ready way, this is what already happens in the wealthier and better-endowed countries. It manifestly does not happen, however, in the great majority of the developing countries, where the only solution, at least for some time to come, seems to lie in the establishment of the three-level system within an area much greater than a single country. The North African countries, from Morocco to Egypt, could easily and logically form such a supranational region, based on the important laboratory already existing in Cairo, and it is not difficult to think of others.

ETHICS OF CONSERVATION

The conservator has obligations not only to the antiquity or work of art he is treating, but also to its owner or custodian and to his professional colleagues. With this in mind, the American Group of IIC appointed a Committee on Professional Standards and Procedures, and a code of ethics for art conservators – one notices the constant emphasis on art, as if museum collections consisted of nothing else – was produced in 1968, setting out the principles and practices which should be observed in conservation. These were considered under the following headings:

1. *Obligations to the Work of Art.* The conservator must respect the integrity of the object, undertake appropriate treatment only within the limits of his professional competence and facilities, maintain the highest standard of treatment and respect the 'principle of reversibility', that is, avoid the use of materials which cannot be removed if necessary in the future without endangering the object. There is considerable controversy regarding reversibility. Three factors are involved. In the first place, one should obviously do everything possible, within the limits of one's knowledge and abilities, so make good the damage which has resulted from the passage of time and from past neglect. This, however, can be done only with the materials and techniques which are available at the time when one carries out the work. In five or ten years a far better method may well be available. Also, the best of conservators is no more than human. It is impossible for him to forecast with any accuracy what will happen either to the object or to his own work on it during the next 50 or 100 years. From the best information he has, he may have good reason to believe that the materials he is using are harmless and that they will be able to be removed at some time in the future. But these materials may quite possibly have properties which are unknown to him and to everybody else, but which will reveal themselves over the years. Is he to do nothing because he is unable to guarantee reversibility? To adopt such an attitude is both irresponsible and lacking in courage. If everyone behaved in this way, no progress would be possible. One must inevitably allow for accidents and for the unpredictable. The principle of reversibility is sound enough, but to follow a principle blindly and unswervingly makes no sense.

2. *Responsibilities to the Owner or Custodian.* The conservator should honestly advise what he considers the proper course of treatment after he has

Mobilier National, Paris. Formed to conserve material in the national collections, it has special facilities both for carrying out repair work and for training skilled staff.

made an adequate examination of the condition of the object, and keep a record of materials and methods of procedures used which should be revealed to the owner or custodian.

3. *Relations with Professional Colleagues.* A conservator should share his knowledge and experience with his colleagues, and should be prepared to consult with another conservator, if requested to do so by the owner or custodian, or if he himself wishes advice on a particular aspect of the proposed treatment. It is unethical behaviour for a conservator to encroach upon the professional employment of a colleague or to volunteer adverse judgement on the qualifications of a colleague unless such comment can be to the mutual benefit of all concerned.

4. *Obligations to the Public.* Every conservator should endeavour to educate the public in the aims of his profession, and take his part in safeguarding the public against illegal or unethical conduct. He should also give proper advice when it is requested by those seeking relief against negligent practice or incompetent work.

This code of practice is generally regarded as representing the aims of all who are concerned with the conservation of antiquities and works of art and who wish to maintain and increase the professional status of the conservator in the museum service.

OTHER CONSERVATION
ACTIVITIES

A conservation service has to concern itself with a number of closely related activities. These include:

(*a*) *The Transport of Museum Objects.* The increase in the number of works of art and museum objects being sent to national and international exhibitions has caused concern among museum curators and conservators that objects for which they are responsible may be damaged. Mechanical damage may result from inadequate packing and/or careless handling and general deterioration may be caused by changes (often rapid) in temperature and relative humidity of objects sensitive to their environment. The risk arising of pressure changes must be taken into account in air transport. Conditions in transit can be satisfactorily controlled by having recourse to special packing techniques and by studying adequately in advance the climatic conditions to be encountered and by taking appropriate measures. This has been shown in transport involved in some recent international exhibitions, for example, the transport of 'La Gioconda' from Paris and the 'Pietà' from Rome, the exhibition of Tutankhamun treasures, and the Chinese exhibition. ICOM and the International Centre for Conservation in Rome have encouraged the study of controlled environment for works of art during travel and they have sponsored the publication of a booklet by Dr Nathan Stolow setting out the general principles, the research that has been carried out and the characteristics of the 'ideal' container. In the published proceedings of the IIC Conference on Museum Climatology the specific problems of the transport of art objects by air are dealt with by Dr K. Toishi. (*b*) *Protection of Cultural Property in the Event of War.* The serious dangers to which cultural property may be subjected in time of war have naturally attracted attention. The problem has been intensified with the advances in techniques of destruction, principally as a result of the development of nuclear weapons. The question of protective measures has been discussed on an international level under the auspices of UNESCO, and a manual, written by M. Noblecourt, Chairman of ICOM's Committee on Security, was published in 1958. This contains a systematic account of the possible hazards, develops certain general ideas with regard to protective techniques, deals with the organisation of protection on the international and national levels and concludes with technical recommendations for the guidance of everyone who is concerned with security problems.

The special measures which were taken for the storage of the paintings from the National Gallery and the collections from the British Museum during the Second World War provide instructive examples of what can be achieved in practice.

INTERNATIONAL CO-OPERATION

Brief reference has already been made to certain international bodies which are concerned with the problems of conservation. In more detail, their functions are:

1. *ICOM Committee on Conservation.* This Committee is constituted on an international basis, the secretariat being attached to the International Centre for Conservation in Rome. It is composed of a Board for directing policy and a series of Working Groups, each concerned with a particular sector in the conservation of cultural property. Each Working Group is directed by a co-ordinator; the programme and composition of each Group and the choice of the co-ordinator are approved by the Board. The aim of the Working Groups is to offer all specialists interested in conservation an organised framework within which they can co-operate in research at an international level. The whole Committee holds a triennial plenary meeting during which progress reports are submitted for discussion. These reports constitute either a critical bibliography on a particular topic or interim or final accounts on research. The texts of the reports are available from the Documentation Service of the International Centre for Conservation.

2. *International Institute for Conservation of Historic and Artistic Works (IIC).* This Institute is administered by an international Council. There are four categories of membership: Fellow, Associate, Supporting Institution and Honorary Fellow. Members of Council are elected by the Fellows. The Institute is concerned with the whole field of conservation of cultural property, whether in museums and libraries or exposed out of doors. With the approval of the Council, Regional Groups have been organised as autonomous units in the United Kingdom, the USA, Canada, Mexico, Poland and the Scandinavian countries. Recently the American Group has become, for legal reasons, an independent corporation.

These groups form centres for the exchange of professional information among members and hold periodic meetings. At intervals of two or three years international congresses are held in different countries. An important function of IIC is that it includes in its membership professional conservators working independently outside the ambit of governments and institutions. They are enabled to have personal contacts with their colleagues at home and abroad through IIC's publications, congresses and regional groups. This service is particularly valuable for members who are geographically isolated. The headquarters of IIC are in London, at 608 Grand Buildings, Trafalgar Square, WC2.

3. *International Centre for Conservation* (*ICC*). This Centre (originally set up as the International Centre for the Study of the Preservation and Restoration of Cultural Property), with its headquarters in Rome, is an intergovernmental autonomous institution created by UNESCO in 1959. It counts at present fifty member-countries spread throughout the world. The constitution provides for a General Assembly made up of representatives of member-countries and meeting every two years to approve the programme and budget; of a Council of specialists and of a Secretariat responsible for the preparation and execution of the Centre's programme. The Centre maintains a library and documentation service dealing with all aspects of the conservation of cultural property and sponsors publication of basic works. Courses are held annually for training of conservators. These are in (*a*) architectural conservation; (*b*) conservation of mural paintings, and (*c*) fundamental scientific principles of conservation. Several forms of expert assistance are offered to member-countries, such as technical correspondence, expert missions, organisation of pilot work sites and urgent rescue missions. Also the Centre organises regional seminars to aid the development of conservation and the study of specific problems.

Collaboration between these international organisations is helped by the joint discussions which take place from time to time on publications and congress programmes. Publications are organised through an International Committee for Co-ordination of Publications which is composed of representatives of the ICOM Conservation Committee, ICC, IIC, and also ICOMOS.

As Georges Henri Rivière has pointed out,[7] 'the museum world is becoming increasingly aware of the scientific nature of the conservation of museum objects. Enormous progress has been made since the first museum laboratory was set up in Berlin in 1888.' Even so, he reminds us, whether we are thinking of institutions, courses, or publications, 'we are still a long way from achieving all the co-operation and co-ordination we need'.

This inadequacy of co-operation and co-ordination is not so much between different countries as between the different kinds of specialist involved in conservation. 'Works of art and archaeological material', observes Mr Rivière,

are still, for many people, the 'noble subjects', worthy of the most extreme veneration and sacrifice, in comparison with other human achievements and with the works of nature. Even on the international level, meetings between experts concerned with cultural material and experts whose field is nature continue to be exceedingly rare. Buried in their special subjects, the experts hardly ever take part in interdisciplinary discussions about their material or the results of their researches, and, as a result, they run a serious risk of reaching only fragmentary conclusions.

More serious, 'laboratory training courses which are being recommended to developing countries with very limited resources only deal with a section of the relevant disciplines, and pay no attention to either the natural heritage or the cultural heritage, whichever the case may be'. This is specialisation gone mad, and Mr Rivière, who is a museologist of great international repute, has performed an admirable public service by drawing attention to it, in his university courses in Paris and on many other occasions. Fortunately, as he has noted, there is a growing reaction against such a stupid and dangerous state of affairs, and with ICOM firmly committed to the cause of interdisciplinarity, there is good reason to be optimistic and to believe that conservation, like other aspects of museum work, will be a good deal more broadly based in the 1980s than in the 1970s.

3 Museum Buildings

'Most of the time', wrote the Indian museologist, Mrs Smita J. Baxi,[1] 'museums have to be housed in existing buildings which were not specially designed for the purpose.' Mrs Baxi's own excellent museum, the Indian National Museum of Arts and Crafts, is in such a building, an office block, and it is easy enough to understand her longing for something more suitable and encouraging, which she will, no doubt, secure before many years are out. The theme of the museum is of great importance to India and one cannot imagine the present cramped and difficult accommodation being considered adequate for much longer.

Meanwhile, partly for the sake of her own morale and partly in order to encourage the Government to think and plan at the right level, Mrs Baxi has very sensibly kept her sights fixed on a dream-museum. 'Let us', she says, 'assume the ideal conditions, where we have a choice of site and freedom for planning.' There should, of course, be room for future expansion and

it should be easily accessible and not too far from the town centres. A site within a park or garden may be ideal, as it gives a good atmosphere and natural setting, but it should not be located in the far interior of such parks or gardens and should be easily accessible from the main roads. The building should have enough open space around it, giving a good amount of natural light and ventilation.

Western Australian Museum, Perth. A building offering great flexibility.

All this is no doubt true and these are the criteria for selecting the perfect site. Some of the world's museums are fortunate enough to have been given such a site. One thinks, for instance, of the M. H. de Young Memorial Museum and the Museum of the California Academy of Art, in Golden Gate Park, San Francisco; the Wilanow Museum, in Warsaw; the National Historical Museum, in Buenos Aires; the National Anthropological Museum and National Museum of Modern Art, in Mexico City; and the National Museum of Ghana, in Accra. Here are the space, trees, lawns and freedom to breathe that, in Mrs Baxi's view, make the task of the museum so much easier. Many new museums, one hopes, will be established in similar surroundings, but meanwhile the situation is, in some ways regrettably, in some ways fortunately, very different.

Before discussing this in detail, we might usefully mention two more important points made by Mrs Baxi, since they are of fundamental importance, typical of a great deal of informed opinion in the museum world and, to some extent, controversial.

'Suppose', she ways, 'the museum is the only public building of the town' – as in many parts of the world it may well be. In that case, 'it will be a centre for all kinds of cultural activities, like theatrical performances, lectures, concerts, exhibitions and meetings'; and 'these amenities will have to be provided on a larger scale than needed only as accessories for museum activities'.

Then, she continues,

the style of the building should be representative of its age and should be at least contemporary, if not ultra-modern. The interiors of the exhibition galleries as well as other related rooms should be architecturally pleasing, but should not be a centre of attraction and should be subordinate to the purposes in view.

This amounts to saying that, both externally and internally, the museum should look and feel like today, not yesterday; that a good building is one which allows work to be efficiently carried out inside it; and that both the building and the site should be able to cope with changing ideas of what the task of a museum is.

With all these conclusions there can be little disagreement, but, having said that, one is forced to point out that the majority of the world's museums are at present not housed in this ideal way, or in anything approaching it. Many of them are cursed with ninteenth-century buildings which defy even the most ingenious attempts to make them suitable for present-day purposes. Those who planned museums four and five generations ago had an instinct for installing the collections, usually of paintings, sculpture and antiquities, either in a superannuated palace or in a new building designed to look like a palace. There were magnificent staircases, vast rooms with high ceilings, and as much marble, carving, mural-painting and mosaic as the budget would allow. It was grand, inflexible, expensive and intimidating.

THE VICTORIAN LEGACY

One of the most magnificent of Victorian entrance halls is still to be seen in its original form at the Fitzwilliam Museum, Cambridge, which was opened in 1848. Here the exhibition galleries are decorated in the style of a prince's palace, with marble floors, columns of scagliola and elaborate moulding ceilings. Few museums of the nineteenth century had the money needed to reach the level of the Fitzwilliam, but throughout the century and even later it remained the ideal. The staircase was particularly important. In the Fitzwilliam, as in the National Museum at Stockholm and the Kunsthistorisches Museum, Vienna, the principle was to make visitors toil upwards to begin their tour of the Museum, in order to induce a suitably elevated state of mind. The fact that such stair-climbing was tiring and inconvenient was of no consequence.

What was then called the South Kensington Museum, and is now the Victoria and Albert, took from 1860 to 1876 to build. It incorporated – one can still see them and marvel at the concept and effect – mosaics, tiles, coloured glass and frescoes in superabundance. The lecture hall façade was given a frieze of carved terracotta figures. Much of the external decoration, at South Kensington and elsewhere, resulted from the increasing use of roof-lighting, which produced large windowless areas of outside wall. The niches, statues, friezes, plaques and ornamental panels were designed to relieve this, in an age in which a large, plain wall was taken to be evidence of either poverty or of meanness of spirit.

The Rijksmuseum in Amsterdam was conceived in 1862 and born twenty-three years later in 1885. It was to be

Exterior of Wichita Art Museum, Kansas, USA.

an architectural embodiment of the history of the Netherlands, with replicas of medieval rooms, painted-glass windows containing portraits of Dutch heroes and worthies, and the names of great historical figures carved on the façade. Once inside the entrance hall, visitors were inspired by murals of scenes from the national past, and along the galleries, staircases and passages the process of spiritual enrichment was continued with quotations from the Netherlands' most famous poet, Vondel.

By modern standards, the museums and art galleries of the Victorian period were ill-lit, under-heated, difficult to supervise, costly to maintain and not infrequently damp. This has been taken to indicate that the architects were in-

competent and lacking in imagination and that the people who employed them were vainglorious and out of touch with reality. The criticism is unfair on three counts. Firstly, the architects were experimenting with new materials and techniques in order to try to meet the demands of a new kind of institution, a public museum, to be visited by a cross-section of the population in large numbers. They were learning to use iron and glass as major constructional materials, to come to terms first with gas-lighting and then with electricity, to install central heating and to understand the possibilities of lifts and turnstiles. Secondly, it has to be remembered that these much-maligned buildings were intended to meet nine-

Fitzwilliam Museum, Cambridge, England. Gallery V I I A – discreet modernisation of a Victorian Gallery.

(below) *Entrance hall and grand staircase.*

teenth not twentieth-century conditions. If the twentieth century has failed to replace them with twentieth-century buildings, the nineteenth-century architects can hardly be blamed. And thirdly, these Victorian museums were felt to be attractive and satisfying by the people who visited them and worked in them when they were new. They were frequented, with regularity and enthusiasm, by millions of people of all classes, which is why they were built. To that extent, the architects were successful.

In a sense, they were over-successful, because a high proportion of the museums they created were so solidly built and of such architectural distinction that it was difficult to think of pulling them down. They grew into the cities to which they belonged and became local landmarks. A hundred years after they were built, it is almost as unthinkable to get rid of them as to demolish a cathedral.

But they certainly present today's directors and curators with a series of extremely serious problems, not least of which is the vast amount of unwanted, unusuable space, in the form of staircases, corridors and high ceilings, which has to be heated, cleaned, painted, ventilated and, if the museum has that amount of money, air-conditioned. Moreover, the nineteenth-century museum was not planned for flexibility. Its collections were installed as if they were never to be moved or changed. The notion of temporary exhibitions might be suitable for a commercial art gallery, but it was certainly not appropriate to a temple of scholarship and self-improvement, which is what a Victorian museum was. In addi-

Modern exhibition techniques in a museum building of the monumental type. Exhibition of Jain art in the Key Gallery of the Prince of Wales Museum of Western India, Bombay.

(below) *Entrance front of Prince of Wales Museum, showing impractical grandeur of Imperial style.*

tion to being rigid and final in their structure and room layout, these museums had a balance between exhibition galleries on the one hand and

offices, storage space and workshops on the other, which does not match today's needs at all. A further disadvantage, by modern standards, is that the pre-automobile age built its museums in city centres with little or no space around them for the car-parking that is demanded now. The nineteenth-century museum was planned for people who arrived on foot or by tram and who were remarkably honest, non-destructive and well-behaved, and respectful and obedient towards authority.

To adapt a building of this kind to twentieth-century ideas of what a museum should be and do is as difficult and expensive as converting an eighteenth- or nineteenth-century house and its large gardens, designed for an ample supply of cheap servants, into an establishment which can be run satisfactorily by two or three people. One understands very well why directors and curators so often long to pull the whole place down and start again, and there

is no doubt that in many instances this would be much the wisest and cheapest thing to do.

As an example of a museum in this category, let us consider the Indian Museum, Calcutta. It was established by Act of Parliament in 1866. Initially it was called the Imperial Museum, but soon acquired its present name. The original collections belonged to a body known as the Aesthetic Society, which donated the land on which the Museum was built. The Society was originally to have its headquarters in the Museum, but in the event it received compensation in exchange for this.

When one enters the Museum, the resemblance to the Victoria and Albert Museum in London is immediately obvious. There are the same great masses of masonry, the same garden courtyard, the same corridors, the same staircases. It is placed directly on a busy street, like an enormous department store, which in a sense it is. The Indian

Museum is Western Europe transplanted intact and complete to India. The process occurred at a time when there was a great deal more money available in Calcutta than there is now, and when the priorities of government were very different. The disaster, from the Museum's point of view, is that the shell of the old system remains, but without the means to support it. The building and the form of administration are inseparable.

The buildings and collections are owned by a Board of Trustees. This is a highly conservative body, which is extremely unlikely to generate any ideas of a radical nature. Its eleven members include the Governor of Bengal; the Vice-Chancellor of the University of Calcutta; the Accountant-General of West Bengal; the Mayor of Calcutta; and the Secretary to the Ministry of Education. Before India achieved its independence, all these officials were British. Now they are, of course, Indian, but they are remarkably similar in their tastes and habits to the members of the Imperial ruling class whom they replaced. They are not, one would guess, a body to which change comes easily, certainly not change of the kind which involves tearing down the Indian Museum, selling what must be a very valuable site, and starting all over again on the edge of the parkland with which the city of Calcutta is generously endowed.

The Museum has six sections: Art, Architecture, Anthropology, Geology, Zoology and Botany. For many years each section was looked after by a separate body: the Geological Survey of India, for example, was in complete control of the Geology section. The Museum was, in fact, and to a large extent still is, little more than a benevolent landlord. In 1961 the first Director was appointed – the Museum had survived for more than a century without one, which is some indication of the power of conservatism – primarily in order to provide an administrative link between the Board of Trustees and the Survey officers of the various sections. He had no galleries in his charge.

In 1965 a very different kind of man became Director. For ten years before his appointment he had been Keeper of Art at the National Museum in Delhi. He had studied at the Louvre in Paris and in London, and he was, in every sense of the term, a museum man. Understandably, his main interest was museum management, not property

management, and he achieved some success, in that he now has direct control of the Art, Architecture and Anthropology galleries. The remaining three are outside his jurisdiction and he cannot influence or change their displays in any way. The result is that remarkable and fascinating phenomenon, a museum of museology, in which three sections are pure, vintage nineteenth-century and three mid-twentieth-century. The Director himself would be the first to admit, however, that, even with the three sections which he has the power to modernise – and with which he has, in fact, achieved miracles – he has been fighting an obsolete, impossible building all down the line. The money available to run the Museum and to maintain its huge, expensive fabric is quite inadequate. Since 1965 there has been only a very small annual increase, not enough to compensate for inflation. Sometimes it is difficult even to find what is required to pay salaries and wages. Development is impossible, and, for a museum of this importance, the staff is absurdly limited. There is a conservation officer, trained in Rome and at the British Museum, but no Assistant Director, Deputy Director or Keepers of individual sections. One modeller, an extremely skilled man, has to cope with all the work in the museum and is, inevitably, grossly overworked.

Meanwhile, the Director and the Trustees watch the Museum's fabric slowly crumbling year by year. This is a building which, under today's conditions, can no longer be maintained, and which could never, even with a fortune spent on it, provide suitable housing for a modern museum. Nothing but nostalgia can justify its retention, a situation which can be paralleled in city after city throughout the world. Those who object to a once splendid building of this kind being demolished usually advance the argument that to do away with it would be iconoclastic and philistine. An historic monument would be swept away and the city would suffer as a result, rather as if a front tooth had been lost. To this one can only answer either 'How bankrupt must a museum become before the decision is taken to house it in a way which fits the money available?' or 'It could well be that, even if the Museum were to leave it, the building could be converted to some other use, with new owners or tenants who could afford to modernise and maintain it.'

One has to distinguish between two

types of old museum building. The first is a large, usually eighteenth- or nineteenth-century palace-like structure, which is not identified with the contents of the museum; and in the case of the second the building and its contents are indissolubly linked. In the first instance the collection would usually greatly benefit from being transferred to a more up-to-date, easy-to-run and cheap-to-maintain setting, in the second a very great deal would be lost. More precisely, the contents, staff and finances of the Indian Museum would gain if the Museum were to be accommodated in a modern and less pretentious building, but to continue to think only in terms of India, the Nehru Museum, now arranged in the great statesman's former official residence, would certainly have nothing like the same appeal or significance if it went elsewhere. The premises of the Nehru Museum are, in any case, modest, reasonably easy to care for and not a serious drain on the Museum funds. Visitors come to see the building and the gardens, which are rich in associations with Pandit Nehru, almost as much as they do the objects inside, chosen and arranged to illustrate his life and career.

On the other hand, it is entirely suitable that the British Raj in its heyday should be commemorated in such a piece of architectural fantasy as the Victoria Memorial in Calcutta. This great white stone hybrid of a mausoleum and a wedding-cake, in its magnificent parkland setting, has no associations with Queen Victoria at all. Neither she nor any member of her family ever slept there, ate there or attended any kind of official function there. The Museum was, in fact, not opened until after the Queen's death. The extravagance of the building is completely in tune, however, with the glories of the Raj that are displayed inside it. Together they present not only the details but the flavour of a period in India's history that no longer has any reality, but which Indians themselves take an extraordinary pleasure, and possibly pride, in remembering. Far more people visit the Victoria Memorial, which is about Britain at least as much as about India, than the Indian Museum, which is wholly Indian. The reason can only be that the Victoria Memorial provides a more pleasurable experience than the Indian Museum, a touch of colour and drama in the midst of a harsh daily life.

FITTING THE BUILDING TO ITS CONTENTS

The subtle relationship of a building to its contents is the most important part of museum showmanship, without which a public museum inevitably fails. If the building is at war with the contents, or gives them insufficient sympathy and support, the result can only be failure. But if, on the other hand, the building, the theme and the contents are all in step, very inadequate museological techniques cease to be of great importance. There are, one might say, certain buildings in which even the most inept curator can hardly go wrong.

One thinks, for instance, of Beethoven's birthplace in Bonn, the spirit and appeal of which have somehow survived the gross vulgarisation and commercialisation of the old city which has taken place during the past twenty-five years. It is impossible to believe that the composer's personal belongings and the details of his family and career could possibly have as great an impact in a neutral building as they do here in the house in which he was born. It is a compact house, and it would be no problem to dismantle and re-erect all the significant rooms inside a large museum somewhere else, where, no doubt, they could be more satisfactorialy preserved against fire, theft, woodworm, fungus, and all the other perils that beset old buildings, and where Beethoven could be 'presented in his contemporary context'. But to do this would be both a folly and a crime. The old house is an integral part of the story. This, we can say, is where the baby Beethoven cried and kept his mother and father awake at night. There are the stairs he crawled up. This is the kind of house his parents could afford. It places the Beethoven family in their social context.

Similar associations arise naturally at several points in Vienna and Salzburg – Mozart's birthplace; the house in which he wrote *The Marriage of Figaro*; the house where Schubert died; the house where Beethoven wrote his Fifth Symphony and quarrelled with his landlady. Every country has these places and dozens of them are turned into museums each year. One can do little more here than list a few examples which illustrate the range and the possibilities of this kind of museum. None, it should be noted, is air-conditioned and all contain features which, if he knew about them, would drive a scientifically trained conservationist to despair. But it is absolutely right that such house-museums should exist and become more numerous. The buildings, the furniture, the books and the pictures should, of course, be looked after and supervised with all possible

Buttolph-Williams House, Wethersfield, Connecticut, USA. A house-museum, owned and maintained by the Antiquarian and Landmarks Society, Hartford, Connecticut.

(below) Hempsted House, New London, Connecticut, USA. Also owned and maintained by the Antiquarian and Landmarks Society.

care – there is no virtue in neglect – but the right balance has to be kept between maximum safety and maximum enjoyment. It would be wrong to allow visitors to handle Beethoven's ear-trumpet and shout down it to test its efficacy, but it would be equally wrong to keep the original ear-trumpet in an air-conditioned store and display only a replica.

Much of the charm of these personal – perhaps one should say personalised – museums lies in the sense of wonder one has at seeing the actual pen, violin or sword the great man used and the boots and trousers he wore. The technique of showing such objects is a very old one. The medieval Church was fully acquainted with the drawing power and profitability of pieces of the True Cross or of the Holy Shroud, as of the bones, hair and toenails of the Saints. One hopes and believes that museum curators draw back with horror from the modern equivalent of manufacturing pieces of the Cross and Shroud, but the temptation is undoubtedly there. There are modern equivalents of the Crucifixion and the Saints in the political sphere and one can only assume, as true believers undoubtedly do, that the relics of them which are to be seen in museums are as genuine as the labels suggest.

A number of these house-museums have become somewhat faded and mouldy with the passing of time and no doubt much of this could have been prevented if adequate funds and skill had been available. But adequate funds and skill are never available and one can only sigh and accept the results with gratitude. With £100,000 to be spent on each, a wonderful improvement could be produced at, say, Wagner's house on Lake Lucerne, or Edvard Grieg's house near Bergen. The portraits and documents could be stopped from decaying further, the lighting, heating and ventilation could be attended to, the piano repolished, restrung and refelted, the composer's hat sent to a first-class conservation workshop. Or, as an alternative, everything could be swept away to safekeeping in the city and selected items released for a special exhibition once every ten years. These things are most unlikely to happen, however, and very imperfect house-museums will continue to draw the crowds for years to come, until everything in them becomes so decayed and decrepit that the name 'museum' ceases to be applicable.

In the meantime, the house in which Georgi Dimitrov, the leader of the Bulgarian Communist Party, lived from 1888 until 1912 can be visited. So, too, can the mud hut near São Paolo in which Dom Pedro I spent the night before uttering his famous cry of 'Independence or Death'. In Chang-sha the school attended by Mao Tse-tung has been carefully preserved as a museum, complete with photographs of his teachers and a selection of the books he read and enjoyed during his schooldays. In France, at Villeneuve-Loubet, there is a Museum of the Art of Cookery, in the former home of the great chef Auguste Escoffier. It contains a signed portrait of the singer Nellie Melba, for whom Escoffier created the nowadays sadly debased Peach Melba. All these museums would lose half their point and attraction by being in any other buildings. The building, in each case, is an essential part of the museum and the reason for its existence.

The same is true of hundreds of site-museums which are not identified with famous people, but which would become something quite different if their contents were to be transferred elsewhere. One might mention in this connection the little building at Ølgod, Denmark, which, as the first co-operative dairy in Denmark, could be said to be the pioneer of a great national industry, or the Salt Museum in the salt-mines at Berchtesgaden in South Germany, which have been operational since 1577. Archaeological and historical museums of this kind are becoming increasingly more numerous and more popular throughout the world. They might, perhaps, be rechristened 'atmosphere museums', since it is the thoughts and feelings which they produce in the visitors which are the source of their popularity. One can see an excellent example of this at Freiberg, in the German Democratic Republic. Here there are two examples of the little chapels in which miners used to hold prayer meetings before going down the pit to their work, and again at the end of the shift, as a token of thanksgiving for still being alive and uninjured. One chapel is now in the town museum and the other, equally excellently preserved, is at the Alte Elisabeth pit, by the site of the old shaft, which is now itself a museum. There is no doubt as to which of the two chapels makes the deeper impression. In the Alte Elisabeth chapel one can feel the presence and the fears of long-dead silver-miners; in the

museum one is looking at what has become merely a curiosity, a piece of quaintness.

Freiberg is, of course, a readily accessible place and many thousands of people visit both the museum and the Alte Elisabeth pit each year. A major problem exists, however, in the case of sites of great historical interest which are not near large centres of population, away from good roads and off the main tourist routes. Every developing country had dozens of such places, most of which would have been carefully preserved and publicised had they been in, say, France or New Zealand.

POTENTIAL MUSEUMS

As an example, we may take Bagamoyo, in Tanzania, which can be reached, by those with sufficient stamina and determination, in two hours from Dar-es-Salaam, over an exceedingly bad road. Bagamoyo has a remarkable history. A century ago it was both politically and commercially far superior to Dar-es-Salaam, the present capital, which was then no more than a small fishing village. Its development began in 1832, when Sultan Said, the Imam of Oman, transferred his capital there from Muscat, in Zanzibar. Because of its proximity to Zanzibar and of the fact that dhows could cross the channel at all times of the year, it became a great trading centre. A trade route was created from Bagamoyo to Lake Tanganyika. The starting-point of this track, which linked the coast with the heart of Africa, is still clearly indicated by a blockhouse, with loopholes and fire-steps, which was built in 1889 by the Germans. This was where many journeys of exploration started. A plaque set up near the beach and not far from the blockhouse commemorates the first of these expeditions, undertaken by the British explorers, Burton and Speke, which set off from here on 27 June 1857.

Bagamoyo was not only a starting-point. For many thousands of slaves it was the end of a terrible march in chains right across East Africa. This was probably responsible for the change in the town's name from Bwagamoyo, which means 'throw off melancholy', to Bagamoyo, 'crush your heart'. There was never a slave market at Bagamoyo, but there was a gathering point, a caravanserai, where a great many slaves must have laid down their hearts before being shipped away by dhow to Zanzibar. Others were fortunate enough to be set free on payment of a ransom, paid for the most part by the Roman Catholic Mission, founded here by the Holy Ghost Fathers in 1868. The mission, which came into existence in order to liberate slaves and to educate them once they were free, is still there, much as it was in its early days. One of the buildings now contains a little museum setting out the history of Bagamoyo. Its collection includes a beautifully written register of slaves ransomed by the Mission, with the name of the slave, his age, where he came from and the date of his baptism.

It was the same mission which took care of Dr Livingstone's body when it was brought back here in February 1874 by a party of exhausted men who had carried it for hundreds of miles. The church in which it rested overnight has gone, but the tower still stands, as does the Grotto of the Blessed Virgin, which was built by former slaves as an expression of gratitude to the missionaries. Another witness to the Mission's care for the sick and the poor is the old hospital, built in 1897 with funds provided by a rich Indian, and run by nuns until 1912, when it was handed over to the Government.

During the Arab revolt against German rule in East Africa, the German military commander made Bagamoyo his headquarters. The German cemetery and four large bronze plaques commemorate the German officers and soldiers who were killed during the fighting. The large fort-like building, now used for area administration, was constructed by the Germans as their headquarters. The old German Customs House still stands and opposite it are the stone and iron foundations of a German warehouse. It was raised above the ground and had a moat around it, which could be filled with water when required, in order to prevent members of the local population from entering the store. There is also, in the town square, a double-faced German-made clock, dated 1900, with the maker's name and address on it.

This ancient town, developed and ruled by Arabs, Germans and English, before it became part of an independent Tanzania, remains a centre of traditional Swahili culture. One sees evidence of this in the beautifully-carved doors, of which there are a number of examples. The carving contains a great deal of symbolism – the lotus as a symbol of generation; the date-tray denoting plenty; the fish, fertility; the chain, security; and frankincense, wealth.

At the present time, Bagamoyo is neither particularly neglected nor particularly cherished. Its museum and tourist potential is very great, however, and it would be surprising if, during the next twenty years, it failed to become one of Africa's most important and interesting eco-museums. Nowhere shows better the different layers of foreign culture which were laid on Africa during the past 150 years and the extent to which they have assimilated or by-passed. To carry out the necessary renovation and signposting would not be a considerable task. The whole town is a wonderful museum-in-the-making, waiting only for the Government to recognise that its possibilities are as great as those of the National Museum, but that different skills are required to interpret them for the benefit of the public, and to conserve them.

The great value of a place like Bagamoyo is that it needs no heavy expenditure in order to transform it into a museum. It is a museum already. All the necessary buildings are there. The only thing lacking, so far, and this will surely come, is the will to regard it as a museum with a status equal to those of the conventional kind of museum, and to acknowledge that it deserves the best and most imaginative museum-skills that can be found.

THE DISTRICT AS A MUSEUM

Somehow, what we might call the Bagamoyo-lesson has to be got across, that every town and every site can be thought of as a museum, if not for today, then for tomorrow. It is interesting to notice how quickly this new concept is spreading. Two English examples will help to make the point. In 1974 an excellent museum of shoes and shoe-making was opened in the small Somerset town of Street. This is a one-industry town, which has grown up around a shoemaking business which is still controlled by the same family that established it 150 years ago. The whole town is a monument to the family enterprise and to the development of the industry. What is officially called the Museum is no more than a central information centre, the hub of a wheel. All around it is the evidence to show the ways in which the community has grown under the owning family's paternalistic direction. One sees the large houses built for their own occupation by the members of the family; the Meeting House which recalls their Quaker connections; the former Library and Institute, now empty and awaiting conversion to some other use; the new Library, a gift of the family; streets of very pleasant, solid houses built for the workers; the swimming pool, another family gift; the hotel, owned and run by the company, with a ban on alcohol as a sign of proper Quaker principles; the new Technical College, with its fine theatre which was built for public performances and financed by the family trust. And, as the source of the money with which the town was built, the factory itself, expanded and adapted over the years to meet changing demands and manufacturing methods.

Without the town and the district as a background, the Museum loses half its meaning. Planned to show both the historical development of shoe making, from Roman times onwards, and the story of the family itself, it has admirable displays of footwear, advertising material, tools and techniques, photographs and mementoes, and it is located, as it should be, in part of the house in which the founder of the firm lived. A separate modern building would have been out of place. The first stage was to get the Museum established: the second, now being planned, is for the Museum to, as it were, throw its arms around the town and to make sure that visitors know what to look for. This involves a new policy of making the Museum outward-looking instead of inward-looking, and of turning it, in effect, into the interpretation centre that it deserves to be. Administratively and financially, the step is not a difficult one to take: the main problem is one of local public relations, to persuade the people who, so to speak, live in the Museum that they will not be peered at by visitors like monkeys in a cage.

At St Austell, in Cornwall, the area affected is much less compact and less densely inhabited. This is the most important centre in the world for the production of china clay (kaolin) and in 1975 a museum was opened to show the history of the industry since its beginnings 200 years ago, and especially during the past fifty years, when the techniques of extracting and processing the clay have undergone revolutionary changes. The Museum has been established at an old works, long out of use, where the clay was purified, dried and packed for shipment. Parts of the works have been restored, so that visitors can see the old equipment in its context, and an explanatory museum set up in a former storage building, an impressive piece of archaeology in its own right.

It is impossible even to reach the Museum without realising what the local industry is, since the huge white tips of waste sand, removed from the clay, are very obvious in all directions. They are a part of the archaeology of china clay production, and one which is being added to each day. What is not at all obvious, however, is the human history of the industry, and it is to be an important part of the new Museum's work to document this and to preserve significant sites in the area which relate to it. Two examples will illustrate the types of building which are relevant.

In the early days of the industry, and indeed until the outbreak of the Second World War, the wages paid were low and, in order to support themselves at a reasonable standard, many of the china-clay workers living in rural cottages, where they could have a large vegetable garden and keep poultry and a pig. These cottages were often primitive affairs, with a beaten earth floor, and they were, in the majority of cases, at a considerable distance from the place where the man worked, involving him in a long walk morning and evening. The Museum plans to restore one or two of these clayworkers' cottages to something like their original condition, with appropriate furnishings, and to plant out the garden to show how it would all have looked half a century ago. It intends, too, with the co-operation of the trade union concerned, to show visitors the office where the Union's organiser worked before 1914 and from which he covered this very hilly district on foot and on a bicycle. In the days to come, a visitor to the China Clay Museum will have a great deal to absorb his energies and his attention.

But – and this is very important – every museum of this kind needs a centre, where the visitor can be given his bearings before he sets out to explore what we might term the outlying exhibits. There is no need for this orientation centre to be elaborate or

Ulster Museum, Belfast, Northern Ireland. Picture store.

expensive, either in its building or its display, but it needs to be well done, in order to provide people with the right balance of curiosity, knowledge and confidence to make their subsequent explorations stimulating and fruitful. This task, a great test of museological expertise, has been admirably fulfilled by a number of the American wildlife parks – the true pioneers of the method – and subsequently by national parks in other countries, notably France, Poland, Czechoslovakia and Kenya. The effect to be aimed at might be best described as simple sophistication, and to achieve this demands both taste and skill of an exceptional order. Any building designed to function as the core of an open-air museum or a national park must meet two requirements:

(*a*) It must be in character with the museum or the park as a whole, and reflect its purpose.

(*b*) It must give the visitor the impression that the interpretation centre or the keynote-collection is a small thing and the museum itself a big thing. It must be modest, self-effacing, informal and encouraging.

MODERN MUSEUM ARCHITECTURE

There are very few people anywhere in the world who are able to devote their

whole time to designing new museums, as distinct from museum displays. In Britain, Michael Rice and Company has been working continuously for a number of years on planning new museums for the Arab States, and Robin Wade's office is wholly occupied on museum projects within the British Isles. Another member of this select band of specialists is the German architect Professor Manfred Lehmbruck, of Stuttgart, whose best-known achievement is probably the German National Museum in Nürnberg. From looking at new museums as a whole, as well as from working out plans himself, Professor Lehmbruck has felt able to suggest certain things which should and should not be done in the future. It may be useful first to summarise his recommendations and then to relate them to particular museum buildings which have been completed during the past twenty years in various countries.

1. The museum of today, and even more, so far as we can judge, the museum of the future, has to meet the growing demand for more information, more interpretation, more communication and more activity. It has to reckon with the strong possibility that the areas in which the collections are actually displayed may take up only a relatively small proportion of the total museum-space.

2. The museum seems to be in the process of transforming itself from a display and conservation centre to a cultural centre, 'a general and multi-purpose centre serving emotion as well as contemplation'.[2] In order to do this, he says, 'the museum should be built as if it were a host'.

3. Since one cannot forecast what the changes in feeling and thinking of the next fifty or so years are going to be, one can only anticipate them by designing highly flexible buildings. Ideally, the museum building should be nothing more than a shell, a shelter, within which all divisions, floors, stairs, and lifts can be easily rearranged as new needs arise.

4. Partly as a result of (3) there is a serious risk that the architect will produce what Professor Lehmbruck calls an 'over-generalised' building, that is, a building which could be used for a wide range of purposes, including, almost incidentally, a museum. One must not go too far along the road of 'technical, rational thinking'. A really successful museum building must reflect the central idea of the museum. If the museum has no central idea, the result can only be a bad building.

5. The museum building has to express the society for which it has been created. What is right and fitting in Brazil is not necessarily right and fitting in Belgium.

It is useful to measure a selection of recent museum buildings against these criteria, with which, of course, not all museologists would find themselves in complete agreement. One might begin with one of the newest of all, the Museum of Popular Arts and Traditions in Paris, which opened its doors in the Bois de Boulogne during the summer of 1975, after establishing an international reputation in its former not very satisfactory premises.

The site is wooded and pleasant, with a welcome feeling of space. Despite this, however, no car-parking has been provided. Visitors are expected to park along the side of the road, in the traditional Parisian manner. This gives the impression, which may or may not be correct, that not many people are expected to be visiting the Museum at any given time, or that a high proportion of those who come are likely to be schoolchildren arriving in buses. The size of a museum's car-park is an interesting indication of the number and type of visitors that are expected.

The building is the standard type of steel and glass structure, used for office accommodation all over the world. The Museum is on the ground floor and the staff and technical facilities are in a tower block adjoining. One looks at the exterior, and it could be that of a computer centre, a precision-engineering factory, the Paris headquarters of some international manufacturing concern. There is nothing particularly French or museum-like about it, and, by Professor Lehmbruck's standards, these are serious weaknesses. On the other hand, the building is certainly flexible. There would be no great difficulty in adding to it, or of completely changing the display layout inside. For that matter, it would be an easy building to convert to some completely different use if the Museum were to go bankrupt and to be forced to close down. The Museum could move out today and IBM or the World Bank could move in, if not tomorrow, then the day after tomorrow.

It is, in brief, a totally undistinguished, characterless building, and with no more warmth and welcome than one would find in any well-provided office block. Whether it can be called an efficient building depends entirely on what kind of museum the Director and curators wanted to create. Quite clearly, certain basic requirements had to be met – the building had to be weatherproof, the air-conditioning had to be reliable and of a high standard, the floor area and ceiling heights had to be adequate. These tests, presumably, have been passed. One cannot suppose that those who commissioned and designed the building would have been satisfied with anything less.

But the building structure is essentially neutral. It contributes nothing at all to the atmosphere and appeal of the Museum. It does not announce to the world that it is the home of the Museum of Popular Arts and Traditions. What the museologists have done, in fact, is to remain in total control of the Museum's impact. They have created, within this efficient, impersonal shell, a museum which has to be regarded as a work of art in its own right. One either likes it or one does not, but there is no denying its brilliance. Exhibits, cases, passages, lighting, cubicles for switching on slide-tape commentaries and explanations – everything has been conceived as a unit. 'This', one can almost hear the staff saying, 'is our masterpiece. Take it or leave it. We are supremely well informed and competent, we have taken the best possible technical advice, no expense has been spared to get it right. Everything you need to know, or should want to know, is here. Buy your ticket, admire and learn.'

In time, no doubt, there will be changes in both the exhibits and techniques, but at the moment it is difficult to image them. The comparison with IBM is not far-fetched, both in the massive display of confidence, the grand style, the knowledge that one is selling the best and the most up-to-date, that the world will inevitably beat a path to one's door. But a museum or a company of this kind, the super-efficient, must inevitably find it difficult to think of the general public as an equal partner in the enterprise. One leaves the Museum of Popular Arts and Traditions or IBM feeling that one has been shown marvels and delights, but that one's own opinion is not particularly welcome. The enterprise, in short, depends for its success on professional expertise, not on feedback or on a dialogue with the public. It presents itself to its visitors as an impresario or prima donna, rather than, in Professor Lehmbruck's excellent phrase, as a host.

This particular museum provides an enormous amount of information, interpretation, aesthetic pleasure and, in its way, communication; but very little activity. It is not a place in which one finds it easy to ask questions with any great hope of having them answered. Its efficiency lies in giving, not in taking, and there is no doubt at all that the building contributes a great deal to this atmosphere. It is, one need hardly add, a very silent museum, in the sense that no background sound is provided and visitors do not become noticeably excited.

It is an interesting fact that the great majority of the 'efficient', expensive new museums in the world are quiet places, in which there appears to be little evidence of any wish to hear visitors reacting and responding with their voices. The exceptions are the museums, such as the National Museum of History and Technology in Washington or the Danish Technical Museum at Helsingør, in which visitors are encouraged to make the exhibits

Detroit Institute of Arts. The extent and growth of the buildings.

work and which are not planned on the assumption of silent contemplation.

The main difficulty facing both museum directors and museum architects is to decide whom the building is really for. Is it intended primarily for scholars and students, who know what they want to see and are, by definition, quiet, methodical and orderly, or is it for a heterogeneous and unpredictable general public? If it is for both, where is the priority to lie? Which is to be allowed to set its mark on the museum and to earn its reputation? Is it to be a building in which entirely unscholarly people will feel immediately at ease, or one in which the general public will be disciplined to think and act in ways which do not come naturally to them?

There is a school of thought, not infrequently found among architects, which believes that at any given time there is a recognisable concept, among people of all classes and degrees of education, of what a prestigious building should look like. If a public building does not measure up to this concept, it will, so the theory goes, lack appeal and esteem. If, on the other hand, it matches the stereotype, certain other kinds of prejudice will not arise. Many architects feel that the ideal which large numbers of people have in their minds at the present time is in the airport—classless, modern in its materials, style and function, and with the proper associations of technical efficiency, ample money and progress. To be suc-

cessful, therefore, any public building, whether it happens to be a school, a shopping-centre, a town hall or a museum, should suggest an airport. For previous generations, the supremely desirable public building was quite different – a palace, a cathedral, a castle – and architects of other types of large building did their best to fit in with the prevailing mood.

There is, of course, a difficulty in such an approach. A few airports – one thinks for instance of Washington International, or Düsseldorf – have been blessed with exceptionally gifted architects, who have been able to create buildings which are outstandingly beautiful and efficient. Most airports, however, are singularly dull to look at and grossly inefficient to use. One would not wish to inflict their ordinariness or miseries on any new museums. This, though, is beside the point. What the public requires of a new building is that it shall say to them, in effect: 'This is your kind of building, designed, constructed and fitted out with you in mind.' It must, in other words, be a democratic building first and foremost. If, as a bonus, it happens to be a work of beauty and genius, so much the better, but only for the minority which appreciates these things. The majority will not notice. It is the flavour, not the details, which matters.

The museum building which is neither old or new is in a different position. As an example of this, one could

take the Mining Museum at Bochum, in the German Federal Republic. The original building here was completed just before the Second World War, in a fortunately rather chaste and simple version of the Nazi monumental style which was almost *de rigueur* at the time. Some damage was caused by bombing, but this has been made good, and the pre-war buildings now form the core of a much larger complex which reproduces the original fairly closely. The ceilings are, by modern standards, absurdly high and the whole effect, both inside and out, is somewhat chilling and forbidding. The Museum has recently been given landmark status, and added distinction, by an enormous pit-head gear, which was brought from a nearby coalmine and re-erected to tower above the Museum and to straddle it like a giant giraffe; but so far as the buildings themselves are concerned what one now sees is a solid mass of excellent brickwork of unmistakably 1930s vintage, which, in the mid-1970s, is unlikely to lift the spirits of visitors very high. Inside, there are huge cathedral-like volumes of space which the Museum cannot possible expect to fill and in which the exhibits are dwarfed by the amount of emptiness above them and around them.

This, one feels, is a Museum which has suffered from having had too much money at its disposal. The collections are superb, but the great halls swallow sound like a sponge absorbing water, so that, through no fault of the curators, the Museum becomes dehumanised and even quite large exhibits are reduced in scale. The contrast between the exhibition rooms and the artificial mine which has been constructed below the Museum is very striking. In order to be convincing, the mine galleries have to be their correct size, with authentically low ceilings, and as a result the equipment in them, which is mostly in working condition, is seen in its proper proportions, and against a meaningful background of coal. Upstairs in the Museum, very similar items of equipment have been domesticated and changed into mere toys by being placed in an environment which takes away much of their significance, although heroic attempts have been made to 'interpret' them. The Museum buildings and the Museum collection do not help one another or carry the visitor along in the same direction, although each is impressive in its own particular way.

In the Mining Museum at Bochum, as in the Louvre, the British Museum or most other large museums, the division between the study collections and the public exhibition is complete. Scholars and visitors need never meet one another, think of one another or be aware of one another's existence. This is not everywhere the case, however. At the Museum of Popular Arts and Traditions in Paris, the two types of collection are separated, but not barricaded off. The explanatory galleries are on the ground floor and the study collections, equally skilfully but more soberly displayed, are in the basement. Anyone is free to walk from one to the other and in this way the Museum is given a welcome and refreshing unity. The new Zoological Museum in Copenhagen adopts a similar policy, with the Museum divided effectively into ecological exhibits, which are primarily for the general public, and systematic study collections for students. The building is uncompromisingly modern and equipped to the highest standards, but it is a museum building in a way the new home of the Museum of Popular Arts and Traditions is not. It is not, in other words, a museum-machine, a title which could be given to a number of new museum buildings, including that of the State Picture Gallery of the USSR in Moscow. This is a good-looking, well-proportioned rectangular block, designed for the sole purpose of housing and caring for a

huge collection of paintings. It is fully air-conditioned and some idea of its size can be obtained from the fact that a visitor who set out with the intention of seeing all the pictures on display would have to walk 6.5 kilometres. A great deal of money has obviously been spent on it and, simply as a machine for showing and safeguarding pictures, it would be difficult to beat. Many superlatives have been lavished on it, most of them justified, but even its most enthusiastic friend could hardly call it an exciting or stimulating building. It is, in fact, museum technology in its purest and most uncompromisingly efficient form and, seen in this way, it does certainly achieve what Professor Lehmbruck says a good museum building should achieve – it expresses the society for which it had been created. The Soviet Union is a society which gives the highest importance to technology, and the State Picture Gallery is a monument to technology quite as much as a monument to painters. It is certainly not a romantic building and equally certainly not a cultural centre or an activity centre. The architects' brief was to provide a structure within which a large number of paintings could be shown and looked at under conditions which would cause a minimum amount of damage to the paintings. This they have done and they cannot be blamed for failing to design a museum which would be a pulsating, activity-filled cultural centre. Nobody asked them to do so.

A comparison with the Museum of Modern Art, in New York, and the San Francisco Museum of Art is interesting. In the United States it would be difficult to design or run an art museum which was not to some extent a cultural centre, and the New York and San Francisco museums appear to have accepted this role very willingly. The evidence for this is of two kinds, the building and the programme of activities. The Museum of Modern Art has one of the most pleasant restaurants in New York City, which is well known for providing exceptional value for money. This, and the sculpture garden which adjoins the restaurant, would be sufficient to make the Museum a popular social centre, even if the Museum itself did not exist. As it is, the exhibition galleries and the facilities for sitting, eating and drinking flow into one another and form an agreeably varied entity, in which talking is as normal and respectable an activity as looking at pictures,

sculpture and photographs. The Museum of Modern Art is, in fact, one of New York's best clubs, with a few galleries and several million pounds' worth of art as one of its features. Its building was designed with this in mind. It is, in every sense of the word, a cultural centre, a place where people with artistic interests congregate.

So, too, is the San Francisco Museum of Art, which is as unmistakably a reflection of California as the Museum of Modern Art is of New York. This is a museum where the average age and income of its visitors is probably a good deal lower than it is in New York and where people are more inclined to want and expect to touch the pictures and sculptures, a problem which causes the management a certain amount of concern. It has a large auditorium, in which youthful musicians play extremely noisy music to equally youthful audiences. Hearing this as he enters the Museum, a stranger may well feel that he has come to the wrong place, but, as he becomes more accustomed to the atmosphere, he will notice the habitués make no clear distinction between, on the one hand, looking at the pictures and arguing about them, and on the other standing packed shoulder-to-shoulder in an impossibly crowded hall, rocked and shaken by a volume of sound which threatens to damage the hearing, and almost certainly does. Visitors drift in and out of the galleries, backwards and forwards between the pictures and the music, much as Catholics drift in and out of Mass in an Italian or French cathedral. This, in other words, is a museum created to provide experiences and sensations, or, at least, taken over by people whose primary demand of a museum is that it shall provide sensual rather than intellectual satisfactions. Faced with such a requirement — and it shows every sign of growing rapidly in most countries – an architect cannot possibly proceed as he would if his task had been to design a new home for the State Picture Gallery in a People's Democracy.

Museum buildings form a spectrum, with silent, scholarly establishments at one end and chattering, popular, participating places at the other. It may well be true that, over the next twenty or fifty years, the first type is destined to become rarer and the second a good deal more numerous, but, since both the rate and the extent of change are difficult to predict and since all but the

70

Museums for the 1980s

smallest of museums are likely to continue to have some scholarly function, new buildings should allow for the maximum amount of flexibility and old buildings should be prepared for some drastic internal reconstruction.

This, of course, has happened before. In Denmark the National War Museum is housed in a pleasant and roomy medieval church, which can hardly be something the original builders envisaged, and in London the Museum of Man, the ethnographical department of the British Museum, has taken over, ingeniously but not altogether satisfactorily, a building which once accommodated the Civil Service Commission and in which candidates for Government appointments sat their examinations until a few years ago.

Museum architects, like all architects, are creatures of fashion, and the buildings they design date and become obsolete like any others. The brilliant building – and brilliance is a very rare quality – will survive and settle down into its place in the landscape. The remainder, inevitably, will become gradually more useless, more irritating, more irrelevant, more ridiculous, more nothing at all. The National Museum of Anthropology in Mexico City is a brilliant building, brilliant in its appearance, its workmanship and its practical efficiency. It looks good and it works. One feels safe in deciding that it will not date.

It is, in fact, one of the very few museum buildings anywhere in the world which meet all Professor Lehmbruck's requirements. Its skill in taming the sun and the heat, its confident extravagance and grandeur in the midst of appalling poverty, its splendid and entirely successful mingling of tradition

and innovation reflect Mexican society to perfection. There is never, from the moment one sees it at a distance, the slightest doubt that it is a museum and nothing else. Under no conceivable circumstances could it belong to IBM or adapt itself to the needs and habits of IBM. It is extremely flexible. The whole of the internal arrangement could be radically changed without affecting the basic structure or the outside appearance in the slightest. There would be no great difficulty in moving it steadily further in the direction of a cultural centre, in adapting it to new techniques and new views of communication and interpretation. Reducing the amount of permanent display space and correspondingly increasing the proportion given over to temporary exhibitions would present no problem. The adaptation to new philosophies, new emphases and new experiments would be comparatively painless and, even more important, cheap.

This, in short, is a new building that justifies itself, which one certainly cannot say of all new museum buildings. There is no virtue in newness for its own sake, and, whatever the pressure may be from architects and other vested interests, the rule should be: 'A new building only if we must.' 'Must' may, however, need interpretation and it could be translated as follows:

1. If the existing building is in a structurally hopeless condition and if the restoration and modernisation would cost a fortune.
2. If maintenance and servicing charges are so high for the present building that moving to something cheaper and more efficient is the only practical possibility.

3. If the museum has beyond all question outgrown its present site and no further extension and adaptation are possible.

Even then, it may be possible to find an old building which could be converted satisfactorily for museum purposes and which would be a pleasant place to work in and to visit. The problems of hot countries and temperate countries are not, of course, quite the same in this respect. In recent years, the cheapest kind of large building to construct almost anywhere in the world has consisted of a steel or concrete frame, with glass or plastic panels to form the cladding for the walls. Many new museum and office buildings have used this method of construction, either for the whole building or for parts of it. The low initial cost has proved to be a false economy, since, with soaring oil and electricity prices, a building of this type is extremely expensive to maintain at a tolerable temperature summer and winter. The traditional masonry walls may cost more in the first place, but they provide far better heat insulation, inwards and outwards, and for this reason they can offer considerable savings in the annual budget.

MUSEUMS AND THE NATIONAL CLIMATE

The balance between initial cost, efficient running and pleasantness in use is never an easy one to strike, since operational costs, and notions of what constitutes efficiency and an agreeable atmosphere, are continuously changing. What does not change, however, is the climate with which the building has to function and a great many idiocies have been perpetrated through a failure or refusal to acknowledge this. What may be extremely suitable in Rio de Janeiro or Beirut can be totally unsuitable, both technically and aesthetically, in Lille, Manchester or Vienna. Far too many architects design for a dream climate which bears no relation to reality. In North-West Europe, for instance, one constantly sees buildings with finishes which would be perfectly satisfactory in a hot, dry climate, but which are disastrous when faced with the rain, wind, frost and snow which are

Ontario Science Centre, Toronto, Canada, showing parkland site and integrated car-parking area.

normal in Germany or Belgium. The same criticism can be made of the ubiquitous flat roof, which is serviceable enough in Mexico or the Middle East, but invariably leaks in Europe, where there happens to be a lot of rain, a fact which architects conveniently overlook but which their clients have to reckon with. Many European museums and libraries, and no doubt many in tropical countries, with a heavy seasonal rainfall, have had good reason to curse a flat roof, after looking at the damage caused by water pouring in over the valuable contents inside.

What this really amounts to is a recommendation to treat architects with caution and with only a limited amount of respect. However wonderful it may look as a drawing or a model, a building which is not designed first and foremost with the national climate in mind is a bad building, and with the development of architecture as an increasingly international profession, the number of prestigious buildings which are irrelevant to local conditions has shown a regrettable tendency to increase. To buy fashion can be dangerous and a luxury which only the very rich can afford.

This is not, of course, to suggest that all modern buildings, or even all steel and glass buildings, are inefficient and lacking in stamina. As an example of one which has proved very satisfactory, we could consider the Swiss Transport Museum in Lucerne, Switzerland. Planned to a tight budget, but with an unusually watchful and knowledgeable Museum Director in constant attendance as the work progressed, the buildings are modern, simple and free from arrogance, brashness or pomposity. Agreeably situated near the lake, and well surrounded by trees, they could be easily modified, added to or even demolished without any worries about vandalising a national monument. There are no enormous staircases up which the unfortunate visitor has to toil, no miles of corridors and acres of entrance halls to light, heat and maintain. It is cheap to run, even with the

complications of a Swiss winter, and the buildings perform admirably their essential function of sheltering the exhibits and of providing a flexible shell within which displays can be arranged and changed round with a minimum of difficulty and disruption. Here, the glass walls have been used to great advantage, not merely accepted as a necessary evil dictated by the budget. Large exhibits, such as a pleasure steamer which once carried passengers up and down Lake Lucerne, railway locomotives and aeroplanes are placed outside in the grounds, but, like the trees and the grass, they are always temptingly in view through the walls. The glass unifies the museum.

A good site, such as that occupied by the Swiss Transport Museum, should be used to the full: the disadvantages of a bad site should be concealed as much as possible by making the museum self-contained and by cutting off the outside world. In some cases, however, the attractions of the site lie downwards as well as outwards, and a skilful architect will base his design on this welcome bonus. An outstanding example of this can be seen at a museum to which reference has already been made in another connection, the Römisch-Germanisches Museum in Cologne. Here, partly as a result of wartime bombing, a magnificent Roman tessellated pavement was revealed, close to the Cathedral and, as a result of the accumulation of rubbish and debris over the centuries, at a considerable depth below the present street level. The decision was wisely taken to build the new museum above the pavement and to make it the central feature. Since this was to be a museum devoted to Roman civilisation in the Rhineland, the presence of the pavement could only be regarded as God-given; and full advantage was taken of it. Visitors look

down at the pavement from a dramatically-placed gallery built around it and this huge and wonderfully executed piece of Roman art anchors the Museum to its site and gives it an added dimension of reality.

This is, one could say without exaggeration, one of the most brilliantly conceived museum buildings of the past fifty years and one which, like the National Museum of Anthropology in Mexico City, is certain to have a far-reaching influence on subsequent designs. Three of its features should be particularly emphasised. The first is that the Museum forms part of a most ingenious and satisfying reconstruction of the whole area surrounding the Cathedral. If one is praising the Museum architects, one must at the same time praise those responsible for the new broad terracing which links the railway station and the Cathedral to the streets and squares in the immediate neighbourhood and which creates the Museum's site and context. The second and very important point is that the workmanship and finish of the building are superb. As in the Mexican Museum of Anthropology, everything is of the highest quality. The design has been given a chance to succeed, without cheeseparing and without any need to tolerate the second best. And the third feature of the Römisch-Germanisches Museum which makes the building so noteworthy is that it is, in a sense, never closed. The sculptures arranged under a canopy running along the outside of two sides of the Museum can be seen and studied at any hour of the day or night. They are part of the street scene of the new Cologne which has grown up from the devastation of the wartime air-raids.

In this same connection one should mention the enterprise of the Louvre in enriching, if not the city's street scene,

The Römisch-Germanisches Museum Cologne, GFR. Exterior, showing terrace for 24-hour display of museum objects. The Museum forms part of the replanning of the central area of Cologne, carried out with great skill and imagination after war-time bombing had reduced much of the city to rubble.

at least its underground scene by turning the platforms of the Louvre Métro station into an outpost of the Museum. The splendidly designed cases and exhibits have metamorphosed what was previously a very drab and ordinary railway station into one of the attractions of Paris. Remarkably, they have been treated with great respect by the travelling public and there are no signs whatever of vandalism or graffiti. A metro exhibition of the same kind in, say, Leningrad, Prague or Montreal might well meet with the same success, but one shudders to think what would happen to exhibitions like this in London or New York, where the behaviour of the metro-going public is a good deal less civilised or possibly less well supervised.

THE MUSEUM WHERE IT HAPPENED

One would hope that the distinction between different types of museum is likely to become increasingly blurred. To call the Römisch-Germanisches Museum a site-museum would not be strictly accurate, although it certainly embodies and shelters an important archaeological site and greatly benefits from it, but at exactly what point a museum ceases to be a site-museum and becomes something else is impossible to say and probably unnecessary to decide. The museum at the excavated Roman palace at Fishbourne, in England, is unquestionably a site-museum. It exists in order to safeguard the foundations of the old building and to display and explain material found there by the archaeologists. Like most of the world's so-called site-museums, the museum is housed in a simple building, erected comparatively cheaply. It is efficient, seemly, modest and entirely suitable for its purpose, but it would make no claim to architectural distinction. The Arin-Berd Museum at Erevan, in Soviet Armenia, is on an altogether more ambitious scale. The Museum is based on the excavated eighth-century citadel of Erebuni, and the needs which had to be observed in designing the building were:

1. preserving effectively the excavated remains of the citadel;
2. displaying the citadel and other finds to their best advantage;
3. the eventual reconstruction of the most important buildings in the citadel.

The solution which the architects decided on was a gigantic umbrella, covering the whole site. The handle of the umbrella is a central steel pillar, from which a triangular concrete roof is suspended. The roof is weatherproofed with PVC emulsion, which provides a coating that is elastic and resistant to frost and cracking, and the building is, in other words, designed for the year-round weather experienced at Erevan.

There are thousands of archaeological sites scattered over the world and the museological problem is always to decide whether to build a small museum on the site, with all the difficulties of supervision and security that involves, or to more or less leave the site to its fate and to transfer what has been found on the site to a conventional type of museum in a nearby city. There are major differences of opinion about this, and the decision is usually taken on economic and political, rather than on museological grounds. In Pakistan, for example, ex-President Bhutto is an enthusiast for archaeological site-museums and this fact must certainly have influenced the decision to establish a considerable network of site-museums in a country which has to observe a strict order of priorities in apportioning its somewhat slender resources.

It is curious that some countries take to open-air museums like ducks to water, while others have shown themselves very resistant to them.[3] In this connection, one might usefully quote what the present author has written in another place[4] about the situation in Finland. 'It has been said,' he notes,

unkindly, but not altogether un-

Fishbourne Roman Palace Museum, near Chichester, England. Walkways for viewing excavations on the site of the Palace.

Indigo Dye-House Museum, Papa, Hungary. The Museum is in the early nineteenth-century dye-house and preserves its original equipment and furnishings.

truthfully, that the Finnish recipe for a museum is to buy a small field, scatter old wooden cottages, pig-houses, sauna-baths and cowsheds over it, with a windmill and a rural distillery for good measure, and then to open the results to the public between the beginning of May and the end of September. This is a fair description of the raw material of at least a third of all the museums in Finland, but it ignores two important facts: one that the task can be carried out either with or without skill and imagination; and the other, that all or any of these wooden buildings house historical collections of one kind or another. Good or less good, however, these open-air museums are popular, non-sensational and non-vulgar and they allow a lot to be done on a small budget.

What goes for Finland goes for a number of other countries as well. Belgium, the Netherlands, Norway, Sweden, Denmark, Bulgaria, Britain and the Soviet Union, for example, all have open-air museums of this kind, to which small buildings, mostly from rural areas, have been brought together from different parts of the country, partly for safety, partly for purposes of comparision and partly in order that more people can have the opportunity of seeing them than if they had remained on their original sites. The distinction between a good open-air museum and a bad one has now become clear. The bad one, or perhaps it would be fairer to say, the old-fashioned type, has been primarily concerned to provide a place in which pensioned-off buildings can rest quietly during their old age. The good ones aim to do more than this, to show the cultural pattern into which the exhibits fit, and for this some kind of interpretation centre, however modest, is essential. Nowhere has this been achieved better than at Britain's latest open-air museum, the Weald and Downland Museum, near Chichester, which fully deserved its Museum of the Year title, awarded in 1975. Here the interpretation centre is in an old barn which, like all the other exhibits, has been dismantled and re-erected at the Museum. The centre demonstrates, simply, but with great clarity and elegance, the building materials and techniques used in the region during the past 500 years, the agricultural methods, the occupations and the crafts. After a very agreeable

Open-Air Museum, Rivoal, France. A farmhouse which forms part of the Museum.

quarter of an hour here, the visitor is adequately equipped to tour the beautiful site and to make proper sense of the houses, corn-stores, charcoal-burners' huts and other old buildings scattered over it.

Most open-air museums have so far relied too much on allowing the story to be told piecemeal by each individual building, without first presenting the whole picture in some kind of orientation centre. More will be said about this in the next section, when we shall be discussing methods of presentation, but for the moment it seems necessary to make only three further points. The first is that open-air museums can only very rarely be planned as a whole. They grow as new items are acquired and for this reason they usually have something of a haphazard quality about them. Although architects frequently and normally have the opportunity to wrestle with the problems of museums of the conventional in-a-building kind, they have never so far been asked to meet the challenge of designing an open-air museum from the beginning and *in toto*. Occasionally an architect or a designer may be employed to work out a scheme for labelling or signposting, for producing brochures, for landscaping or for an interpretation centre, but not for the complete project. The results which such a revolution in museum practice would bring would be extremely interesting to study.

The third point of special relevance from the buildings point of view,

where open-air museums are concerned, is that in the majority of cases where there is some sort of interpretation centre it is to be found in an old building, not a new one. This situation has probably arisen not so much from a lack of money as from an instinct on the part of those responsible which has caused them to feel that visitors who come to see old buildings may respond better to guidance which is offered to them in another old building, almost as if the old building itself were advising and informing them. The instinct is almost certainly a sound one.

It is impossible to devise an interpretation scheme which makes no mistakes. The way in which exhibits are presented, the form of wording used on captions and labels, must necessarily be tentative and experimental. This applies with particular force to industrial sites, where a new tradition of explanation has to be established, with curators feeling their way very cautiously until the reaction of visitors can be observed. At Ironbridge, which is now, after five years of development, Britain's best-known and best-publicised open-air museum, the policy has been followed, especially at the Museum's Blists Hill site, of leaving interpretation and labelling at a very rudimentary stage until more information could be gathered about the people visiting the Museum. Only then, it was felt, could the right level and amount of explanation be decided on with any confidence. Most other museums prefer to learn from their mistakes, sometimes in an *ad hoc* fashion, sometimes systematically. In Norfolk, England, for instance, the County Museums Service has carried out careful surveys of the reactions of visitors to the interpretation panels placed at historic sites in various parts of the county. It was found that there were significant differences according to the time of day, the weather, and the sex of the person concerned. No attempt has so far been made to correlate criticisms with age or educational background. Comments ranged from 'What is a staithe?' to 'The board is too small', and from 'Tell us more about the mill and its construction' to 'What about an aerial photograph, with key?'

A major problem is to make up one's mind now as to the kind of site-museum which is likely to be of interest to future generations. A copy-book instance of this dilemma can be seen in Tanzania, near a place which has already been referred to at some length, Bagamoyo. Here there is an extensive area of saltings, covering perhaps 50 acres. The brine is allowed to run into shallow ponds and to evaporate. The coarse salt produced in this way is brought from the beds by men carrying two flat baskets, one at each end of a carrying-pole which they rest on their shoulders. It is taken into enormous thatched storehouses, built on a wooden framework, with matting walls and floors. At the moment this process is still going on and there is no question of turning the saltings and the warehouses into a museum, but the time will probably come in East Africa, as it already has in Europe and America, when the demand for salt and the wages of men will both become too high for the traditional methods of production to continue. At that point, mined salt, probably imported, will take over the market and the old works will close. Ideally, the decision to turn the saltings into a museum should be taken long before production finally ceases, so that films and recordings can be made and photographs taken, and so that the possibility can be explored of keeping some production going in the interests of visitors. If this can be done, both the interpretation centre and the preserva-

tion of the site and its buildings can be planned in good time, before decay and neglect make this work more difficult and, of course, more expensive. At Bagamoyo, the choice would almost certainly have to be a new building, probably of wood, for the interpretation centre, in order to achieve some measure of security for the material inside. Such a building might well be placed inside one of the storehouses, so that it would not be obtrusive, a building within a building. The main problem, however, is not of this kind, but to make the authorities aware that a salt museum at Bagamoyo is as reputable, interesting and valuable as any other kind of museum.

NEW MUSEUMS INTO OLD BUILDINGS

This section can be summarised by two parables, both of which are entirely true and factual.

The first concerns the National Museum of Yemen, at Sana.[5] Here there was a great deal of discussion as to whether the Museum should be in a new building or an old building. If the decision were for a new building, in what style should it be? Since there is a distinctive Yemeni style of architecture, anything else would obviously be out of place, but it appeared that such Yemeni architects as there were were more likely to be practising abroad than in the Yemen and that neither they nor good foreign architects would respond very favourably to the suggestion that they should design a brand-new building in the old style. There was no real precedent, since none of the four existing museums was of the size or importance contemplated for the National Museum. The problem was eventually solved, to more or less everyone's satisfaction, by taking over the former police headquarters, which had been built as a palace in 1938, in the Yemeni style and without much attention being paid

The Tanks of Taweela, People's Democratic Republic of the Yemen. The site of the planned National Ethnographical Museum.

to expense. The police now have a new headquarters, the Museum is very suitably and pleasantly housed, and an excellent building has been preserved.

The second parable relates to Japan, which, after the United States, has more museums than any other country in the world. This situation is the result of what can only be called a post-war explosion in museum building.[6] All over the country municipalities decided that it was essential for any town worthy of the name to have a museum, preferably a large and impressive museum. Hundreds of new museums were therefore built, but it was then discovered that the collections to go into them did not yet exist. There were conservation laboratories, but nothing to conserve; offices for directors and curators with nothing to direct or care for; empty galleries and cases; air-conditioning plant with no work to do; lighting experts with nothing to light. This meant that for many years these museums have had to depend on one

loan collection after another and that the local Museum of Art or Science or Ethnography was not exactly what its name might suggest to the uninformed. This appears to have been an exclusively Japanese situation, without parallel anywhere else in the world.

Japan has, however, another unique achievement to her credit, and one which other countries might well consider copying. The Tokyo Museum of Modern Art moved into new buildings in 1969, and at a slightly later date the Kyoto and Nara National Museums also acquired new premises. In each instance, the old buildings have been designated Important Cultural Properties, representing important examples of buildings in the European style designed by Japanese architects. This extremely enlightened policy has relieved three museums of an incubus and at the same time preserved interesting local landmarks for other uses.

The museum which is housed in a specially designed building is the

exception. It has been estimated by ICOM that 80 per cent of the museums in existence today are in buildings which were originally designed for some other purpose. This is not, of course, to say that 80 per cent of the world's museums are in *unsuitable* buildings. On the contrary, for many a move to a brand-new building would be either absurd or a disaster, since the building is an integral part of the museum. How many people would visit, for instance, the National Goethe Museum in Weimar, if it were removed from its present location in Goethe's former home and transferred to a steel and glass shell on the outskirts of the town?

So far as one knows, no survey has ever been carried out, either nationally or internationally, to discover what proportion of museum directors or curators consider they are in a building which meets their needs. If this were to be done, one feels that most of the seriously dissatisfied directors would be those running relatively large museums. Small buildings are, on the whole, much easier to adapt to museum purposes. A large building, like a large school, on the other hand, must be regarded by those who work in it as a plant, to be judged to some extent by industrial standards. Seen in this way, it is either an efficient or an inefficient plant, and most large museums in old buildings are, one has good reason to believe, very inefficient plants indeed. They are difficult and expensive to heat, light, ventilate and clean, they waste a great deal of space, they contain rooms which are either too high or too low to be really suitable for museum requirements, and it is often far from easy to move people and goods around them. Worst of all, they are nearly always, from today's point of view, in the wrong place. A large museum needs a great deal of space around it, for car-parking, for deliveries and for outdoor storage, and this is precisely what the city-centre museum so rarely provides.

It is a useful exercise to look at a list of museums in a major city, such as New York or Tokyo or Paris, and decide which of them would benefit from moving into another building, either new or put up long since. A

National Museum, Nara, Japan. This combines modern construction with traditional Japanese forms.

check through the list of the museums in London suggests that, if the money existed, 10 per cent should go straight away into a brand-new building and a further 10 per cent as soon as possible. The remaining 80 per cent, which include nearly all the small museums, are, by any reasonable standard, either adequately or very well housed, and one can see no particular reason for putting them anywhere else. This is not, of course, to deny that in a number of cases modernisation and redecoration would be very desirable.

If this figure of 80 per cent reflects the position elsewhere, then one has to be somewhat sceptical of some of the claims made by members of the museum profession, especially when these relate to small museums. In the next ten or fifteen years money for new museum buildings is going to be very hard to find in most parts of the world and there is a strong case for saying that the bulk of the funds which are available should go to rehousing large museums, especially those devoted to science, industry and technology, subjects particularly ill-suited to buildings which were not built for the job. A visit to the present premises of the National Museum of Science and Technology in Ottawa or to the Museum of Arts and Trades in Paris will make the point clear.

The plight of another Paris museum, the Palace of Discovery, is even worse. To say, in this case, that the building is inadequate is a massive understatement. Palatial it certainly is, but it is the palace of a bankrupt duke, who is totally without the funds needed to maintain it. The imposing entrance is protected by a wooden case, to prevent pieces of masonry and plaster from falling on the heads of visitors, the grandiose staircases have long lost whatever charm they once had, the vast rooms are a nightmare to heat and clean, and the glass roof presents constant problems. Within this idiotic framework, the Director and his staff have done their heroic and enthusiastic best to create the national museum of science. To say that they have performed miracles is no more than just, but this does not in any way alter the fact that the sooner the Palace of Discovery is pulled down, the better for France. This is a building with no future whatsoever, and it is ironical that, with the National Museum of Science so inadequately housed, a fortune should have been found from public funds to build the enormous Georges Pompidou Centre, at Beaubourg, in Paris, so that modern art is now sumptuously accommodated, while science, on which the economic development of France depends, should continue to languish in near-slum conditions. The amount spent on Beaubourg would have provided half-a-dozen magnificent new science museums, strategically located in different parts of the country. Society can have a strange order of priorities, determined, apparently, by considerations other than logic and prudence. It is worth mentioning in this connection that certain highly industrialised countries, notably Belgium and Switzerland, have, as yet, no national museum of science and technology at all.

One should not, however, leave this discussion of museum buildings without drawing attention to some very wise words, spoken in Tokyo in 1976[7] by Dr Eric Westbrook. 'Very frequently,' he said, 'at least in Australia, architects and engineers are commissioned to build or renovate one museum building and then do not again approach the same highly specialised problem for many years, if at all. This has the double disadvantage that each time the material has to be covered afresh and it is then allowed to gather dust on the shelves of an architect's office.'

I believe [Dr Westbrook continued] that in this region there is a very high level of architectural ability and knowledge and it seems wasteful that this is not utilised to the full. I would therefore suggest that serious consideration be given to creating a central pool of information about both new and renovated museum buildings which could be drawn upon by any country, together with practical assistance from the architects who have contributed the information.

The value of this suggestion is certainly not confined to Asia and Australia. Regional information banks, such as Dr Westbrook proposes, would benefit architects and museums throughout the world and prevent many unnecessary and expensive mistakes from being made. One hopes that the creation of such banks will be one of the achievements of the next decade.

4 The Museum and its Visitors

THE MUSEUM'S 'COMMUNITY'

In some countries, the United States especially, museums are much given to talking about their 'place in the community' and their 'service to the community'. The habit is misleading and unhelpful, rooted in sentiment rather than logic. 'The community' is, in fact, at least four communities. They might be roughly defined as:

(a) *Local* – say a five-mile radius around the museum.
(b) *Regional* – up to two hours' travelling distance from the museum.
(c) *National* – whatever the size of the particular country may be.
(d) *International* – such countries as may provide the museum with visitors within a particular year.

An analysis of the entries from Easter to the end of September 1975, in a small, but excellent, museum in an English provincial town, on a well-used holiday route, showed that approximately 45 per cent were what we have termed local, 22 per cent regional, 29 per cent national and 4 per cent international. What, then, is this museum's 'community'? There is no reason to suppose that these proportions are either typical or untypical. Rich countries with good roads and with car ownership widely and thickly distributed throughout the population are likely to provide a small provincial museum with one pattern of visitors, poor countries with few cars and bad roads with quite another. The size and character of a community depend to a considerable extent on its public and private transport system.

This being so, it seems wiser to talk of visitors, rather than the community, and to consider the relationship of a museum with its visitors instead of its relationship with the community. One recognises, of course, that 'visitor', like 'community', is a blanket term. It includes people who come once and people who come a dozen times a year, people who are students and people who come to while away a morning, people of eighty and people of ten. An essential part of a museum's business is to monitor, regularly and systematically, the men, women and children who come to see what it has to offer. Without this information, it is aiming blind.

But – and the point is an important one – monitoring is essential not only to obtain information about the people who do come, but also about those who do not. Serious attempts to attract the non-visitor may produce quite different skills and techniques from those which are apparently meeting the needs of the existing visitors reasonably well.

It is possible and practical to consider this huge and amorphous subject of the relationship between a museum and its visitors under four headings – Communication, Participation, Taking the Museum to the People, and Feedback. The division is, however, entirely arbitrary, and each section overlaps the others to a considerable extent. Participation is, for example, an essential part of Communication, as one cannot achieve satisfactory communication without reliable and imaginative feedback to assess the results of one's efforts. The four headings simply reflect different aspects of the same problem.

THE NATURE OF COMMUNICATION

'Communication', as an abstract concept, is meaningless in the museological context. One can only try to communicate something to somebody. It is reasonable, therefore, to ask a museum curator three questions:

1. What are you attempting to communicate?
2. With what kind of people do you want to communicate?
3. How do you measure your success or failure?

In many cases, unfortunately, the only honest answer to all three questions is that the curator does not know, that he has never thought about his work in these terms. The honest answer is not, of course, what one is always given and determined pressure to obtain it may cause embarrassment. Even so, all museum people, like all writers or broadcasters, should be asking themselves these questions every day of their lives. To face up to them is a salutary discipline.

The list of possible answers to the first question is a long one.

(a) This painting/carved jade/piece of porcelain is beautiful. I am trying to display it in such a way that people will see immediately how beautiful it is.
(b) The workmanship of this desk/pistol/engraved glass is superb. I should like you to understand my reasons for saying this.
(c) This is a model of James Watt's steam engine and this is how it worked.
(d) These are all the butterflies which can be found in Brazil and these are their names.
(e) This is roughly what a giraffe looks like in its native environment in Africa.
(f) Here are some of the things that archaeologists found when they were excavating this Bronze Age village and this is what they tell

us about the people who lived there.

(g) Balzac was an untidy man and wrote very fast. This is a page of one of his manuscripts.

And so on.

If one talks to a number of people whose task it is to work out museum displays that they think and hope will interest the public, it becomes clear that they divide themselves into two groups. Those who fall into the first group have a mainly didactic purpose: they are trying to teach their visitors something or, at least, to encourage and help them to learn something. The members of the second group are much more interested in pleasing, amusing, frightening, stimulating. Group One, it could be said, aims primarily at the intellect, Group Two at the emotions. The qualification 'primarily' had to be included, since no museum professional, whatever his temperament and inclinations, would be aiming wholly at educating or wholly at entertaining. Each activity would necessarily contain a leaven of the other. This can be easily illustrated by considering the practical implications of the answers (a) to (g) above. It may possibly be easier to use (g) than (c) as a source of entertainment, but each, suitably interpreted, contains excellent raw material for both instruction and entertainment. This has certain very important museological consequences, which can be best explained, perhaps, but making a comparison between museums on the one hand and reading and television on the other.

Television, like films, is an excellent medium for stimulating interest and modifying attitudes, but a very poor medium for communicating factual information. Research carried out in a number of countries during the past ten years has shown that viewers remember extremely few of the facts which have been presented to them, whether in a news bulletin, a documentary programme or in a programme specifically designed for educational purposes. They may well be interested, and even fascinated, but that is quite another matter, since one can stay with a speaker for the sake of his charm, but absorb absolutely nothing of what he has said. One can, of course, take in some facts from television, but, since the programme must move along at a predetermined pace and cannot be stopped or run back for one viewer who has missed a point or would like to check something that

was shown 30 seconds before, it is, of necessity, a very rough and ready way of coming to grips with a subject. For exact, detailed learning, suited to one's own pace, temperament and ability, there is still no substitute for the book or the article.

But, and this is both the difficulty and the opportunity, television and films have an enormous, unequalled prestige. In today's world, nothing exists until it has been seen on television, and children who have grown up with television have become accustomed to learning about the world through visual impressions. They may well, as a result, have a very inaccurate knowledge of a great many things, but that is another matter. What is significant in the present context is that years of exposure to television causes people to have certain expectations. They are used to material being presented to them in the television way and they find it difficult to consider any other possibility.

The matter was argued with some heat during a seminar held in 1967 at the Museum of the City of New York. The seminar was concerned with the 'exploration of the ways, means and values of museum communication with the viewing public',[1] and the participants whose voices were heard most frequently were Dr Marshall McLuhan and Harley W. Parker, of the Royal Ontario Museum, Toronto. Both objected very strongly to what they called the story-line approach in museums.

> Museums in the past [said Mr Parker] have tended – museum curators tend today – to write a story line and then use the artefacts to illustrate it. In fact, if they were writing a book they would do exactly the same thing, except that in this case the artefacts would be photographed and used as illustrations, but there is no essential difference. In other words, they think of a museum as a book.

Dr McLuhan then became ecstatic about the international exhibition held in New York, Expo 67. It was, in his opinion,

> the first world fair which had no story line whatever. It was just a mosaic of discontinuous items in which people took an immense satisfaction precisely because they weren't being told anything about the overall pattern or shape of it, but they were free to discover and participate and in-

volve themselves in the total overall thing. The result was also that they never got fatigued.

He well remembered experiencing as a child, he told the seminar, 'that museum feeling, a kind of claustrophobia and exhaustion which settles upon you as soon as you get inside those straightened avenues and alleyways. Once you move into a world of continuous connected spaces – visual space – you quickly discover exhaustion setting in, because there is no means of participation.'

There is certainly some truth in this, but fashions have a way of generating hostile reactions to them, and it is possible that if all the world's museums were eventually to be of the impressionistic, participating type advocated by Dr McLuhan a new style of quiet, orderly, story-line museum would have to be created in order to meet the needs of people who found participation unhelpful and repulsive. In a disorderly world, a few oases of order and discipline can be extremely attractive.

The real issue is whether museums should try to play the part of books or of television. Are they to be, can they be, primarily media for conveying information or is their real function to stimulate, to implant or to intensify interests? Do they, in other words, belong to the instructional world or to the entertainment world?

Fifty years ago, ninety-nine museum professionals out of a hundred would have answered without any doubt in their minds, 'To the educational world', but in recent years attitudes have changed, mainly because the line between education and entertainment is no longer as sharply drawn as it used to be. Most good teachers have, in any case, always, in any period, known the value of mixing entertainment with instruction, but publicly and officially the two have tended until recently to be kept fairly strictly apart. This has been partly for financial reasons. It may be perfectly in order to finance instruction or even education from taxation, but to finance entertainment from the same source is quite another matter. The more serious-minded an establishment can make itself out to be, the more likely it is to get either the public or the private money it needs. To attack this as hypocrisy is to show oneself sadly ignorant of the essence of politics and bureaucracy. Museums, regrettably, have to live in a real world and

certain aspects of that world are unpleasant.

But, even so, some museums do undoubtedly provide a great deal more excitement and entertainment than others and it is difficult to believe that the difference is accidental. It will be understood, of course, that neither excitement nor entertainment need be noisy or obvious and that what stimulates and amuses one person will not necessarily have the same effect on another. It is reasonably certain, however, that, so long as museum-going remains a voluntary activity, the museum which is visited by a great many people is considered to be more interesting, size for size, and local population for local population, than the museum or exhibition which is visited by very few people. One says 'reasonably certain' because it is always possible to attract visitors by not altogether honest publicity and for these visitors to be disappointed at what they are actually offered once they are inside the doors. This is true of any kind of tourist attraction, of course. There must be a large number of people in the world who have come away from Stratford-on-Avon wondering why the town had failed to come up to the tourist literature.

If a museum says clearly and unmistakably what it is trying to do, one is in a position to judge how successful it is in presenting itself and its collections to the world or, in other words, how well or how badly it is tackling the task of communication.

In 1974 Mr Mahmoud Mesallam, at that time the energetic and enthusiastic Director of the Museum of Science and Technology in Cairo, reviewed the progress of the Museum since it had been established five years earlier. His unusually plain and straightforward analysis, written for UNESCO, as a working document for this book, is a minor classic of museology.

The ground was well prepared.

Ironbridge Gorge Museum, Shropshire, England. Demonstration of printing in the nineteenth-century printing shop at Blists Hill. This kind of museum activity causes no difficulties with the Factory Inspectors. Other kinds of industrial process may be officially regarded as dangerous to visitors and, if they are permitted, expensive safeguards have to be taken.

(below) *North of England Open-Air Museum, Beamish. Group learning to make corn-dollies.*

'Committees of experts were set up, studies of the aims and methods of big museums in Europe and the United States were carried out, missions were sent to these museums and a plan was drawn up.' At that point, however, when the infant Museum had to acquire and develop its resources, things began to go wrong. 'Objects, models and samples were collected from the Ministries of Irrigation, Agriculture and Communications, and from some scientific institutions. The models were silent and big, and occupied a great deal of space in a haphazard way. The arrangement could tell no story.'

Mr Mesallam was completely dissatisfied with the collections, 'But I was aware', he recalled, 'that the people responsible for financing national projects would not be generous until they saw something done.' His judgement was sound, since soon after the inauguration of the Museum an encouraging budget was allocated, a number of the staff were sent abroad for training and proper workshops were set up. It should perhaps be explained at this point that the Museum building had been one of the palaces of the former King Farouk and that, although roomy and in some ways even luxurious, it was not ideal as a home for a science museum. Mr Mesallam did his best with what was available, however, and, being a man with a strong sense of humour, decided to put the section devoted to Light in the ex-King's bedroom.

About 2000 people visited the Museum on the first day – a science museum was a great novelty in the Arab world and Mr Mesallam's pioneering had attracted a good deal of newspaper publicity – but after that the total slumped to only 300 a month. Something was obviously wrong and a questionnaire left no doubt as to why visitors were dissatisfied. Mr Mesallam summarised the main failings as follows:

1. The exhibits were built to interest those who designed them and did not meet the needs of the different sectors of the public.
2. The models were too big for the ideas they had to illustrate.
3. There was no sequence. The exhibits were put in the positions which best suited them, and not according to any logical sequence.
4. The exhibits were silent and could not arouse the interest of the visitors.
5. There were too many words to explain each exhibit. Visitors do not want to come to museums to read books. [Mr Mesallam might have added that a high proportion of Egyptians either cannot read or find reading very difficult, so that captions of any length must have been largely wasted.]
6. The exhibits were much too crowded.
7. There should have been demonstrations of big national projects.
8. There were no exhibits to show the recent scientific and technological achievements in developed countries.

The Museum was, in plain terms, uninspiring. It communicated next to nothing and it was necessary to take urgent and drastic action. Mr Mesallam took a number of important decisions. The first was to set a large room aside specifically for international exhibitions. In the first year, there was an exhibition from the United States on recent developments in medicine; two exhibitions, one from the United States and the other from the USSR, on space research and space travel; an exhibition from Czechoslovakia on the development of sound recording and reproduction. The Russian exhibition provided an unexpected bonus, since all the exhibits were afterwards made over the Museum as a gift.

This done, Mr Mesallam felt he had 'to get in contact with those who are responsible for carrying out big national projects and to ask them to carry out their responsibility towards their fellow citizens and to show what is being done for them to raise their standard of living'. The appeal succeeded and the required information was quickly forthcoming. The Museum's technical staff made sectional working models for the various plants and dams, which were self-explanatory, with very short captions.

'Children', says Mr Mesallam, 'are the men and women of the future. They should be encouraged to meet that complex future. We should begin to encourage them not to fear what appears to be complex in science and technology.' A great deal of effort and imagination was devoted to this. Push-button exhibits were designed, to arouse curiosity and interest, science clubs were set up and a special Science Centre was created for particularly talented children, some of whom were given the opportunity to visit similar centres abroad. Summer camps, each lasting a fortnight, were organised for members of the Centre, to allow them to carry out fieldwork. The camps were provided with specially designed small laboratories and with a library.

A slogan was adopted: 'The Museum services should reach the villages.' Special village-exhibitions were therefore organised, with film shows, usually of cartoon films. Before the exhibition takes place, a Science Club is formed in the village and one or two exceptionally able young men or women are selected for a special training course, 'so that they can carry out the job on behalf of the museum staff, as they are more able to speak to their friends and relatives in the language they can understand'.

The urgency of putting across modern scientific ideas did not mean that the Museum should neglect the past. On the contrary, it should be concerned with both the past and the present of science. Egyptians and Arabs have made great contributions to scientific progress. They were the first to study mechanics, chemistry, algebra, geometry, medicine, light and astronomy in a systematic way, the first to describe the circulatory system, to perform delicate surgical operations, to know about bilharzia and water pollution and to write prescriptions.

From the beginning a firm decision was taken that the Museum should give film and slide shows and arrange short courses for teachers. To allow this to be done, the Museum has twelve projections, a stock of more than 2500 scientific films and a large collection of slides.

Most of our new exhibits [reported Mr Mesallam] were shown in television programmes, which produced a rush of both schoolchildren and adults to the Museum, so that in a short time the number of visitors increased from 300 a month to 2000 a day. The Museum is open from 8 in the morning until 9 at night, and we have noticed that some boys and girls who have come with school parties during the day come again, either alone or with their parents, in the evening. They examine the samples and models carefully, make notes, ask questions and consult books.

The Museum of Science and Technology in Cairo was set up in a poor and seriously undeveloped country in which educational opportunities, especially for girls, are still, by modern standards, quite inadequate and in which very many people are unable to read or write. In such a situation, a museum such as this has quite a different kind of role to plan, compared with a museum in an advanced country like Germany or the United States. As Mahmoud Mesallam has put it, 'the museum is an effective educational institution, which preserves the national heritage and continuously adds to man's knowledge, helps him to understand and protect his environment and prepares him for a better life'. This is true of all countries, but it has a special significance and force when applied to a developing country like Egypt, it is a fresh and powerful assertion of one's national identity. The thirst for knowledge which undoubtedly exists there today recalls the situation in Europe and America a hundred years ago. 'A better life' does not mean the same to an Egyptian as to a Frenchman or a Canadian, where the line marking poverty from comfort and education and ignorance is drawn at a different point. If one is educated, well fed and well housed, visiting a museum is a luxury to be measured against other luxuries; under the conditions of a developing country, it can be a first step towards education, a better job and a more tolerable existence.

THE SOCIAL BASIS OF MUSEUM PRESENTATION

To belong to a Science Club in Egypt is to watch a door beginning to open, whereas in America it is, in most cases, little more than an agreeable hobby. This means, inevitably, that, provided they feel that the museum is giving them what they want and need, Egyptians or Ghanaians or Indians are not likely to be critical of the style of the displays. They are prepared to accept very basic forms of presentation and to work hard to understand what they are shown, whereas Europeans and Americans nowadays resent any trace of the take-it-or-leave-it approach and expect a museum, like a shop or a hotel, to take pains to flatter, to please and to be fully up to date. A sophisticated style, although possibly not the most sophisticated, is taken for granted in most establishments which cater for the public, and anywhere which fails to provide it will probably find its cus-

tomers disappearing. One could put this another way, by saying that in a technically and museologically advanced country even a good museum has to face considerable competition from other types of attraction and that, if it wants to stay in business, it must present its wares in ways to which a demanding and pampered public is accustomed.

It must, in other words, be continually asked: 'How can this exhibit be made more eye-catching, more intelligible, more interesting?' This usually means, 'How can we achieve originality and avoid clichés, in a field in which so much is being done all the time? How and where can we discover some new ideas?' But one needs to remember that what is an overworked, boring cliché to one person may seem dazzlingly original to another and that, in museums as in architecture, the theatre, films, television, music or literature, most published criticism consists of one professional writing about the work of another professional. The voice of the ordinary consumer is rarely heard and he may well find refreshing and exciting what the hardened expert, who has grown cynical in the service, considers merely a tedious repeat performance.

Designers, like television producers, are frightened of boring other people in the same line of business as themselves. For this reason, they feel themselves to be under a constant compulsion to achieve something new and, if possible, revolutionary. To a considerable extent, designers design for other designers and architects for other architects, in the sense that they value the opinions of their colleagues and competitors more than those of the people whose needs they are theoretically supposed to be meeting. This is partly because one designer understands, or thinks he understands, what another designer is saying. They speak the same language. To establish a fruitful dialogue between a designer and a curator (who in turn has to create a dialogue between himself and the public) is a far from easy matter, but it is a problem which somehow has to be solved if a museum is to have any success at all. Both the designer and the curator have to ask themselves constantly, not 'Is this a good design, or a good exhibit?' but 'Good for whom?'

A very relevant story from a special branch of design, not connected with museums, may help to make the point

clearer. A few years ago the present author was visiting a university in the North-West of England, and, after spending a couple of nights in a new residential block normally used by students – it was during the vacation – he commented to the Vice-Chancellor of the university that he found the layout, furnishing and décor of the room extremely pleasant. 'Yes,' said the Vice-Chancellor, 'you consider it very good, I consider it very good, and so do the architect and the designer. But a high proportion of our students find it cold, frightening and unfriendly, and do their best to change it for something else as quickly as possible.' He went on to explain that many of the students came from working-class and lower-middle-class families and had been brought up in small terrace-houses, where the walls were covered with flowery paper and pictures, the mantel-shelf above the fireplace was crammed with ornaments and family photographs, and the rooms were so full of furniture that it was difficult to cross from one side to the other. The rooms at the University, with their plain white walls and functional, un-fussy furniture, belonged to another culture altogether. They were in enemy territory and they were frightened and angry. The design of the rooms might be good in the eyes of the architectural journals, but it was not good for them.

In 1972, the British periodical *The Designer* devoted a large part of one issue[2] to a consideration of the problems facing museum designers. A number of the best-known and apparently most successful designers contributed to and some useful points were made, but, extraordinary and impossible as this may seem, the people who visit museums, the general public, are hardly mentioned at all. A careful analysis of the tone and content of these articles, which are entirely typical of what one finds in design periodicals and at design conferences all over the world, shows how inbred and narcissistic a business museum design and presentation have become.

John Hayes, the Director of the London Museum, had been closely involved in the planning of the new Museum of London. He had noticed, in the course of many discussions, that designers and curators tended to be very suspicious of one another. They had been differently educated and trained and they had 'different kinds of intelligence, different attitudes of mind, different pressures to face and, possibly, though less so nowadays, different tempi of work'. Given 'mutual confidence and forbearance', however, and 'a harmonious relationship between curator and designer', Mr Hayes was sure the problem could be solved to the satisfaction of both parties.

The initial impetus [wrote Mr Hayes] will come from the curator's own enthusiasm and knowledge about the subject concerned, but he will then expect a designer to immerse himself in that subject and eventually to produce a visual response perhaps far removed from whatever ideas about possible methods of treatment he may have envisaged himself. The deeper the designer's understanding of the subject, the more imaginative and truly original the visual response is likely to be.

This is no doubt true, but the aim of museum presentation is not to produce an imaginative and truly original response on the part of the designer. It is to achieve the maximum possible degree of communication between the exhibit and the people who look at it. It may well be that a brilliant design will make visitors want to study more closely what is being shown, and indeed help them to do so. If it achieves this, it is a good design, but if all it really does is to attract praise for its originality, then a great deal of money has been wasted.

In fairness to Mr Hayes, his article suggests that he realises this. For the Museum of London, he points out,

the problem is to tell the story of London in 38,200 square feet, an area disposed on two floors round a central courtyard; and to tell it in a consecutive and easily intelligible way, as an unfolding visual experience. Needless to say, we shall maintain the very highest standards of scholarship; but the achievement of a close rapport with the ordinary museum-going public is regarded as of paramount importance, and in the course of our work we shall endeavour to anticipate some of the questions about London's history to which they will wish to have answers.

Three important questions arise from this: first, how does Mr Hayes or anyone else define 'the ordinary museum-going public'? Second, what form is the 'close rapport' to take? And

third, if the wrong questions about London's history have been anticipated, is it proposed to make any radical changes in the Museum? This, after all, is no mere temporary exhibition, but a big, prestigious museum, on which a correspondingly large amount of public money has been spent. Until it opens, nobody knows what the reaction of visitors is likely to be. What happens if the guesses and the intuitions prove wrong? Will the Museum of London turn out to be what more than one pessimist has forecast, the last of the dinosaurs? Or is there sufficient built-in flexibility to allow mistakes to be put right?

Any curator or director can only base his predictions and strategy on what he knows already, but to make far-reaching changes in a layout or style of display is an expensive matter and, with budgets as they are today, few museums are in a position to regard all their presentations as experimental and expendable. It is certainly for this reason that consumer research surveys are regarded with such suspicion by many museum professionals. If the public dislikes what has been so carefully prepared for its benefit, the curator would prefer not to know.

But to return to Mr Hayes' term, 'the ordinary museum-going public'. As a result of investigations carried out in a number of countries, we now know quite a lot about the people who visit museums voluntarily – this excludes school parties – and especially about their ages and educational backgrounds. We have incontrovertible evidence that the typical museum visitor, whether in a socialist or a capitalist country, is extremely unlikely to be someone who left school at the earliest possible moment, who does unskilled or semi-skilled manual work and who is over forty years of age. We know, too, that women of all ages visit museums less than men. Yet, and this is where Dr Marshall McLuhan undoubtedly has a point, plenty of unskilled manual workers, women and people over forty years of age did visit Expo 67, which therefore succeeded where most museums fail. One could put this another way, by saying that the ordinary world's-fair-going public is considerably wider than Mr Hayes' 'ordinary museum-going public' and it is reasonable to wonder why. If the composition of the museum-going public is to be regarded as static, then one could perhaps accuse museums of defeatism.

If, on the other hand, some museums expect and want to attract people from a social and educational spectrum, which comes closer to that of the population as a whole, then quite different techniques of publicity and presentation may have to be adopted.

The experience of television producers is relevant here. Television, as those who work for it are never allowed to forget, is not for minority audiences, and for a programme to attract and hold millions of people certain rules have to be followed. They can be simply stated. One has to:

(a) paint with a very broad brush and make positive assertions. The details and the qualified statements beloved of scholars are inadmissible;

(b) personalise a story as much as possible, or at least to emphasise its human associations;

(c) remember that, for most people, the emotions are more important than the intellect;

(d) be extremely cautious with any assumptions about what people do and do not know;

(e) remember that one's audience includes the very stupid and the very intelligent, the very tolerant and the very narrow-minded, the uneducated, half-educated and highly educated;

(f) never forget that people who are suspicious, hostile or bored are extremely unlikely to absorb or even consider the information one is anxious to set before them. One has to please before one can begin to instruct.

This amounts to saying that one cannot cater for 10 or 20 million people in the same way as one could and probably should for half a million. The question which then has to be put to Mr Hayes, or to anyone else who may be planning a museum is: 'What kind of audience do you have in mind? Is it of the half-million or the 20 million type?' The answer will almost certainly have to be that of the half-million variety, that is, that the 'ordinary' museum public is seen to be extraordinary if it is compared with the rest of the population.

This is not true of the children who are brought to museums in school parties. For these age groups museums have a genuine cross-section of taste, temperament and intelligence, such as they never attract again. Adults, in general, will go to Expo 67, but, left to their own devices, they will not go to museums, except in very unusual circumstances or to a very unusual museum, such as Anacostia, which has risked its existence on its ability to communicate with the whole of the community.

The true situation can be confused and concealed by a number of factors. Anyone entering the Louvre, the British Museum or the Prado between the beginning of May and the middle of September might well be excused for thinking that the millennium had arrived and that museum-going was at last a popular activity. A more careful investigation, carried out with both the eyes and the ears, would reveal that a high proportion of the visitors are foreign tourists, for whom the museum is just one item on a prescribed list of places to be seen; that the number of women is, by comparison with the museum norm, exceptional – they are visiting the museum only because they are on holiday with their family or with a package tour; and that a considerable number of these holiday-making visitors get little further than the postcard and souvenir counters, But, statistically, they are all visitors to the museum, which can congratulate itself that it is doing a good job. In such circumstances as these the word 'communication' means very little. The British Museum, like the Tower of London, Notre Dame and the Eiffel Tower, communicates merely by existing. So far as the bulk of visitors are concerned, no more is required.

But extremely few museums, fortunately, are in the Pyramids and pigeons in St Mark's Square class. All the others have to float or sink by their merits, one of which is the capacity to identify the kind of person who is likely to come to the particular museum and to do everything one can to communicate with him by using all the resources at one's command.

THE CURATOR AND THE DESIGNER

Mr Robin Wade, who is Britain's leading museum-design consultant and a man with a world reputation in this field, has strong views about what the relationship between the curator and the designer ought to be. He resents any suggestion that the designer is purely a visual man, that 'the curator is the intellectual and organises the job and the designer makes it look pretty', and

refuses to be cast in this role, 'as it denies involvement in the really creative and enjoyable aspect of the complete idea, story, concept or whatever you like to call it, of the exhibition'.

The designer also, in Mr Wade's opinion, carries out the function of a carrier of ideas into the museum from the outside. He is, if not exactly the voice of the people, at least *a* voice of the people. 'As a layman, in museum terms, he can sometimes see the complete picture from the point of view of the general public more clearly than can the scholarly specialist.'

Two of Mr Wade's most successful projects have been for the new Greek and Roman rooms at the British Museum, where the problem was to select from an overabundance of material and somehow display it effectively in a frustratingly limited space; and for the Fishbourne Roman Palace Museum, where a precisely opposite situation presented itself – there was plenty of space and too little first-class material.

I have come to believe [says Mr Wade] that in the latter type of situation, where the objects to be displayed do not necessarily speak for themselves, an editor (someone with journalistic experience) is an essential member of the planning team. He has the talent and training to present the story to the public in terms that they will understand. The success of Fishbourne Museum is an almost perfect illustration of effective journalism. While journalism may not always be the saving component of every museum, this example does suggest the need for an open-minded and flexible approach to museum design.

Mr Wade makes a very important point here. It amounts to saying that museums are too serious a matter to be left to museologists, and that it may be necessary, when planning a new museum or a new exhibition, to enlist the help of experts in quite different fields, whose main recommendation is that they have a great deal of experience in communicating with people in other contexts. In the case of Fishbourne, it is interesting to observe that Mr Wade

Fishbourne Roman Palace Museum, near Chichester. Construction of wooden building at this site-museum, with 'newspaper-type' displays.

speaks of 'presenting the story', an approach which what one might describe as the school of Marshall McLuhan has long since abandoned as irrelevant and absurd. The fact remains, however, that, whatever Dr McLuhan may say, the story-line is by no means obsolete and it is still both useful and necessary for some purposes. One gets nowhere by pinning one's faith entirely to either the story or the impressionistic method of presentation. Both are valuable and both need using with common sense and discrimination, a point of view which is not likely to commend itself to leaders of crusades.

The display at Fishbourne has had considerable influence throughout the world. It was brought into being by the combined efforts and expertise of a journalist, a professor of archaeology and a designer. It was from the start a journalistic project and, we emphasise this, received a subsidy of £20,000 from Times Newspapers Ltd. There was an accumulation of bits of evidence which required some form of didactic presentation if it was to have any meaning at all for the general public. The logic of the displays indicates the main historical sequence of events at Fishbourne, but, as well as helping to describe the site, fragments of little superficial interest have been brought to life by being related not only to the history

of the settlement but to everyday life in Roman and modern times. An important feature is the use of a newspaper-style arrangement of captions, explanatory text and photographs, a method of presentation which, *pace* Dr McLuhan, most people find as normal and acceptable as the techniques used by television.

'We have been beaten at our own game', said a professional museologist about Fishbourne, and went on to say with remarkable generosity that it was a success in which his own profession could claim no part.

At the British Museum the aim was to present a mixed and comprehensive exhibition of Greek and Roman art in chronological order. The previous system had been chaotic and confusing. New exhibits had been incorporated into the Museum's collection where space permitted and more or less as they were acquired. Sculptures and vases were in different parts of the building and anyone wishing to put the complete picture together for himself needed to have great determination and organising ability.

The designers were faced, as a first step, with the problem of taming the overpowering architecture of the nineteenth-century museum. They did this by concentrating on that part of the area which was at spectator-level and by using screens to make the remainder less obvious. One of the main objectives was to transform the museum into a less drab and more enjoyable place to be in, both for the ordinary visitor and the

scholar, and to enhance the objects themselves by reproducing something of the qualities of their original, usually Mediterranean, settings. These qualities were defined as 'serenity, logic, simplicity and the suggestion of bleaching light', and if they could be recaptured in the Museum most of the communication problems would have been solved.

The quality of the light is perhaps the most striking feature of the design. It has been achieved not only by lighting from above, but by reflected light from the new honey-coloured floor. The effect was greatly helped by the Museum's new mud-pack technique for cleaning marble, which brought back the original clear tones of the sculpture. To increase the feeling of Mediterranean light, the repainting of the walls and ceiling was mainly white, with the occasional use of sky blue or earth brown.

'The redesign of these galleries', the designers told their employers and the world, 'is a statement in favour of popularisation.' The Museum's then Director commented on this by saying that although scholarship and popularisation were at opposite ends of the spectrum, the task of his Museum was to 'share the documentation of human achievement with as many people as possible and at all levels of scholarship'. The phrase 'documentation of human achievement' is a good one. This is what museums are about and the basis on which their special kind of achievement rests.

It is interesting to compare Fishbourne and the Greek and Roman galleries, which were deliberate and clearly defined essays in popularisation, and for which outside consultants were employed, with the British Museum's new Ethnography Department, for which all the work was carried out by the Museum's own Exhibition Office. The idea behind the new museum, which had to be accommodated in a large and very unpromising Victorian Government office building, with a monumental staircase and a multitude of small rooms with high ceilings, was to present ethnographic material relating to primitive cultures on a semi-permanent basis, so that selections from the Museum's huge collections could be shown to the public 'in digestible quantities and to the best possible advantage'.

Opinions on the result vary, as they will of course with any new museum, but it is difficult to feel that the achievement is as remarkable as at Fishbourne or in the Greek and Roman galleries at the British Museum itself. Whether as a consequence of this or not, the Museum of Mankind lies much further to the scholarly end of the spectrum than the other two do. The approach is strongly didactic. There are long explanatory texts on the wall of each room and, in some instances, the ratio of text to objects verges on the absurd. The essential museum strength, visual impact, is lost. The cases and other exhibits are close together and the result is an unpleasant, claustrophobic feeling.

It is a dead museum. There are no sounds, slide-tape presentations, music, dioramas or dramatic lighting. Even when, as in the Yoruba room, the exhibits are arranged around a hut-courtyard, there are no human figures to bring it all to life.

The publications are excellent as far as they go. The postcard section in particular is good and the quality high. But the booklets, all costing over £1, contain very little to stir the imagination of comparatively ignorant people, or to give them their bearings in what may well be completely unknown territory. Entrance is free and the Museum is

British Museum, London. The Archaic Room, part of the redesigned Greek and Roman Galleries, within an early nineteenth-century building.

close to the much-frequented areas of Piccadilly and Regent Street, but the attendant in one of the galleries, the Yoruba room, remarked sadly to the present author, 'Hardly anybody comes here', and at that particular moment, 3 o'clock on a Saturday afternoon, this was indeed very obvious.

Yet the material is wonderfully good. How, then, is one to explain this apparent failure to attract large numbers of visitors? The answer can only be that the administrators and curators are more interested in scholars than in the general public and that they have not set out to produce a museum which is visually exciting or which communicates easily with the kind of people who grasp easily what Fishbourne has to offer. There are many things which the outsider cannot know about such a situation. Robin Wade has revealed that, when planning the Greek and Roman galleries, he fought and won a great battle with the Museum, and therefore indirectly with the Treasury, over the tiles he insisted on for the floor. They were expensive and, as is always the case in negotiations with bureaucracy, he was told to find something cheaper. As a powerful, independent figure in the design world, he was fortunately in a position to override the opposition and to get exactly what he wanted, but a staff designer would almost certainly not have had the same weapons to fight with. To what extent the Museum of Mankind as the public now sees it represents the original intentions and wishes of either the designer or the curators is difficult to decide. One can only comment on the results as they are, but the general point is worth more attention than it normally gets. When one is dissatisfied with a museum exhibit, one should always ask oneself – and the museum authorities, if they are available and willing to talk frankly – 'Is it like this because the people responsible knew no better, or because they were kept too short of money to do the job as they knew it should be done?'

MUSEUMS WHERE FAILURE IS DIFFICULT

The examples of the British Museum, Fishbourne and the Museum of Mankind happen to be English, but this is of no particular significance. They could equally appropriately have been taken from Czechoslovakia, Sweden or Turkey, and one hopes everyone who reads this section will feel inclined to apply the same kind of critical approach to the museums of his own country. The multiplication is equally valid, no matter the language in which it is recited. Some museums are fortunate enough to have a built-in appeal. They communicate because of qualities that have nothing at all to do with museological skill, because they are places with interesting associations; the Mu-Museum of Mankind has no interesting associations, it is entirely what its staff have made it. The Tel Aviv Museum, however, starts with enviable advantages, even before the visitor has seen a single one of its exhibits. It was established in 1931 by Meir Dizengoff, the founder and first Mayor of Tel Aviv, who used his own home as the nucleus of the new museum. In the explosive and fervently nationalistic atmosphere of the 1930s and 1940s, it quickly became the cultural centre of the young town. As well as providing a place where the permanent collections and temporary exhibitions could be displayed, lectures and concerts were frequently held there. And within its walls, which were so closely linked to the spiritual and practical renaissance of Jewish life in its ancient homeland, the State of Israel was proclaimed in 1948. The Tel Aviv Museum, which has since expanded considerably beyond the limits of Meir Dizengoff's house, is bound into the fabric of Israel and one cannot visit it, even as a non-Jew, in the same neutral and objective frame of mind as one would say, the National Museum in Stockholm.

A similar comment can be made of many of the monuments, now museums, of national resurgence and notabilities throughout the world. In many of the countries of Africa and Asia, houses have been preserved as mementoes of the early years of the republic and as memorials to the men who were responsible for the creation of the new state. Many of these buildings are very simple and with no pretensions to architectural distinction, but, in one case after another, one notices the devotion and expertise which have been applied to preserving the old building and to converting it into the kind of house-museum it now is.

The Museum of the Culinary Art, at Villeneuve-Loubet, near Nice and Cannes, falls into the same category, although it engenders a different kind of national pride. It is in the family home of the most famous master-cook of all time, Auguste Escoffier, and it is a memorial both to the life and achievements of Escoffier and to French cuisine at its most notable and distinguished. It includes something which would be possible only in France, a Panthéon Culinaire, a Culinary Hall of Fame, with mementoes of great chefs and gastronomes of every nationality, 'to whom', the Museum modestly announces, 'France owes its supremacy in the art of cookery'. But, and the point is worth emphasising, the arrangement of the Museum is distinctly old-fashioned and owes nothing to the techniques, materials and theories which have characterised museological development during the past quarter of a century. Its rejection of current fashion is, in fact, one of its great strengths. It is peacefully and refreshingly Edwardian and no one who visits it would wish it otherwise.

A high proportion of American and Australian museums have established emotional links of another kind with their visitors, and with the communities within which they are situated. Local people have provided the money to build and run the museum and have gathered the collections together and, in some instances, helped to arrange them. The museum consequently has the flavour of a special kind of community-temple, to which people bring their gifts and oblations. Under such conditions, communication between the museum's collections and the adults and children who come to look at them is of a warm and instinctive kind. The objects which are preserved and shown are expressions of the culture of previous generations of families still living in the district and the museum has a certain quality of ancestor-worship about it.

The Bright and District Historical Society Museum, in Victoria, Australia, is accommodated in a superannuated railway station. Its leaflet says:

We welcome you to our Museum, and trust that this display relating to our district's history will be of interest. Our members have spent considerable hours preparing this exhibition, finding enjoyment in working amongst so many items of an era that has passed. The Society would appreciate any information relating to our district, and of any items which could provide added interest to our Museum.

The important thing to notice is the reference to 'our Museum'. The French visitors to the Louvre do not refer to 'our Museum', even though it is maintained and run very largely on the money they have contributed as taxpayers. Since they do not identify themselves with it, they judge it by a different set of criteria, which amount to deciding whether 'they' are doing a good job of presenting the collections to 'us'.

Between the Bright and District Historical Society Museum at one extreme, and the Louvre at the other, there is the complete range of degrees of identification between the museum and its visitors. Towards what might be called the Bright end of the spectrum there is, for instance, the Western Development Museum at Saskatoon, 'dedicated to the memory of the men who pioneered the Great Plains of Western Canada. Its collections of machines, implements, tools, household furnishings and utensils are designed to keep ever fresh the Saskatchewan culture of the homestead days.'

The scale of the Western Development Museum makes it necessary for it to have professional management, but the help and involvement of people who live in the area are sought and welcomed all the time. In addition to the static exhibits there are annual displays and working demonstrations, in which the Museum's equipment comes to life, with local people dressed in period costumes to give a human dimension to the machinery, the wagons and the tools. In a museum like this it is difficult to say where presentation ends and public relations begins, since each is so tightly interwoven with the other.

An equally lively kind of museum, but one intended for tourists rather than for local inhabitants, is exemplified by Barkerville, British Columbia, where the theme is 'The Gold Rush Town Lives Again'. Here, as the publicity tells anyone who is willing to listen,

restoration is bringing back the original face of Barkerville. You can look into the bar-room of Kelly's Saloon, the cluttered general store, the barber shop of Wellington Moses, and many other authentic exhibits. See Billy Barker's mine shaft and the grave of Cariboo Cameron. Sit on the time-worn pews of St. Saviour's Church. Slake your thirst with root beer at the Barkerville Hotel, or enjoy a meal at the Wake-up-Jake Cafe.

Come for fun. You can take your family on a stage-coach ride, pan for gold and visit the Theatre Royal.

Bright and District Historical Society Museum, Victoria, Australia. Myrtleford railway station, now the Museum.

(below) *Platform looking west. The exhibits include a mangle, old school-desk and station nameboard. Their intrinsic value may be, from a saleroom point of view, negligible but, as objects for cultivating the historical imagination, they are priceless.*

City Museum, Bristol, England. Brass-rubbing centre in former St Nicholas Church.

THE 'EFFORTLESS PLEASURE' CONTROVERSY

By Louvre and British Museum standards, the scholarship behind the restoration of Barkerville is not, perhaps, entirely adequate. Corners have been cut here and there and certain aspects of this town-museum are a trifle over-dramatised. One assuredly cannot imagine potential visitors to either the Greek and Roman galleries or the Museum of Mankind being invited to 'Come for fun' and yet one may usefully wonder why. What is the block in the mind at these two museums, or at the Metropolitan or the Deutsches Museum or the Rijksmuseum, which rules out the possibility of 'fun'? 'Fun', after all, is only a short way of saying 'effortless pleasure'. Must all museum-going worthy of the name involve effort and serious application? Is it wrong for museums to provide for relaxation as well as for study?

This question seems to have been usually answered in the wrong terms. It is now more or less accepted that museum visitors get tired and may need refreshment, and to cater for these human weaknesses many, but by no means all, museums provide a few seats and a café or restaurant. But the implication of this is nearly always that the purpose of relaxation of this kind is to allow visitors to recover from one bout of serious effort and to prepare them for

another. There is rarely any suggestion that the museum-going itself might be relaxing or, in Barkerville language, fun.

This, of course, is where Expo 67, the Salon de l'Automobile and the Ideal Homes Exhibition differ from the great majority of museums, and, not incidentally, why they attract so many and such a cross-section of visitors. They are publicised as events, not as potential habits, and people go to see them because they know that large numbers of other people are doing the same and they are anxious not to be left out. They want to be in a position to discuss the exhibition with their friends. Such events are the equivalent of medieval fairs, joustings, and executions.

THE VALUE OF THE BANQUET EXHIBITION

It is perfectly possible for a museum to have one great success of this kind perhaps every two or three years, but hardly more frequently. The great exhibitions of Chinese art and of the Tutankhamun treasures from the National Museum in Cairo are certain to draw large crowds each time they come to rest in one of the world's capitals, but an endless succession of such exhibitions is impracticable.

There is some disagreement among

museum directors as to how much lasting benefit such prestige-exhibitions confer on the museums in which they are held. One side of the scales one has to place the publicity value of attracting so many people through the doors of the museum and the hope that some at least of them will be persuaded to come to the museum on more normal occasions, but on the other side is the sad possibility that the bread-and-butter diet which the museum offers its visitors week in, week out, may compare unfavourably with the banquet-fare provided by the grand special exhibition.

One could put this in another way, by saying that major events such as the Tutankhamun exhibition jolt both the museum and the public out of their usual rut. They set a new, money-is-no-object standard which is normally impossible to achieve and they act as a stimulus in several directions. They are, in fact, a form of shock treatment which brings a quietly-resting body to life. But not every member of the staff of the host-museum finds it agreeable to have his peace disturbed in this way.

AIMING AT CONTROVERSY AND 'SOCIAL RELEVANCE'

In 1968 a travelling exhibition which the local press described as 'art with a shock effect' was given its *première* at Norrköping, in Sweden. It had been commissioned by Riksutställningar,[3] the national organisation for travelling exhibitions, and the group of specialists responsible for it attempted to show by every artistic means available to them the problems faced by the developing countries. The name of the exhibition, Sköna Stund – 'Beautiful Moments' – echoes the name of a pleasure-garden in Stockholm, Gröna Lund, and the designers portrayed Sweden in the form of just such a pleasure-garden, with, to quote their manifesto which accompanied the exhibition,

the bitter-sweet colours, the tinsel, the enticements and allurements, the biting contrasts. We will make a lot of kiosks and stands, rooms full of pictures, events, movement, and things exciting people to participation without anything to inhibit them, and then perhaps they will suddenly realise that all this actually exists in the world around them and not just here inside the exhibition.

Full use was made of short texts and tape-recordings of sounds and commentaries. The catalogue was in the form of a newspaper, and the artists emphasised, although what they had created might have the appearance of an art exhibition, its purpose was social and political, not aesthetic. It was intended to break the crust over visitors' minds and feelings and, by deliberately producing controversy, to force an awareness of the importance of the subject.

It was unquestionably successful in that 10,000 people, representing 15 per cent of the total population of Norrköping, came to see it, but the members of the museum staff eventually came to feel that they were not adequately equipped to deal with the controversy which developed. One woman wrote to the local newspaper to protest. 'I think it is horrifying', she said, 'that museums should be dragged into politics like this. A museum is not the right place. The exhibition would have been admirably suited to the Community Centre. In a museum, on the other hand, one expects to find art.' The correspondent of the conservative Stockholm newspaper, *Svenska Dagbladet*, objected to a public museum being used for what he described as political propaganda. 'It is vital', he told the nation, 'for the museums to adhere to their traditional objective, that is, the setting of the situation of the moment in its proper perspective.'

Before the decision was taken to

bring the exhibition's tour to an end, it had been seen in three museums. The opposition to it had become increasingly strong and in each place where it was shown a panel discussion had been arranged to allow the various bodies criticised and the different shades of opinion to state their case. One of Sweden's leading museum personalities, Lennart Holm, delivered an address to the Scandinavian Museums Association at the time when the heat and fury were at their height. He claimed that museums and exhibitions operate, and must operate, under the same conditions as any other kind of mass media, and that they should quite properly play a part in the creation of

public opinion. He foresaw that the situation which had arisen over 'Beautiful Moments' was bound to recur. Museums of natural history, for instance, were very likely to come into conflict with the establishment and with local and central government over the problem of the conservation of the environment. This, he felt, was a very desirable state of affairs, and one at which museums should be deliberately aiming. It was an inevitable and welcome part of the process of building up a public to which the activities of a museum meant something. To reject controversy was to make it certain that the younger and more active members of a community would turn their backs

Riksutställningar (Swedish Travelling Exhibitions), Stockholm, Sweden. Part of 'Beautiful Moments' exhibition, an attempt to convey information about the problems of developing countries. A group of artists visualised the exhibition as a pleasure-ground, and deliberately aimed at arousing controversy.

(below) '*Cooking in the Ancient World*'. *A 'cabinet' exhibition, produced in twenty-five copies, about the eating habits and domestic utensils of the ancient world. The exhibition includes nine ceramic copies of artifacts, sixteen screens, herbs, and a study-guide. The cabinet, which also serves as a crate, measures $86 \times 75 \times 42$ cm.*

on museums and go elsewhere for stimulus and encouragement.

The furore over 'Beautiful Moments' will probably be seen by historians of museums and museology as one of the key events of the present century. It was not, of course, the first time that an exhibition in a museum or art gallery had given rise to controversy. For many years and in many countries, civic authorities have been in the habit of turning their attention to statues and paintings of nude figures in the local art gallery and of demanding their removal. A ludicrous and typical instance of this occurred in Buffalo, New York, in 1911, when the city's Board of Trustees unanimously passed a resolution demanding that the nude statues in the Albright Fine Arts Academy should be draped. The arguments in the press were remarkably similar to those produced by 'Beautiful Moments'. 'We are willing to wager', declared the *Buffalo Times* in a leading article, 'that sculpture has a future in Buffalo, now that our city fathers are beginning to wake up to its demoralizing possibilities.'

Few people nowadays are disturbed by nudes. That battle at least has been fought and won, and museum directors, like theatre managers, can show paintings and statues of people without their clothes on without fearing for their jobs and pensions. Political and social controversy is quite another matter, however, and this is likely to cause trouble anywhere, since in all countries the control of museum finances is for the most part in the hands of extremely conservative people, who are certain to tread very hard on anything which 'causes trouble'.

It is instructive to examine the statements put out by the more prosperous American museums about their aims and financial basis. The Timken Art Gallery in San Diego, California, for example, assumes that its task is to 'display the paintings under the best possible conditions as well as to preserve them for posterity', and points out to visitors from outside the area that: 'We call our institution the Timken Art Gallery, because of the contributions of that family to art in this community.' The Long Beach Museum of Art, which specialises in twentieth-century American art, is on record as saying:

Patron support is the life's blood of a museum and singularly determines the strength of its programme, if not the very vitality of the institution.

Museum membership is the main avenue of such support and in this Museum is conducted by the Museum Association and the Friends.

'Patron support' is a euphemism for 'providing money', and the fact that nearly all American museums rely for their existence on the funds provided by well-to-do and, in some cases, rich people makes them extremely respectable and conservative institutions. It is almost impossible to imagine an American equivalent of 'Beautiful Moments' finding museums willing to give it house-room. To be involved in any way in political controversy, or to give the slightest hint of non-establishment views, would be a major disaster for most American museums. This, in the opinion of a number of critics, is why museums have little or no impact on the major part of the community. In today's world to be socially and politically neutral is virtually to guarantee decline and death.

NEUTRALITY AND ITS POSSIBLE CONSEQUENCES

The policy of neutrality, at its most impressive, is illustrated by the Solomon R. Guggenheim Museum in New York City. Its remarkable spiral building (1959) by Frank Lloyd Wright, designed to accommodate the performing arts as well as pictures, has been described with some justice as 'the most beautiful building in New York'; and the Foundation's aim as 'to foster an appreciation of art by acquainting museum visitors with significant painting and sculpture of our time'. One doubts, however, if these works of art, or at least the way in which they are presented, would match up to the same definition of 'significant' as the one followed by the artists responsible for 'Beautiful Moments'. The Guggenheim does not set out to be a 'socially relevant' museum. Its emotional level is kept low and anybody who comes out feeling politically excited has only himself to blame.

The Guggenheim Museum is one of the sights of New York, and a considerable number of people visit it each year, partly, one suspects, for the sake of being able to say that they have visited it. It does not seek to interest everybody and it does not appear to consider itself as being in any way within the field of the mass media. Its aim is entirely honest, although there are those who

might nowadays consider this to be misguided or obsolete, 'to foster an appreciation of art'. But, and this is of great importance, it cannot achieve this with people who are fundamentally hostile to everything for which the Museum stands. To derive benefit from the Guggenheim, one must share its basic premises. One cannot communicate with disbelievers, with those who are not of the Faith.

At the same time, however, any curator will, if he is wise, come to terms with the fact that there is no way of guaranteeing that visitors will respond to exhibits in the way in which the museum itself had hoped and intended. Communication is not yet an exact science and, if perfect communication means total ability to transfer information and associated emotions to another person, one hopes it never will be. All that one could and should reckon to achieve, with good fortune, is to ensure that one's own knowledge and intentions are received with a reasonable degree of sympathy and understanding, and with a minimum amount of distortion. But communication is not a one-way process. A museum exhibit is a stone thrown into a pond, and any curator worth his salt is exceedingly interested in the ripples he has been responsible for producing. Communication back from the people who have stood around the exhibit and thought about it is as important and as entitled to the term 'communication' as what goes out from the exhibit to the museum's customers. The ripples, one might say, are as necessary as the stone.

Some museums do not appear fully to understand the implications of their own publicity. Suppose, for example, that one considers what the National Museum of Rhodesia has to say about its dioramas, which are much used at the Museum's Bulawayo, Umtali and Salisbury centres to convey information about natural history, ethnology and archaeology. These, says the National Museum, 'endeavour to answer the questions of the ordinary person – the housewife, the farmer, the industrialist, the teacher and the child. Each can find in one of Rhodesia's museums something which will give a greater understanding of his own complex environment and his place within it.' The exhibits in the National Museum would certainly be reckoned by the Director and his staff to be both non-political and non-controversial, but they have been selected and

arranged on the basis of certain prejudices. Without these, or given another
set of prejudices, the same material
would be presented in quite a different
way and have quite a different impact.
It is difficult to believe that one of the
Museum's dioramas or other exhibits
will produce the same thoughts and
emotions in a black Rhodesian as in a
white one. A group of black people, preparing and eating their food around a
fire in the open air, with a replica of part
of the natural landscape around them,
may, as a diorama, represent in theory
nothing more than an accurately and
objectively observed scene. The white
visitor to the museum may see it in this
way. The black visitor, on the other
hand, may see such exhibits as racialist
and insulting. To show his recent
ancestors as half-naked and with a
primitive way of life may not be pleasing to him at all. The fact that other
vanished cultural patterns are illustrated by dioramas of white people in
nineteenth-century surroundings will
not necessarily be a comfort to him
since, however uncultivated the life of
the South African whites may have
been a century ago, it was the life of the
master race. To present the history of
white settlement in South Africa in a
politically and socially neutral way is,
under present conditions, almost impossible, however good the intentions
may be.

There is a fairly widely held view that
natural history, archaeology, music,
fine art, the physical sciences and technology are 'safe' subjects for a museum
to handle and that history, literature
and the social sciences are dangerous.
As a corollary of this, the first group of
'subjects' can be presented to the public
in an objective, scientific way, since one
is attempting to communicate facts, but
the second involves great problems.
Objects connected with an historical
event or personage can easily generate
wrong thoughts on the part of the visitor, thoughts which even the most
skilful of impresarios is powerless to
control. The distinction is, in fact, nonsensical. One cannot separate facts and
attitudes in this way, convenient as it
might be to do so. Every good scientist

*National Technical Museum, Prague.
Section devoted to metallurgy and iron-
working. Simply but effectively displayed, this fine collection documents the
eighteenth and nineteenth-century
achievements of the Czech ironfounders in
a way that does justice to their skill.*

has an attitude towards science, not
always publishable, and many literary
and historical works are so safe or so
dull as to make the multiplication table
seem explosive.

The nature of the communication
attempted and achieved by museums of
science and technology is especially interesting in this connection. The view
of Dr Josef Kuba, the Director of the
National Technical Museum in Prague,
that technical museums are, as he puts
it, 'centres for the infection of science'
is now fairly well known. This basic
theory has, however, been subject to a
certain refining process in recent years,
and Dr Kuba now sees the importance
of such a museum in slightly different
terms. The main purpose of a museum
devoted to technology is, in his opinion,
to show the visitor:

(a) how important technology is,
     and how impossible it would be
     to exist or make progress without
     it;
(b) how ignorant he himself is.

The combination of (a) and (b) should,
if the museum has been successful, send
the visitor away feeling small, stupid
and determined to learn some science
with all possible speed. The museum
should provide him, on his departure,
with some elementary booklets to encourage this process of self-improvement. The museum can do this in complete good faith, believing that without
scientific knowledge nobody can be his
proper size. The person without science
is destined – quite rightly, in Dr
Kuba's view – to feel permanently in-

ferior and unworthy of a place in the
modern world. This might be described
as Dr Kuba's attitude towards science,
his motivation, and it will be noticed
that it contains a number of value-
judgements, which, by definition, cannot be scientific. In order to create and
run a good technical museum, one must
therefore approach the matter in a way
which is to some extent emotional and
there is no need to feel guilty about that.

A combined technical and scientific
museum, as Dr Kuba sees it, should
cover physics, astronomy, mathe-
matics, chemistry, biology, agriculture,
industry, advanced technology, simple
and complex power principles and systems, mineralogy, geology, prospect-
ing, meteorology and the full range of
engineering applications. It can, he
says, 'awaken vocations, complete cur-
ricular education, inform adults about
modern progress, bridge the gap
between traditional and modern technology'. It will be

an information centre for all technical, technological and scientific problems, which will infect everybody
with curiosity about modern techniques. In the future, this type of
museum must be, not merely a single
institution in a single building, but
the headquarters of a network of
local, regional and rural science
centres, science clubs, science fairs
and mobile units.

Since, Dr Kuba goes on, 'a museum of
science and technology is attractive to
a very large public', and since, 'being
essentially three-dimensional and self-

explanatory, it is accessible to all, including technical illiterates, it must be considered to be a powerful communication medium and, as such, should be included in any policy of mass-communication at the national level'. To claim that a science museum is in itself a 'communication medium' shows remarkable confidence. Others might feel that a museum requires communication techniques in order to communicate what it contains and has to offer, but there is undoubtedly much to commend Dr Kuba's point of view.

His plans for the extension of his own at present very inadequately housed museum stem from the general philosophy outlined above. They envisage an overall emphasis on science, rather than on technology, so that the building would have two functional divisions:

1. *Technology.* This would be, in effect, the Humility Centre, to make the visitor feel small, weak and determined to improve.
2. *Science.* Here the penitent – the religious terminology arises very naturally, since there is something fundamentally theological about Dr Kuba's approach – would strive to liquidate his ignorance.

Possibly because of the traditions in that part of Europe, Dr Kuba comes down firmly on the side of what he calls 'the classical museum', that is, the museum arranged on straightforward, didactic principles, with good design, no gimmicks and a minimum of 'showmanship', which, like most professionals in the socialist countries, he regards as part of a personality cult, suitable, perhaps, for an actor, but not for a museum director. The showman-director may, he feels, achieve temporary successes and bring the museum to the notice of the public, but he is a dangerous figure, who prevents the museum from achieving the continuity and stability which it needs to have in the long run. A much-travelled man, with wide knowledge of museums in other countries, Dr Kuba has some illuminating comments to make about the face which some of the best-known museums present to the world. His attitude to the Swiss Transport Museum, for instance, could be summed up as follows:

(a) It is a remarkable museum, created and run by a genius.
(b) When this genius dies or retires, the museum will collapse.

(c) The showmanship is too obvious, especially in the Air and Space sections.
(d) The Museum breaks the cardinal rule which should be observed by all museums of technology; it takes quite insufficient pains to make the visitor feel small and humble.

On the other hand, Dr Kuba does not appear to have a high opinion of some museums of science and technology, partly because their ultra-conservatism is a barrier to communication with modern people, and partly because they cause unnecessary confusion by putting all their goods into the shopwindow at once. They are, in short, yesterday attempting to talk to today.

KEEPING THE MUSEUM'S PHILOSOPHY UP TO DATE AND HONEST

The Deutsches Museum in Munich is one of the three great museums of science and technology in the world, and it has been suffering for some time from philosophy problems, which have in turn produced a certain weakening of the massive confidence which has carried the Museum through three-quarters of a century and two World Wars. There is a conflict within the Museum between two groups of people who, for reasons of convenience, may be labelled the Traditionalists and the Progressives. The Progressives find themselves faced with the difficult task of persuading their Traditionalist colleagues that the Deutsches Museum presents its material and organises its educational programme on far too narrow a basis. Up to now, the approach has been concerned almost entirely with objects, with engineers, scientists and industrialists, and with engineering achievements, and hardly at all with the ordinary people who made these achievements possible. There is, for example, a celebrated section of the Museum which deals with tunnelling. It has nothing to say about such human aspects of tunnelling as the wages of the men who built the tunnels or about the casualties they suffered. The workmen, one might say, were incidental to the techniques and materials, very subsidiary pieces of engineering equipment that were of little interest and hardly worth mentioning.

This means, in the opinion of the

Progressives, that the Museum is wilfully throwing away one of the chief ways in which it can communicate with people in their twenties and thirties. What is needed is to abandon the notion of an abstract concept, the History of Technology, and think instead of the part that new machines and new technologies played in the lives of the men and women who had to earn a living by them. The Traditionalists, according to the Progressives, are unwilling to grapple with this kind of philosophy, partly because it 'smells of Eastern Europe' – museum people in the East would smile at this – and partly because it is thought to be 'unscientific'.

As a result of these uncertainties and inner tensions, the Museum has been playing about for some time with what the Progressives call 'pseudo-modernity'. This consists of putting up portraits of the Great Engineers, making machinery move and having all the working models and visual aids that the budget can afford. This, say the Progressives, is merely an irrelevant nonsense. The real and urgent task is to infuse the Museum with a genuine humanity, however politically risky that might seem. Only if this were done would the collections become really relevant to today's world and the vast annual budget be socially and morally justified.

The point about 'pseudo-modernity' is an important one. A museum can be very up to date in the matter of its techniques and equipment, and yet not be a modern museum at all, because its philosophy is obsolete. The most fundamental difference between an old-fashioned and a modern museum lies in the limits within which it permits itself to operate. An 'art' museum which is concerned entirely with the aesthetic and technical aspects of painting is old-fashioned, no matter how modern its building, its lighting and air-conditioning may be. So too is a natural history museum which excludes living creatures or recorded sounds or ecology, and a museum of science and technology which fails to include people and human problems in its displays. There is an ecology of machines, just as much as there is an ecology of birds, plants and animals. Equally, a 'don't touch' museum is not a modern museum, no matter how wonderful its galleries and equipment.

Modernisation and the breaking down of subject-barriers between and within museums is proceeding, as might be expected, in a very piecemeal and haphazard fashion. One can illustrate this very well in the field of Natural History. Here there have been a number of interesting innovations and experiments within the past twenty-five years. Among these are the Museum at Constanza in Romania, with its successful blending of live and preserved exhibits and the Museum of Wildlife Sounds, which is attached to the British Institute of Recorded Sound in London, and which is now, with over 6000 different animal, bird and reptile noises on disc and tape, much the largest collection in the world. Some museums now have equipment which allows visitors to the museum to press a button and then to see a particular creature in a display to be lit up or a picture of it to be projected on a screen, at the same time as noises made by the creature and reproduced from tape. This technique can now be seen at a number of good natural history museums, including those at Oakland, California, and at South Kensington in London.

A few museums have set aside a special stock of stuffed animals, birds and reptiles which are available for visitors to touch, stroke and hold. This is now a well-established and popular practice at a number of museums, but it has been found by experience that touchable creatures lose their freshness fairly quickly. One cannot, for instance,

stroke an owl more than about 500 times without the bird showing some signs of wear!

BREAKING DOWN THE BARRIERS BETWEEN MUSEUMS

The main trend to be observed at the moment in museums connected with natural history is the breaking down of the idea that wild creatures should be observed respectfully or passively. This revolutionary process is being accomplished partly by the methods which have just been described and partly by the rapid disappearance of the difference between a natural history museum and a zoo. One can see an excellent example of this at the National Museum in Nairobi, where one has only to cross the road to pass from stuffed and pickled creatures inside the Museum to the extremely popular Snake Park, with its live snakes, tortoises, crocodiles and alligators inside.

But other barriers are still intact and one can only speculate as to the reasons. Botanical museums and botanical gardens continue to keep their collections very separate, although the links between plants and animals are obvious, and there is no logic in dividing one off from the other. Even more curious is the refusal to merge natural history and agriculture museums. Let us suppose that we are looking at two

fields on the outskirts of a town in England. The first field contains a number of cows and a bull (agricultural museum), a drinking trough (agricultural museum), and a specially sown grass and clover mixture (agricultural museum). A flock of sparrows (natural history museum) is resting in one corner of the field and a rabbit (natural history museum) has just vanished into the hedge (borderline, but probably natural history museum if wild and uncared for, agricultural museum if carefully cut and laid). Along the base of the hedge one can see a variety of wild flowers (natural history museum). Between the two fields is a drainage ditch (agricultural museum), containing frogs, weeds and fish (all natural history museum). In the second field, a man is ploughing with a tractor (agricultural museum). As he turns over the ground, a number of sea-gulls (natural history museum) are hovering above the furrows, waiting to pick up worms and other insects (natural history museum).

One can continue with this nonsense indefinitely. The only point of such an example is to demonstrate the ridiculously meaningless way in which the two types of museum split their territory. Such an arrangement does violence to the way in which the ordinary person, the non-specialist, sees the world around him. The division between natural history and agriculture is not the only one, of course. Another runs between agriculture and local history and a third between growing and rearing food and processing it for human consumption. To have, for instance, a museum of bread and baking in one place, as is brilliantly done at Haifa, and an agricultural museum in another makes little sense and serves nothing but administrative convenience. Only the complete picture is justifiable, in both museological and educational terms. The same, too, could be said of art museums. How much more interesting and alive these would become if, before they saw any pictures or statues, visitors were shown how the artist's materials were prepared at different periods, how the colours were ground, the canvas or wood panel prepared, the brushes and palettes made, the stone

Bristol City Museum, England. Children handling items from a school natural history loan collection.

quarried and selected. How many of the world's sculpture galleries show the tools the sculptor required or indicate how they were used? By removing the craftsman element from art, and turning art museums into temples for connoisseurs, museologists have not only attempted to turn the artist himself into a rarefied, intellectualised creature which he never was and never could be, but have wilfully rejected the one element in an art museum which could be guaranteed to attract and interest a wide range of visitors. The technology of art is fascinating, explicable and, above all, democratic. It may be that art museums will only begin to communicate with more than a small section of the population in any country when they find the courage to redefine themselves as technical museums, or possibly as the painting and sculpture departments of a technical museum. As matters stand at the moment, most visitors to art galleries have no idea at all of the technology of art. They are not encouraged to think of works of art from a technical point of view. Chinese porcelain has to be viewed and admired by people who are kept in ignorance of the methods used by the potters to produce these beautiful objects, Greek and Roman sculpture by people who know nothing about the qualities of the different types of stone or about the hardness and temper of the tools used to get it out of the quarry and shape it afterwards. How many visitors to the Louvre or the British Museum are aware, for example, of the extreme difficulty involved in cutting and polishing the red porphyry of which some of the finest Roman portrait busts and vases were made?

It is interesting to imagine London's National Gallery, or any other prestigious art museum, replanned so that the visitor has first to spend a few minutes in a technical orientation centre before he is let loose on the pictures. Such a centre would include, for example, an historical account of the methods used by painters to prepare the wood or canvas for painting.[4] There would be cross-sections of paintings, or coloured photographs, or models of cross-sections, to show the different layers of a painting and the effects of time, humidity and temperature on these layers. The visitor would also learn how a different kind of craftsman, the restorer, attempts to put damage to paintings right. There is no reason whatever why the restoration department of a museum, not only an art museum, should not be brought out of the background and into the public gaze, or why there should not be regular demonstrations, showing how artists worked with the old materials and techniques. One does not have to be a scholar to understand and enjoy these things, and an interest in an artist's techniques can very easily lead to an interest in his finished work.

The same advantage can be obtained by explaining to visitors the physical and economic conditions under which artists have worked at different periods – the kind of light they had to accept and use in their particular part of the world, the type of room that was available to them as a studio, the patrons, money and customers they had, the place they occupied in the community. Once one knows these things, one is beginning to tread on solid ground and to feel that art galleries are not the impossibly élitist places one had always believed them to be.

There is a growing feeling, especially among the younger museum professionals, that really effective communication cannot be achieved in any kind of museum until the old academic compartments and barriers are swept away, and until the collections of every specialist museum are seen to be only arbitrarily placed there, rather than in a completely different kind of museum. Why, for example, should Van Gogh's paintings of the peasants in the Borinage be considered to belong inevitably to an art museum and not to an agricultural or history museum? What is the appropriate kind of museum for jewellery, make-up and hairdressing? What kind of museum specialist can claim a monopoloy of human vanity? The way towards this deliberate and creative removal of the traditional distinctions between one category of museum and another is admirably pointed by the Senckenberg Museum at Frankfurt in the German Federal Republic. This old-established and distinguished natural history museum devotes constant attention to making its collections visually attractive and to arranging stimulating special exhibitions on matters of urgent social importance, such as population control and the pollution and degradation of the environment. It achieves this by blending art and scholarship in the most skilful and enthusiastic manner, using a combination of both to increase the impact and significance of the information that the museum is trying to communicate. The result is a natural history museum that would have seemed utterly strange fifty years ago, a science museum which aims at touching the visitor's emotions as well as his brain.

CHANGING CONCEPTS OF 'EDUCATION'

One of the best statements ever made on the subject of museum communication came thirteen years ago from the Director of the National Museum of Leiden, in the Netherlands, Dr Peter H. Pott. It formed part of an address delivered at the ICOM meeting in The Hague in July 1962,[5] and we can do no better than quote it here. Dr Pott was speaking particularly about museums of history and folklore, but his remarks are equally relevant to every kind of museum. The museum director, said Dr Pott, requires two qualities above all, 'pluralism of interest and flexibility of imagination'.

'What should distinguish him from his predecessor', Dr Pott went on,

is his consideration of the interests of his potential public rather than his own tastes and special hobbies. It need hardly be said that we as museum directors have particular subjects that interest us more than others, and about which we may think we know more than other people do. It is only human that we feel an urge to occupy ourselves with these subjects, when the collections of our museums give us the least chance, and to want to show and explain that which has stimulated or moved us to a wider public that is not reached by our scientific publications. But as directors of museums of history and folklore, we cannot permit ourselves this luxury. Before all we must ask ourselves what will interest our potential public and how we can present these objects in such a way that this public will feel at home in the museums. This means in the first place the maintaining of contacts with the multiform public, not only so as to know where its interest lies but to know how we can best fit in with those particular interests. Only then will we have a realistic basis from which to approach the potential visitor; he will then suddenly find in the museum elements familiar enough to enable him to follow them easily and at the same time be prepared to make some effort himself when he finds himself faced with something less familiar.

Our potential public is made up of individuals, each with his own interests, knowledge, and capacities, as well as his own approach to what is offered to him. Therefore a director must not aim at one particular cross-section of his potential public but must from the very beginning take into account their wider range of capacities and interests by making his presentation many-sided. He will thus provide presentations for the individual prompted by aesthetic feelings, others that invite the romanticist or escapist, and still others in which thematic explanations are given which nevertheless leave room for personal interpretation. In addition to this plurality of approach to his public, he must have great flexibility of imagination, in the sense that over and over again he must find new and varied aspects of life to bring to the fore, aspects that are of topical interest and that he can present comprehensively and distinctly by means of techniques proper to museums. By doing so he makes it possible for certain groups of visitors to use his presentation as a short, encyclopedic picture but one keyed to the intellectual capacity of his public. Above all he must reach this public as living individuals and not as an abstract audience which may take or leave what is offered to it.

Here is the point at which he must be most aware of the other sources of mass information that influence his public. Nothing is more irritating to the public than to be confronted with a presentation of a subject that seems childish when compared to what it has been given on the same subject by the illustrated press, radio and, especially, television. A childish presentation immediately produces a reaction of complete rejection; people feel that instead of receiving answers to reasonable questions asked by reasonable mature persons they have been treated like children given a sweet and sent off to play.

All this results in two main consequences: the maintenance of very close contact with other educational media by actively cooperating in their activities, and the presentation of specific subjects in ways that the other media cannot realize.

In practical terms, this means a shifting of the museum's activities in the direction of so-called 'extramural' work, using a flexible form of presentation which draws the visitor into a personal involvement in that with which he is confronted.

There is no more dead element in this type of museum than a dull succession of stiff and lifeless period rooms or of an accumulation of curiosities, rooms full of objects that may be related to one another but in a way that is not immediately apparent to the visitor. A varied presentation, on the contrary – one in which the visitor encounters now a habitat group which invites his participation in a situation, followed by a very distinct and comprehensive documentation on a factual situation by means of photographs, copies of a few important charters, and so on, with an accompanying text which in a few sharply formulated captions give the quintessence of what is exhibited, once again followed by the confrontation with a really first-class piece of art or craftsmanship in the intimacy of a small room which can do full justice to it – all immediately gives a much more lively character to such a museum. As a result of this kind of presentation a large part of the collections will be doomed to consignment to the storage rooms where they are accessible to specialists and experts and do not confound the average visitor.

Dr Pott is implying two things here: first, that we have a duty to plan and run museums in a way which meets the needs of the modern world; and, second, that those needs are in various significant ways different from what was required fifty or a hundred years ago. If this is correct, then the difference probably stems from a much wider and more elastic concept of what education is about. In the Victorian age, which was the first great period of flowering for museums, education was for the most part and for most people equated with the acquisition of factual information. Today, this view is considered totally inadequate, and the one factor which the great number of philosophies of education have in common is their insistence that education is about the growth and development of the complete person, and that the gathering and ordering of facts is only part of this total process. It is not an

accident that, until comparatively recently, the words 'education' and 'instruction' were used almost as synonyms by those who had the task of organising and administering the schooling of those who were to carry out the nation's work. It is not an accident that for most of its history the relevant ministry in France was called the Ministry of Public Instruction.

In his introductory address to the National Museums Symposium on 'The Role of National Museums in Education', held in Colombo in 1966, the Sri Lanka Director of Education, Mr E. H. de Alwis, expressed a widely-held view that 'one of the primary purposes of a museum is Education, although the organisation of museums to serve this purpose is of recent origin'. He went on to observe that this reflected a new attitude. 'At one time', he said, 'museum officials were content with what they considered their main duties; acquisition, conservation and research and perhaps some display particularly designed to satisfy the evanescent curiosity of a passive audience.'[6]

What Mr de Alwis had in mind was that education is a deliberate process, which only happens if it is planned and organised. To insist on this is to take a very narrow view of education, which is and must be a very unpredictable, haphazard affair, continuing throughout a person's life and stimulated by the most unlikely and unrelated events and objects. Basic education, the grammar of coming to terms with society and of acquiring the intellectual tools with which one can earn a living, is another matter and, in the developing countries, museums can certainly play an important part in this. But – and the point needs to be made with all possible emphasis – to be educative a museum does not need to be didactic. Many of the most informal and unprofessional museums are profoundly educative, in the sense that they arouse curiosity and provide a great deal for it to feed on. Museologists who insist on fully structured learning and teaching within a museum are misguided.

A debate which shows no signs of reaching a conclusion is centred around what one might call the pleasure element of museums. At bottom, it is an argument about the rights and wrongs of puritanism, and as to whether it is proper for public money to be spent on providing the opportunities for 'pure' enjoyment. There is no possible end to this, since one person can obtain extremes of spontaneous delight from something which is a grimly serious piece of learning to another. To claim that 'entertainment', 'amusement', 'pleasure', or whatever term one chooses to employ, is nothing more than the bait on the hook, the sugar on the pill, is either stupid or dishonest. There is absolutely no reason why a museum should not arrange a display, a demonstration or a concert which gives enjoyment for its own sake. One does not have to feel guilty about it, or to pretend that the provision of entertainment is merely a cunning way of tempting new customers across the museum threshold, rather in the manner of loss-leaders in a supermarket. Good things can exist in their own right and a museum should feel proud of making them available, without striving to give the impression that it is preparing its visitors for some unknown examination.

The ethic of museum work can be defined in the following way. One has a duty to make one's collections as interesting as possible to as many people as possible, but to attempt to endow objects with a bogus or irrelevant interest is immoral. The curator of a technical museum who presents a piece of machinery or a tool in order to emphasise its aesthetic qualities, as if it were a piece of sculpture, is guilty of an immoral act. He is behaving in precisely the same way as a motor manufacturer who drapes nearly-nude girls across his cars at the annual Motor Show, as a way of attracting people for whom the cars alone would have insufficient appeal. But to offer material to the public in an imaginative way, so that it jumps out of its background and says 'look at me', is what professional skill is all about. A splendidly-produced book is not *ipso facto* a bad book. A plain woman is by no means always more virtuous than a beautiful woman.

A wise museum communicates with its public in every possible way, by the atmosphere which it creates, by the sensible use of all the modern media, by forging links between itself and the immediate community, by understanding and using the language of its customers, by a broad programme of educational work and by its political and social attitude. A sensitive observer can tell immediately he enters a museum whether it is really interested in communication or not. The clues are everywhere.

There is, for example, absolutely no doubt that the Palace of Discovery in Paris, which has been severely criticised above from the point of view of its building, is extremely interested in communication, and it is equally clear, from the reactions of its visitors, that it succeeds, despite the dowdiness of its surroundings and the old-fashioned character of many of the displays. This is an outspokenly didactic museum, run by people who are convinced of the importance of teaching the principles and applications of science. The visitors, overwhelmingly, are young and, to stimulate their interest, a high proportion of the exhibits can be made to work, either by pushing a button or, in the case of more complicated and potentially dangerous apparatus, in the form of demonstrations at fixed times throughout the day. This is a museum which is 40 per cent laboratory, 50 per cent exhibition and 10 per cent university lecture room.

Like other science museums in the Western world, the Palace of Discovery encouraged industrial concerns to sponsor exhibitions dealing with their own particular speciality, partly in order to take some of the pressure off the museum's budget and partly to show boys and girls the career opportunities which exist in the fields of science and technology. The museum is anxious to show that science is real, with an important part to play in the modern world, and it very naturally regards industry as an ally, not an enemy.

In 1976, for example, the Palace of Discovery mounted an exhibition called Jeunesse de Gaz, which showed how the technology of producing and distributing gas has developed, especially during the 1945–75 period, and the opportunities which exist for technically-minded boys and girls within what is obviously a rapidly-expanding industry. Visitors were provided with leaflets, prepared by the national gas corporation, Gaz de France, to tell them exactly what kind of recruits were required, what training facilities existed, and where to make applications.

The Palace of Discovery rates communication of all kinds very highly. It is essentially and by deliberate intention a communications centre. With more money and a more suitable building, it could achieve this considerably better than is possible at the moment.

PARTICIPATION

Participation is a much-favoured word nowadays, but its use is as likely to lead to confusion as to understanding. In the museum context it means, when it has any precise meaning at all, the active role which the suitably encouraged and steered layman can take in the running of certain aspects of the museum and in taking advantage of the facilities it offers. 'Participation' is seen as an essentially modern, democratic attitude, in contrast to the take-it-or-leave-it philosophy which is, rightly or wrongly, taken to characterise the museum in its autocratic, élitist days. The 'participating' museum is one in which the visitors and the community have an acknowledged and officially approved share.

The concept of a museum as an institution to which one can belong, and to which one pays an annual subscription, is widespread and deeply rooted in America. It resembles closely the American system of church membership, by which one not only attends religious services in a particular church and shares in its general programme of activities, but makes regular and agreed payments to church funds, which amount to a subscription, although the word is never used in this context.

Americans, it has been rightly said, are great joiners and the person who is not a member of something can hardly be said to exist. Museum membership consequently fits very easily and naturally into the American pattern of life and there is no doubt that American museums owe a great deal to the support and finance they have obtained in this way. The Directory of the American Association of Museums gives details of the different grades of membership and subscriptions which each museum has, and to a non-American these make fascinating reading.

The Warner House Museum, at Portsmouth, New Hampshire, offers seven grades. Those who subscribe the minimum of $2 are entitled to be known as Helpful members; $5 brings the label of Timely; $10 Encouraging; $25 Solicitous; $50 Beneficent; and $100 Munificent. A gift of $1000 puts one on the top of the ladder as a Life Member. Some museums have thought up even more impressive titles for their members. At one, in the Mid West, a $500 annual subscription brings the honour of being called Steam Boat Captain, although the museum itself has nothing to do with river transport. The American system applies to all museums, great and small. Junior museums, of which there are many in America, usually offer membership on a family basis.

'Membership' of a museum is not a uniquely American idea, but it is one that is still not widely found elsewhere. In other countries, museums are more likely to have Friends than Members. The earliest Friends were groups of members of learned societies, formed in the early nineteenth century, in Europe, with the aim of using museums as a means of bringing science, history and the arts to the masses. At the same time, however, quite a different kind of Association of Friends began to grow up, composed of people who had made donations to a museum and who in this way acquired privileges as benefactors.

As the present Secretary-General of ICOM, Luis Monreal pointed out in his address to the first conference of the Friends of the World's Museums, held in Barcelona in 1972, the character of today's Friends varies greatly, according to the country and museum in which they are active. Broadly speaking, however, one can say that present-day Friends exist in order to provide a museum with moral and material support and to help with the work of educating the public. What is now required, and what is now happening in a number of places, is that the Friends should begin to regard themselves as a form of consumer organisation, or, in Mr Monreal's words, that 'Societies of Friends should aspire to be the spokesmen of a body of opinion, the regular visitors to the museums, who until now have been largely ignored, in an era of mandarinism'.

'We firmly believe', he told the Barcelona conference, 'that the establishment of public power would help to balance each side of the scales, which are at present occupied by "administrative" and "curatorial" powers.'

Before the Second World War, Friends of the Museum were mostly confined, outside North America, to a few of the larger museums. Once the war was over, however, the situation began to change and the movement spread more widely. The Museum of Knitted Textiles at Troyes, in France, was exceptionally early in the field, with the establishment of its Association of Friends of the Museum in 1947, but nowadays in all countries almost any museum of any size is likely to have its

Friends, although they are not necessarily called by this title. With the spread of the Friends idea, its character has changed somewhat, at least outside America. In Europe, before 1939, Friends were, with rare exceptions, only to be found in art museums and in cathedrals. They existed primarily in order to raise funds to buy and restore works of art, and to maintain ancient and decaying cathedrals in a safe and attractive condition. During the past thirty years the Friends method of getting for museums of all kinds money and amenities which cannot be obtained in any other way has become widespread, not least in the socialist countries, where voluntary action is seen to produce benefits very similar to those obtained within the capitalist system.

The Museum Society of Bombay is a good illustration of what can happen when there is an energetic organiser with plenty of free time to devote to the work. It was set up in 1962 – the first in Asia – after a visit to India by an American couple who had been associated with the Friends of the Boston Museum. To begin with, the programme of activities was designed mainly to meet the interests of comfortably-off women, who welcomed another activity within the cultural-public service field in order to alleviate the boredom of a leisured, highly-privileged existence, and the meetings were held in the afternoons. Soon afterwards, however, meeting times were changed to the evening and at that point membership broadened out considerably. The annual subscriptions (1976) are:

Individual members: 15 rupees
Students, artists and art teachers: 10 rupees
Family membership: 20 rupees
Life membership: 300 rupees

To put these figures into perspective, it may be useful to mention that the average monthly salary of a teacher, a senior clerical worker or a skilled mechanic is about 300 rupees, which is the same as Life Membership of the Museum Society. The Society receives donations as well as subscriptions, and it should be noted that under Indian law gifts made to the Museum are not tax-deductible, but money given to the Museum Society is, and a good deal of support from rich people, with whom Bombay is well endowed, has un-

doubtedly come to the Society for this reason.

Membership is small, when one considers the size of Greater Bombay, but people attend regularly. No entrance fee is charged for lectures, which are advertised in the local press and which can be attended by the general public. There are between eighteen and twenty-four of these lectures a year, given by both Indian and foreign scholars. The subjects are always connected in some way with either art or archaeology and, to a foreign observer, both the subjects and the style of treatment appear somewhat formal and old-fashioned, but one has to allow for the Indian taste in such matters. The lectures are held at the Museum in a room holding about 200 people, for which the Museum makes no charge to the Society.

In addition to the lectures, the Society organises a wide range of activities. During the past five years these have included a talk on the Kanheri Caves, followed by a bus trip to look at them; dance demonstrations; a summer art course for eight- to fifteen-year-olds; a visit to the Regional Handicraft Design Centre; and house tours to look at private collections.

The Society forms a bridge between the Museum and schools. When the Society was established, there were no guides for children in the Museum. The Society therefore arranged for a suitable person to be trained and paid to carry out this work and also made itself responsible for organising school visits to the Museum. Another venture is the Children's Creative Centre, built in the Museum's grounds, but financed and run by the Society. The Society is adept at fund-raising for special purposes. Money for a publications bookstall at the Museum came from a successful Moghul evening.

The Museum Society's Secretary, Mrs Nalini Haridas Swali, is helped by a very devoted band of workers, including her husband, who is employed by a bank and assists mainly with proofreading and mailing the Society's literature. Mrs Swali believes that, in the circumstances in which all public institutions in India find themselves, the Society is likely to play an important part in the Museum's work for many years to come, and there is no reason to doubt her judgement. What is particularly important to stress, however, is that the money-making aspect of what the Society is doing is not the most important. The Society functions not only as a group of Friends of the Museum, but as Friends of the Museum staff, giving them invaluable psychological support in conditions of penury and shortages which must frequently seem intolerable. Relations between the Director and the Museum Society are excellent in Bombay, a welcome feature which is not, unfortunately, to be found everywhere.

As it happened, there was no Museum Society in Bombay during the years of British rule, but there could well have been. Such an activity would have fitted excellently into the social life of the Raj and one can easily imagine the character and atmosphere of its meetings, which would almost certainly have taken place in the afternoons and been noticeably female-dominated. Elsewhere in the former European colonial territories this was certainly the case and after the coming of independence these countries have been faced with the difficult problem of adapting a former colonial institution to a completely new kind of society. What happened in Ghana makes an interesting case-study.

Here, what Europeans called civilisation existed before independence only in a narrow coastal strip, centred on Accra. There was a museum, set up and run by the British, and it had a Friends of the Museum Society. The members were the wives and daughters of British officials, and of the diplomatic and business representatives of other European countries. There were no African Friends at all, and activities were very much of the coffee-party, culture-is-good-for-the-complexion type. After thinking the matter over for some years, the Ghanaians who now found themselves in control of the National Museum came to the conclusion that the wisest step would be to abolish the Friends and make no attempt to revive the organisation for a number of years, not because the idea of having Friends of the Museum was bad in itself, but because both the country and the Museum needed a different kind of Friend. After a ten-year interregnum, the institution was re-created, but this time the qualification required of a Friend was not merely or even neces-

sarily an annual subscription, but the fact of having given something to increase and improve the collections of the Museum, or of having helped in some similarly practical way. Since the Museum's policy was to acquire mainly African material, it was certain that the new Friends would be mainly African. There are, as it happens, some European Friends in the new organisation, but they are there for the same reasons as the Africans and on what might be called African terms.

It is clear that Friends of the Museum or Members of a Museum Society must reflect the habits and philosophy of the country in which the museum is situated, just as the museum itself will and should reflect that community. Countries like the German Federal and Democratic Republics and the Soviet Union, in which academic people are held in great respect and in which the distinction between professionals and non-professionals, bureaucrats and non-bureaucrats, is drawn with extreme and unmistakable clarity, cannot regard its Friends in the same way as America, Britain or, to a lesser extent, France, where the distinction is not so clearly or sharply made. One can usefully ask, when studying the programme or the aims of the Friends of any particular museum or art gallery, 'How Belgian or American or Japanese is this? How much of

it is transferable or adaptable to my own country?' It is an excellent museological discipline.

As an example, we can examine the brochure *An Invitation to Join the Friends of the Ironbridge Gorge Museum*. This museum, partly indoors but mostly open-air, is one of Britain's most successful and most innovatory postwar museums, the world's first National Park of Industrial Archaeology, organised as a private trust, but drawing some part of its income from public funds.

'The Friends of the Ironbridge Gorge Museum', says the brochure, 'is an organisation formed to co-ordinate voluntary activities on behalf of the Museum.' It then goes on to list the activities on which the Friends are mainly engaged:

1. Publicity. To make known as widely as possible, by both formal and informal means, the objects and achievements of the Ironbridge Gorge Museum.
2. Fund-raising. Through annual subscriptions and special money-raising functions. Money raised by the Friends is normally spent on specific projects in the Museum by arrangement with the Director.
3. Staffing of sales points and information centres.

Ironbridge Gorge Museum, Shropshire, England. Museum volunteers de-rust a nineteenth-century iron canal boat.

4. Guiding duties in all parts of the Museum, for which special training sessions are arranged.
5. Practical work on museum sites. Numerous projects are in hand, requiring a variety of types of help, both skilled and unskilled.
6. Research and special project groups. One group is currently collecting information on the ceramics industries of the Ironbridge Gorge and another is cataloguing documents deposited with the Museum. A photographic section is carrying out a survey of buildings in Ironbridge.
7. The organisation of special functions at the Museum.

'By becoming a member of the Friends', prospective subscribers are told, 'you will be supporting one of Britain's most important conservation projects and helping to create a Living Museum in the birthplace of modern industrial technology.

In return, membership of the Friends brings you the following privileges:

1. Free admission to all [the Ironbridge Gorge] museum sites, whenever they are open.
2. Copies of the Museum's bulletin, *Ironbridge Quarterly*, and of the *Friends' Newsletter*.
3. Special reduced rates from time to time on publications and other items sold by the Museum.
4. An active programme of lectures, visits and social events.

Examples are given of what volunteer workers have achieved at the Museum – the removal of machinery and equipment from a local tile-works and its transport to the Museum; the dismantling and re-erection of several stationary steam-engines; the organisation of the Museum's twice-yearly Open Days; and there is a forecast that 'the scale of the Museum's plans is such that voluntary help and support of all kinds will be needed for a long time ahead'.

MAKING THE MOST OF AMATEUR HELP

The Friends of the Ironbridge Gorge Museum are obviously not the same kind of people, nor are they giving the same kind of help, as the Friends of Canterbury Cathedral, but there is a link between the activities of the two which marks them off as distinctively British. The ladies who embroider hassocks, provide and arrange flowers and polish brass in English churches and cathedrals are working without payment, within the same national tradition as the people who dismantle and clean steam-engines for the museum at Ironbridge. They are making a contribution with their hands and their time, rather than with money, and, under today's inflationary conditions, this can be an enormous help to the budget. The Friends of the Ironbridge Gorge Museum are, in fact, an interesting modern hybrid of volunteer workers, research assistants, guides and fund-raisers. The Museum is, one might say, their hobby. In some countries it would be very difficult to organise Friends on this basis, either because of trade union opposition to the employment of unpaid labour or because a tradition of working-for-love has never become established. One must in fairness admit that 'Friends', of the Ironbridge type, would be more difficult to absorb into the activities of certain other types of museum. An art gallery, for instance, would probably not welcome amateur help, however enthusiastic, for cleaning or restoring paintings, and a natural history museum would almost certainly prefer to confine itself to professional taxidermists. In all museums, of course, a clear distinction has to be made between those tasks which are essentially for the full-time staff and those which can safely and usefully be entrusted to volunteer helpers. At one extreme we find the Friends of the Belgian Royal Museums of Fine Art, who are essentially passive supporters, receiving in exchange for their annual subscription free entrance to any of the museums and publications at a reduced price, and at the other, the Friends of the Ironbridge Gorge Museum, who represent an unpaid labour force of considerable size. It is clear from the proceedings of the two conferences of the World Federation of Museums which have so far been held that the majority of Friends so far belong to the Belgian rather than to the Ironbridge type. The recently established National Technical Museum at Helsinki, in Finland, is attempting to make the fullest possible use of volunteer helpers. These have been recruited exclusively from retired engineers, who are happy to spend one or two days a week at the Museum, mostly cleaning and renovating machinery and equipment. They attend regular lectures on the aims and techniques of conservation and their unpaid work allows the Museum to carry out a more ambitious programme than would otherwise be possible.

Many museums, especially in the English-speaking world, use volunteers as guides. The Americans make extensive use of this system in their smaller museums, most of which would not be able to function without it, since their financial resources do not make it possible to employ more than the bare minimum of paid staff. American influence has made itself felt in other parts of the world. In Bangkok, for instance, the Museum Volunteers Programme was directly inspired by American experience. Its beginnings do not lie far back. In 1969 a group of American women living in Bangkok, and needing some way of filling their over-ample leisure time, offered to provide free tours in English at the Museum. The offer was accepted and the first group of fifteen volunteer guides spent several months studying the Museum collections in depth and in detail. Since then, the Volunteers have become an integral part of the Museum's rapidly-expanding educational programme, both for adults and for children. In addition to guided tours in English there are now, on a regular basis, tours in French, German and Japanese. The Volunteers also run a monthly *Newsletter*.

The results of using volunteer guides are not always predictable, and any sensible museum learns and improves by trial and error. Difficulties are most likely to be experienced when the social and educational background of the guides is markedly different from that of the visitors whom they happen to be guiding. The American Museum in Britain, at Bath, learnt this truth the hard way. For many years it has employed, as part-time guides, middle-aged women who have always been, in the English sense of the word, ladies, that is, people who come from, or sound as if they come from, the upper 10 per cent, economically speaking, of the population. They are renowned for their helpfulness and for their knowledge of the collections, but an investigation showed that they were having only mixed success with school parties, of which the Museum has a great many. Broadly speaking, they got on well with young children, but less well with the over-thirteens. When this puzzling fact was looked into more carefully, it became apparent that the young children regarded the guides simply as pleasant women, but that, to many of the older ones, who had acquired their life-stock of social prejudices by that time, the same people represented an alien culture, a different and hostile class. There are those who argue that prejudice can be by-passed, if not altogether avoided, by using audio-visual guiding systems, which are supposed to be objective and neutral, instead of human, face-to-face guides, who may represent an emotional barrier between the museum and the public.

The point has been discussed recently by Mr Keith Pennyfather, in his excellent British Government publication, *Interpretive Media and Facilities*.[7]

To some extent, [he says] it can be argued that direct personal contact with the visitor, provided by an expert ranger or guide, is the only really effective method of communication, and that all the other examples – trails, hides, binoculars, dioramas, gadgets and so on – are poor substitutes. In an ideal situation with no restraints on manpower or finance, interpretation by a *good* ranger is the best method of all, but in practice this ideal is rarely attainable, not least because skilled manpower is in short supply. In those cases where interpretation is considered necessary but individual contact with visitors is impossible, the wise use of other media is probably better than no interpretation at all.

There is a real problem here, but it is not always recognised in its correct terms. The fundamental difference of opinion is between those who, instinctively, temperamentally or by training, want every aspect of museum work to be under complete professional control, and those who believe that people, all people, only learn by doing something for themselves, by having their performance criticised and by asking questions. If one holds the first view, then the less direct contact one has with the public the better. The visitor picks up his recorded guide-cassette and moves through the museum along the prescribed route, looking at the prescribed things. He never meets his guide in the flesh and the cassette

neither receives nor answers questions. That the explanations on the tape are authoritative is never in doubt. At the Metropolitan Museum in New York, the Introductory Tour is recorded by no less a person than the Director himself, and in one sense one is well served. But – and there is a but – a recorded commentary, however well done, is necessarily a take-it-or-leave-it form of communication. There is nothing one can do with it but listen, switch off or throw it to the floor. Thousands of people visit the Metropolitan each week, and it would be beyond the limits of possibility to have enough guides to take them all round personally. Many people in any case have no wish for a guide; they want to be left alone and to walk around in peace. Participation, whether in the form of stroking stuffed owls, pressing buttons to make models work, cleaning machinery or even asking questions, is not everyone's idea of pleasure. A considerable number, however, do appreciate help of some kind, particularly the opportunity to talk to someone knowledgeable, and there seems to be no good reason why volunteers should not be used for this purpose, provided they have been carefully selected and given a certain amount of training. This need not be in any way elaborate or lengthy. At the Belgian National Railway Museum in Brussels, railway enthusiasts, many in their teens, are often on hand in the Museum galleries to answer questions, as a spare-time activity, and it is difficult to believe that any professional museologist could

know more about railways than they do. A museum should use expertise thankfully, wherever it happens to be found.

In a number of countries, it is, unfortunately, difficult for trained museum staff to find work and, where this situation occurs, the use of unpaid volunteers is hardly likely to be popular. In the United States, for instance, the output of what are somewhat quaintly called 'historical archaeologists' has for a number of years been considerably larger than the labour market can absorb and any attempt to make use of volunteers on projects nowadays meets with fairly strenuous resistance. The situation is not dissimilar in West Germany and France. Opposition may be found at all levels of work. With growing unemployment in most Western countries, museums have to tread warily in getting even the simplest manual tasks carried out by people who are not normally mechanics, carpenters, bricklayers or painters and who are without a union card. On the other hand, anything which helps to bind a museum into the fabric of the local community is surely to be welcomed, even when times are difficult. A museum which begins to be talked about as 'our museum' is well on the road to success.

WINTERTHUR: A PUBLIC RELATIONS CLASSIC

Paradoxically, one of the most community-involved museums in the world

Technorama, Winterthur, Switzerland. Interior of machinery store.

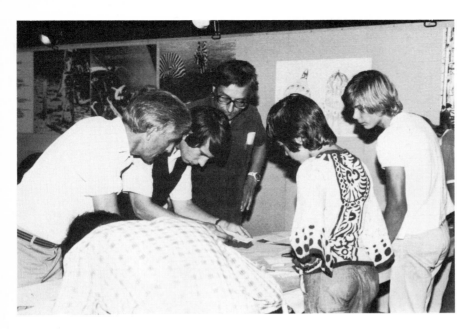

is one which has not yet been built, Technorama, the Swiss Technical Museum. The plan to establish a national museum of industry and technology in Switzerland goes back a long way. The prime mover, in the 1950s, was an engineer on the staff of the major employer in Winterthur, Sulzer Brothers. He began to collect and store material for the future museum, which an advanced industrial country like Switzerland badly needed, and to arouse interest in the project among industrialists, the Cantonal and Federal Governments and the public generally.

In 1965 he obtained funds of 150,000 francs from the City of Winterthur, and 150,000 from Canton Zürich. A group of architects was engaged to prepare plans for a building and the City gave a 50,000 square metre site, with an adjacent 70,000 in reserve. At this point a decision was taken to set up the Technorama Foundation with a full-time Director.

The Director was told by the Cantonal and Federal Governments that he had to 'prove interest' in the Museum, and that the way to do this was to raise money. This he did, with considerable

success, and by 1970 he had promises of 2.4 million francs. At this point, unfortunately, difficulties arose over the plans. The Federal Government asked, in the normal way, for an independent assessment, and as a result of this the architectural merit came in for criticism. It appears to have been a case, again very normal, of one architect not liking the work of another. Prices were meanwhile rising, and new plans were drawn up for a smaller building, known as Project 72. These plans were submitted to the City of Winterthur and to the Federal Government, which ordered a local referendum. This was held in 1973, after a well-organised publicity campaign to tell the people of Winterthur what they were voting for. The preparations for the vote included sending a party of journalists and other opinion-formers to the Deutsches Museum in Munich. Eventually, the referendum approved Technorama and the scheme then went back to the Federal Government for the final approval. By then, however, the international financial situation had deteriorated even further and, although approval in principle was given, the actual construction of the Museum has had to be deferred. Meanwhile, Technorama continues with its programme of temporary exhibitions and other activities, in such premises as it can find.

The point of the story is that the inhabitants of Winterthur have been involved in the planning of the new museum, and in the controversy surrounding it, to an extent which it would be difficult to parallel anywhere else in the world. In the matter of museums, as of everything else, the Swiss do not take democracy lightly.

CLUBS, WORKSHOPS AND HANDICRAFTS

The absence of an exhibition building, however, has compelled Technorama

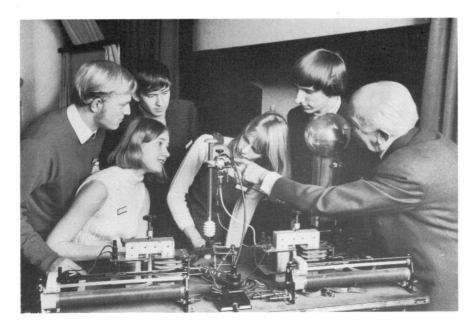

to concentrate its energies on projects of a different kind, so that when the building does come, as one day it must, it will grow out of a thoroughly tested philosophy of community participation. It will be, in other words, a relevant museum.

Two of Technorama's activities illustrate how this is being achieved. The first consists of experimental projects carried out by boys and girls, with the help and encouragement of Technorama. In 1974 there were, for instance, 2000 school pupils engaged in making model rockets. Technorama is not, of course, the only museum in the world to be engaged in this kind of work, although in Switzerland the circumstances are unique—clergy without a church, so to speak. The Technical Museum in Stockholm is also very strong in this field, with a specialist member of the museum staff allocated full-time to it.

The other Technorama activity which seems particularly worthy of mention is the formation of the archive of tapes and transcripts of retired professors of the Swiss Federal Institute of Technology, describing what is now yesterday's technology. This invaluable record, which no other country has attempted in the same systematic and thoroughgoing fashion, will ensure that when the Museum does eventually open, it will have a personal as well as an object content. The absence of a permanent building may turn out to be a blessing in disguise, since it is forcing a concentration on what might be called the lively side of a museum's activities.

The most important criterion for a museum to have in mind when it is deciding whether to devote time and money to a particular activity must be, 'Is anybody else doing it already?' If, for example, science clubs or nature clubs or research projects are being perfectly adequately organised by the schools, there is no reason for the museum to do the same, unless, of course, it is convinced that the other people are grossly incompetent. In many parts of the world, however, the door is wide open for museums to pioneer in this way and exceedingly valuable work is being accomplished as a result. The same solutions do not, of course, apply everywhere, and methods

have to be adapted to meet the needs and conditions of each situation. One does not, for example, have the same order of priorities in a poor country in which the majority of the people are illiterate as in a rich country where at least minimum standards of reading and writing are taken for granted. In the first, the museum may well find itself in a truly pioneering situation, spearheading the national advance; in the second, it is likely to be supplementing other forms of education.

With this provision, however, it is useful to know what is being done in the educational field in a number of very different countries and conditions, both for children and for adults. One of the most successful ventures has been the variety of what are called workshops at Muse, a centre for teenagers and adults, at the Brooklyn Museum, New York City. In these workshops members can receive expert instruction and follow their own interests at their own pace. Among the possibilities are:

Having Fun with Words (for children aged 6–8)
Writer's Workshop (9–12)
Anthropology Workshop (10–14)
Photography Workshop (17 upwards)
Dance Workshop (15 upwards)
Aviation Workshop (15 upwards)

New York has great problems with its educational system. Many of its children come from poor families, City taxes provide insufficient money to pay the teachers that are required and to give

them adequate materials to work with, and a considerable proportion of the school buildings are not up to present-day standards. Muse makes it possible to add a dimension to the lives of teenagers and young adults which their schooling has denied them.

The Bal Bhavan children's centre in New Delhi has a very similar function. Teaching in Indian schools is extremely (and as many Indian educationists think, inhumanly) book-centred, with practically no opportunity for children to engage in art and handicrafts for themselves. That a country with such magnificent artistic traditions as India should be able to find neither the time nor the money for art in its schools is a great educational irony, and one which gives museums both a real opportunity and an essential function. The popularity of the Bal Bhavan proves beyond doubt that the demand for artistic expression exists, and those children who are fortunate enough to be granted membership have to be strictly rationed to a few hours' attendance each week. It has excellent workshops for painting, pottery, music, drama and dance, and there is also a children's museum which is used mainly by visiting school parties, although it is also available to members of the centre.

The National Museum of Niger has gone even further, by providing actual apprenticeships for boys who want to become craftsmen. This remarkable achievement has to be seen in its context. The Museum was created in order

National Museum, Niamey, Niger. Mechanical engineering apprentice.

National Museum, Niamey, Niger. (top left) *Museum workshop for the blind and physically handicapped.* (top right) *Blacksmiths'* *and goldsmiths' workshop.* (bottom left) *Craftsmanship from the jewellery workshop.* (bottom right) *Potter at work.*

to make the citizens of Niger aware and proud of their traditions and to help towards the creation of national unity. Craftsmen were brought together from all over the country in order to build traditional dwellings and to make furniture, cooking utensils and other articles of everyday life. Visitors can see these things being made and, a matter of great importance for the Museum's budget, buy them. Sales are now running at nearly 30 million francs a year, and more than seventy craftsmen are working full-time at the Museum. They are not employees; they sell what they make at market prices. One should emphasise that in this country, as elsewhere in Africa, the craft-tradition is central to national awareness and development. It is not part of the luxury fringe, as it is in Europe and America.

Great care is taken to select only the best possible craftsmen, partly in order to have first-class work to sell and partly to provide exemplary training facilities for apprentices, of whom about twenty are recruited each year. Before being considered for an apprenticeship, a boy must have attended primary school up to school-certificate level – the Museum is, in other words, producing the literate craftsmen that Africa so badly needs – and there are now many more candidates than can be accepted.

Like a number of other African museums, the Niger Museum has felt obliged to take on some of the functions of a Design Centre. In most African countries, crafts are encouraged as part of the tourism programme and for this reason they are usually promoted through the Ministries of Tourism or Culture. The general system is that craft-objects are made either by individuals or by groups working together in co-operatives. Either of these may operate a shop and sell their work directly or they may supply some form of central government agency. In the case of Uganda, this is the National Handicrafts Shop, which sells to the general public, mainly tourists.

The National Museum of Niger has gone to great pains to extend the potential market for its handicrafts, by preparing a splendidly designed and printed catalogue for world circulation. In this way, it hopes to be able to sell the Museum's products to people who have never visited either Niger or the National Museum.

Each left-hand page is devoted to illustrations of the objects described on the right-hand page. The text is in three languages, French, English and German, and the size and weight of each object are given, together with the material from which it is made. Few museums in the world, including the largest and richest, have so far shown the same degree of enterprise.

Many African handicrafts have been improved through the use of better-quality materials, such as dyes. Some, however, have been modified – the word can be a considerable understatement – to suit the tastes of tourists, and in the process become debased to an unacceptable extent. There are, for example, musical instruments which are sold as such by craft shops, when in fact they are no more than toys. They are defective in construction and they have no musical qualities. The Niger Museum prevents this, at least in the case of those goods made by the craftsmen working within its organisation. Nothing is offered for sale which is badly made or which offends tradition. It would be a thoroughly good thing if every developing country had some kind of craft council, which could well be linked to a museum, and which would offer guidance to the craft shops on the standard of the items offered for sale to the public. UNESCO, it should be noted, has two projects in the planning stage at the present time, aimed at showing how excellent craftsmanship and traditional designs can be perfectly compatible with commercial success.

The position in India is interesting and not entirely satisfactory. There is, in New Delhi, a Crafts Museum, and there is also a Design Centre. They are many miles distant from one another. Both are responsible to the same Government organisation, the Handicrafts Board, but co-ordination and even information between the two are very difficult, as the Handicrafts Board is divided up into more or less autonomous sections, which never seem to link up with one another. Consequently, the splendid examples of old crafts in the Crafts Museum are of little help or inspiration to the men who are employed by the Design Centre and who work on its premises, the Indian Design Centre being a curious combination of factory and showroom, which shows and sells only what it designs and makes. Few people visit it, owing to its remoteness from the centre of the city, and its influence is correspondingly much reduced. In India, as elsewhere, a good craftsman can make money only if he can find an organisation to market his products efficiently. This means, for the most part, marketing abroad or to tourists, since craft items are now considered an expensive luxury in India, where the housewife demands something cheap, practical and easily cared for. The results are plain to see in the Design Centre's showroom. There has been a great deal of compromise, if not precisely debasement, in order to meet the requirements of modern buyers.

Museum of Modern Art, New York. Gallery of Toys at the Children's Art Carnival.

The Niger Museum has neither the funds nor the human and technical resources to engage in advisory educational and social work to the extent it would wish, but it has been able to arrange a cultural and literacy programme in association with other organisations, such as Niger Radio and Television, the Niger Red Cross, and the Franco-Niger Cultural Centre. The mornings are taken up with a wide range of activities, which include first-aid, do-it-yourself techniques, handicrafts, story-telling, music, drawing and painting; the afternoons are devoted to reading and writing classes for illiterate children, given by a teacher assigned to the Museum by the Ministry of Education.

In a more developed way and on a much larger scale, the Niger Museum is fulfilling the same kind of social and educational functions as the experimental slum-area museum at Tacubaya, in Mexico City, which has already been described. At the moment, it is certainly doing what no other body is able to do. In time, no doubt, some of these tasks will be taken over by more specialised institutions, but meanwhile the National Museum of Niger is justifying its existence in ways which would have been considered quite outside a museum's field fifty years ago, and which demand a considerable widening of the definition of the word 'museologist'.

It is possible to argue that in many countries the museum facilities provided for children are far more intelligent, relevant and successful than those which are considered suitable for adults, even in the same museum. At the Metropolitan Museum in New York, for instance, the Junior Museum has an excellent section called 'The Artist's Workshop – Tools and Techniques'. This shows the variety of techniques which have been used in the pictorial arts from ancient times onwards; how artists make mosaics and tapestries; what materials they use; how they paint in watercolours, tempera, oil and fresco on such different substances as wood, clay, glass and canvas; and how an artist's choice of

Objects in Gallery of Toys, Children's Art Carnival.

medium affects his work. There is a reproduction of a Renaissance painter's studio, films, slide-stories and peep-hole viewers. A considerable number of original works from the Museum's collections are shown, including tempera panels, an Albrecht Dürer wood-block, a Florentine altar-piece and El Greco's 'Adoration of the Shepherds'. 'The aim', says the Associate-in-Charge of the Junior Museum, Louise Condit,[8] 'is to interest children in materials and methods, to encourage them to look beyond the subject of a picture and find out all they can about how it was made, with what materials, in what kind of studio.' Why, one asks, does such an admirable approach have to be reserved for children? Why are adults forced to continue to be second-class citizens when visiting a museum?

It is a short step from showing people, of whatever age, the tools and materials artists use, to giving visitors an opportunity to handle these things for themselves. Such an approach allows communication and participation to flow into one another. The distinction between the two is, in any case, shadowy and unreal. One of the most original and successful of all art exhibitions designed for children, the 'Children's Art Carnival' has been shown in a number of countries since it was first created by Victor D'Amico and his colleagues at the Museum of Modern Art in New York in 1942. It continues to be presented each year at the Museum and there is a replica in New Delhi, the gift of ICOM and the Asia Society. The Carnival is in two parts, an introductory area and a workshop area. The introductory area, which is in semi-darkness, contains a number of specially-designed toys, displayed in pools of light, with background music to add to the wonderland atmosphere. Children between the ages of four and twelve are invited in to play with the toys; others look on through glass panels.

There are no words, either spoken or printed, but as the children play with the toys they are unconsciously being introduced to colour, texture, rhythm and good design. Stimulated and, if one may dare to use the word, conditioned, by Area One, the children emerge into the brightly-lit and colourful Area Two, the Studio Workshop. This has adjustable easels along the walls and round tables with tools and materials in the centre of the room. The children can do whatever they please here for an hour and they are allowed to take home the constructions, paintings or collages which they make. The Carnival has proved equally successful in all the countries where it has been shown. Barriers caused by language, cultural background or lack of previous art experience do not seem to exist.

American museums are much given to organising after-school, vacation and Saturday morning creative art classes and workshops of all kinds for children from the age of three upwards. Each class is usually for a fairly narrow age-range. The teachers are more likely to be artists than teachers and the museum charges a fee just sufficient to cover the cost of materials and instruction. Some major museums, such as the Museum of Modern Art in New York, and the Junior Arts Center in Los Angeles, cater for as many as 3000 children a year in this way.

Non-active, non-participation courses are even more common. In 1973 the Junior Museum of the Art Institute of Chicago offered a fifteen-meeting course (Saturdays, 1–3.30) on 'Movies – the Story of a New Art' and the Cleveland Museum arranged 'Viewpoints in the Galleries' for seven-to eight-year-olds, in which a musician, a writer and a dancer showed how the Museum's collections relate to their particular art. The Junior Museum at the Metropolitan runs a vacation course for twelve- to fifteen-year-olds each summer, with series on 'How to Look at Works of Art', 'History of Painting from the Renaissance to the Present' and 'Learning to Look'. During the summer of 1969 the Brooklyn Museum arranged a Black Art Seminar for teenagers. Thirteen boys, aged twelve to sixteen, attended the sixteen sessions which were wholly devoted to African, Afro-American and Haitian art.

LECTURES AND DEMONSTRATIONS

By comparison with workshops and creative art classes, lectures and demonstrations are cheap and easy to organise, and it is not surprising that so many museums prefer to concentrate their energies on this kind of educational activity, especially when money is hard to come by. The Science Museum in London is a case in point. The Museum has no clubs or activity centres and confines itself to lectures. Its well-organised lecture service is available to any type of party, from ten-

State Art Collections, Dresden, GDR. The museum's restorer explains the function of firearms of the sixteenth to eighteenth centuries, as part of a series of special days when the work of the museum is explained to boys and girls.

year-old children to university graduates and other adults. The service is free and the lectures offered are of two kinds, Request Lectures and Ticket Lectures.

For the Request Lectures, arrangements have to be made at least fifteen days in advance. 'As much information as possible about the parties should be given to the lecturers,' says the brochure, *Science Museum Party Visits*, 'so that lectures are prepared to suit the ability and special interests of the audience.' The choice is offered of lecture tours of the Museum galleries, for a maximum of twenty people, or of lecture-demonstrations in a theatre.

The Special Ticket Lectures, for which free tickets have to be obtained in advance, are announced in a leaflet which appears three times a year. There are also Joint Industrial Lectures, given by invited lecturers, usually scientists and technologists working in industry, who demonstrate the application of pure science to industrial processes. The Museum considers these lectures to be primarily for senior students.

Public lectures, taking the form of introductory talks or demonstrations relating to particular collections, are held in the Lecture Theatre, usually on Saturday afternoons and during school holidays. 'Public Lectures', the Museum warns, 'are not intended for school parties and teachers should not bring parties to them unless it is absolutely impossible to make arrangements for a request lecture. When school parties are brought to public lectures, the lower age limit (10 years) must be strictly observed.'

Teachers planning school visits are 'strongly recommended to make a personal visit to the Museum beforehand. If distance makes this too difficult, a letter enquiring about any particular gallery or exhibit and making certain it will be available could prevent a disappointment.' Two lists of 'suggested lecture topics' are given, thirty-five for Gallery Talks and thirty-two for Theatre Lectures. The choice ranges from 'Electricity and Magnetism' to 'Typewriters' for the first, and from 'Studying the Weather' to 'The Rise of Steam Power' for the second.

National Museum of Science and Technology, Milan, Italy. Adult members of the experimental physics group in the Museum laboratory.

There are also film shows at 1 p.m. on Wednesdays, Thursdays, Fridays and Saturdays, with a weekly change of programme. Films considered especially suitable for children are shown every weekday at 12.30. 'Only films with scientific or technological interest are shown', announces the Museum.

The London Science Museum is not, in the modern sense of the term, a participating museum. One could very well put it in the category of mandarin museums. The fact that, like the Palace of Discovery in Paris, it has many models and displays which visitors can make work does not make it any the less mandarin. It does not have activities, clubs or centres, it does not use volunteer guides or indeed volunteers for any purpose at all, and it has no Friends of the Museum system. Everything about it gives the impression that People Who Know are providing exhibits, lectures and demonstrations for People Who Should Know. It is efficient and well run in a curiously formal and old-fashioned way, a comment that has been made earlier about the Deutsches Museum in Munich. One should not fail to point out in this connection, however, that British schools are reasonably well endowed with science clubs, so that, in contrast to the situation in many other countries, there is less need for a museum to provide them.

The difference between the Science Museum, established in 1857, and the Birla Museum, established in 1959, in Calcutta, is very marked. The Birla Museum provides extensive educational services outside its own premises. Self-contained mobile science exhibitions, each consisting of twenty-four working exhibits, cover a wide area; small regional science museums have been set up in rural schools; extensive school services are available, in the form of demonstration lectures, hobby centres and teacher-training programmes. The teacher-training programmes show science teachers how to run the hobby centres and make demonstration exhibits. Other educational activities include an annual model-making competition and a science fair for adults.

There is no doubt that many museums, especially science museums, would like to organise more activities, but are prevented, or believe they are prevented, from doing so because of a shortage of money. This argument should not always be taken at its face value, however. Museum activities are a matter of willingness and determination, quite as much as of finance, and it is perfectly possible, as many museums have shown, to run children's clubs on a shoestring, by keeping the arrangements simple, by ignoring the traditional 'administrative problems', and by drawing heavily on the goodwill and expertise of volunteers.

ACTIVITIES AND THE MONEY PROBLEM

Two quite different matters, getting the public involved in museums and making the maximum use of the museum premises, are easily confused, but need

to be kept distinct. The National Museum of Science and Technology in Milan illustrates the point very well. Like most Italian museums, it is permanently and chronically short of money, It balances its books each year only by hiring out the Museum's excellent rooms and facilities for meetings and conferences and by using its cinema for commercial film shows. The cinema was built and equipped in the first place in order to show films concerned with science and technology and this does still happen once a month. Nowadays, however, the cinema is used, twelve hours a day and six days a week, to present recent releases of general-interest films which can be seen on the ordinary commercial circuits, and the Museum makes a lot of welcome money as a result. Pressed to explain why the public should choose to visit this cinema, the Museum suggested four reasons:

1. The no-smoking rule, which is rigidly enforced.
2. The exceptional comfort of the seats and amount of leg-room.
3. The general pleasantness and orderliness of the Museum cinema.
4. The relatively easy car-parking, in a city where parking is one of the major tribulations.

Subsidised in this way and by contributions from the State, the City of Milan, industry, the banks and other private sources, the Museum is able to continue to function and to maintain the greatly-appreciated programme of educational work carried out in its Physics Centre. Although there has been some improvement during recent years in the science-teaching facilities in Italian schools, they are still far from adequate and schools from all over Italy are in the habit of sending their more interested and talented pupils to the lectures and demonstrations at the Physics Centre, where they can be assured of first-rate teaching and equipment. These parties are drawn both from primary and secondary schools and they normally have a whole day at the Museum. Those living at a distance spend one or two nights in Milan. During the past five years, between 40,000 and 45,000 boys and girls have attended these sessions

each year, the peak month always being April.

This example from Milan illustrates:

(*a*) an attempt by an important national museum to find ways of balancing its books and of adding to its income in a reputable and not altogether irrelevant fashion – this is essentially a management, not a museological, problem;
(*b*) a traditional and essentially passive approach to the task of using a museum for educational purposes.

Both (*a*) and (*b*) get people across the Museum threshold, and some of them, no doubt, may be persuaded to take an interest in the Museum's collections and displays as a result. But neither method does anything to involve the people concerned in the day-to-day running of the enterprise. They attend, but they do not participate. They do not help to change the Museum's policy in any way, although they may certainly have a certain public relations value, in making the Museum better known.

Holding concerts in museums may bring similar advantages, although in many cases the museum is little more than an agreeable background to the music, which does nothing whatever to bring the collections alive. Some concerts, however, are more relevant than others. The Guimet Museum in Paris, for instance, is in the habit of putting on concerts of Asian music, which fits in well with its displays of Oriental art.

One can see that museums use the

word 'activity' in two quite different ways. It may describe either an occasion on which the museum itself is active – organising a concert would be an 'activity' in this sense – or one on which the public, suitably stimulated and encouraged by the museum, was active. One can perfectly well argue that at a good museum lecture the minds of the audience are very active and that, for this reason, to label a lecture as a passive event is incorrect. It would certainly be absurd to insist that an 'activity' must involve physical activity of some kind, but anyone who has attended lectures or demonstrations is well aware of the difference in atmosphere produced by the lecturer who, as it were, throws his arms around his audience and invites questions or comment as he goes along. The 'participating lecture' exists, and it is not at all the same as the lecture which expects reverent silence from beginning to end. Participation involves effort from all the parties concerned. The form which such effort takes is immaterial.

The modern museum is always saying, in effect, 'We want people to know about us and we want our collections to be used to the maximum possible extent. That is why we exist.' The collections need not be used on the museum premises. They can be circulated physically and three-dimensionally in the form of travelling exhibitions or kits or illustrations to lectures, or two-dimensionally, as reproductions. In either case, the purpose must be to excite comment and curiosity, both of which are entitled to be called activities.

John Judkyn Memorial, Bath, England. Selecting material for an Indian kit, for circulation to schools.

KITS

A number of museums now offer kits for use by schools. These are of two kinds, packaged selections of objects, with accompanying explanation, on loan to the school, and folders of pictures, cut-out models, texts, and sometimes slides and gramophone records, which can be bought and kept permanently.

One of the best-developed kit services in the world is organised by a museum which exists entirely for this purpose and to prepare special exhibitions, the John Judkyn Memorial, at Freshford, near Bath in England. The John Judkyn Memorial is part of the same foundation as the American Museum in Bath and has close working connections with it. Its collections of Americana of all kinds are constantly in movement between the Memorial and schools and colleges all over Britain.

The system is very popular and there is a long waiting list for the kits, but unfortunately no further expansion is possible until some way can be found of financing an increase in the staff, which at the moment consists of only three very overworked people.

The John Judkyn curator monitors the results of the kits and exhibitions very carefully, both by meeting teachers who come to the museum for the purpose, and by visits to schools which are using the kits. The curator, a friendly man who rates the arts of communication very highly, bases his annual programme on the feedback from his previous efforts. If something obviously fails to arouse interest, it is dropped as soon as possible; but long experience seems, however, to have produced a remarkably sure touch.

The excellence of its Teaching Kit sold, remarkably cheaply, by the Weald and Downland Open Air Museum in

England was partly responsible for the Museum's success in winning the Museum of the Year Award in 1975. It comes in a large cardboard envelope and contains the following items:

1. A large drawing of the Museum site, showing the topography and the position of the buildings already transferred to the site.
2. The Museum Guide, explaining the various buildings and the problems involved in moving and re-erecting them.
3. A Guide to the Museum, specially written for younger children by a teacher of long experience.
4. A copy of the second edition of the Handbook for Teachers, by the same author, which comments in its Preface that 'although most school visits continue to be extremely successful, it is a matter of considerable regret that there

Weald and Downland Open-Air Museum, Singleton, near Chichester, England. Cardboard cut-out of granary at the Museum.

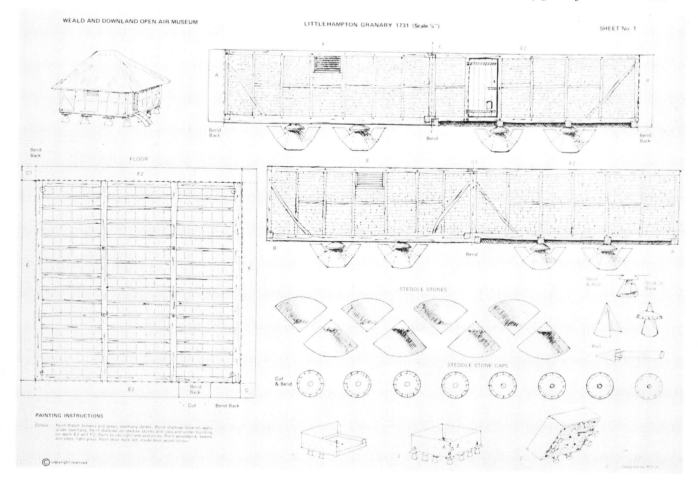

are schools, particularly secondary schools, whose visits have been far from satisfactory. This jolly day-off-school type of excursion, the needs for which are surely far better met by a visit to a fun fair or the beach, have been increasing at a disturbing rate. There was a marked decline in behaviour in 1974. Groups have been arriving with no fixed purpose and with some teachers not even prepared to give supervision to the children in their charge. Despite all the Museum's requests for co-operation, the damage, and complaints from other schools and the general public, have now reached a position which can no longer be tolerated. We do therefore urge all teachers to consider very carefully the reasons for their visits, and ask for the utmost co-operation to ensure the highest possible standards of educational use.'

5. A brochure describing the Children's Nature Trail.
6. Sheets containing outline-drawings of the principal buildings, with spaces in which children can write their own notes.
7. A number of very attractive postcards, made from drawings by the Museum's architect.
8. A large card, carrying a reproduction of the charges given on a mid-nineteenth-century toll-board preserved at the Museum.

Each item in the Kit can be bought separately, in whatever quantities may be required for class use. The excellent Publications hut also sells cut-out sheets of some of the principal buildings, for painting and assembling, and superb explanatory sheets describing and illustrating old farm implements.

The outstanding features of the Weald and Downland publications, which are a model for any museum in the world, are that they have been concerned and designed as a whole, with a clear understanding of what the Museum is trying to accomplish and for what kind of people. It is assumed:

1. that the Museum will have three categories of visitor – family parties, with children of varying ages; school parties, again of varying ages; and adults, coming in ones and twos and in small groups, with a considerable pro-

portion of foreigners during the summer months;
2. that a certain amount of self-selection will have taken place before the adult visitors and family parties arrive at the Museum, and that people expecting a noisy, funfair type of outing are very unlikely to come;
3. that, although most of the visitors, schoolchildren included, will have a certain amount of practical and nostalgic interest in farming, old buildings and rural history, their detailed knowledge of these matters is likely to be rather sketchy.

The Orientation Centre, the signposting and labelling on the site and the Publications and Souvenir Centre are planned to meet these four conditions. Participation at the Weald and Downland Museum means, for the most part, walking over the fields and the woodland where the buildings are situated, going into the buildings and, with the help of the various information media that are offered, discovering for oneself what the Museum has to offer. There are no guides, human or electronic, no film or slide-tape shows, and no dioramas. This is, honestly and deliberately, a museum for people who can read, and who enjoy tramping about – the Museum covers quite a large area – and who do not expect to be spoon-fed.

At what point, then, are they reckoned to use the various types of explanatory booklet on sale at the Museum? Most of the answer is contained in the layout of the Museum. One does not arrive at the Publications Centre until one's tour is well advanced. It is a considerable distance from the entrance and most people would be extremely unlikely to make a beeline straight from the car park to the Publications Centre and then back again to the Orientation Centre to begin the visit in the most logical sequence. Only teachers with school parties are expected, then, to digest and use the guiding and explanatory material in advance. Everyone else, on a first visit, will probably buy their booklets and information sheets, and certainly their cut-outs and postcards, to take away with them, to be digested afterwards at leisure.

THE PRINTED GUIDE

Many, perhaps most, museums give the impression of not having given a great

deal of thought as to how and when their booklet guides are to be used. One does occasionally see and hear museum visitors using a museum-guide as if it were a volume of Baedeker or Michelin, but this has become comparatively rare in recent years. Many museologists would feel that the need to tour a museum gallery guide in hand is evidence of failure and incompetence on their part and that a properly arranged exhibit should speak for itself. There are, in fact, curators who are prepared to say publicly that they strongly disapprove of printed guides, partly because such a guide puts the curator in a strait-jacket and makes it more difficult for him to change and rearrange exhibits as often and as much as he wants to, and partly because it transfers attention from the exhibit itself to a description of it, or in other words, conditions visitors in the wrong way. One hears quite frequently nowadays another objection, that a good guide is expensive to compile, print and sell and that, unless the museum is extremely fortunate, there will still be a stock of guides in the cupboard when both the facts and the style are years out of date.

The anti-guide faction have a strong, but not unchallengeable, case. It can be countered partly on grounds of humanity and partly of commercial expertise. Many people like to buy an exhibition or museum guide as an agreeable and, for some, useful souvenir of their visit. The more attractive the guide or catalogue is, the more pleased they are to take it home with them. And, equally, the more they have enjoyed what they have seen during their visit, the more likely they are to buy a souvenir guide at the end of it. They will want their visit to continue long after it has ended, so to speak, and it is surely perverse to deny that this is anything but a good thing. The word 'participation' is used in much too narrow a sense by many museum professionals. Reading about what a museum has and what it is trying to do with it is just as much a form of participation as joining a museum art group or pressing a button to make a model work.

The argument about guide-books going out of date is easily answered. One should plan them with the intention that they will go out of date. Styles of printing, layout and photography change as rapidly as museological attitudes and techniques, and no museum with any pride in itself wants to be embarrassed by quantities of obviously obsolete material of this kind. To avoid such a situation, four rules should be followed:

1. Decide at the beginning that no booklet, leaflet or brochure of any kind is to be offered for sale for more than five years without revision and reprinting. Five years is an absolute maximum. Three, in most cases, is much more satisfactory.

2. Adopt a two-layer system for all guides, one for visitors who want a short, simple explanation of what a particular collection or the whole museum is about, and one for people who need something more detailed and elaborate and are prepared to pay for it.

3. Decide on a realistic pricing policy. This means that one should aim at covering one's costs and making a modest profit, *at the rates which exist when the books, booklets or leaflets are first published*. This means that, in an inflationary situation, the guides will seem better and better value each year, which will help to exhaust the stock. Do not – and this is extremely important – put up the price steadily in order to match a general change in market prices. This is unnecessarily sharp practice, as well as bad business.

4. Always go for a good designer. Not to do so is foolishly short-sighted and a waste of a good opportunity to improve the museum's image.

THE PUBLICATIONS COUNTER

In most museums throughout the world the publications counter is wretchedly poor, largely because the four rules given above have been disregarded, but also because publications, in the sense in which we have used the word, are considered a luxury. A large museum, with its full complement of scholars behind the scenes, all anxious to advance their professional and academic reputation, will always tend to think of two quite distinct kinds of 'publication'. One of these, the higher and really worthwhile category, consists of scholarly articles in learned journals, in which one anthropologist is writing for other anthropologists; and the other, which is not considered to be

in the same class at all, is 'popularisation', that is, attractive booklets and perhaps books for the general public. A few experts with very rare gifts and an unusual amount of daring and courage find it possible to produce both kinds of publication, but, in general, it appears to be necessary to concentrate on one or the other. It would not be entirely fair or accurate to say that the more scholars there are in the backrooms, the lower the standard and the smaller the range of on-the-counter publications is likely to be, but there is, most unfortunately, a good deal of truth in the argument.

Many museum publication displays are not at all what they appear to be at a first glance. An apparently well-stocked counter or bookstall may turn out on closer inspection to contain very few items for which the museum itself is responsible. What is being offered is not, in fact, an opportunity to participate in the museum's collections later and at one's leisure, but a kind of appendage, a bibliography, a course of reading. The museum has not attempted to grapple with its own follow-ups and popularisation problems. It has farmed them out to other writers and other publishers.

Extensive travel has convinced the present writer that the average level of publications produced by British museums, large and small, is far and away the highest in the world. This is mainly because British publications increasingly give the impression of having been planned with the needs and interests of the average visitor in mind. They do not look and read like crumbs from the scholar's table. It does not, therefore, seem necessary to apologise for including what might otherwise be thought to be an unreasonable proportion of British examples in a discussion of museum publications.

A particularly interesting range of material is available at one of the most important and adventurous of recent museums, the Ironbridge Gorge Museum, at the cradle of the Industrial Revolution, in Shropshire. The same designer, Robin Wade, has been used for the booklets as for the Museum itself and the style is immediately recognisable as belonging to this particular museum and to no other. Each item in the series has six pages and is by a different expert author. The illustrations have either been specially photographed for inclusion in the booklet or are reproductions of contem-

porary prints, painting and maps which have been very little published in recent times.

The intention is that visitors shall use these booklets as their personal guides through the area covered by the Museum and to particular sites and buildings within it. What is logically the first guide is called *Coalbrookdale: a walk through Coalbrookdale to explore its historic buildings and sites*. The first few lines will indicate the approach, the style and the level of information aimed at. There is a sketch map of the village on the facing page, and the figures in brackets refer to that.

Iron was made here more than four hundred years ago and casting continues to the present day. However, Coalbrookdale is known principally for the series of momentous innovations which took place in the eighteenth century and for its artwork in cast-iron in Victorian times. The Museum and Furnace site illustrate these aspects of Coalbrookdale history. This guide will show you Coalbrookdale as a unique iron-making community, the houses, churches and pubs which served it and how its landscape has changed over the last two hundred years.

Begin your walk at the Great Warehouse (1), built by the Coalbrookdale Company in the 1830s. The window lintels, frames and sills and the arch over the loading bay are of cast-iron. The clocktower, also of cast-iron, was added in 1843.

From the Great Warehouse pass under the railway arch and then turn right. The viaduct (2) carries the former Great Western Railway line which ran from Wellington and Shifnal to Buildwas Junction on the Severn Valley Railway. It was opened in 1864, carried passenger traffic until 1962 and is still used by coal and oil trains going to the Ironbridge power stations.

After going parallel with the railway viaduct for about 200 yards, turn left at the T-junction. On your left you will see how the fine houses once occupied by the iron-masters stand close to the cottages of their workpeople. The first large house, a five-bay structure with a balcony on the first floor, is Dale House (3), which appears on a plan of 1753 and engravings of 1758, but has since been much altered. In 1851 it was occupied by Mrs. Lucy Darby, her daughter and four servants. The next house, another building of five bays, with black quoins and an elegant classical doorway, is The Grange (4), which is probably the house begun by the first Abraham Darby but not completed until after he died in 1717.

And so on. The text is by the author of the authoritative book on the history of Coalbrookdale; and the simple, straightforward style of the booklet conceals a considerable amount of scholarship and research. What the reader is being told, in effect, is, 'You have come to have a look at Coalbrookdale and the Ironbridge Gorge Museum. You know something about the place already, but probably not a great deal, and you would like to get as much as you can out of your walk around the area. In the Visitor Centre, which we know you have already visited, because you bought this booklet there, we have tried to give you a general idea of why Coalbrookdale is such an interesting and important place. What you now have in your hand,

as you start your walk, is a set of bearings, to point your feet in the right direction and to make reasonably sure that you miss nothing of significance.'

After entering into the spirit of the place and absorbing some basic facts with the help of this first pamphlet, the visitor can broaden his knowledge with other titles in the series. Here is a selection, to show the care that has been taken to help people to use their time and their eyes to the best advantage:

The Iron Bridge: A short history of the first Iron Bridge in the world.
Blists Hill Open Air Museum: A guide to the site and exhibits.
The Unnatural History of Blists Hill: A guide to the plants and wildlife of the museum site.
The Tar Tunnel: A one thousand yard tunnel under Blists Hill.
David and Sampson: A pair of blast furnace blowing engines.
The Hay Inclined Plane: How tub boats were raised and lowered between the Shropshire Canal and Coalport Basin.

It is most unlikely that anyone will read all these booklets on the occasion of his first visit to the Ironbridge Museum, but, by making it cheaper to buy the whole set at once, the Museum feels, with good evidence, that people will come several times and, ideally, regularly. To encourage the museum habit still further, there is a free, four-page news-sheet, *The Ironbridge Quarterly*, which provides up-to-date information about the Museum and related matters in this form:

Work started in March on the second phase of restoring the Iron Bridge. The project, which will occupy two years, was begun in the Spring of 1972 and is designed to prevent further inward movement of the bridge abutments, which have been crushing the arch. Last year the first phase, consisting of the excavation of the north abutment and the insertion of reinforced concrete diaphragm walls to support the ashlar facing and new road deck, was completed by the Roads and Bridges Department of the Shropshire County Council. The work to be carried out

during the Summer of 1973 involves excavation of a trench in the bed of the river and the insertion of a reinforced concrete invert arch between the two abutments which will hold them in constant relationship to each other.

The contract for this second and major phase of the operation has been let to Tarmac Construction Ltd., who have already established site buildings on the adjacent railway station area and driven a test pile for one of the coffer dams which will provide a dry river bed for construction of the arch.

Work is due to be completed by the early Autumn, before the level of the River Severn rises to a height which might flood the workings.

In the Ironbridge context, this news item is a clear invitation to regular visitors to come and see the progress of this difficult and ingenious civil engineering job for themselves. The very existence of the newsletter implies a public which takes a continuous interest in the affairs of the Museum and which consequently deserves to be kept adequately and promptly informed of new developments.

A noteworthy venture is a concertina-type folder, called *The Young Visitor's Ironbridge*. This lavishly-illustrated publication, aimed at boys and girls below the age of thirteen, has proved extremely popular. The language is much simpler than that of the main series of booklets and the author makes even fewer assumptions about the amount of knowledge that visitors are likely to have.

Do you know why this bridge is so famous? [she asks her readers]. There are lots of bridges that are older or longer or higher. But this bridge was the first one in the whole world to be made of iron.

Two hundred and fifty years ago there was no bridge over the River Severn between Buildwas and Bridgnorth. It can be a very dangerous river to cross by boat. So some men who lived near Madeley decided to build themselves a bridge.

In those days bridges were built either of wood or stone. But because there were a lot of iron works on the banks of the river, the men of Madeley were used to making everything of iron.

Supplementing the booklets, there is a large selection of postcards illustrating

Ironbridge Gorge Museum, Shropshire, England. Layout of Museum area, as shown in booklet produced by the Museum.

the history of local industries and the exhibits at the Ironbridge Gorge Museum itself. The cards, which are of very high quality, are styled in the same way as the other printed material.

Many other museums in the world besides Ironbridge have excellent post-cards, introductory guides for children and adults, and newsletters. What makes Ironbridge exceptional at the moment is that from the beginning its publications have been planned as a whole, in the firm belief that to cater for real visitors and real needs is the way to encourage people to participate in what the museum is doing. Ironbridge, in other words, gives a very high priority to its publications and regards investment in them as not only wise but essential. This is a museum which, because it is spread over a considerable area of hilly countryside, must have physically active visitors. Since, however, it wishes to encourage mental as well as physical activity, it has committed itself from the beginning to a thoroughgoing programme in which education, publicity and signposting are inextricably and excellently mixed. The subject-matter of the museum – industrial archaeology – can be understood and enjoyed without years of scholarly preparation, and, presented as it is at Ironbridge, it is neither socially nor educationally divisive. Ironbridge has never made any secret of the fact that it needs large numbers of visitors in order to survive, and, with proper gratitude, it sets out to cater for them.

Other museums and other countries will say that Ironbridge is a new museum and that it has been exceptionally fortunate in many respects. To some extent this is true. A museum which is only five years old has had no time to encumber itself with obsolete publications and obsolete ideas. It has been free to decide to do things in the best possible way. In ten years' time, however, seasoned observers may say, Ironbridge will find itself faced with the usual problems of conservatism, inadequate finance, unenterprising staff and ageing plant and equipment. Let it enjoy its golden years while it can.

This attitude conveniently ignores the fact that some museum directors are more intelligent, more enterprising, more adaptable and more energetic than others. It also fails to acknowledge that some directors are frankly snobs, with little genuine interest in the ordinary members of the public, and that others have remarkably little taste or,

incredible as this may seem, visual awareness. If the average level of publications in British museums is exceptionally high, the basic reason for this may well be that the number of intellectual and social snobs running British museums is exceptionally small.

The correlation is an interesting one and worthy of further investigation. One of the least snobbish museum directors anywhere in the world is Mr Hamo Sassoon, who is in charge of Fort Jesus Museum at Mombasa, Kenya. Mr Sassoon is a white man in a black man's country. He has spent more than twenty-five years working in Africa and, like his wife, speaks fluent Swahili. His life is modest, but comfortable, and his chief wish is to avoid being identified with the colonial settler type, which he in no way resembles.

The museum staff consists of himself, an educational guide and various drivers and attendants. About 15,000 people visit the Museum each year, a high proportion of the adults coming from what are known as the ethnic group, that is, Indians and Arabs. Many of the local people are suspicious of the Fort, in the belief that it is haunted by evil spirits – it was used as a prison until comparatively recently – and the Director is trying hard to overcome their resistance.

The Curator is an unusually imaginative man, who believes in using the Museum's assets to full advantage. He labels the trees in the Museum precincts, in order to get visitors interested in them, and does the same for the different kinds of stone of which the Fort is built. With his visitors almost equally divided between Kenya residents and people who are in Kenya on holiday or on business, and with both groups representing a number of different races and nationalities, publications are not an easy matter. For the time being, Mr Sassoon has decided to use English as the language for both his *Guide*[9] and his *Newsletter*. It is interesting and surely significant that the tone and style of these two publications is very similar to that which is found at Ironbridge, although the appearance is entirely different. The Museum at Mombasa has not been able to employ a designer, the *Guide* is the work of a local printer whose skill and equipment are not the equal of those which are available to Ironbridge, and the *Newsletter* is issued in duplicated form. But, when one reads it, the Fort Jesus *Guide* feels like the Ironbridge *Guides* and its *Newslet-*

Fort Jesus Museum, Mombasa, Kenya. Men and a crane from the Kenya Navy salvaging old cannon for the Museum. This service was provided without cost to the Museum.

ter bears a strong resemblance to the one published at Ironbridge.

Throughout the month [the August 1974 issue begins] work has continued on the cleaning and painting of the twelve 18-pounder cannon in front of the museum. The cannon are having the rust, pitch, earth, etc., chipped and scraped off them. Then they are given a coat of red oxide and zinc chromate paint to inhibit rust and are finally painted matt black. The concrete and wood stands are also being repainted dark grey. Five more 18-pounders have been moved up from the sea-front to the Fort entrance, and some time soon the effort will have to be made to get them into the Fort. Once again we are indebted to Dhanjal Bros., the storm-drain contractors, who provided a large earth-mover to carry the cannon up from the sea-front.

The parallel with Ironbridge is exact, even to the mention of the name of the contractors. Elsewhere in this and other issues of the Fort Jesus *Newsletter* we find other evidence of an Ironbridge type of the extent to which local people are involving themselves in the work of the Museum and of the Museum's efforts to create links of all kinds with

This painting, with a proportionate distribution of orange, green and white colours, makes a balanced composition to which a fresh charm is added by the dramatic clouds in the sky, which is an outstanding feature of Bundi painting.

and

The Summer Elephant
Rajasthani School, Bundi, circa 1750 A.D.
Size 22.7 × 30 cm.

Against a bright yellow and pink background is seen resting an elephant, disconsolate from the scorching summer heat. Another elephant is wading through the lotus pool. One of the two elephants in the background is seen climbing the pink and blue rocks, apparently maddened by the blazing heat depicted effectively by the radiating golden sun and flaming red sky. A monkey is seen resting on the branch of a tree to the left, while another is running to seek shelter in the rocks.

A Braj Bhasha Kavita by the poet Karna, which very aptly compares the advent of summer to the onrush of an intoxicated elephant, can be freely translated as follows:

. . . behold the heat blazing like fire,
And the quarters overspread with dust,
The scorching summer comes storming in
Like the onrush of an intoxicated elephant.

English-speaking visitors can be nothing but grateful for the trouble the Trustees of the Museum have gone to on their behalf, but they may well wonder why similar efforts have not been made for Hindi-speakers. It is, of course, true that every large national museum is at the same time an international museum, but there are grave dangers in appearing to put the needs of overseas visitors first and those of one's own people a poor second. To this it can easily be objected that most Indians are neither able nor prepared to pay the kind of price for publications which Europeans and Americans find entirely normal and indeed very cheap, and that, if one wants to achieve a high standard in this branch of the museum's work, it is essential to go for

the community. At the annual Mombasa Show, the Museum was awarded Third Prize in the Government Class for its 1974 stand; a Son-et-Lumière performance took place in the Museum courtyard; members of the crew of HMS *Llandoef*, which was visiting Mombasa, spent four days moving four cannon at the Museum to new positions ('This sort of extra-curricular activity, although hard work, is popular with crews, who would otherwise have to spend their time scrubbing decks, or worse'); a retired schoolteacher has begun the difficult task of translating all the Museum labels into Swahili ('The sort of thing that has to be translated is "sherds of transitional Ming with floral designs in manganese and underglaze blue"'); a local resident is busy at an archaeological site connected with the Museum, numbering all the carved pieces of stone and plotting them on a plan of the tombs and mosque. All this is what 'involvement' and 'participation' can and often do mean in a developing country.

If the publications are a fair guide, many of the world's museums give the impression of believing that their best days were in the past and that there is no particular point in devoting much energy or imagination to the task of building bridges between yesterday and today. In such museums, one feels that the intellectual and emotional investment was made a long time ago and that it has not been topped up very much since. Their original public has

dwindled and disappeared, and its successor has not so far revealed itself. They create an atmosphere of nostalgia and faded glories.

Some of the older museums offer visitors wonderful and unrepeatable bargains at their publication counters, beautiful pictorial material and explanatory texts which were originally produced, many years ago, at a fraction of what today's cost would be. The superb reproductions of Indian paintings which are available at the Prince of Wales Museum in Bombay are a case in point. Once the present stock is exhausted, it is extremely unlikely that the Museum will be able to find the money to order and pay for a reprint, and, from one point of view, it is probably undesirable that a reprint should ever be undertaken. These excellent coloured reproductions, each enclosed in a pleasant folder, have explanatory texts in English. Here are two examples:

Hour of Cowdust
Rajasthani, Bundi, Mid 18th Century A.D.
Prince of Wales Museum, Bombay
Size: 28 × 18 cm.

In this scene the cowherd god, Krishna, accompanied by two friends, is returning home at eventide with his cattle. Two gopis are watching this event from the shaded balcony of a house. Brahma, Vishnu, Siva and Narada are standing in the background.

a good market, rather than a poor one. In any case, it will be said, those Indians who are genuinely interested can all read English.

One can sympathise with this view, while continuing to insist that it misses the main point altogether. Any museum which does not aim first at meeting the needs of the people who are citizens of the country puts itself in a very weak political position and, sooner or later, is certain to find funds diminishing and public support slipping away. Every possible effort must be made to persuade ordinary people to feel that the museum is their museum, planned, arranged and run in their interests. Élitist museums or tourist-worshipping museums are very vulnerable to attack from democratic and nationalist movements. The publications counter is the museum's barometer. It expresses the philosophy and ambitions of the management more clearly than anything else does, and it deserves extremely careful attention and a high priority for this reason. Whatever the difficulties, financial or otherwise, may be, some way has to be found of getting well-designed, attractive, intelligible material into the hands of people with low incomes at prices they can afford, which may turn out in the event to be no more than token prices. Once a visitor to a museum has bought something there, he is to some extent involved. He has proved his interest, both to the museum and to himself.

A NEW LOOK AT CARDS

It may be that the best kind of museum publication for mass consumption is not any kind of booklet or leaflet, but a card. Up to now, museums have always thought in terms of postcards, cards to be mailed to one's friends with good wishes. There is therefore a picture on one side, to provide something to interest the recipient of the card, and space for the address and a brief message on the other. The card has to be of a certain shape and maximum dimensions in order to meet the requirements of the postal authorities.

Nearly the same result can be achieved by giving the visitor something useful and attractive to take away with him. A number of the world's larger museums now make explanatory leaflets available in each section or gallery, describing briefly what it contains. The best leaflet of this kind is to be found in the Museum of the Louvre in Paris. The material for them has been prepared by the staff of the Department of Paintings and help with the design and the cost has been given by the public relations service of Kodak-Pathe.

The series has the general title, *The Louvre, Room by Room*, and is obtainable only inside the Museum, after one has paid the entrance fee. In that sense, it is not free. It is not available, even for payment, at the Museum's publications counter. Each leaflet has four large pages. The one for the Main Gallery, which is devoted to French paintings of the first half of the seventeenth century, will illustrate the method.

Page 1 gives a short history of the Gallery, outlines the development of French painting between 1600 and 1650 and lists the main works on display. Page 2 lists all fifty-three paintings in the Gallery, locates them on a plan and illustrates and describes nineteen of the more important. Page 4 has biographies of the painters represented.

It is difficult to see how the task could have been better accomplished, and one hopes that in time other sections of the Museum will follow the example of the Department of Painting.

But there is no need to think of cards in this limiting way at all. From personal experience and from conversations with one's friends, it is clear that a high proportion of museum cards are not bought for posting. They are added to the purchaser's own collection, partly as souvenirs and partly for later reference. With steadily increasing postal charges, this tendency is almost certain to increase. To produce and sell postcards which are never likely to be posted is an absurdity and a great waste of the valuable space on the back of the card. Once one begins to regard cards as information media, completely different possibilities begin to reveal themselves.

To begin with, it is, in a number of countries, possible to sell them more cheaply, since educational material carries a lower rate of tax than stationery. Secondly, by breaking away from the crippling restrictions imposed by postcard size, one can do a great deal more with the card. Even a 25 per cent increase in the surface area gives the designer far more scope to produce something which conveys a great deal of information and is visually attractive. Once the message-address stranglehold is removed, one can have pictures and text on both sides of the card. The whole card can be conceived as a unit.

Information cards of this type can be produced to meet the needs of different kinds of visitor. Some people may need, at least to begin with, nothing more than a route and set of signposts round the museum, and this can be achieved much more successfully with a card, which can be held easily and firmly in the hand, than with a leaflet or booklet. Others will want to know about particular rooms and particular exhibits. Children have to be given the information in one form and adults in another. Foreigners will be grateful for cards in their own languages.

The card system has great virtues, which are well suited to today's conditions. To begin with, it is extremely flexible. One can build up one's own loose-leaf guide at a very small cost for each unit, and one need buy only those parts of the guide which one finds interesting. From the museum's point of view, there is no need to regard the guide as final. Individual cards can be revised, added or deleted as required and bulk sales of particular cards are possible. By printing the cards from film, it is no longer necessary for the museum itself to hold a large stock. Repeat orders can be quickly executed by using the film which has been kept filed by the printer, a particularly useful advantage when, as will always happen, some cards prove more popular than others. And there is no difficulty in having some cards in colour and some in black and white, which is more difficult and more expensive in the case of a booklet-type guide or catalogue.

No museum has yet had the courage to embark on the card method in a thorough going fashion, but there have been a number of experiments in this direction which show what might be achieved by full-scale pioneering. In the German Democratic Republic, Dr Otfried Wagenbreth has prepared for the Ministry of Culture a set of cards on industrial monuments in the GDR. These are on sale in museums, and the whole of the back of the cards is taken up by text, indicating that they are intended to be kept and studied, not posted. But the cards are of conventional postcard size and appearance. They make no attempt to break new ground in the matter of design, and they are not identified with any particular museum, so they do not contribute to the creation of working links between a museum and its visitors.

The Metropolitan Museum of Art in New York has patented what it calls Supertexts. These have been developed in response to a survey 'that showed that more people buy postcards to keep than to send'. The invention consists of an adhesive label in two parts which reproduces the back of a normal postcard and which can be peeled off the backing with which it is supplied and re-fixed to a new-style postcard on sale in the Museum. These new cards have information printed all over the back and, of course, a picture on the front. Those who wish to keep the cards need not bother about Supertext, but, by using the Supertext label to cover up the information, a message and address can be written and the card posted 'The recipient reads the message, peels off the Supertext, and has an illustrated lecture on an object from the Museum selected by you.' 'Isn't it nice', says the envelope containing the Supertexts, 'when an invention pleases both the majority and the minority?' con-

veniently ignoring that sad fact that the invention is essentially a compromise and consequently a second-best. If postcards had never existed, no designer would set about producing museum information cards in this way. He would certainly see no need whatever to keep to the glossy, but expensive, pictures which have become traditional in the postcard world.

THE NEED FOR A RELEVANT AND ENTHUSIASTIC PUBLICATIONS POLICY

Much of the extreme conservatism shown by museums in the matter of publications is due to an anxiety to recoup the maximum possible investment on the original outlay. This can lead either to ridiculous over-ordering in the first place, so that ancient stock hangs around the museum's neck like an albatross, or to unwise reprinting of old publications without revision.

Metropolitan Museum, New York. 'Supertext' lecture card, 'Tutankhamun crowned by Amun'. The text on the back reads:

'Egyptian, XVIII Dynasty, ca. 1360 B.C.
Indurated limestone.
Height: 6 inches.

Smenkhkare was succeeded by Tutankhamun, possibly another half brother of Akhenaten. When he was a child of nine or ten, Tutankhamun was already married to the third of the Akhenaten daughters – a marriage that strengthened his claim to the throne. Tutankhamun's brief life ended before he was twenty. His modern fame rests chiefly on the magnificent treasure with which he was buried, discovered in 1922 by Lord Carnarvon and Howard Carter, but he had lived long enough to return to Thebes and restore the property of the god Amun.'

The rule should always be to under-order rather than over-order. If the publication is expensive but has become out of date in the course of time, no harm is done by allowing it to go out of print and to become a collector's item for the few people who really need it and who can buy it on the second-hand market. If it is cheap, it should, after five years, have sold in sufficient quantities to cover its first cost and to make a profit. Something else should then take its place, with today's and not yesterday's conditions in mind. There is only one thing more depressing than the antiquated stock one so often sees on museum sales counters, and that is a large selection of material from ordinary commercial sources but next to nothing from the museum itself. To get the visitors involved in its work and its aims, a museum must have its own publications and they must be good, which means that they must be both immediately interesting to a wide range of people and show considerable ingenuity in overcoming the cost problem. In the next ten years very few people indeed are going to buy the coffee-table books[10] and the large scholarly works that museums have, quite rightly, been so proud of producing during the past half-century. The meaning of the word 'publication' is undergoing a radical and much-needed change. Those museums which have given proper thought to the problem – and they are still, unfortunately, in the minority – are concerned to see that everything the museum 'publishes', that is, sets its name to and sells, shall in some way improve the public image of the museum, give visitors a worthwhile and tangible memento of their tour and, most important of all, summarise and emphasise a part of what the museum is trying to achieve. This is what is meant by 'having a publications policy'. Merely to have a selection of books, pamphlets and cards for sale is meaningless. It may yield cash, but it yields little else. Its cost-benefit value is very low.

This is not to say, however, that a museum cannot make money from selling well-designed, well-chosen articles. On the contrary, a well-run and imaginatively-stocked museum shop can be very profitable. It is essential, however, that its contents are fully relevant to the aims and atmosphere of the museum. To have a shop which exists solely to make money is a professional crime. One of the best examples of a properly planned and organised shop is at the RAF Museum, Hendon, near London. It offers a large range of kits for making model aircraft, an excellent selection of books on aviation and plenty of badge replicas and other souvenirs that come within a child's budget. The profits from the shop, which, like the Museum itself, has been open for only four years, have already paid for the recently-opened museum extension.

TAKING THE MUSEUM TO THE PUBLIC

'The public', says Maud Linder,[11] 'has become lazy', and she attributes this to what she calls 'the new forms of mass-communication'. Now there are only three new forms of mass-communication: the cinema, radio and television. Newspapers, books and magazines are old forms, and they, we are asked to

believe, did not make people lazy. We are faced, we are told, with a different, more insidious and more widespread form of mental and physical laziness and the major villains are broadcasting and the cinema. Before we accept or reject the argument, which is frequently heard, we should examine certain of its implications more carefully.

First, to what extent is it true that reading, theatre-going, concert-going and museum-going are 'active' pursuits, carried out by energetic people with minds of their own, and that watching films and television and listening to the radio are, by contrast, 'passive'? Why is it 'passive' to play records or tapes of music in one's own home, but 'active' to sit in a concert hall or an opera house? The answer cannot be that one involves personal choice and effort and the other does not, since at some point a book or a record or a magazine has to be selected and paid for, an act which requires at least as much

effort as buying a theatre ticket. Having made the purchase, one usually sits down to enjoy it, and whether sitting down in public is more energetic and praiseworthy than sitting down in private can only be a matter of opinion. A play in a theatre makes no greater demands on an audience than a play on television. For what reason, then, is the television viewer guilty of laziness, and the theatre-goer innocent? What does Maud Linder really mean?

She might possibly mean that a person who makes a journey to see something is to be considered more worthy than someone who sits at home and waits for the play, the concert, the football match, or whatever it may be to come to him, that the man or woman who buys a book in a bookshop is a better person than one who orders it by post. This attitude would be extremely difficult to defend, and it is much more likely that, if pushed to explain exactly what she had in mind when she accused

North of England Open-Air Museum, Beamish. (left) *Front of publicity leaflet.* (right) *Back of publicity leaflet.*

Metropolitan Museum, New York. A magazine advertisement for the Museum Shop.

the public of being lazy, she would say it was not that they exercised their minds at home instead of in a public place, which would be unexceptionable, but that, faced with an ample supply of extremely undemanding television programmes and background radio music, they had become content not to use their minds at all. Given the same opportunities, the Victorians would almost certainly have behaved in exactly the same way.

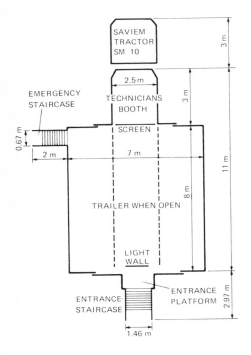

Floor plan of the Linder Museobus.

The process feeds on itself, of course. Using one's mind is a habit and, if one is accustomed to live in a half-awake condition, a fairly powerful stimulus is needed if the dozing intelligence and emotions are to be jerked into activity. This can only be achieved if the stimulus and the person who is destined to receive it are brought into physical contact. It is quite impossible if they are a mile, five miles, ten miles apart.

The mobile museum, in its many forms, has been created on the assumption that Mahomet either will not or cannot come to the mountain and that, short of admitting total and permanent

defeat, the only course of action to adopt is to take the mountain to Mahomet and see what happens. The Linder museobus, designed to present original paintings, did precisely this. 'We are living', wrote Mrs Linder, 'in a time of promotion, advertising, ostentation, large-scale posters, blaring sounds and loud colours. Amid these various claims on people's attention, if we are to stand any chance of getting them to appreciate art, the first step must be to show it to them.'

The Linder vehicle is ingenious. The side walls and the roof are telescopic, extending by means of hydraulic jacks. On the road, the width is 2.5 metres, but, for exhibition purposes, it becomes 7 metres. This gives visitors a feeling of space and the area, 56 square metres, is large enough to allow the paintings to be viewed from a proper distance. The floor is carpeted and the walls are covered with woven material, with aluminium edgings. The interior is that of a pleasant room, not of a bus or lorry. There is a wide entrance stairway, which also helps to counteract any feeling of entering a caravan or trailer.

Great pains have been taken to make sure that the works of art are safe while they are in the Museobus. All the materials used are either non-inflammable or have been fire-proofed. The electrical equipment is designed and built to the highest standards of security, with very sensitive circuit-breakers, should anything go wrong. There is an air-conditioning system and double-wall thermal insulation to keep the temperature and humidity constant and at safe levels. In transit, the paintings are in crates, securely fastened to copper rings in the centre of the bus.

While the bus is on the road, it is accompanied by two armed policemen on motorcycles; when it is parked, two policemen, also armed, act as guards. 'So far as we know,' says Mrs Linder with justifiable pride, 'no museum is better guarded.' The technical precautions are equally impressive. Each picture has its own alarm signal, which is set off by any attempt at theft. There are, of course, fire-extinguishers and an emergency exit. A gauge connected to the dashboard monitors the pressure of all the tyres, and there is an electric decelerator, in case the brakes should fail.

It is possible to show thirty average-sized canvases on the walls and extra space can be provided if necessary by fixing screens running at right angles to

the walls. Pictures can be hung easily, securely and quickly on a rail with sliding rings, which runs right round the inside of the room. Either direct or indirect lighting is available, from spotlights fixed to tracks built into the ceiling. Power points in the floor allow different lighting effects, which are particularly useful for sculpture exhibitions, when it is often an advantage to be able to have play of light and shade. Films and slides are back-projected from the technician's booth, and there are also facilities for background music.

The Museobus tours France and sets up shop in provincial towns for two, three or four days. The first two exhibitions, paintings by Georges Rouault and Fernand Léger, were visited by an average of more than a thousand people[12] a day, a third of whom said they had never been inside a museum or an art gallery. 'Most of them', reported Mrs Linder, 'saw the film about the painter which we showed, and listened with a healthy curiosity to the explanations given by the Curator or the museum guides.'

The Linder Museobus is very probably the best equipped in the world. It is equally probably the most expensive. To say, however, that it is the best is not necessarily true, because 'best' is not an absolute term. One has to ask 'best under what conditions?' The Linder bus was designed to operate on good European roads, at relatively short distances from its base and from skilled mechanical attention, should it break down, and in a country where police protection was not difficult to arrange. None of these advantages would apply in most of, say, Brazil, India or Tanzania. In areas such as these, something altogether more rugged, more basic and more self-contained is required, if a mobile museum service is to operate with any chance of success. And, it may be added, something a good deal cheaper. The Linder mobile museum sets a standard which all museums, certainly all art museums, can usefully bear in mind and at which, within their own local limitations, they can aim. But few are able even to dream of obtaining the money with which to buy and equip a travelling museum of this kind.

The Linder bus, one has to realise, had to be expensive if it was to exist at all, because of the type of museum-merchandise it was carrying. A load of thirty paintings by Rouault and Léger represents several hundreds of thousands of dollars, which the museum would be unwilling to lose or have damaged. If such an exhibition is to be moved about at all, it must travel in safety, and this requires all the technical refinements which have been described above. An exhibition of reproductions would obviously not demand the same super-careful treatment. Nor, too, would a display of models, archaeological specimens, simple scientific equipment or photographs. The technical facilities one needs depend to a large extent on the fragility, expend-ability and, from a criminal's point of view, desirability of what one is offer-ing.

There are those, without doubt, who would consider it eccentric and possibly perverse to want to take such valuable material from town to town around France, or any other country, in the hope that people might be interested to see it. As a missionary endeavour, it cer-tainly has its curious aspects, but to concentrate on this is to miss the point altogether. A museum is not an event: the arrival of this mobile treasure-house in a provincial town is very much an event and something which is almost certain to create, if not a sensation, at least a major talking-point. If an exhibi-tion is in town for only two days, one had better go and see it quickly. If it is permanently available, there is always tomorrow and so, eventually, one never goes at all.

There could hardly be a greater con-trast between the lavishly equipped Linder bus and the mobile museum run by the Indian Museum in Calcutta. This was established in 1969 and since

then it has travelled all over India, except in the extreme south, for the most part over roads which bear no comparison with those in France. It is often away from its base for as long as five months at a time, with the Museum's Assistant Curators looking after it for a month on a rota. This single-decker vehicle, with a specially-built body, has done its work very well. It travels with a driver/mechanic, two assistants and a guide-lecturer, who is as well qualified as those at the Museum in Calcutta.

The procedure is always to prepare a journey in advance by getting names of schools and colleges from the local Inspector of Schools. The Museum then writes to the head of each of these establishments, offering the services of the Mobile Museum and asking if ac-commodation for the staff could be pro-vided. This accommodation is usually of a very basic kind. The guide-lecturer and his colleagues are given a daily allowance of money for food while they are away from home and it is up to them to make the best bargain they can.

No charge is made for the Museum. If electricity is available, the school is asked to provide it free; but if not, the bus has its own generator. The unit carries twenty-eight small cases, each containing a diorama illustrating the development of man from the earliest times until the eighteenth century. The Museum in Calcutta holds a stock of forty-five of these dioramas, all made by the modeller there, and they are inter-changed as necessary, to suit the area and the people the bus will be visiting.

Films are also shown, with such titles as *A Century of Indian Archaeology*, *The Life of Snakes* and *The Dances of South-ern India*. The guide has a book in which visitors record their reactions to exhibits on the bus. Those who cannot read or write record their impressions on a tape-recorder, which they enjoy doing. A selection of publications of various kinds is also carried.

There is a fundamental difference between the people who visit the Indian Museum bus and the Linder bus. The French people could visit an ordinary museum or art gallery but have chosen not to; the Indians, for the most part, live too far from a major city or are too poor to be able to afford a visit. The first might perhaps be called lazy, the second certainly could not.

During the past twenty years, mobile museums have been introduced, with varying degrees of success, in many countries. When they have done badly, the reason has not been far to seek; the guide-lecturer, curator, or whatever he may happen to be called, has had the wrong temperament and personality for the job. The person who does well is always enthusiastic, friendly and as anxious to learn as to teach. He must, of course, have a good knowledge of whatever material he may be taking with him in the bus, but his prime task is to get people interested, to draw them out to open up new horizons for them. This is not the traditional blend of talents required in a museum curator and it is consequently not surprising that really good staff for a mobile unit are hard to find, especially since their life is likely to contain quite a lot of dis-comfort. Men and women who do this very demanding work, or who have done it, often reveal that the experience has changed their whole attitude to-wards museums, museum priorities and museum skills. Most museological training begins with the object and moves slowly and unsteadily from it to the needs and characteristics of those who, as visitors to the museum, are likely to look at the object. The staff of a mobile museum have to work in a pre-cisely opposite direction, by getting on terms with the visitors first and then bringing the objects into a human con-

Queue waiting to see the Mobile Museum on location from the Indian Museum, Calcutta. The photograph shows how the show-cases on the side of the vehicle greatly increase the number of people who can visit the Mobile Museum each day.

text, which any good teacher, whether of adults or children, will always do.

If it were possible to organise an international conference of people with considerable experience in running mobile museums, one can be fairly sure that there would be considerable agreement on aims, techniques and equipment. The successful staff would also be seen to possess remarkably similar characteristics, no matter which countries they might come from. Where differences of opinion did occur, these would relate mainly to views on the urgency and importance of the task to be done. The representatives of the advanced countries would certainly appear enthusiastic, but they would probably not be prepared to say categorically that mobile museums were essential for national progress. They would see them as useful, rather than vital. The delegates from the developing countries, on the other hand, would mostly feel inclined, one suspects, to echo the wise words[13] of Mr R. M. Chakraborti, who is responsible for the mobile science exhibitions of the Visvesvaraya Industrial and Technical Museum, at Bangalore:

In India the villages contain 75 per cent of the total population. To meet their needs, to make them conscious of science and technology and of their duty towards mankind, to the environment, the land, health, family institutions, society, education, employment – all influenced by science and technology – special methods are required. The city dweller does not feel lost among the many changes taking place about him; he is directly or indirectly involved. Moreover, various agencies are engaged in bringing new knowledge and understanding to city dwellers.

The picture is completely different in the villages. There, people are shielded from all these influences, and their prevailing attitude towards their environment is non-scientific. They are never brought to imagine that a scientific temperament is essential to them. Neither do schools deal with this problem, nor is there any agency seriously interested in wiping out the ignorance of villagers. Dynamic science education, in a proper perspective, may be the only solution. Since the considerable number of illiterates makes the problem more acute, no formal education can change the situation overnight.

But a quick, interesting new method can solve the difficulty. Plenty of imported audio visual systems already exist, but unfortunately they are not tailored for the rural population of our country. To bring the rural population to the city for such education would in no way be possible or advisable.

The Visvesvaraya Industrial and Technical Museum has consequently developed science exhibitions on wheels which are taken to the places where they are most needed. Before discussing the techniques that are used in creating and using these exhibitions, which are one of the most important educational experiments in Asia or, for that matter, anywhere in the world, it may be helpful to examine the word 'illiterate' more closely. Mr Chakraborti clearly means it to indicate people who cannot read, but, in museum and educational terms, it can have a much wider significance. There are, for example, historical illiterates, who have no feeling for the past and who are without the bearings needed to find their way through the jungle of events which took place before they were born; artistic illiterates, who are not conscious of the fact that the artist has his own way of seeing and understanding the world around him; and, of course, scientific illiterates, who are unaware of the possibilities of applying a methodical, experimental, number-based approach to the solution of human problems. Each of these three types of illiterate – and there are many more – may need to have instructional material brought to them in the places where they are normally to be found, if there is to be any hope at all of cracking the thick crust of prejudice and indifference which lies on top of their intelligence and potentialities. Although on the surface these problems may appear very different, the Bangalore mobile science units and the Linder art bus are attempting to deal with what is fundamentally the same situation, people who are greatly handicapped by the social environment in which they live. It is precisely the situation of the Mexico City slum-dwellers, to which reference has been made earlier.

The Bangalore Mobile Science Exhibition presents themes which can be easily shown to be relevant to lives of village people. This means, for the most part, that they are confined to hygiene, in its various aspects, and to

agriculture. 'The exhibits', says Mr Chakraborti, 'should be simple, concise, impressive and coherent. They must be easily understood and impress the memory.' To achieve this, extensive use is made of what are called 'participatory exhibits', that is, models which visitors can work for themselves. These have to be simple and strong, 'so that the ordinary man may find pleasure in playing with them', without wrecking them. The exhibits are in standard-sized cabinets, $990 \times 732 \times 298$ mm., and the finishes and materials are chosen to minimise maintenance.

The unit is in two parts, a lorry carrying the crew, technical equipment and certain stores, and a trailer, for the exhibition. The design of the trailer is ingenious, with an outside flap running the entire length, so that a complete row of exhibits can be viewed from outside by people standing on the ground. This greatly increases the number of persons who can be usefully accommodated in the area of the trailer at any one time. Inside the van, adequate ventilation is maintained by means of a forced-air fan.

The Bangalore system is to send a unit out on sixty-day tours, allowing a three-to five-day stop at each place. The programme is arranged, so far as possible, in co-operation with the centres to be visited. A questionnaire, dealing with specific requirements, and an illustrated pamphlet explaining the aim of the tour and briefly describing the exhibits are sent to all the schools in the area which is to be visited. The final itinerary is drawn up only when the returned questionnaires have been examined and when the extent of local support can be estimated with some accuracy. Once the route and the time-table are fixed, schools and local authorities are notified and posters about the exhibition are sent out in advance. When the exhibition reaches the site, the trailer unit tours the area with a public address system to give more details of what is being offered. Advertisements are also put in local newspapers.

The team of four consists of a guide-lecturer, an attendant, a driver and a technician/mechanic. The guide-lecturer, who is usually a young science graduate, is the team-leader and belongs to the permanent staff of the Museum. Before the exhibition is opened, he picks a group of particularly interested boys or girls from the host school to work as demonstrators and to explain the exhibits to visitors. From that point on, the entire proceedings are managed by these students, with the guide-lecturer doing little more than act as a supervisor. The amateur guides, it has been found, go to great pains to do the job well and often become the nucleus of science clubs which are established afterwards in the schools.

At Dar-es-Salaam the Education Officer at the National Museum goes out with the Mobile Museum himself, together with an assistant and a driver. He is a teacher by training and he often goes to teachers' seminars in different parts of Tanzania to explain how the Museum can help them. The Mobile Museum is no more than an addition to his other extra-mural duties. The vehicle which the Museum owns and runs for this purpose is large, unwieldy and unsuited to the bad roads over which it is forced to travel. It is hoped to replace it by one or two Land Rovers, which would cope much more satisfactorily with the terrain. The kind of display the Museum takes out can be mounted on panels and a huge vehicle is not necessary for this. The National Museum has not reached the point at which it feels it could reasonably allocate a large part of its resources to buying and operating a mobile unit of the Bangalore type, and in India, indeed, these elaborate and expensive facilities have been possible only because of financial support from industry. In any case, the National Museum's mobile unit is concerned with archaeology, ethnology and folklore, not with science. Tanzania does not yet have a museum of science and technology, although one is planned for Morogoro, 120 miles from Dar-es-Salaam, in an area which contains mining and sugar plantations. There is also the possibility of setting up a Museum of Natural History. It should be pointed out in this connection that a Museum of Science and Technology would, under present arrangements, be somewhat strangely under the control of the Department of Antiquities, not of the National Museum, so that any mobile unit which might be formed would have to develop its own methods and traditions, and select and train its own specialist personnel. It could not necessarily depend on the experience so far gained by the National Museum's team.

No country has anything like the number and variety of mobile museums that are to be found in the United States. To own one is almost a status

necessity for any museum with any claims to be important or up-to-date. Not to have one is almost to confess that one is failing to serve the area in a way that the community has a right to expect. It is not altogether easy to understand why this situation should have arisen. Americans, of all ages and social classes, are the most mobile people on earth, with practically no difficulties in going anywhere they feel inclined to go. A mobile museum is not an essential for them in the way it is for people living in rural Mexico or India. Yet they feel they must have them, and even a selection of what is available makes impressive reading.

There are a considerable number of mobile art exhibitions, some operated by individual museums, some by foundations and societies, and some by a particular State. The City of Concord in California has its Mobile Muse; the Virginia Museum of Fine Arts has provided itself, on a lavish scale, with Artmobiles I, II, III and IV; Michigan State Council on the Arts has invested in an Artrain, based on Detroit; the State of Hawaii's Department of Education sponsors Artmobile Hawaii Ho'onani; and the Wichita Art Museum Members' Foundation finances the Mobile Gallery.

In the field of Mobile Art Workshops, as distinct from Mobile Art Museums, one could mention Van Art (Columbus Gallery of Fine Arts); the Roving Art Cart (City of Pittsburgh); Color Wheels (Albright-Knox Art Gallery, Buffalo); Trip-Out Truck (M. H. de Young Memorial Center, San Francisco); and the more soberly named Arts Resource Transportation Service (South Carolina Arts Commission).

There are many History Mobiles both in the United States and in Canada, often with exotic or impressive names: the Louisiana Arts Traveler (Louisiana State Museum, New Orleans); the Canal Packet (Canal Museum, Syracuse); The Rolling Stock (Manitoba Museum of Man and Nature); the Northeast Wyoming Mobile History Laboratory; the Children's Traveling Unit (Museum of New Mexico, Santa Fé).

Science Mobiles in America are, if not exactly two-a-penny, at least very common in North America. The American Museum of Atomic Energy at Oak Ridge, Tennessee has its Mobile Exhibit Hall; the Science Museum of Virginia its Trans-Science; the Royal

Ontario Museum, Toronto, its Museumobile; and the Buffalo Museum of Science its Haul of Science.

The American mobile museums cover the full range of museum specialities and activities, from the California State Centennial Commission's Historical Coach to the Cleveland Museum of Natural History's Travelling Trailside Museum, and from the Senior Citizens' Van of the Columbus Gallery of Fine Arts to the Yellow Submarine of the Children's Museum, Nashville, Tennessee.

Why, one might reasonably ask, are the Americans so obviously enthusiastic about mobile museums, when it is so easy for Americans to visit the mother-museum from which the mobile museum comes? Five answers suggest themselves:

1. A mobile museum is often the gift of a wealthy individual, the Friends of the Museum or an industrial or commercial concern. It is a financially self-contained package, which can be paid for as a complete unit and readily identified with the donors.
2. A mobile museum is a convenient and impressive way of showing the flag, the museum's flag. It is an excellent, practical and dividend-earning form of investment.
3. A mobile museum suggests that the museum is actively doing something, striving to make itself known and useful to the people at large.
4. A mobile museum is a very handy way of making use of surplus exhibition material that one might otherwise not know what to do with and of occupying designers and technicians in their odd spare moments.
5. A mobile exhibition is an excellent way of training staff, especially young people, to understand what the public is really like. It is a form of public relations which can modify the expert's attitudes considerably.

North America is, of course, a continent which expects salesmanship and holds salesmen in considerable esteem. An institution which holds back from advertising and selling its wares by all possible means is clearly not in the first rank, or even worthy of attention at all. By going out to meet the customers with a load of samples and promotional material, the mobile museum is engaging in a very normal and natural American activity. It is as reasonable and welcome to find a mobile museum outside a school or in a shopping centre as to see an ice-cream van parked there. A mobile museum is no more than an efficient and convenient way of carrying one's goods around and displaying them. It avoids the problems of finding and paying for premises, unpacking and packing exhibits and arranging lighting, which are inevitable if one sets about the business in any other way.

THE REAL SIGNIFICANCE OF MOBILE MUSEUMS

The main importance of a mobile museum, it may be suggested, is not technical or logistic. Nor is the mobile museum itself the major innovation. What matters most is the effect such a unit has on the museum organisation which sponsors and organises it. Once the decision has been taken to embark on a venture of this kind, nothing can be the same again. The museum has begun to market itself and to interest itself in marketing techniques. Priority has been given to the customers, not to the collections, and this must influence the attitudes of the base-museum to which the mobile museum is attached.

This is well illustrated by the way in which the Ontario Science Centre has developed. The Centre, which has the good fortune to be housed in a new and architecturally brilliant building, probably has a higher proportion of exhibits which allow visitors to participate than any other museum in the world. Over the years, the staff have become accustomed to designing material which would stand up to almost continuous manipulation. They have developed what amounts to an instinct for thinking in terms of exhibits which involve visitors in some way.

The Centre's mobile unit is a natural extension of this. It forms part of what is known as the Outreach programme, to make the museum available to the whole province of Ontario. A large trailer takes everything required to outlying cities. At Sault Ste. Marie in the autumn of 1975, for example, the exhibits attracted 40,000 visitors in sixteen days. The project involved thirty members of the staff going to Sault for a few days each, to demonstrate the exhibits, show films, put on scientific demonstrations and visit all the schools in the neighbourhood. In order to do

this, they were required to be many-sided people – practical, resourceful, knowledgeable; and anxious and able to communicate the ideas the Centre stood for.

Once the position has been reached when, in any given country, many teams of experts – agricultural experts, literacy experts, birth-control experts, health experts, arts and crafts experts and museum experts – are moving about from place to place, trying to interest people in new ideas and to change their habits, expectations and ambitions, a substantial and influential new class of teachers has been created, all with similar techniques and with the same fundamental aim, to break down prejudice and widen horizons. Those who are successful in such work are likely to have similar temperaments and skills, and to share similar satisfactions and frustrations, no matter what their speciality may be. They can all learn from one another. The staff of a mobile museum is simply one group of modern-type educators among many.

All the developing countries have such people and need many more. They are essentially crusaders, willing to take advantage of any occasion which looks promising. The staff of the Nairobi National Park go to all agricultural shows of any size and particularly to the Nairobi Show in September, where they have a permanent stand. At these shows they present photographs, three-dimensional exhibits and films about the Parks, their locations and what can be seen in them. They often take along, too, live creatures from the Animal Orphanage. It is quite possible that a mobile museum would be a more sensible way of accomplishing most of this, although the live animals might not be altogether easy to display, but there is an equally strong argument for having a stand, like everyone else at the Show, in order to make the point that the National Parks are a normal part of the life of Kenya.

The advocates of mobile museums base their case on one of two beliefs:

1. that the people reached by the mobile museum are extremely unlikely to be reached in any other way and that the chances of the majority of these people even being able or willing to visit an ordinary kind of museum are remote;
2. that the primary function of a mobile museum is evangelistic,

and that, once the appetite for museum visiting has been stimulated in this way, the number of museum visitors will increase.

On the evidence that we have so far, (1) seems the more probable. In all countries and among all age-groups, people do what their friends and neighbours do, and it requires courage, individuality and strength of character of a very high order to acquire habits which are abnormal in the social and family group to which one belongs. To suppose that the citizens of Clochemerle would decide to make for the nearest large town *en masse* and spend Saturday morning at the art gallery there, after the visit of the Linder Museobus, seems to contain a fair amount of wishful thinking. It is possible that one or two might do this, but if they should happen to take such a bold step they would almost certainly keep it hidden from their friends, because of a fear that it might be considered to be some kind of cultural treason, a mark of disloyalty to one's group, a friendly foray into enemy territory.

Some of the most honest thinking on this subject has been carried out, not by museums, but by design centres. What has been discovered and discussed there is very relevant and helpful to museum work.

The International Design Centre in West Berlin was opened in the spring of 1970 and by the end of that year the Director, François Burckhardt, and his colleagues were finding themselves increasingly dissatisfied with what they were doing. Burckhardt is a Swiss architect, with a strong sense of social purpose. Before coming to Berlin he had been doing a similar job in Hamburg and, as a non-German, he probably saw and understood certain features of German society with exceptional clarity. The Berlin Design Centre is at the end of the Budapester Strasse, close to the most fashionable of Berlin's streets, the Kurfürstendamm. It is the area of expensive restaurants, cafés and shops and everything about it suggests money and luxury. This image inevitably rubs off on the Design Centre, exactly as it does on the London Design Centre, which is in a very similar kind of district. Mr Burckhardt's Design Centre became, from the beginning, a meeting place for well-to-do people and their sons and daughters, with a few visiting foreigners thrown in to lighten the mix.

The exhibitions were imaginatively planned and well carried out: 'Adventure Playgrounds'; 'Advertising'; 'Eating at Work'; 'Fashion and Fashions'; 'Good Design'—an exhibition of the year's prize-winning awards—and they attracted considerable numbers of visitors. But, as the staff at the Centre were well aware, the people who came tended to be all of the same type and quite unmistakably from the top quarter of the Berlin population. The members of the working class recognised this and stayed away. It was not their kind of place, just as the Guggenheim Museum in New York and Dumbarton Oaks in Washington are not their kind of place.

Mr Burckhardt was far from happy about this. It was not by any means that the Centre was ignored or underused. A steady 500 people a week came in to ask for advice on colours, materials, catalogues, room design and furniture; the exhibitions were much frequented and apparently well liked; the evening discussions received excellent support. But it was all bourgeois-talking-to-bourgeois, yet another club and pastime for the Berlin middle class. The people who most needed help, advice and encouragement, the families on the city's huge working-class apartment estates, never came near. The Centre was in the wrong place to be able to do any real good.

Since then, experimental advice-centres have been set up in the lower-income areas of Berlin, greatly helped by the contacts that had already been made by a remarkable and subsequently remarkably successful designer of children's play equipment, who had been working in association with the Centre. These experiments have proved, like very similar efforts in Stockholm, that, when educational work is carried on where the people concerned live, it immediately acquires an extra dimension. If someone comes to the Centre for advice and asks what colours he should use to make a small room look and feel bigger, one can create a great deal more confidence and talk better sense if one is in a position to offer then and there to come to inspect the room and to give one's advice on the spot. To anyone living in one of Berlin's working-class blocks, any suggestions made in the Budapester Strasse would be almost certain to sound remote, cold and lacking in interest, always assuming that such an enquirer had been able to summon up the courage to enter the Design Centre in the first place, which is unlikely.

To a great extent, the problem of contact and understanding between members of different cultural groups is linguistic. The barrier is not so much one of ideas and knowledge as one of finding a language and a pattern of language which the two people have in common, and, if this barrier is to be broken down, or at least reduced to a manageable height, an exceptional degree of patience, tolerance and adaptability is required on the part of the adviser and helper, as well as unfailing missionary zeal. Some experts, whether they are employed by museums or design centres, are quite incapable of this, and they need to be kept well away from where-the-customers-live work.

What is quite wrong, however, is to regard the mobile unit or the small branch centre as a poor second-best. This type of work demands immense skill of a special kind and there is no point in regarding the outposts as mere temporary affairs. If any progress at all is to be made with the appallingly difficult task of creating even the beginnings of a widely-shared culture, at least some of those who regard themselves as the agents of culture will have to be prepared to leave the comfort and delights of a headquarters existence and do what missionaries have always seen as an essential feature of their task, live among the people. The short-stay missionary achieves little of any value, whether he comes with a Bible or a mobile museum, unless, as in the case of the mobile museums at Bangalore and Cairo, he is able to leave others behind to continue and consolidate his work. To imagine that because two thousand small-towners have passed through one's mobile art gallery in two days their lives and attitudes will be permanently changed for the better is a dangerous illusion. Most of the world's cultural outposts will require to be permanently manned.

There is, of course, absolutely no obligation for a museum or any other kind of cultural or educational institution to concern itself with more than a small fraction of the population. Some things may always be destined to be only for minority consumption. All one is entitled to demand is honesty of purpose. If money, time and people are invested in neighbourhood museums, mobile museums or any other form of decentralisation, those responsible for such enterprises should understand and say clearly what the purpose of such pioneering is. 'To be in the fashion' or 'to appear democratic' are not adequate or politically wise answers.

One should probably make a distinction between those kinds of museum or museum activity which can help a person to advance in his career, and those which are, in so far as such a thing is possible, purely cultural—between, in other words, the vocational and the non-vocational. There is no doubt that many, perhaps a great many, boys and girls have been introduced to a completely new world as a result of the pioneering activities of the mobile science units and science clubs in the developing countries, and one can be quite sure that, with their imagination and their ambition fired in this way, they have been prepared to make every possible effort to read, to visit museums in large cities and to continue their education in order to qualify for a scientific career. What seems less probable is that more than a very small number of the people who are introduced to archaeology, ethnography or art in this way will be motivated to the same extent. This is not in the least to say that science museums are more worthwhile than art museums. It is simply to point out that the science missionaries may have an easier task than the art missionaries when it is a matter of pushing interest and awareness further down into the social structure.

DISPLAYS IN NON-MUSEUM
SETTINGS

But the concept of mobility includes much more than the use of trailers and lorries to move museum displays into the countryside. It rests on a belief that the museum ought to be where the people are, and that it should adapt itself to the times at which its potential customers are free. In the developed countries, museums have not, for the most part, made any significant effort to follow the migration to the suburbs and to the community areas even further afield. Libraries and churches have done a good deal better. Museum opening-hours, too, tend to be arranged to suit the convenience of the staff and the administration, not of the public. To be open only from 10 to 5 from Monday to Friday, when most people are at work, is to perform a public service in a very inadequate and unimaginative manner. In many places, 2 to 9 would be more realistic and more appreciated.

As matters stand, the mobile museum is often doing little more than trying to make up for the inadequacies of the big-city museum to which it belongs. It is the small boat sent out from the great luxury liner which lies permanently moored in port, with its engines broken down.

There is a school of thought which holds that, in cultural matters, infiltration is likely to be more successful than frontal attack. With this in mind, many art museums throughout the world have developed the habit of displaying parts of their collections in non-museum settings, offices, factories, shops and restaurants. It is difficult to say whether this policy has been suc-

cessful or not. If it is carried out consistently and over a long period, it may well gradually condition people to accept as normal what was originally regarded as abnormal, disturbing or outrageous, and if acceptance is defined as the ability not to notice, the policy has presumably justified itself. But the really great artistic achievement never loses its power to surprise and to excite. When the Pirelli building in Milan or the International Airport at Washington were first completed, they stood out immediately and forcefully from a mass of contemporary mediocrity. They still do. They have never become buildings which have ceased to attract attention. One fears, however, that at least 99 per cent of the works of art which find their way into factories or banks are not of this quality and that after a short time they become no more than part of the furnishings.

This, say enthusiasts for this kind of display, is not the point. If twenty women, doing boring, repetitive work in a factory, look up from time to time at a painting fixed so as to be in their line of vision, and if they do this every day, five days a week, for two months, the picture must have had some effect on them. They may:

(a) have found the picture an agreeable change from a girder or an overhead heater;
(b) have enjoyed the colours, without bothering themselves overmuch about the details of the picture;
(c) have developed a certain fondness and friendliness towards it, much as a prisoner does for the bird that perches outside the bars of his cell each day, or the mouse which appears through a hole in the wall.

Subconsciously, and without making any effort, they may have absorbed the picture's shapes, tonal range, and composition. The picture has, in other words, not left them as it found them. No intellectual activity need have taken place. The factory workers or the clerks in the bank can finish the week as they begin it, with no idea of the name of the painter or of when and where he lived. They may not have liked the painting. But if it is something which they would otherwise have been unlikely to see, and

Bristol Brass Rubbing Centre

A FASCINATING OPPORTUNITY: you can choose from a selection of exact replicas all moulded from original brasses in churches in the Bristol area. They include merchants and mayors of medieval Bristol and brasses selected from the surrounding area to give a comprehensive collection showing the development of armour and fashion. The brasses are made by specialists who supply replicas to churches for use by brass rubbers.

TAKE HOME YOUR OWN RUBBING: you can rub any of the brasses on show. They make beautiful wall hangings and gifts.

ADMISSION IS FREE! you need no experience we will show you how and provide all the materials needed. A charge is made for every rubbing which includes the cost of materials and a royalty to the churches.

ILLUSTRATION: the brass to Thomas the Magnificent, 10th Lord Berkeley, 1392.

mon - sat 10 am - 5.30 pm
st nicholas church
and city museum
city centre - Bristol

St Nicholas Church Museum, Bristol, England. Bristol Brass Rubbing Centre. Front of leaflet.

if, under no conceivable circumstances, could they have had anything like it on the walls of their own homes, their experience has been to that extent broadened and the picture that replaces the first one will not be received in quite the same way. It is interesting to speculate what would have happened if a number of Picasso's paintings had been exposed to working-class and lower-middle-class view in factories, banks and offices during the 1920s and 1930s, and not to the eyes of the *avant-garde* and initiates in art galleries.

The motives of the employers who sponsor this kind of art exhibition are, in most cases, very mixed – a paternalistic wish to brighten the lives of their workers, a vague hope that the pictures will increase concentration and prevent boredom, a satisfaction in being thought progressive. Such exhibitions have often been described but very little discussed or analysed in any satisfying depth. The Swiss tobacco firm of Burrus and Company, for example, accommodated an exhibition of non-representational art at their factory in October and November 1968. If there was any research into the attitudes of the workers to the exhibition, the results have not been published.

One very considerable problem arises when works of art are put on show in premises designed for quite different purposes. The temporary exhibition site may and probably will break all the conservationists' rules. The lighting will be too intense and its quality may be destructive; the humidity may be at an unacceptable level; there may be a considerable amount of vibration from machinery. 'The curator', says an article in the *Museums Journal*,[14] 'has every right, if not moral obligation, to demand that certain guarantees be given by the borrower so that the conditions in which the work is transported and exhibited will not diverge significantly from the conditions to which it has been acclimatised.' The author goes on to say that he believes that the main consideration the curator has to face is, 'Will the work of art suffer significantly as a result of this loan? Or will its future be virtually unaffected?'

THE LOANS PROBLEM

During the past ten years ICOM has devoted a good deal of attention to the matter of international loans. Its 'Guide-lines for drawing up a loan-agreement' were adopted by a meeting of experts held in Paris in 1974 and published, together with recommendations concerning insurance, in *ICOM News*, no. 3/4, 1974. Individual countries are now getting down to the task of applying these suggestions in a way which will suit their own particular national circumstances.

In Britain, a Working Party set up by the Museums Association has drawn up a detailed Conditions of Loan document, for which it has been trying to obtain international acceptance. If it is successful in this, the result must be, as it points out, 'a reassessment of the policy of many museums and art galleries towards temporary loans'. This would certainly make most of the more adventurous kinds of temporary exhibitions impossible to arrange. No factory, office block, department store or college could conceivably meet all the conditions laid down in the Museums Association document, and the paintings would have to continue to rest securely in a museum's air-conditioned store-room, where nobody but the museum staff could see them. The situation is a difficult one. On the one hand, it is absolutely right to determine what the museum profession calls 'the minimum conditions required to safeguard our national cultural heritage', and to do everything possible to see that these conditions are met; but, at the same time, one has to think very carefully about deciding to put the well-being of objects before the well-being of people. It is certain, and the point has been stressed repeatedly in this book, that a very large proportion of the world's people will, from choice or necessity, never make their way to city museums, or indeed to the traditional kind of museum at all. What does not come to them, in the places where they live and work, they will never see at all. To say, in effect, 'So much the worse for them. Our prime duty is to our collections', is not humane, constructive or an answer. One can only work towards a useful answer by putting another question, 'How expendable should we be prepared to allow our museum collections to be?' When one considers the treatment given to works of art in the past – looted and taken across Europe in horse-drawn carts, packed away in salt-mines and disused prisons to escape bombing, attacked by madmen with knives, cut from their frames and kept rolled up in a damp shed for a year or more – the insistence on a minimum standard of exhibition conditions can at times appear a little unrealistic. It also has to be recognised that at the present time many paintings are being kept in such abominable conditions that almost any change of scene would benefit them. Those who are unconvinced by this argument have only to visit the town halls of Europe and America and inspect the portraits, many of them very fine, in the Council Chamber, along the passages and up the stairs and in the basements. To be taken from such a wretchedly damaging environment and put on exhibition in a well-used public building can do little but good. The new location may, by strict conservationist standards, leave a good deal to be desired, but, from the picture's point of view, it may mark a considerable advance. This is, alas, an imperfect world; and museology, like politics, is the art of the possible.

If however, the attempt to move works of art around the country and around the world meets, as seems likely, with increasing opposition from the major museums and galleries which own them, other possibilities will have to be developed. Three in particular suggest themselves.

Approved replicas. It is perfectly possible, given the will and the money, to produce remarkably good copies of paintings, certainly good enough to meet most of the requirements of an exhibition in a school or a factory. These copies can be regarded as entirely expendable. No attention need be paid to environmental considerations, transport and insurance can cease to be the problems they are at the moment and the security headache disappears overnight. They are, in fact, exhibition copies; and the term, once officially approved and in circulation, could and should become entirely honourable, with no derogatory flavour to it whatever.

It is of great importance that the copies should be made in the same way as the originals. An oil-painting must be copied in oils, and on the same kind of ground, a watercolour must have a watercolour reproduction. Once the principle became accepted, it would be possible to create a great deal of regular and much-needed employment for artists, some of whom would undoubtedly acquire an international reputation for their skill and would be paid accordingly.

Making new works of art specifically for exhibition purposes; or, in the case of such things as furniture, pottery or glass, building up a stock of duplicates which one intends from the beginning to move around.

Sorting through one's reserve collections and deciding that, from now on, this and that item shall be permanently on tour, to return periodically to base for checking and servicing, in much the same way as a hire-car does.

It should, however, be firmly stated that the organised international body of museologists, as represented by ICOM – this is not quite the same as the Museum establishment – pins its faith and its reputation to the exhibition of original material. It does not, in general, approve of duplicating. There are two main reasons for this. The first is that an original object is imbued with magic ('psychological impact') in a way that no copy can ever be. This assumes, of course, that the visitor knows what he is looking at. Magic is essentially in the eye of the beholder and, to anyone who is ignorant of the deception, a replica possesses magical powers fully equal to those of the original. Deception is, however, completely unthinkable among reputable museologists. If an object is a copy, one has to say so.

The second reason for objecting to replicas and for insisting on the circulation and exhibition of original material, even if a certain risk is involved, is that what is now called the National Heritage must consist of original material. If ICOM, UNESCO or any other body is concerned to preserve the National and International Heritage, it cannot afford to weaken its case by admitting that, under this or that set of circumstances, reproductions would do as well as originals. It has always been one of the major arguments of the anti-preservationists that copies, models or photographs are a perfectly adequate means of documenting the past. If one gives way on this point, the whole case for preservation and conservation is seriously weakened and may well collapse altogether.

The present system of bringing works of art together in one capital city from all over the world, so that they can be seen in one another's company for a precious two months, is appallingly expensive and one wonders how much longer it can or should continue. However large a subsidy the exhibition may receive from the Government or the museum subsidising it, in order to keep the entrance fee down to a price the public is prepared to pay, the money has to come from somewhere. In today's terms, that means from the taxpayer's pocket, and in every country hard-pressed taxpayers are showing signs of revolt. In any case, even when these mighty international art circuses are organised and on the road, they are going to be seen by a very small proportion of the population in each country they visit, in most cases, only by people who live in the capital or very close to it. It may well be that the magnificent Rubens and Picasso and Rembrandt exhibitions which have been a feature of the museum world for the past fifty years are rapidly pricing themselves out of the market, much as international Grand Opera is doing.

THE POSSIBILITIES AND LIMITATIONS OF TELEVISION

There are those who believe that only television can solve the problem and that we are at the beginning of an enormous worldwide development of museums-by-television. Before discussing some of the achievements which have already taken place in this field and making certain forecasts of what is likely to happen during the next ten years or so, certain general statements have to be made about what television can and cannot do. Like all media and methods of communication, it possesses certain powerful advantages and certain serious drawbacks.

In order to get value for the very large investment which has to be made in creating a television programme of any quality, and to cover the technical costs of transmitting it to the public which is waiting to receive it, the potential audience has to be considered in terms of millions. This means, inevitably, that any possibility of appealing to a minority audience has to be disregarded. The situation is not, however, quite as bad as it may seem, because a programme originally made for showing in, say, Britain may afterwards be sold to North America, Australia, Germany and Sweden. If the minority audiences in each of these countries are added together, the total may be very considerable indeed, possibly of the order of 50 million people, and once this happens, the original cost of the programme will have fully justi-

fied itself. Even so, the custom is growing of making sure of this kind of international co-operation before, not after, a major programme or series is embarked upon, particularly if expensive filming abroad is involved. Most television programmes, however, are made on the reckoning that they are for home consumption only, which means that they are required to appeal and be intelligible to people covering a very wide band of taste, knowledge, education and opinions. What this amounts to in practice is that the producers aim somewhere just below the middle of the band and hope that the results will be satisfactory all round, not too baffling at the bottom and not too boring or insulting at the top. Specialists are nearly always irritated by television programmes made within their special field, but they should remember that the programme has not been planned for them.

As we have mentioned earlier, television and radio by themselves are quite good at education, but poor at instruction, if we define instruction as communicating facts and education as establishing or modifying attitudes. The qualification 'by themselves' is important, because broadcasting, with or without pictures, can be used in conjunction with booklets, gramophone records and tapes which remain in the possession of the student and to which he can refer again and again, to suit his own pattern of work. There is no need to think of any one of the media in isolation. Good broadcasters and good producers of broadcasts have an instinct for talking round and illustrating a theme, and of humanising it whenever possible. They know that one cannot hope for success by merely confronting a television or a radio audience with a series of facts. The texture of a broadcast has to be kept very open, with a few facts, but only a few, woven into the pattern. This again is very likely to annoy the specialist, who lives day by day with the facts of his subject and cannot understand why other people are apparently unable to do the same.

The third, and obvious, limitation of both television and radio is that they give the public no immediate opportunity to ask questions or to answer back. Many countries have attempted to lessen if not to overcome this weakness by providing phone-in and write-in programmes, but these are very much a second-best, compared with having a speaker or a demonstrator there on the spot, to explain and clarify. Like most professionals, television producers tend to lead a somewhat self-contained, not to say incestuous, intellectual and cultural life. Unlike teachers and guide-lecturers, they rarely meet the people who make up the audiences for their programmes and, unless they are kept exceedingly and regularly well informed by experts in the business or audience research, they may and do make serious errors in planning their programmes and in assessing the results.

'In general,' reports John Read,[15] an experienced BBC producer, 'mass communication is a new experience for museum and gallery staff. They have got used to their "private views" and press days. They are familiar with the requirements of publishers, and write and publish books themselves. They have even understood the need to publish postcards, but there, sometimes, the matter ends.' This is, on the whole, true of the staff of major national museums, but it is much less true of the people who work in small local museums, who have always found it more difficult to fence themselves off from the public.

What has been happening during the past twenty-five years is that André Malraux's 'museum without walls' has shown strong signs of becoming a reality. As John Read puts it, museums have 'become part of a system of leisure, arts and education. Their collections are used as well as conserved. There is a new demand for a new kind of knowledge from a new public. This public is familiar with the techniques of television and often expects more of an exhibition than the museum has ever imagined trying to give'. The concept of 'using' a museum's collections is both novel and frightening to many curators, people to whom 'using' is synonymous with 'exposing to danger' and 'wearing out'. The miser's tradition of hoarding one's treasure, rather than spending it, dies hard in the museum world. One should, however, by a little suspicious of Mr Read's use of 'demand'. This is a word widely used by salesmen and manufacturers, who are much given to referring to a 'public demand' for a particular line of goods, when the fact is that the manufacturer first makes something and then does his best to create a market for it. It is very doubtful if there really is a 'new demand for a new kind of knowledge', at least in any positive or conscious

sense. There may be a market for it, but that is a different matter. People in the communications business prefer to be thought of as 'satisfying a demand', rather than 'selling to a market'.

Television programmes about museums are rarely satisfactory, partly because it is difficult to find a convincing shape or theme and partly because the viewing public is apt to become too interested in what both the museum and the producer would consider to be irrelevancies. In a BBC film about the National Gallery, for instance, one of the most curious and fascinating features of the Gallery turned out to be the voices of many of the curatorial and administrative staff, which were caricatures of the British upper-class, academic accent. The producer had certainly not set out to expose this. His aim was to show what went on behind the scenes of the Museum – purchase, conservation, restoration and security – and to use this as a link which would hold together a representative selection of what was on display and in store. The voices were an unplanned bonus, which added considerably to the entertainment value of the programme and prevented viewers from taking the museum experts as seriously as they obviously took themselves.

Television producers are accustomed to regard the world as a quarry, from which they will extract, as of right, those stones best suited to their immediate purpose. Museums, so far as they are concerned, are simply one kind of quarry among many. It is for them, not the museum authorities, to decide what should best be shown. It is, as they not infrequently feel obliged to point out, their programme, not the museum's, and their responsibility to decide what will interest the public. 'There is', says John Read, and all television producers would agree with him, 'no reason at all to suppose that a museum offers a ready-made programme. A collection is not a script, and a catalogue is not usually any more interesting to read than a telephone directory. Some kind of theme has to be found. Dramatic values have to be established.'

At this point museums may well feel inclined to ask the television organisation who is doing whom a favour. 'Who', they may say, 'needs whom most?' The answer from the television side would be either:

1. This is a potentially fruitful partnership between two sets of

people who are in a position to help one another; or

2. This is a wonderful, God-given piece of free publicity for the museum, publicity on an enormous scale.

Of these, (2) is almost certainly not true. One recalls, for instance, the number of museum exhibits which Lord Clark used in the course of his BBC television series, *Civilisation*. These were undoubtedly useful to the programmes, but all the museum received in return, apart from a fee, was a mention in the credits at the end. How many viewers, one may ask, either noticed or remembered the names of the museums which provided the objects? What kind of publicity did they, in the event, receive? As to whether any television programme can be regarded as a partnership between the museum and the producer or his employers, it is difficult to say. If it is a partnership, it is likely to be of the unequal kind that exists between the cook and her greengrocer, with one party supplying the raw materials and the other the artistry.

On the other hand, says John Read, and many of his colleagues would echo his words,

I would certainly not like to underestimate the debt we owe to harassed museum officials who suddenly find themselves involved in our activities, about which they often know little, and for which they get little credit. My own film about the Tate Gallery would have been impossible to make without the whole-hearted support of almost every member of that institution's staff. The gallery was invaded, night and day for two weeks, by a team of up to eight people. It meant special security arrangements. Staff had to be found to supervise our activities. Overtime schedules had to be arranged. Cables and lights had to be installed in every conceivable position. We sometimes needed to exclude the public while we were working. Often we worked in galleries with the public present and being filmed themselves. Exhibits had to be moved. Fragile and quite priceless works of art were taken out of their respective showcases. Trustees had to be informed and soothed. Heads of departments were consulted and nagged. The library was placed at our disposal and the gallery photographer was given nightmares preparing colour transparencies for our needs. The entire restoration department was involved in a day's shooting, and the Director of the Tate, firmly pinned behind someone else's desk, was gently persuaded to lift a few veils from the secrecy that usually surrounds a museum's affairs. The paper work was formidable. Owners had to be traced, copyright clearances obtained.

This was certainly co-operation and hospitality on a formidable scale; but if it was partnership, there was no doubt as to which of the two partners was in command.

It is possible, however, that the heyday of co-operation between television and museums may be drawing to an end, at least in some countries. Realising that television producers can be in command of large budgets – the BBC's *Civilisation* series cost more than $600,000 – museums have begun to charge enormous reproduction and facility fees. If it now costs $200 to show a photograph of a single painting for ten seconds or less, and if the museum then demands the return of the transparencies, for which they have already been paid, in order that these may be hired out later to someone else, television arts programmes could well be priced out of business. What is clearly required, and what must eventually come, is an agreed international scale of charges, with a single payment that would allow the television company full rights to repeat its programmes and to have them shown in other countries. As it is, the stage has nearly been reached when it would be cheaper to commission an artist to make an original painting than to use a colour transparency of an existing work.

A number of museums, mostly in the United States, have experimented with making their own television programmes, for transmission on the public service networks. One of the most successful pioneers was the Milwaukee Museum, which appointed a Television Co-ordinator in 1952 and, after a number of pilot projects, launched five types of programme. These were:

1. *The Explorers' Club*, a natural history programme for children, developed in association with children's activities at the Museum. A bulletin, *Explorers' Log*, was produced and circulated in conjunction with the programme.
2. *Let's Experiment*, which featured a scientist in a museum laboratory, and demonstrated basic principles in physics and chemistry.
3. *Diorama*, a programme with a large family audience, which covered hobbies, public issues and general cultural matters.
4. *The World to You*, which dealt with the local implications of scientific and historical topics.
5. *No Doubt About It*, a quiz programme about 'mystery objects' from the Museum's collections.

An article in *Curator*[16] summed up what has been learned from the series. 'The natural differences in the methods of television,' it said,

with its tendency toward the bold, broad strokes of Madison Avenue, and the museum, with its preference for quiet restraint and thoughtful precision, presented understandable difficulties. But, as the professional scientist learnt the values of showmanship, the professional broadcaster gained an increasing respect for scholarship. Methods were developed to set the dramatic highlight against the background of solid information, to check extreme erudition with popular appeal, and to maintain accuracy in spite of simplification and focus. The result was highly effective museum television.

In 1958, however, television was still a relatively cheap and simple tool, compared with what it has since become. Even as late as 1967 the present author recalls watching when in New York a talk on Picasso, in the breakfast-time *Sunrise Semester* series, where the production technique, if it could be called that, consisted of keeping the camera fixed on the speaker's head and shoulders throughout the talk, with no change of shot at all. From time to time, when an illustration was required, the very competent lady giving the talk merely picked up a book containing the picture from the table beside her and held it up in front of her face, so that viewers could see what was being referred to.

As television became more sophisticated and more expensive, most of the American museums which had at one time been producing programmes dropped out of the race, either because of the cost or because too much staff time was taken up in preparing the programmes or, in one or two cases, because no suitable presenter was available. Of the handful of museums which still broadcast regular programmes, the most successful is probably the Boston Museum of Fine Arts. This has four full-time television staff and puts out two half-hour programmes, *Images* amd *Museum Open House*, each week. $100,000 was spent in wiring the Museum's galleries and once this had been done the annual budget was between $35,000 and $40,000. The programmes are pre-recorded on videotape, by a technical unit from the local educational television station. Each programme is reckoned to have a local audience of about 45,000 and a total audience of perhaps half a million, since it is transmitted on all the stations of the Eastern Education Network.

In an article, 'The television environment', which they published in 1974 (*Museum News*, vol. 52 no. 5, Jan/Feb), Billy Adler and John Mangolies pointed out that between the ages of two and sixty-five the average American is likely to spend nine full years, a quarter of his waking life, watching television. For this reason museums, Adler and Mangolies concluded, could not afford to ignore television. Over a period of three years they made slides of television programmes, taking the photographs in their own living-rooms in the course of watching programmes. From these photographs they selected a thousand 'slide images', which were built into an exhibition shown in five American museums in 1971. This used twelve projectors, 'flashing still frames of evocative TV vignettes around the walls'. At the same time, 'four TV sets within the installation carried live local programmes, serving to bring the immediate communication environment into the gallery, as well as providing a social collage to augment the slide image'. At this point, most of the world's museum curators are likely to sigh at the impossibility of ever laying their hands on twelve automatic slide projectors, to say nothing of the elaborate and expensive programming which is needed to co-ordinate and direct them. An important American museum, however, would find it no more strange to have twelve projectors than to have twelve telephones.

For a second series, shown in 1972, Adler and Mangolies projected their slides in a sitting-room setting. 'By recreating the context in which television is usually experienced,' they said, 'we believe the implications become more difficult to escape. The exhibition-goer becomes part of the exhibition, as he settles down in the living room to watch television.'

Another American team, James Howard and Sylvia Lanford Marchant, believe that only moving pictures are effective. Slides, in their opinion, are as impossibly old-fashioned as magic-lanterns. Their work for Electragraphics, the quaintly-named audio-visual department of Greenville County Museum of Art, South Carolina, has convinced them that 'the contrast between the generations reveals word-oriented adults and visually-oriented teenagers'. In an interesting article, published in the American journal *Museum News* (vol. 52, Jan/Feb 1974) they express their belief that

> boys and girls who have been brought up on the sophisticated presentation techniques of commercial television may not recognise quality content but they are unimpressed [sic] and consider deadly dull so-called educational slide programmes and film-strips. Adults who recognise significant educational value in audio-visual materials cannot expect to reach students who are tuned in to the media, by handling these aids as supplements to print or by using visuals unskilfully.

Howard and Marchant make use of colour video-tape, film projectors and tape control. These are the core of 'interpretation, amplification and support programmes', and for showing artists and craftsmen at work. Programmes for older student and adult viewers are designed to raise questions which 'serve to analyse the significance of paintings, sculpture, and other objects in the galleries'. Certain programmes, they say, 'may serve as entertaining channels of information, while others deliver commentaries, interviews or opinions by artists, jurors or critics. Paramount, however, is the aim to provoke questioning responses by the viewer that lead him to make discoveries of his own within the Museum environment.'

This is television used as a working tool, by people who belong to the museum and understand its aims. It is effective, but expensive. At the present time most of the American museums which use television or radio do so for publicity purposes, usually when there is a new exhibition or some other feature of special interest, and in general news or magazine programmes. A survey carried out in 1969 showed that, of those museums which said they took advantage of television facilities, 70 per cent used local commercial stations, and paid for the air-time they were given, and 47 per cent educational channels.

TRAVELLING EXHIBITIONS

There are few, if any, countries which do not at some time make use of travelling exhibitions for museum and educational purposes, but two, Sweden and the Soviet Union, have developed a co-ordinated national system which is, in both cases, extensively used. During the next ten years, it seems probable that other countries will come to see the great advantages which carefully thought out national planning can bring to travelling exhibitions and, for this reason, the Swedish and Soviet examples are worth discussing in some detail.

The Swedish organisation Riksutställningar (Swedish Travelling Exhibitions) was set up in 1965, after a Government committee had decided that museums were increasingly unable to meet the educational and cultural demands which changing social conditions were making on them. Swedish Travelling Exhibitions (STE) was given the task, first, of investigating the role of the exhibition in contemporary society; and, second, of creating a nation-wide service which would provide the kind of exhibition for which there was evidently a market and at the lowest possible cost. The two functions have, from the beginning, been carried out simultaneously. Surveys are regularly made to discover what kind of people visit the exhibitions and how successful they are. The results of these surveys are used in the planning of new exhibitions. STE has a built-in research element.

There is a central studio and workshop in Stockholm, which, in 1975, had a permanent staff of about fifty people. A number of designers, including some of the most successful, are also employed on a freelance basis. Audio-visual material is extensively used as a supplement or an alternative to exhibitions. Exhibition packages for schools usually include short films or film strips.

One or two examples will show the range of activities which form part of the work of STE and illustrate its possibilities and its method of operation. Few Swedes, whether children or adults, ever have the opportunity to see original Greek or Roman artifacts. The only collections of any size are in the Mediterranean Museum in Stockholm, which is, of course, a long way from the towns where a large part of the population lives. The Museum was anxious to

John Judkyn Memorial, Bath, England. Preparing labels for the exhibition on American Presidential Elections.

find ways in which its collections could be made accessible to a wider public and came to STE for help. One of the first fruits of this collaboration was a 16 mm colour film, *Gifts to the Gods*. This runs for six minutes and illustrates ancient religious beliefs, as these are expressed in different kinds of votive offering. The film is backed up by pottery replicas of votive objects, commissioned by STE. STE has also worked with the Mediterranean Museum to produce exhibitions which re-create daily life in the ancient world. The first of these, *The Kitchen in Ancient Times*, consists of pottery replicas of cooking utensils, pictures, an explanatory booklet and a number of recipes which pupils can try out for themselves.

STE has also experimented with ways of making museum archive material available for school use, so that schoolchildren can study history in the original sources. The facsimile collections published in England (*Jackdaws*) and in France (*Documents*) are commercially possible because of the size of the English and French-speaking markets, but the Swedish linguistic unit is very small by comparison and this creates great publication problems for books of all kinds. To see what might be possible in Swedish, given the necessary financial backing, STE produced a Jackdaw-type folder dealing with Swedish emigration to America in the second half of the nineteenth century, a subject which is abundantly represented in the collections of every local museum in Sweden. It was hoped that the STE facsimiles would stimulate school pupils to undertake follow-up work in the museums and relate the material to their own family history, since a very high proportion of Swedish families have relatives in America. The STE collection, which was given the title, *The Land in the West*, is intended for pupils to keep and includes emigrant recruitment brochures, crash courses in English, letters, land prospectuses, broadsheets warning Swedes about the evils of emigration, folksongs, boat-tickets and labour-contracts.

The Land in the West is part of a larger exhibition for schools. This has large mounted pictures, tape-recordings of Swedish-American dialects, catalogues of contemporary emigration exhibitions at various Swedish museums, and statistics and maps which can be projected with an epidiascope.

STE has also developed a series of exhibitions on countries outside Europe, especially the developing countries. This is a continuation and extension of an idea pioneered in the Netherlands, at the Ethnographical Museum in Leiden, where schoolchildren studying the culture of a particular country can put on its native clothes, attempt to play its musical instruments, cook and eat its food and perform simple and largely unrehearsed plays. The first of STE's exhibitions of this kind, developed jointly with a teacher-training college, dealt with Tanzania, an African country in which Sweden takes a special interest and in which many Swedish volunteers work. It begins with colour illustrations to show the people and their environment. These are of two types, plastic-covered postcard-sized pictures which can be handled without being damaged and eight large folding pictures which serve as a background to cut-outs or models of plants, animals, vehicles and implements which the children make themselves. Replicas of everyday objects can be used for discussion purposes and there is a strip-cartoon picture covering such problems as education, employment and ecology in the particular country.

A large and extremely popular STE exhibition, *Discovery and Experience*, was concerned with some of the major aspects of aesthetic education in schools. It was shown in museums for two years, and every museum which accommodated it had to agree to provide an area in which both adults and children could use various kinds of simple and cheap materials for self-expression.

In 1970 STE produced its first exhibition, *Our Culture – in Textbooks and Real Life*, which was specially designed for a teachers' course. The aim was to suggest a new method of teaching the history of art and music between 1910 and 1920. The exhibition took the form of a room containing furniture from the Nordic Museum, in Stockholm, and paintings from the National Museum showing an art historian's study. On two of the walls, as a contrast, were photographs of scenes from working-class life during the same period. The other two walls dealt with the disintegration of popular culture and the growth of a new kind of urban culture. The exhibition was shown at museums throughout Sweden. Curators added local material to it and co-

Riksutställningar, Stockholm, Sweden. 'To the Land in the West', a travelling exhibition on the history of emigration.

operated with the regional educational authorities in arranging study-days for teachers.

STE has also produced a number of exhibitions to be used in conjunction with various types of adult education programme. *The People's Music* was planned in co-operation with the Workers' Educational Association and the National Concert Tour Scheme, to provide a basis for discussion in groups studying music. It illustrates the role of folk music in Sweden and suggests the need for a more popular form of musical culture than the one which is found at the present time. The exhibition is assembled from standard modules, the size of a fishbox, which are built up into three-tier semicircles for display purposes and into seats on which people can sit to listen to music played on a tape-recorder which is fixed into one of the boxes. The *What are Handicrafts?* exhibition was designed to allow members of handicraft groups, which are mostly concerned with practical activities, to discuss the history of handicrafts in relation to other forms of art and to social developments in general. Large plastic-covered screens and samples of material are used to stimulate answers to such questions as: 'Is this a domestic craft, a handicraft, or an industrial product?' Typical rural and urban domestic interiors are illustrated by folding cardboard models.

The *Immigrants in Sweden* exhibition was produced to try to get rid of some of the ignorance and prejudice which can give rise to considerable social problems in a country with a high rate of immigration. Four hundred copies were printed and the exhibition was accompanied by a collection of short articles, subsidised and sold cheaply, and a brief catalogue to the exhibition, in Swedish, Serbo-Croat, Italian, Greek, Finnish, and German. The catalogue was issued free.

STE regards its main duty as the education of ordinary men and women. It co-operates with the Swedish Adult Education Association and the Board of Education to discover ways of adapting its exhibitions to attract new categories of people. Part of its budget has been used to equip information centres, which deal with questions and with requests for practical help.

In the Government-sponsored experimental scheme for the use of television and radio in education, a series was broadcast with the title *We Call Them Developing Countries*. To accom-

pany the radio and television programmes, there was an illustrated handbook and an exhibition produced by STE, in 300 printed copies for group use, covering topics included in the course. The basic exhibition was on three screens and with it went a number of symbolic objects from the countries in question – a hoe from Zambia, a piece of printed cotton fabric from Tanzania, an earthenware vessel and a printed picture of Buddha from Ceylon, a piece of sugar cane and a 'literacy flag' from Cuba. A fourth screen showed the work of UNESCO in the developing countries.

In 1973 STE produced exhibitions, with excellently illustrated large-page textbooks, to accompany two television series on the industrialisation of Sweden, and its human consequences, between 1850 and 1915. The material was intended for use by study-circles, and STE, the Workers' Educational Association and the broadcasting authorities were all anxious that the projects should encourage people to carry out research on their own. To encourage this, tapes were provided, containing extracts from the reminiscences of old people talking about their work. There was a section giving instructions as to how to take the kind of photographs which were required as documentation of industrial history, and another which told members of the groups where to find archive material and how to make use of it.

Since it was set up in 1965 STE has become one of the main centres of experiment and innovation in the museum world. Its work is based on the conviction that the range of people visiting museums is far too narrow and that imaginatively planned and designed travelling exhibitions are one way, and an important way, of helping museums to extend their influence both socially and geographically. It believes that by concentrating resources and talents a much greater impact is possible on a comparatively modest budget. STE is, above all, an organiser of co-operation. Much of its remarkable and undoubted success can be attributed to its skill in acting as an informal consultative body for museums and for other makers of exhibitions. It sees no point in originating material itself, when other people have already done the fundamental work in a perfectly satisfactory manner; but it feels that it is important that the exhibitions made by museums and other bodies should

reach as many people as possible, and, with them in mind, it has devoted a large part of its resources to taking over, adapting and promoting already existing exhibitions, so that they can be sent round the country with every hope of success.

What particularly characterises the exhibitions sponsored by STE is their technical excellence – the best people in the country are employed to design and make them; the strong sense of social purpose; and what can best be described, perhaps, as their open-endedness. STE considers that an exhibition has succeeded if it provokes discussion and a wish to find out more about the subject. Any information it provides is secondary to this main purpose of stimulating thought and personal action.

The travelling exhibitions organised by the Polytechnic Museum in Moscow have a different aim. The Museum's very large collections are concerned entirely with industry and technology, and it is consequently that it should also be the headquarters of the All-Union Society for the Dissemination of Scientific and Technical Information. This body, known from the initial letters of the Russian title as Znanie, organises travelling exhibitions which are sent out all over the Soviet Union. The system is to have twenty exhibitions in circulation at any one time, and to introduce five new exhibitions each year to replace those which have become outdated, from the point of view of the style of presentation or of the information. Each exhibition visits up to six towns each year and remains for one or two months. Znanie undertakes the planning and design of the exhibitions in collaboration with Ministries, scientific institutes, industrial concerns and specialist societies.

The exhibitions fall into three categories:

(*a*) Popular science exhibitions on scientific and technical developments.
(*b*) Specialised exhibitions, for people with an expert knowledge of the subject.
(*c*) Exhibitions built around items from the collections of the Polytechnic Museum.

A list of the exhibitions currently available is widely circulated and Znanie then has the task of deciding, from all the requests received, which museum, scientific society, factory, cultural centre or research institute can be allocated an exhibition and when this can be arranged.

The information needed by the design studios is provided by the relevant section of the Museum, which will probably have collected it from a number of sources. An explanatory booklet is produced to accompany the exhibition and a member of the Museum section immediately concerned travels to each location in order to supervise the installation. For specially large exhibitions, he will remain on hand throughout the time they are on display.

Every effort is made to make sure that as many people as possible from the area see the exhibition. Publicity is given to it in local newspapers and on radio and television. Group visits are arranged for schoolchildren, students and teachers, and meetings are usually held in connection with the exhibition.

The subjects of the exhibitions are selected to meet what are believed to be the most urgent national needs at the moment. For a number of years during the 1960s, for instance, a high priority was given to new developments in chemistry, and especially to those relating to synthetic materials and to agriculture. In the Soviet Union, as in other countries, there was considerable suspicion of synthetics for many years, largely, one fears, because many of the early products were of such obviously poor quality. Exhibitions were therefore prepared to convince both the specialist and the lay public that synthetic materials were a good thing. One, *Polymers in the National Economy*, included posters, photographs, statistical material, diagrams and a large assortment of samples, which could be picked up and handled. Visitors were instructed in this way in the physical and chemical properties of the new materials and of articles made from them, in their economic advantages and in the production processes. There were films and lectures by a specialist from the staff of the Museum. The exhibition was on tour for two years in the Soviet Far East, Central Asia and in northern and European Russia.

Two years later, as a follow-up, the Museum's chemistry section arranged a number of more specialised exhibitions on polymers. These had such titles as *Synthetic Glues and Methods of Adhesion*; *Polymer Materials in Building*; and *The Use of Fluoroplastics in Technology*. It was assumed that the visitors to this second series of exhibitions would already know about the subject and would be directly involved in it in some way, as teachers, technologists or scientists.

Polytechnical Museum, Moscow, USSR. International travelling exhibition, 'Achievements of the USSR in Space Exploration'.

(below) *International travelling exhibition, 'The History of Soviet Automobiles'.*

During the summer months there are travelling exhibitions on river boats. These move along the Volga and the Oka and stop at all towns of any size.

The Polytechnic Museum exchanges exhibitions with other socialist countries, under scientific and cultural agreements. *Hydro-electric Construction* and *Atoms for Peace* went to the Technical Museum in Prague, and *What is Automation?* to the Technical Museum in Warsaw. In return, Prague sent Moscow *From the Rushlight to the Fluorescent Lamp* and Warsaw's contribution was *From Copernicus to Space Flight*. Following this series of exchanges, the National Technical Museums in Prague, Dresden, Moscow and Warsaw jointly organised a large exhibition, called *Technical Museums and their Contribution to the Polytechnic Education of Young People*, a title which would almost certainly not have commended itself to National Travelling Exhibitions in Sweden, but which fitted naturally enough into the more sober educational and museum atmosphere of the socialist world. In this monumental travelling exhibition, Moscow dealt with museum work with schools; Dresden with the history of photography; Warsaw with energy and the attempts to harness it; and Prague with man's use of stone and the history of sound recording. The exhibition was shown successively, for a year at a time, in each of the four cities which had contributed to it.

No greater contrast is imaginable than between the travelling exhibitions organised by the Moscow Polytechnic Museum and the Swedish National Travelling Exhibitions. Both are the result of a national scheme and in both cases the people responsible would certainly argue that what they were providing was very much in the national interest. There are certainly superficial resemblances – co-operation with other bodies, careful research and planning, good materials and graphics – but these conceal a fundamental difference in philosophy between the two types of exhibition. The Russian aim is to provide information, in the clearest and most intelligible way possible; the Swedish is to modify attitudes and to persuade people to see facts, developments and ideas in their social context.

The travelling exhibition of the future? Interior of Hungarian worker's apartment.

The style and organisation of the exhibitions reflect this.

What the Russians and the Swedes certainly have in common is a conviction that if museums are to make any real impact they must find ways of taking the museum to the people. The Russians prefer to do this in a majestic fashion, with a relatively small number of exhibitions going on their rounds at any given time and with ample funds for the purpose. The Swedes always have to think very carefully about their budget and have become very ingenious in providing good value for money. Their travelling exhibitions are much less didactic than the Russian ones and appear to assume, as the Americans do, that the hook must be skilfully and attractively baited before the man-in-the-street will take it, a consideration which seems to worry the Russians very much less.

SPREADING THE WORD INDIRECTLY

Mobile museums and museums-by-television imply that the people aimed at have no museum facilities available. They represent a direct approach from the museum to the public. It is possible, however, for a large museum to use its influence indirectly, by working to improve small local museums, which as a result will be able to offer the public a better service, and, under certain conditions, it may be wiser to spend money this way, rather than on equipment such as mobile museums.

New Zealand has followed this policy, for geographical, historical and financial reasons.[17] New Zealand is divided into three main islands, which are long and narrow and divided by a high central range of mountains for most of their total length of 1500 miles. This makes it difficult for people to get to the country's four main museums, in Auckland, Wellington, Christchurch and Dunedin, and has encouraged the development of a network of smaller museums, provincial and local. These usually have no full-time professional staff and are open for only restricted periods during the week. It is often easier to raise money to establish a small local museum than to collect funds to develop and maintain it.

What New Zealand has, in fact, is a large number of display points scattered over the country, which, properly used and encouraged, provide facilities for showing the collections of the four principal museums over a wide

area. With the help of a small Government grant, this is now being done by travelling exhibitions, by sending display experts to arrange exhibits and train local staff, and by showing curators how to make their museums more relevant to the area in which they are situated. These activities are linked to a developing service to schools, by which display cases and collections of artifacts are lent by the major museums for extended periods, with advice to teachers on how to make the best use of them.

The methods used by New Zealand in an attempt to widen the museum's area of usefulness are not necessarily applicable to other countries. They have been developed by a particular set of national circumstances and their success can be judged only within that context. What is universally valid, however, is the determination and the need to find effective ways of taking the museum to the people, in the certain knowledge that if this is not done both the number and the range of museums will continue to be frustratingly limited.

One must, of course, allow for differences in national temperament and traditions. It is not possible to apply the American experience to the Soviet Union, or the Swedish experience to India, without a great deal of skilful adaptation and interpretation. This is not merely a question of money or technical facilities. To be successful and to possess stamina, experiments must grow out of the local soil. Terms and institutions change their meaning when they are transplanted. The overtones of words like 'television' and 'mobile museum' are not at all the same in a developing country as in an old and prosperous one. To employ currently-used American phrases, they possess a different degree of 'excitement-potential' and 'normality-value', according to the society in which they operate.

FINDING OUT ABOUT ONE'S VISITORS

In 1972, MUSE, the activity-subsidiary of the Brooklyn Children's Museum, was attracting 100,000 visitors a year, and that, as the Director, Lloyd Hezekiah, noted,[18] was without any advertising at all. 'If we really tried to advertise,' he said, 'we could never accommodate the people who want to come to the building.' Asked if he had ever tried, in a methodical way, to find out anything about the social and educational background of the 100,000 or even where they came from, he replied that he had not. 'We just know they're coming from everywhere, even the surrounding states,' he told the interviewer. In time, he hoped, he would be able to produce scientifically-gathered evidence to prove the point, but meanwhile he was reasonably content simply to see the visitors coming through the door in such large numbers and returning for more.

This attitude, which contains a great deal of common sense, is not very fashionable nowadays. Museums, like most other organisations which provide goods and services for the public, are anxious to know who is buying what they have to sell and whether their customers like what they are being offered. This can, of course, develop into a neurosis, and an expensive one at that, since modern market research and consumer surveys use time- and labour-consuming techniques which have to be paid for. Unless he is seriously worried about the way things are going at the moment, a museum director certainly does well to think twice about committing himself to spending money which might well be devoted with greater profit to some other purpose.

There are, even so, cheap surveys and expensive surveys, each of which can be good of its kind. The cheap variety are mostly concerned with discovering where people visiting the museum come from, how old they are and how many of them arrive on different days of the week and at different periods of the year. The money-hungry type of survey is looking for information about the social and educational background of visitors and for opinions on the exhibits and the activities of the museum. Purely statistical surveys are not difficult for a museum to carry out with its own staff, but anything more elaborate will almost certainly involve professional help.

A questionnaire sent out by the present author in August 1973 revealed that a surprisingly large number of the world's most important museums had never carried out any form of systematic enquiry into the opinions and wishes of their visitors. A list of these museums may be of some comfort to those who have felt that their own museum is falling hopelessly behind in the race for status and prestige. It is included here merely for information and not with the least hint of blame or accusation. The museums in question may have excellent reasons for not indulging in this form of activity, and one or two of them, of course, may have commissioned a survey since 1973. The list is given as Appendix 1 to the present chapter. It includes such large and well-known establishments as the Museum of the History of Art, in Vienna; the Natural History Museum, Paris; the German Museum, Munich; the Science Museum, London; the Museum of Modern Art, New York; and the Prado, Madrid.

In 1961 the Americans Duncan F. Cameron and D. S. Abbey made an assessment of what had been accomplished up to that time in what we might call Category 2 research, the kind which is concerned with the attitudes, habits and mental equipment of museum visitors. They found the situation profoundly unsatisfactory.

'For over thirty years now,' they wrote,[19] museum workers in North America have been using scientific methods in the study of museum audiences [sic]. Unknowing visitors have been tracked through galleries by observers armed with stop-watch and clip-board. Thousands have been accosted by interviewers at the turn-stiles, in the exhibit halls and in the street. Yet in spite of these many and varied endeavors, the useful knowledge accumulated is slight, and the value of such investigations remains a matter of diverse opinion in the museum profession.'

This clearly means that in 1961 a substantial proportion of the people engaged in museum work in the United States, and presumably in other countries as well, was not prepared to accept visitor research, carried out as it had been so far, as a useful, reliable professional tool. The sceptics may have felt – Cameron and Abbey do not say – that the sampling methods had been inadequate, or that the questions were badly phrased or irrelevant. They may, on the other hand, have believed that any attempt to quantify people's reactions to museums is misguided and that, by channelling and shaping their answers in the way any questionnaire inevitably does, surveys distorted the response of the public to what museums offered them. Many excellent and far from antiquated curators would say that they learn as much by walking round the museum watching and listening to visitors as they would from any scientifically-planned research operation.

One has to remember, however, that the planning and analysis of surveys is now a considerable industry throughout the world and that a great many highly-trained and highly-paid specialists, particularly in the United States, earn their living this way. It would therefore be unreasonable to expect that what the professionals, whose careers are devoted to the application of scientific method, would call mere conversation, eavesdropping and intuition could have any degree of public prestige, any more than one would reckon that the habit of taking a walk in the country would be popular among those who find their livelihood in the leisure industries. The professional has to defend his existence in every possible way, and a much-favoured weapon is to attack and ridicule the amateur. There is no need, however, to take an extreme view in either direction. Questionnaires, listening and watching, and following one's instincts are all valuable methods of checking the effectiveness of one's work, and any one of them can be carried to excess. To avoid unnecessary and sterile quarrels between those who believe in surveys and questionnaires and those who prefer to rely on the results of keeping one's ears and eyes open, it may be necessary to develop a science of looking and listening, so that the professionals can continue to

feel needed and involved and an indispensable method of gathering information may receive the prestige it deserves.

The city of Portsmouth, in England, has six museums, all under the same administration. The Director of Museums has devised a technique for making exceptionally detailed and useful records of attendances which makes a minimum demand on staff time.[20] Each entrance desk is provided with printed forms on which the number of adults, children, and people arriving in parties is entered for every hour for which the particular museum is open. When a sheet is full it goes to a senior attendant who extracts the daily totals on to a calendar. Every month these figures are extracted and filed. The result is a body of statistical evidence which is completely reliable and which provides a solid foundation for future planning, when used in conjunction with material available from other sources.

It had been reported, for example, by the staff at two of the museums that there was a demand for the museum to remain open after 6 p.m. The opening hours were consequently extended, as an experiment, until 8 p.m. It was then shown from the daily record sheets that 8 p.m. was exactly the wrong time to close, because the evening visitors came between 7 and 8. The closing time was then extended to 9 p.m., and imme-

diately attendances increased in a spectacular fashion.

By studying the statistics carefully, it is possible to adjust staffing to meet the hour-by-hour and day-by-day fluctuations in attendance. Any changes in the pattern of attendance can be met by changes in the pattern of labour distribution and the statistics are an invaluable source of reference when the Museums are asking for more money from the City Treasury.

A good example of the wisdom of using several sources in order to obtain apparently simple statistical information is provided by a survey of visitors to a special Rouault Exhibition in Manchester City Art Gallery in the summer of 1974.[21] This major exhibition, which was partly financed by the Arts Council, was shown nowhere else in Britain. The Council was at that time developing its policy of promoting the regions at the expense of London and it used the Rouault Exhibition as something of a laboratory experiment, devoting an exceptional amount of money to publicity of various kinds in order to find out more about the best ways of marketing exhibitions in the provinces. Part of the research took the form of a survey of visitors, 'to find out the characteristics of the people attending the exhibition and where they came from; the extent to which those coming may have been influenced by advertising; the extent to which they have read'.[22] At the same time, the Art Gallery decided to make a survey of its own from the signatures in visitors' books at the Gallery, having previously discovered that the number of signatures was always in proportion to the number of visitors, one signature for every six visitors.

The overall attendance figure for the eight weeks was 27,029, which was 114 per cent more than for the previous summer's exhibition, *Munch Graphics*, which had not had the benefit of the special Arts Council publicity campaign. Nearly a third of the visitors were making their first visit to the gallery. About half of them had come specifically to see the Rouault Exhibition. As might have been expected, the Greater Manchester area provided the highest proportion of visitors, with the figures dropping according to distance. There were, even so, a considerable

PLACE:

	11 a.m.	12 noon	1 p.m.	2 p.m.	3 p.m.	4 p.m.	5 p.m.	6 p.m.	7 p.m.	8 p.m.	9 p.m.	TOTAL
Date: Adults												
Children												
Parties												
TOTAL:												
Date: Adults												
Children												
Parties												
TOTAL:												
Date: Adults												
Children												
Parties												
TOTAL:												

Portsmouth City Museums, England.
Form for recording daily attendances.

number who had come 100 miles and more. Of 296 foreigners who signed the visitors' book 100 were from the United States and Canada, 47 from France and 34 from West Germany, which, for 1974, was almost exactly the same ratio as for tourists to Britain.

The Arts Council questionnaire was presented to a random sample of 236 visitors, by a professional market research organisation, during the last week of the exhibition on different days at different times. This week was chosen because it came at the end of all the different types of publicity which had been used. Full details of the questionnaire are given in Appendix 2 at the end of this chapter. The answers to it showed that 60 per cent of the visitors in the sample were under thirty-six and that 27 per cent were students, figures very similar to those obtained by Daniel Yankelovich (52 per cent under thirty, 25 per cent students) in the survey which he carried out for the Metropolitan Museum in New York.[23]

Of these 236, 78 per cent were aware of the Rouault Exhibition, mostly as a result of paid press advertising and press reviews – a party of sixteen prominent art critics from the national newspapers came up from London on free rail warrants for a press preview lunch. The newspapers mostly read by visitors to the exhibition were from the top end of the list, the *Sunday Times*, *Guardian*, *Manchester Evening News* and *Observer*. A third of those attending had listened to commercial radio at some time during the previous week.

The Art Gallery and the Arts Council obtained a great deal of useful information as a result of the publicity campaign and the survey. This could be summarised as follows:

1. The national Sunday newspapers are extremely valuable in publicising provincial activities, a fact which had not previously been realised in the museum world.
2. Paid advertising in newspapers and on commercial radio fully justified itself.
3. One gets what one tries for. No publicity was aimed at working-class institutions, such as clubs, and few working-class people visited the exhibition.[24]

This Manchester survey was of the simplest kind. It went solely for facts and made no attempt to discover the opinions of visitors, either in connection with the Art Gallery or its facilities in general, or with the Rouault Exhibition. Even so, it provided extremely valuable information, notably on the feasibility of attracting visitors to a provincial museum from a much wider area than had been previously thought possible and on the relative advantages of different kinds of publicity material. Posters, for example, proved much less successful than had been previously thought.

The more elaborate type of investigation, which aims at finding out not only the kind of people the museum is attracting, but why these people have come and what they think about the things they are offered, is exemplified by a survey carried out at one of Britain's most enterprising and successful regional museums, the Norwich Castle Museum, during 1971 and 1972. The survey was intended to serve as the basis for future planning and expansion and it was consequently prepared and carried out with great care and thoroughness.[25]

Outside interviewers were used, to ensure impartiality, and a random sample of respondents were interviewed as they left the museum. This was done during four periods, chosen to illustrate the different pattern of attendance throughout the year: 5–11 July 1971; 2–8 August 1971; 17–30 January 1972; and 24–30 April 1972. Over this total of thirty-five days, 1597 people were interviewed, 74 per cent on Monday to Friday, 17 per cent on Saturday, and 9 per cent on Sunday afternoon. The questionnaire contained thirty-six questions, some with multiple-choice answers, and the results were analysed by computer.

Norwich is an important regional centre, both for those who live in the eastern part of England and for the tourist industry. It is also an area in which there has been considerable social change in recent years, especially as a result of the establishment of a new university in the city and of the administrative headquarters of the Government publications department, HM Stationery Office. It was important for the Museum to know where its visitors came from and to which social and occupational groups they belonged, and to relate this information to the way in which the Museum was used.

Over the total period of thirty-five days covered by the survey, 60 per cent of the Museum's visitors lived in the area and 4 per cent were on holiday there, the proportion of local visitors being considerably higher in the winter than in the summer. The age-distribution, shown in percentage form, was as shown in the table.

Age	Percentage
Up to 8	2
9–12	8
13–16	16
17–19	9
20–29	20
30–39	16
40–49	11
50–59	9
60–69	7
70 and over	2
	100

Castle Museum, Norwich, England. Entrance hall, also used as supplementary café area during busy months of the year.

Two comments were made on this by the authors of the survey report.

1. The youngest age-group was inadequately sampled because the children were reluctant to take part.
2. Comparison with the age structure in the United Kingdom population figures showed an over-representation in the museum of people under forty and an under-representation of those over forty.

An examination of the occupations of visitors to the Museum demonstrated very clearly that, by comparison with the British population as a whole, the middle class was over-represented in the sample and both the skilled and the unskilled working class seriously under-represented. Of all visitors, 14 per cent came alone, 34 per cent in pairs and 9 per cent in parties of more than ten people. The lone visitors and those in pairs were most numerous in January and least numerous in August.

The average time spent in the Museum was between sixty and ninety minutes, visits tending to be shorter in the winter than in the summer. The winter and summer visitors evidently used the Museum in different ways. The August visitors tried to see the whole Museum, and came with that intention, but the January visitors came to see a particular section only, and a greater proportion of them, incidentally, used the Museum's very pleasant and efficient refreshment facilities. The winter visitors are much more likely to have visited the Museum before. Of the August visitors, 18 per cent had made a previous visit within a month, while the figure for January was 28 per cent.

The most frequent visitors, among those who lived in Norwich, Norfolk or Suffolk, were in the 13–16 age group, of whom 33 per cent had been in the Museum more than five times in the six months before the interview. The average was 20 per cent over the whole age-range, with 50–59, 60–69 and 70+ scoring the next highest figures. At all times of the year, the natural history section of the Museum was the most visited, followed by archaeology and fine art. Unskilled and semi-skilled

manual workers saw most of the Museum, followed by the skilled manual, schoolchild and housewife groups, in that order. Fine art was more popular in January than at other times, while the peak for natural history was in August, and for archaeology in July.

Visitors were asked if certain services were adequate in the Museum. The percentage of 'no' answers was: seats (17 per cent); facilities for children (17 per cent); signposting (11 per cent); opening hours (10 per cent); floor plans (9 per cent); bookstall (9 per cent); toilets (7 per cent); refreshments (4 per cent). These figures varied very little with the season of the year.

The Norwich survey was not, by modern standards, particularly elaborate or particularly expensive, but it required three things which are difficult or impossible to obtain in many countries – professional help in planning the questionnaire; skilled and experienced staff to carry out the field-work; and a computer to analyse the results. In case this should be found depressing and discouraging, it should be pointed out that as late as 1968 it was possible for one observer of the situation in Britain, Philip S. Doughty,[26] to point out that until that decade 'there was not a single British museum with published results of surveys to discover who its visitors were, how effective its displays were, what the public liked and disliked'.

Mr Doughty had been responsible for the first major visitor-survey to be carried out at a museum in Britain, at the Ulster Museum. The survey was commissioned as a ground-clearing operation before the Museum began a large extension and reshaping programme. It was conducted on five weekdays in July. On these days, every person over the age of seven was asked to complete a questionnaire and about half of them did so. The questionnaire first aimed at discovering certain personal details – age, sex, place of residence, occupation – and then asked visitors if they had visited the Museum before, how long had they spent there on this particular occasion and why had they come. For this last question, there were five possible answers – to look at the whole Museum, to see a particular section or exhibit, to make an enquiry, to have an object identified, to pass the time. Visitors were also asked which parts of the Museum they had visited, which they liked best and least, what form of transport they had used in order to reach the Museum, whether they had ever taken part in any of the Museum's activities, such as film-shows, and what improvements, if any, they would like to see introduced.

As a way of finding out how much of the Museum had been seen, visitors were presented, as part of the questionnaire, with a selection of exhibits which were in the various galleries. Any item

Ulster Museum, Belfast, Northern Ireland. Exhibition of contemporary ceramics.

which had been noticed was to be ticked. Included on the list was a wholly fictitious item, which did not exist at all, but, most regrettably, a considerable number of respondents ticked it, which demonstrated that material yielded by surveys needs to be treated with a certain amount of caution.

The public's opinions of the Museum's amenities could be accepted with a good deal more confidence. The survey left no room for doubt that these were not highly regarded: 'staircases are barriers, lifts are not clearly marked, seats are uncomfortable and only discovered by diligent search, and there are no facilities for refreshment'. Since the report on the survey was published, most of these failings have been

remedied, and in this respect the Ulster Survey has certainly justified itself. It has, however, met with considerable criticism from other points of view.

One of its most serious weaknesses, which it shares with most other museum surveys, is that it was concerned only with the minority of people in Belfast and Ulster who visited the Museum and not at all with the majority who did not. It made no attempt to discover information about the habits and opinions of its potential customers. This lack of balance has since been restored to some extent by David G. Erwin, in his investigation into what the Belfast public as a whole knew or thought about the national museum in their midst.[27] He made use

of a short, simple questionnaire and applied it to a random sample of the city's population. These people were asked to give their sex, age, postal district, and occupation, and then to provide answers to the following questions:

1. Have you ever been to the Ulster Museum? *Yes/No*
   If the answer is *No*, then
2. Have you ever heard of the Ulster Museum? *Yes/No*
   If the answer is *Yes*, then
3. How did you hear of it? *Press/TV/ Poster/A friend/Don't know/Other*
4. Where is it? *Armagh/near Queen's, Belfast/N. Ards Road/ Cultra/Don't know*

Ulster Museum. Department of Technology and Local History. Engineering Hall, with industrial steam-engine display and related graphics.

5. Why haven't you been? *Not inter-ested/No way of getting there/Can never find the time/Other*
6. What would attract you to the Museum?

The most important new information provided by this second survey was concerned with the ways in which people said they had learned about the existence of the Museum: 43 per cent said they knew of it from a friend, 37 per cent from television and 20 per cent from newspapers. The high figures for television and newspapers were particularly interesting, because, up to that time, the Museum had never engaged in either a television or a newspaper campaign to draw attention to itself. Any publicity which had occurred in these two ways must therefore have been incidental, probably in the form of news items.

It is quite clear, from both Doughty's and Erwin's surveys, that a large number of people in Belfast had never been to the Ulster Museum at all. At that point, some kind of decision, formal or tacit, had to be taken as to how sensible or justifiable it was to chase the non-visitors and to attempt to persuade them to visit the Museum at least once. Philip Doughty, who was certainly speaking not only for himself, believed very strongly that it was foolish and morally wrong to devote too much attention to what has become known as the consumer-oriented museum. Such a policy, he was sure, would mean that other branches of the Museum's work would be impoverished and neglected. One should, so to speak, look after the people who did not come and not worry too much about the people who did not.

This amounts to saying that the same piece of market and consumer research can cause one person great anxiety and another hardly any. If a museum is assumed to be for serious-minded people, the absence of non-serious-minded people is not a matter of any consequence, but if, on the other hand, it is seen as an invaluable way of persuading improbable people to take an interest in fields which are completely strange to them, then a narrow range of visitors must be regarded as a failure.

Philip Doughty belongs to the first group, the serious-minded. His views[28] are not, however, universally accepted. In 1955, Dr D. B. Harden, a scholar and a greatly-respected figure in the museum world, gave it as his opinion that, for most people, a museum was

essentially a place of entertainment and amusement. This belief was echoed, after the publication of Doughty's report, by C. A. Sizer,[29] who criticised the deductions made from it, and declared that 'the more museums try to educate the public, the more resistance they will encounter'. Sizer's own opinion was that 'the general public wants its money's worth (even if it does not pay for admission) and perhaps regards museums as another type of trade fair, agricultural show, or stately home'. Many museum professionals would still greatly resent the establishments in their care being compared with trade fairs or agricultural shows, but there is little doubt that a large part of the general public does think in this way. One could put the matter differently by saying that, if the organisers of an agricultural show should happen to carry out research on their visitors, they would be very disappointed indeed to discover that what they had provided with such expertise and at such expense was being patronised only by people from a comparatively narrow social and educational band.

One of the very few countries to have grasped this point is Canada, and the large and very detailed report, *The Museum and the Canadian Public*, which appeared in 1974 as a Government publication, is therefore of exceptional interest. It was based on an unusually elaborate and expensive market re-

search project, almost certainly the most ambitious that has ever been undertaken. The project had the clearly-defined aim of discovering to what extent the national museum policy could be said to be working. That policy, introduced in 1971 and given considerable publicity, rested on the twin principles of democratisation and decentralisation. 'One goal of that policy', says *The Museum and the Canadian Public*, 'was that the largest possible number of Canadians should have access to the collected resources of our human and cultural heritage.' It went on to point out that 'a major handicap to implementing the national museum policy has been our ignorance about the actual and potential audience for museums'. The potential audience, it correctly emphasised, had been almost entirely ignored by previous surveys – Sizer's researches in Belfast were an honourable and notable exception. As a result of this, there was 'little knowledge about people who do not attend museums and other cultural and leisure facilities and events. Comprehensive audiences and non-audience information has been lacking.'

The Canadian survey of behaviour and attitudes towards museums was conducted during April and May 1973. A total of 7230 people aged fourteen and over were interviewed, the sample being designed to represent all regions of the country. Only those people living

Level of participation		Frequency of participation		
		Frequent	Occasional	Rare
Watching movies, drama or sporting events on television	97*	57†	33	10
Reading newspapers, magazines and books	96	72	22	6
Attending or participating in sports and recreational activities	69	49	35	16
Working on indoor or outdoor hobby, craft or art	69	49	38	13
Going to zoos, conservation areas, nature parks, etc.	69	21	52	27
Going to movies	67	13	39	48
Visiting a Canadian historical site or cultural centre	50	9	47	44
Going to concerts or other musical events	49	15	47	38
Visiting a Canadian museum, art gallery, or science centre	48	9	44	47
Going to see a play	43	11	42	47

* This means that 97 per cent of the respondents said that they had watched these things on television at some time during the past twelve months.
† This means, for example, that of those respondents who said they watched television, 57 per cent did so frequently.

Ontario Science Centre, Toronto, Canada. General view, showing the high proportion of exhibits which visitors can operate.

(below) *Children experimenting with a sound-focusing disc. A whisper directed at the centre of the disc can be heard 36 yards away, at a similar disc.*

in very remote areas (the Yukon, and the North-West Territories), Indian reserves, penal institutions and hospitals were excluded. Three questionnaires were used. The first contained a series of brief questions on participation in a selection of leisure activities, including visits to museums and historic sites, during the previous twelve

months. This questionnaire was completed by professional fieldworkers who visited the interviewees in their own homes. Each person interviewed was then classified as a goer or a non-goer, that is, someone who did or did not visit museums, and he was given one of two longer and more detailed questionnaires to fill in at his leisure and to return by post.

The first questionnaire, entitled *Level and frequency of participation in leisure activities during the past twelve months*, produced the overall results shown in the table on p. 137.

Separate analyses of the questionnaires were made to indicate any differences which might be related to age, sex, region, income, language (i.e. French or English) or education, and the results were very significant. It was noted that there was, for example, a steadily increasing participation in 'culturally-oriented activities' as one proceeded across Canada from east to west, and in particular that 'French-speaking Quebecers report a participation rate in visiting museums, art galleries and science centres that is 21 percentage points behind other Canadians'. Over the country as a whole, people living in rural areas participated considerably less in all the leisure-time activities listed in the questionnaire, with the exception of reading and watching television. There is little sexual difference at any age. The participation level declines everywhere with advancing age.

Income and participation are closely related. Those with family incomes below $6000 are least likely to participate, even in television watching and reading, although on the face of it these activities might seem the least likely to be affected by income level. Major increases in the level of participation take place at both the $6000 and $12,000 levels. On the other hand, the frequency of participation is not related to income. The proportion of frequent museum-goers, play-goers, TV-watchers and so on does not increase to any significant extent as income increases.

The tables in *The Museum and the Canadian Public* confirm the findings of previous surveys of leisure-time activities that both level and frequency of participation are strongly linked to occupation: 'Students, professionals, executives, and white-collar workers are the groups most likely to participate in these activities and to do so frequently.' It is also evident that the level rises with increasing education.

While the pattern is most pronounced for the more culturally-oriented activities like play-going, museum-visiting and concert-going, it also surprisingly applies to such activities as working on a hobby and even participation in sports. Thus, the more highly educated respondent is not only more likely to be a museum-goer, he is also more likely to be a sports participant.

The more highly-educated respondents also report a higher frequency of participation. 'Those with university education are two or three times as likely as those with only elementary school education to report themselves as frequent play-goers, concert-goers, museum-goers and sports participants.

The self-administered questionnaires produced a great deal of evidence about the attitudes of Canadians towards their leisure-time activities. One of the methods employed was to ask respondents to choose which of a pair of contrasting words or phrases best described their attitude towards each kind of activity. The resulting data, it was pointed out by the authors of the report, should, like the information on level and frequency of participation, be viewed comparatively. 'Their most important contribution is in giving us greater insight into where museums stand in relation to other competing activities and why. While they do, at the same time, give some insight into attitudes towards the other five leisure activities, they should not be treated as absolute measures of attitudes towards those activities.'

With this caution, the replies to the questionnaire are extremely valuable as a means of knowing how the public in general regards museums. Each word or phrase, it should be pointed out, was derived, as the report expresses it, 'from pre-testing experiences'. This means that it had arisen either in group discussions or in responses to the pre-test questionnaire.

It will be observed from the table given as Appendix 3 at the end of this chapter that a majority of respondents say that they find each of these activities 'something they like to do', 'stimulating' and, more surprisingly, 'easy on the brain'. On the other hand, when asked the 'always the same' or 'always different' question, a majority felt that there was a sameness about both tele-

Reasons given by Canadians for visiting museums

Reason	Frequency			
	Frequently	Occasionally	Rarely	Not at all*
I wanted to enjoy myself	84	82	78	73
I wanted to learn something	82	87	79	74
I had nothing else to do that day	5	12	15	20
I thought the visit would be good for my education and growth	82	77	65	64
My club or organisation was going	11	9	7	5
I wanted to show the museum to my family or friends	43	41	33	37
I wanted to see a special exhibit I'd heard about	58	41	34	35
I wanted to see all or part of a permanent exhibit I'd heard about	58	44	39	43
I needed some unusual information the museum has available	21	12	6	6
I went to see a film, concert or play	15	10	6	6

* This heading may appear to contain a contradiction. The column refers to correspondents claiming to be goers in the personal interview questionnaire, but indicating in the self-administered questionnaire that they had not attended a museum during the past twelve months.

Canadian visitors' suggestions for improving museums

	Goers	Non-Goers
Make entry to museums free	31	28
Make museum exhibits available to me in my neighbourhood	15	16
Keep museums open longer hours	11	8
Provide more advertising and publicity about what museums are like	18	16
Provide more advertising and publicity about what activities go on in museums	19	13
Provide baby-sitting service in museums	5	4
Provide museum sections designed for young children	17	13
Provide better restaurants in museums	5	4
Make museum buildings look brighter and friendlier and more welcoming	8	7
Hire friendlier and more congenial guides	3	3
Provide the guides with more information about the things in the museum	7	6
Make the information on the signs and labels easier to understand	3	7
Provide free guidebooks and pamphlets about the things to see in the museum	18	20
Give more information on the signs and labels	4	4
Make it easier to locate the things I'm interested in	5	4
Display things in a more interesting way	5	3
Show more things about the present and future	7	6
Let me touch things and operate demonstrations	12	7
Bring in artists and craftsmen and let me watch them create things on the spot	31	17
Change the displays more often	7	5
Use the museums to show more films, plays and concerts	9	4
Provide arts and crafts workshops where I can learn to make things	18	12

vision and museums. Museums are rated as 'for everyone' by only 61 per cent of the population, live performances by only 57 per cent. One in every three Canadians, a disturbingly high figure, believes that museums and live performances are primarily for 'intellectuals', however these may be defined. The facts do not, however, bear this out. There is, the report admits, 'a slight pro-cultural slant' in the museum-goer's activities and attitudes, but it is not pronounced. He is 'not so much a "cultural-snob" as he is an active doer of a wide range of activities'.

As the authors of the report point out, Canadians – and the same could no doubt be said about most other countries – have not yet made up their minds about museums. In the language

of the report, 'visiting a museum has the least clearly defined image of all six rated activities'. This is partly a result of the museum's relative lack of popularity. In Canada, at least, watching television and reading a book have the sharpest images, probably because a large majority of the population takes part in these activities and has the experience to reach a consensus of opinion about them. Even so, the opportunities to obtain this experience are certainly increasing, since between 55 per cent and 60 per cent of all Canadians visited a museum during the twelve months preceding the survey, a proportion that was almost certainly not exceeded anywhere else in the world; and 84 per cent said they had visited a museum at least once in the previous five years. Historical sites and general museums received

the highest proportion of visitors during this period, followed by art museums, science and technology museums, touring museums and maritime and marine museums.

From the point of view of any specific type of museum [it was concluded] the using public consists of two very different kinds of visitors; a large majority who are very infrequent visitors, averaging less than one visit per year, and a small core group who visit frequently and account for a highly disproportionate number of visits. The museum director is thus faced with the dilemma of trying to serve two very different types of users, with very different behaviours and . . . very different attitudes towards the museum.

Asked what had prompted them to make their most recent visit to a museum, visitors replied in significantly different ways, according to the frequency with which they claimed to visit museums. The pattern of response to the eleven questions is shown in the first table on page 139.

At the end of the self-administered questionnaire, respondents were asked to agree or disagree with a list of suggested improvements to museums which might improve attendances. The second table on page 139 shows the percentage of goers and non-goers which agreed with each suggestion.

There are a number of interesting and perhaps curious features about these figures. One is the considerable measure of agreement between the goers and the non-goers, another the size of the demand for practical activities from people who visit museums a good deal, confirming the view expressed earlier in the report that museum-goers are energetic, rather than intellectual or scholarly. The intellectual is unlikely to want more opportunities to touch things, make things or make things move.

The fact that these suggestions are made at all does not mean, of course, that they describe complete innovations. Many museums, even in Canada, do have excellent signs and labels, do allow visitors to touch and operate exhibits, do provide arts and crafts workshops, do display things in an exciting way, do have friendly, con-

Museum of Oxford

Welcome to the Museum of Oxford

Information in this museum is given in French, German, Spanish, Japanese, and Arabic as well as in English.

Soyez les bienvenus au Musée d'Oxford

L'information dans ce musée est donnée en français en même temps qu'en anglais.

Willkommen im Oxforder Museum

In diesem Museum finden Sie alle Informationen neben Englisch auch in Deutsch.

Bienvenidos al Museo de Oxford

La información en este Museo se da en Español además de en Inglés.

オクスフォード 博物館へ ようこそ
当博物館の 情報は 英文と共に 日本文
でも 提示されています

أهــــلا وسهــــلا الـــى متحــف اكسفـورد
المعلــومات فـي هذا المتحـــف، متوفــرة باللغتيـن
العربيـــة والانكليزيـــة

Museum of Oxford, England. Multi language labels.

genial and well-informed guides. A nation-wide survey of this kind is very valuable as a basis for more effective and relevant national planning, but it is bound to be unfair to the best museums. The answers and therefore the information to be analysed are bound to be general, even though they may be based on a personal knowledge of only one or two museums. To say that 18 per cent of museum-goers want museums to 'provide arts and crafts workshops where I can learn to make things' may well mean no more than that for 18 per cent of the people who completed the questionnaire the local museum does not have these facilities. It is, on the other hand, possible, but unlikely, that the 82 per cent who failed to agree with this suggestion lived in or near museums which had excellent facilities of this kind. This is not, of course, to label the statistics as meaningless, but merely to issue a reminder that they should, like all statistics, be treated with caution and that their limitations and possible distortions should be kept always in mind.

Comments made on precise situations have a better chance of being really meaningful and of leading to action than comments on abstractions. One does not, after all, visit an abstraction. One visits a particular museum, with its own strong and weak points, a fact which is rarely even hinted at in *The Museum and the Canadian Public*. The object of one's hate or affection is the Ontario Science Centre, the Willow Creek Historical Museum or the Vancouver Maritime Museum, not some vague synthetic called The Museum. The Ontario Science Centre has a real public, which can be seen and heard. The Museum is visited and managed only by statistical cut-outs.

ENCOURAGING COMMENTS BY VISITORS

The difficulty is, of course, that some visitors do come very close to being statistical cut-outs, and that when they are encouraged to put their reactions into words they do not sound like real people at all. The Guggenheim Foundation has published a large selection of unsolicited comments made by visitors to the Tenth Anniversary Exhibition of what was then called the Museum of Non-Objective Painting in New York. It is now the Solomon R. Guggenheim Museum. These comments were written down after the people con-cerned had seen the collection. There is no way of telling if they are typical or if they would have expressed themselves in the same way if they had been talking instead of writing, but from the evidence we have it is clear that these visitors take themselves very seriously indeed and that they are thoroughly soaked in psychological and sociological jargon, which is, of course, taken as a sign of profound thinking and solid education by many people in the United States.

Their comments are preceded in the printed report by this note: 'The visitors' names and addresses, together with their unsolicited comments, are on record in the Museum of Non-Objective Painting, owned by the Solomon R. Guggenheim Foundation, 1071 Fifth Avenue, New York City. They give evidence that never before has there been art equally effective, equally uplifting and equally practical.'

This, to a non-American observer, might seem to be the language of the advertising man rather than the museum man, of Madison Avenue rather than Fifth Avenue. But it is fully in tune with what the visitors themselves wrote. The two clearly spring from the same national culture, in which all public language is apt to sound computerised and second-hand. One reads: 'This is the only museum I have ever seen which makes me feel that it is sincerely interested in furthering the growth and deepening the insight of all creative endeavors. This museum really serves humanity: I wish there were more like it' – and one has no mental picture of the person who produced it. Somewhere underneath these flat, impersonal, grandiose words there must be a real man or woman, but the Guggenheim's audience-research technique gives him no encouragement to appear.

The report makes remarkable reading. 'The paintings of Bauer', declared one enthusiast, 'are messages of intimations of immortality, of man's communing with spatial profundity.' Others went further and testified, in the language of a religious revivalist meeting, to the miracle-working way in which the exhibition had transformed their lives.

'I had lived in France for years,' wrote one of them, 'then everything was lost. I came to America a broken person. I walked around as if a great weight were on my shoulders. One day someone showed me some prints from the non-objective museum, and I came to see the paintings. Somehow each visit brought subtle changes. I was able to go about building up my life again. People who had not seen me since my arrival hardly recognised me. I felt thirty years of difference on my face. Now I walked as if on air. Non-objectivity has caused this miracle for me.'

Outpourings of this kind are valuable from the museological point of view only if they can be documented in some way. To make them a useful source of information one needs to know as much as possible about the people who wrote them. This would include their age, sex, occupation, education as a minimum, as well, of course, as their address, which the Museum already has. What someone says only becomes meaningful when one knows what kind of person said it. The Guggenheim comments make sense as supplementary research material. By themselves they have little more than entertainment value, except perhaps to a psychologist.

There is no doubt that the remarks made by the visitors to the Guggenheim Museum were conditioned by the atmosphere of the Museum, in the sense that the visitors were part of that atmosphere and used the language they felt to be appropriate to it. One can see and feel the same process at work in the John F. Kennedy Museum in Dallas, Texas, where, once inside the entrance, the visitor is greeted by huge photographic enlargements of some of the adulatory comments cards filled in by previous visitors. Anyone who is rash or pious enough to complete one of these cards himself must find it extremely difficult to write down any independent or objective thought of his own. He is most likely to echo the kind of things that have already been said and that he can read on the wall in front of him. To regard these cards as being in any sense research material is, from a museological point of view, a gross misuse of the term. They are an exercise in group thinking, carried out by people who are fully accustomed to reacting and being asked to react in this way.

The phenomenon is not, of course, peculiar to the United States. To quicken their powers of observation and to encourage them to develop a personal response to works of art, children living in selected cities in the German Democratic Republic have been asked, for the purposes of a research project, to write down their impressions of selected works of art during their visits to galleries.[30] Two examples will illustrate the results. The first relates to a portrait of the President of the Republic, Wilhelm Pieck.

> I am standing in front of the portrait of Wilhelm Pieck. His friendly eyes look straight at me below his bushy eyebrows. The expression on his face shows not only kindliness, but determination. It is like a silent command, not just to keep going forward, but to listen to what he has to say first. His face tells of a life of anxiety and deprivation. The high forehead, the hair combed smoothly back are characteristic of a reflective, studious man, eager for knowledge. One can see he was a man who was driven on to acquire new experiences during every day of his long life.

The second set of comments in the survey from the German Democratic Republic refers to a different kind of painting altogether, Paul Michaelis' 'High School Girl'.

> I don't know this girl personally, and yet she isn't a stranger to me. I understand what she's thinking. On many points, our opinions are the same. I would do many of the things she does. If I were to look for her, I should find her everywhere in our country. I could look for her in Berlin, Leipzig or Dresden and I could find her a hundred times over. She could be one of my classmates, she could be myself. She is a girl with her weak points and her strong points, but she knows what she's aiming at, and she's going to get there. She knows what life's about, for herself and for everyone else.

This, in short, is not a portrait of any high-school girl, but of an approved kind, the officially best kind of high-school girl, the most desirable type. The painter could, no doubt, have decided to depict a shiftless, idle, scatter-brained girl but, for reasons best known to himself, he chose not to. What one therefore has is a circular process; an artist paints an approved subject in an approved way, and schoolchildren write down their approved reactions to the result. From the point of view of a museologist or an educationist, this is feedback of a very special kind. It may well measure observation, but it measures conformity at the same time. A more searching, and one is tempted

to say worthwhile, test of artistic discrimination, cultural development and powers of expression would have been to confront the visitors to the Guggenheim or to the unspecified German art galleries with a Rembrandt, a Turner or a Van Gogh, to see what they made of it. It would quite probably have been found that neither their pattern of thinking nor their vocabulary was equal to the task, which is always a major difficulty with this write-down-what-you-feel kind of consumer research.

But suppose, instead of a German child looking at Wilhelm Pieck's portrait in 1971, we had an English boy or girl faced with a picture of Lord Kitchener in 1914 or of Winston Churchill in 1942. Would their responses have been so very much more original, more unpredictable? In any period and in any country, a genuinely personal reaction is a rare phenomenon, except among very young children. There are fashions of thought and emotion in the United States and Sweden, just as there are in the Soviet Union and Nigeria, and any research, of whatever kind, which is conducted with visitors to museums can do little more than explore the strength of the current fashion, which may not be at all to the taste of many of the museum staff, who belong to a different generation or a different cultural group.

The main frustration and irritation with which the curators of museums, especially large museums, have to contend is that they and the members of their professional staff are highly-educated people, while many, perhaps most of their visitors are nothing of the sort. The curators would naturally like to improve this situation, and to bring at least some of their visitors closer to their own level of taste and knowledge. Market research is often, one feels, undertaken with this aim particularly in mind, as a check on the success one is achieving in the progress towards what, one fears, may be an impossible goal. Some have come to feel that the struggle is futile and that the surveys confirm what they have always believed, that the serious work of the museum must and should go on behind closed doors, while the idiot public is given a museum-circus to keep it amused and contented.

INFORMAL MARKET RESEARCH

It is quite possible that those who are most successful in communicating with

State Art Collections, Dresden, GDR. 'Portrait of Wilhelm Pieck.'

(below) *Paul Michaelis, 'High School Girl'.*

ordinary people are not far from being ordinary people themselves, and that, in the museum field as elsewhere, the mandarin, respect-the-expert attitude is doomed to failure. A high proportion of the world's museums are in the charge of enthusiastic, devoted men and women with no museum training or career ambitions at all. They are the museum curators who rarely attend conferences and never draw up or administer questionnaires or attempt any other kind of investigation into the habits or attitudes of their visitors. The collections for which they are responsible are often, if not usually, arranged in a way which is calculated to make a professionally-trained curator despair, but which the general public seems to like. Museums of this type can become part of the local community to an extent which is almost impossible for the large museum and carry out their own special kind of visitor research inevitably and automatically as they go along. A museum with a large staff of experts and specialists is, inescapably, in a we-and-they position with regard to the general public. The neighbourhood or community museum on the other hand sees no cultural, power or administrative gap between the people who plan and run the museum and the people who use it. MUSE, in New York, has rejected the conventional geographical definition of community in favour of something different and wider. 'I like to think of it', says the Director,[31] 'as something called the "community of interest" or the "community of concern", which cuts across any narrow geographical boundaries around any

one institution. It cuts across social, economic, ethnic and all other kinds of interrelated barriers. It's like a spider's web reaching out wherever it can cling. That's how I define the word "community".'

He is convinced that the idea of a museum as a cathedral or a temple is completely out of date.

> My personal belief [he has made clear] is that a museum is a theatre. There are many parallels. I look at the theatre building as being a museum building. I look at the content of a museum as the play that's running at the theatre. I look at the design of the exhibits as being analogous to the props the actor uses on stage. But the actor has to use the proper props to bring life into the play. And similarly the museum visitor, I think, is the actor, who has to interrelate with what is presented and exhibited to get the juices flowing and to get the production to come alive.

With this as the aim and the method, MUSE has its producers and designers on the stage with the actors. The staff are not, as in most other museums, shut away and segregated in their offices. They spend a large part of each working week moving round among the children visiting the museum finding out how they react to the displays and discovering which exhibits are successful and which are not. This is the MUSE form of visitor research. It is unscientific and it is not statistically reliable, but it keeps the staff in constant touch touch with the public in a way that a computer-

analysed questionnaire can never do. Despite all the technical advances of the past fifty years, the most effective kind of visitor research in museums is still what is known in agricultural circles as the farmer's boot, walking round to see for oneself. This is true of every type of human activity. To take people round a house and then to ask them, 'What do you think of this house? Do you like it? Is it what you want? Does it meet your needs?' is far more relevant and sensible than to ask them 'What do you think of four-bedroomed, detached houses with one bathroom, washbasins in each bedroom, gas-fired central heating and a kitchen 12 feet by 10?' Yet many, perhaps most, museum surveys tend to ask the second kind of question rather than the first, and, equally important, even when they do put the first sort of question, they rarely do so actually in front of a particular object or display, pointing and referring to it. There is no substitute for:

(*a*) Standing with a person or a group of people looking at an exhibit and saying, 'Tell me, honestly and bluntly, what you think of that and the way it is presented to you?'
(*b*) Wandering about incognito, watching people's movement and behaviour in a museum and listening to their comments.

Most curators, if pressed, would say that they did both (*a*) and (*b*) occasionally and that they exchanged experiences, in an informal way, with their colleagues who attempted to put their finger on the visitors' pulse in the same way. What is wanted, however, is something more systematic, in the form of a daily comments diary or log. The entries in this need not, of course, be made by the curators themselves.

THE UNDER-USED GALLERY ATTENDANT

Gallery attendants are, at the present time, used in an extraordinarily wasteful and inhuman fashion. Being always around in the galleries and among the

Unused potential. A gallery guard at the British Museum, London. This policeman is required to do nothing but watch and protect. The Museum authorities are not interested in the conversations he overhears. His possibilities as a valuable research agent are largely wasted.

public, they are ideally placed to see and to overhear. It should be part of their training and duties to note down what they observe, so that what is, in effect, a running report on visitors' behaviour is constantly available for the curators' benefit. More precisely, what is required is a note of:

1. Which exhibits are obviously receiving a great deal of attention and which practically none.
2. Any questions, no matter how apparently trivial these may be, which the attendant is asked.
3. Any remarks which are overheard about particular exhibits, the museum as a whole, or other visitors. It is of the greatest importance that these remarks should be written down in the words that were actually used, together with some indication of the way in which they were said and of the kind of person who said them.

Experiments are already being made with this at the Prince of Wales Museum in Bombay, and possibly elsewhere as well. The habit must surely grow, since it offers such obvious advantages – attendants can give a more intelligent kind of attention to their work, they can feel more closely involved in the aims and activities of the museum, and curators can be provided with a regular supply of information to set against their own impressions and, possibly, prejudices and preconceptions. It is, of course, perfectly true that some attendants would carry out this additional duty more easily and efficiently than others, that some would resist it and that some would demand extra payment. Some countries would undoubtedly find the system easier to introduce than others. This would be particularly true of countries, such as India and Mexico, which have a high rate of unemployment and where many people are working at jobs below their real capacity. A more serious obstacle, and one that should certainly not be underrated, is that far too many museum curators and directors frankly enjoy a tightly organised, hierarchical system and would object to gallery attendants, whom they regard as private soldiers, carrying out functions which are traditionally the preserve and prerogative of officers. One cannot have it both ways. If rank is considered to be more important than information, the museum will have to do without the information. There are certainly battles to be fought on this front. The democratic museum is, as yet, an exceedingly rare institution.

THE OPINIONS OF WORKING-CLASS VISITORS

A fact which is usually ignored or not noticed at all is that museum attendants, because of their social and educational background, can be invaluable intermediaries between the working-class culture of a section of the visitors and the almost wholly middle-class culture of the museum's professional staff. Given the will to do so, they can be used as link-figures and interpreters, and even as research material themselves. How often, however, are attendants asked what they think of an exhibit? The planning imagination of most museums appears to have curious limitations.

This is not, of course, the same as saying that museums are not interested in discovering the opinions of working-class visitors. An interesting and original survey was carried out in Paris during the mid-1960s by Pierre Bourdieu and Alain Darbel,[32] who were well aware of the need to find out what working-class people thought about museums. In the course of their survey visitors to a number of art galleries in Paris and the provinces were interrogated by means of a questionnaire and their feelings summarised and presented partly in statistical form and partly as quotations. Among the questions put to them was: 'Which of these institutions reminds you most of a museum: a church, a library, a court of law, a large store or a court waiting-room?' The replies varied a great deal, according to whether the person interviewed belonged to the working class, middle class or upper class. Of the working class respondents 66 per cent gave the answer 'a church', compared with 45 per cent of the middle class and only 30.5 per cent of the upper class. A museum was compared to a library by 9 per cent of the working class, 34 per cent of the middle class and 28 per cent of the upper class. The other comparisons received much less support from any group. It should be noticed, however – and here one returns to a constant weakness in museum surveys – that the questions were abstract. It was not 'Does the museum in Valence, where you live, remind you most of the parish church, the law-court, the public library or Dupont's department store in Valence?' The proviso is an important one, partly because not all museums, courts of law, churches or department stores are alike – some museums are almost indistinguishable from department stores and others from churches – and partly because most people are at their best when they are asked about real things that they know, not about abstractions. The truth is, however, and it needs to be stated with all possible firmness, that the computer, like any other form of data-processing equipment, deals easily and confidently with abstract concepts and very badly indeed with precise pieces of information, such as the Church of St Séverin and Dupont's department store. Once it is agreed that a survey is to have a statistical base, one has turned one's back on certain kinds of information and understanding, in order to obtain others. The only truly flexible research tools are the human brain, eyes and ears, compared with which the computer is a poor second-best. What it can do, it does fast and accurately, but there are many things which it cannot do at all.

The Bourdieu and Darbel survey contains a number of interesting examples of this. The interviewees were asked, for example, 'In your opinion, what are the best conditions for looking at a work of art? In particular, do you yourself prefer to be with a lot of people or a very few people?' The results could be easily tabulated, as shown below.

Working-class people were more likely to say – the report necessarily talks in generalisations – that they felt happier to visit museums and galleries in groups and that they liked to be provided with a guide, even though they feared, from past experience, that the guide might talk above their head. Educated people, who were the best

	A lot of people	Few people	No preference	No answer
Working class	39	39	18	4
Middle class	11	67	15	11
Upper class	2	70	19.5	8.5

equipped to understand what the guides were trying to tell them, were, paradoxically, the most anxious not to go round the museum with a guide.

This kind off information is within the computer's grasp, and, like Mr Bourdieu and Mr Darbel, one can deduce what one likes from it. That, after all, is what statistics are for. The more personal and individual comments made in answer to other questions in the survey demanded quite different treatment. Visitors to each gallery were asked to give the names of painters whose works they had seen during their tour. Of the working-class visitors, 55 per cent were unable to recall the name of a single painter. Those who could produce a name invariably selected painters, such as Leonardo, Michelangelo and Rembrandt, who lived a long time ago, or those more recent artists, like Renoir and Van Gogh, who had been the subject of films or whose paintings have been much reproduced. It would, it is true, have been possible to report statistically how often Rembrandt or Cézanne had been mentioned and by what kind of people, and the information might have been worth something. What would have been distorted beyond recognition by an attempt at statistical presentation was the list of reasons given for likes and dislikes. The Lille housewife who said 'I like pictures with Christ in them' and the Lens shopkeeper who admitted 'I don't understand Picasso' defy the computer, unless one is willing to have so many classifications and subdivisions that the final analysis and report become so huge and detailed as to be unreadable and unusable. The computer would also have ironed out of existence the Lille factory worker who explained why it was important for him to remain silent in a museum. 'You're frightened

of meeting a connoisseur,' he told the interviewer. 'Anyone like me comes and goes without speaking to anyone.'

The Lille factory worker had good reason to be frightened of meeting, if not a connoisseur, someone who knew or gave the appearance of knowing a great deal more about art than he did. Art galleries, like all other museums, are still overwhelmingly middle-class institutions. A survey[33] carried out in 1973 in four large London museums – the National Portrait Gallery, the Tate Gallery, the Natural History Museum and the Science Museum – showed that visitors came almost entirely from the middle classes and, more particularly, from people whose full-time education had extended to eighteen and beyond. There was, says the report, 'a consistent and depressing absence of working-class visitors'.

THE RESEARCH THAT PREVENTS MISTAKES

Forecasts are always likely to be proved wrong, but it seems reasonably safe to predict that ten years from now most museums will have developed a routine method of discovering the kinds of people who are coming as visitors, and that most of the time, skill and interest of what we have termed feedback will be concerned with finding out what the public thinks about the way a museum is going about its job.

A good deal of work has already been accomplished in this field, especially in the United States. Ten years ago, in a well-known series of experiments, Lee A. Parsons, of Milwaukee Public Museum, tried to discover how visitors were reacting to a specially arranged anthropological exhibit. His conclusions (reported in *Curator*, Vol. 8 no. 2, 1965) were:

(*a*) We are gauging some of our exhibits at too low an informational level. Our museum audience is better educated and more demanding than we realise.

(*b*) Museum exhibit-designers may find it advisable to return to well-filled displays and above all to de-emphasize tricky or extraneous 'art work' in case exhibits. This is not to say that we advocate displays which are truly overcrowded; instead, we recommend some sort of compromise between open storage and the ultra-selective exhibits which are the trend today.

Three years later another American, Harris H. Shettel, was saying (*Curator*, vol. 11 no. 2, 1968) that there were ways of achieving fewer failures in the design of exhibits. 'Ad hoc solutions to these problems', he declared, 'are not only a bad risk; they are becoming increasingly expensive.' Mr Shettel produced what he called an Exhibit Effectiveness Rating Scale, which could be used by the designer and his colleagues while the exhibit was still in the planning stage. This was really a systematic way of forcing oneself to think very hard about an exhibit before, not after, it happened. It is clear, however, that, no matter how good the planning, total success is almost impossible, simply because human behaviour is only predictable up to a certain point. The good museum is essentially a perpetual laboratory, in which the monitored results of one experiment allow one to begin the next with a more adequate body of knowledge. Feedback, to be of any real value, must be continuous and, above all, it must be transformed into action, so that visitors are, probably without knowing it, creating their own museum.

APPENDIX 4.1

Museums which reported in 1974–5 that they had never carried out Visitor Surveys

Australia
Art Gallery of South Australia, Adelaide
South Australian Museum, Adelaide
National Gallery of Victoria, Melbourne
Western Australian Museum, Perth
Art Gallery of New South Wales, Sydney
Museum of Applied Arts and Sciences, Sydney

Australia
Museum of Upper Austria, Linz
Augusteum, Salzburg
Gallery of Paintings, Vienna
Museum of Applied Art, Vienna
Museum of the History of Art, Vienna
Natural History Museum, Vienna
Technical Museum, Vienna

Canada
Manitoba Museum of Man and Nature
National Gallery of Canada, Ottawa
National Museum of Natural Sciences, Ottawa

Cyprus
Cyprus Museum, Nicosia

Finland
National Museum of Finland, Helsinki
Historical Museum, Turku

France
Natural History Museum, Paris

Germany, Federal Republic
Gallery of Paintings, Berlin-Dahlen
German Museum, Munich

Great Britain
National Museum of Wales, Cardiff
National Gallery of Scotland, Edinburgh
Art Gallery and Museum, Glasgow
City Museum, Leeds
British Museum, London
Horniman Museum, London
Science Museum, London
Victoria and Albert Museum, London

Greece
Ethnological and Historical Museum, Athens
National Archaeological Museum, Athens

Hungary
National Gallery, Budapest

Iceland
National Museum, Reykjavik

India
Indian Museum, Calcutta

Ireland
National Gallery of Ireland, Dublin

Netherlands
van Oudheden National Museum, Leiden

Norway
National Gallery, Oslo

Spain
Prado Museum, Madrid

Sweden
National Museum, Stockholm
Nordic Museum, Stockholm

Switzerland
Bern Historical Museum
Natural History Museum, Bern

United States
Children's Museum, Boston
Art Institute of Chicago
Cleveland Museum of Art
Denver Art Museum
Los Angeles County Museum of Art
Peabody Museum, New Haven, Connecticut
Museum of Modern Art, New York
Museum of the Californian Academy of Sciences, San Francisco
Henry Francis du Pont Museum, Winterthur, Delaware

APPENDIX 4.2

Arts Council Questionnaire

1. Male/Female/Under 15/15–25/26–35/36–50/Over 50?
2. Is this the first time you have ever come to the Gallery? Yes/No.
3. (*a*) Have you seen any other exhibitions at the City Art Gallery this year? Yes/No.
   (*b*) If so, which? Manchester Academy Spring Exhibition of Local Artists/The American Frontier/ . . . .
4. (*a*) Had you heard about the Rouault Exhibition before you came today? Yes/No.
   (*b*) If yes, how? . . . .
5. (*a*) Have you seen or heard any (other) advertising for this Rouault Exhibition? Yes/No.
   (*b*) If Yes, where? (Prove) . . . .

6. (*a*) Have you read or heard about this exhibition in the press or from radio or television? Yes/No.
   (*b*) If yes, what? . . . .
7. Where have you come from today? Manchester/. . . . .
8. Where do you live? Manchester/. . . . .
9. (*a*) What is your occupation?
   . . . .
   (*b*) If a student or teacher, is your work involved with the Arts? Yes/No.
10. Where do you work? Manchester/ . . . .
11. Within the past two weeks have you travelled by British Rail in the Manchester area? Yes/No.
12. Within the past week have you listened to commercial radio? Yes/No.

13. Within the past week have you looked in the classified advertising columns for information on art exhibitions? Yes/No.
14. (*a*) Did you look at any newspaper last Sunday? Yes/No.
    (*b*) If so, which? . . . .
15. Did you look at any morning or evening newspapers yesterday? Yes/No (or 'On Saturday' if interview carried out on Monday, 15th). If so, which? . . . .
16. (*a*) Have you come to the exhibition in a party? Yes/No.
    (*b*) If leader of party. Did you know that you can have help towards your travel cost? Yes/No.
17. Any other comments? . . . .

APPENDIX 4.3

Table of Leisure Activities

Percentage of respondents choosing the italicised descriptor

Descriptor	Watching television	Reading a book	Going to a movie	Visiting a museum	Participating in sports	Going to a live performance
Relaxing/Exciting	87*	85	56	54	15	45
Modern/Old-fashioned	80	58	63	49	77	58
Educational/Entertaining	25	70	4	81	12	18
Expensive/Inexpensive	9	8	73	19	41	74
Rewarding/Unrewarding	60	90	48	82	80	68
Something I like/don't like to do	84	80	71	66	72	65
Boring/Stimulating	28	17	21	29	13	28
Always the same/Always different	53	12	27	45	28	24
Sociable/Unsociable	42	33	69	72	85	75
Something I do very often/don't do very often	70	60	20	8	44	14
Convenient/Inconvenient	91	85	46	29	52	30
Easy on the brain/Hard on the brain	88	73	81	74	70	73
For everyone/For intellectuals	97	76	89	61	88	57
Valuable to me/Not valuable to me	58	83	41	62	66	52

* This means that 87 per cent of the respondents chose the first description, 'Relaxing'.

5 Selection and Training of Personnel

Museums are a growth industry. Taking the world as a whole, the number of museums is probably increasing at the rate of about 10 per cent every five years. In some countries, such as Japan, the Soviet Union and the United States, development is considerably faster. Many of these new museums, it is true, are very small and some are community enterprises, run without any full-time professional staff at all. But the distinction between 'professional' and 'amateur' or 'volunteer' is always somewhat unreal. If a small local museum is started by a former 'professional', who left her job in order to marry and bring up a family, and is now happy to devote much of her leisure time to acting as an unpaid curator of a two-room museum in the town hall, is she to be regarded as a professional or not? If she persuades a highly skilled graphics artist, who happens to be a member of the local historical society, to carry out the museum's design work, also for nothing, is he to be branded as no more than a dabbling amateur? In fact, the number of these hard-working amateurs is now so considerable, in countries as different as Canada and the Soviet Union, that one of the major tasks facing the museum profession during the next ten years is going to be to find effective and relevant ways of helping and training them. They cannot be simply argued and ridiculed out of existence.

Museums which have taken the trouble to integrate volunteer staff into their normal working pattern have found this extra unpaid assistance invaluable. One of the best organised systems is to be found at the Toledo

Museum of Art, where the volunteers are organised into four groups:

1. The Endowment Development Group, which concerns itself with discovering major donors to Museum funds.
2. The Art Museum Aides. These are the force behind the membership drive. They also staff Collectors' Corner and the art rental and sales gallery of the Museum and take care of the plants which are liberally distributed over the premises.
3. The Friends of the Museum. Their main task is to enrol new members, but they also help the Aides as hostesses at the opening of major exhibitions.
4. The Docents. These give lectures on art and music. They are carefully trained for the job, and their function is defined as 'bringing the Museum's collections alive and relating it to the school curriculum, from the first grade through high school'. During 1974, they gave lectures to 28,000 children and 2100 adults.

If all these people were paid for the work they did for the Museum, the bill would amount to hundreds of thousands of dollars a year, which the Museum does not have.

According to a survey carried out in 1973 for the National Endowment for the Arts, the total 'museum work force' in the United States, including volunteers, numbers more than 110,000. Of this total, 30,400 were full-time paid personnel – 11,000 professionals and 19,400 non-professionals – and 18,700 were employed part-time. There were 64,200 volunteers. One can interpret this to mean either that without its huge

unpaid labour force the American museum would collapse or, more objectively and statistically, that more than half the people working in American museums give their services for nothing, as a contribution to the welfare of the community.

These proportions were not equally spread over all types and sizes of museum. The survey showed that 84 per cent of the museums employed part-time staff and 60 per cent made use of volunteers. If the distribution of full-time staff is related to the size of a museum's budget, it becomes evident that in 1973 the 5 per cent of American museums with operating budgets of a million dollars and over employed 45 per cent of all full-time employees, and that the 44 per cent of museums with annual budgets of under $50,000 employed only 9 per cent.

The largest proportion of full-time staff, 45 per cent, worked, and presumably still work, in what was described as 'operations and support', i.e. technical, manual and unskilled services. This was followed by administration, 23 per cent; 'curatorial, display and exhibit', 17 per cent; education, 9 per cent; and research, 6 per cent. In each of these areas, except for operations and support, in which 90 per cent of the employees were non-professional, the professionals represented a slightly higher proportion of the staff than the non-professionals. The distribution of part-time staff was about the same as for full-time staff, except that a higher proportion of part-time staff was involved in education.

Roughly 50 per cent of all museum directors said that they need more staff in each of the five job categories. This percentage ranged from 47 per cent in the research area to 61 per cent in curatorial, display and exhibit. It seems possible, however, that staffs in American museums have already reached their peak, at least for some time to come, since reductions in staff, both professional and non-professional, were the most frequently mentioned way in which museums had attempted to cut their operating costs during the previous five years. It might therefore be reasonable to suppose that there are now (1977) 10,000 museum professionals in the United States, which amounts to something like 1.25 per museum, since there are approximately 8000 museums in the whole country. This, however, is a mere average and it is certain, although the National Endowment for the Arts Survey did not investigate this, that the spread is by no means even and that many museums employ no professional staff at all. Given the range of museums and the facilities for training, this is exactly what one would expect.

Even at well-provided museums, the proportion of professional staff can be surprisingly low, a fact which is often concealed by the grandiose names which employees receive in official publications. The Art Gallery at Huntington, West Virginia, provides a good example of this. In 1971 the Gallery went into a magnificent new building, financed by a private benefactor and designed by one of the world's leading and therefore most expensive architects, Walter Gropius. The staff at that time consisted of:

Director
Co-ordinator of Education
Administrative Secretary
Membership Secretary
Education Secretary
Artist-in-Residence
Receptionist
Exhibition Co-ordinator
Manager, Craft Shop
Superintendent of the Plant
Two maintenance men

Of these twelve people, only three, at the most – the Director, Co-ordinator of Education, and Exhibition Co-ordinator – would have been professionals, in the museum sense of the term, and it is quite possible that none of them had, in fact, had any formal museological training. The main task of the staff was to safeguard and administer a valuable property, and to ensure the financial success of the enterprise. The educational function of the Gallery was

secondary to this, although certainly not unimportant.

This is true of many of the world's museums. What might be described as the business or managerial side of museum work has overwhelmed the curatorial and educational side to such an extent that museum-managers are often difficult to distinguish from the people who run commercial or industrial enterprises with no cultural pretensions at all. It is obviously right and sensible that directors and curators of museums should possess managerial skills to a marked degree, and that the development of these skills should form an important part of their training, but it is very dangerous, even so, to assume one can be a satisfactory museum administrator without museological training and experience, as many museums have found to their cost in recent years, especially when directors have been purely political appointments. The first criterion must be a real and proved interest in museums and a conviction that museums are important cultural instruments, to be used with sensitivity and knowledge.

'I have had the museum opened five years,' writes the curator and sole staff of a small local museum in the American West, 'doors never locked, people come and go at their desires. I do not expect to lock the doors until someone takes something, then I will keep them locked from 10 p.m. to 7 a.m.' His museum, he tells us, has

> more than 200 pieces of gourd craft from Ecuador, South America, lots of crafts from Peru as well as crafts and gourds as they are used as containers from all over the globe. Four different persons are making Indian musical instruments and sending them to the Museum. We have two carved by Theo Schoon of New Zealand. He is considered the world's best carver.

This is one extreme end of the museum spectrum. Until the owner and curator of the museum dies or becomes too old to carry on, there is no staff problem and no financial problem of any consequence. One man serves as director, guide, head of the conservation, design and acquisition departments, secretary, and performs, in a somewhat basic fashion, all the other functions which the administration of a museum requires. His museum contains a considerable number of exhibits which the few hundred people who come to see

them each year find interesting. He is very knowledgeable about these objects and how they were made and he enjoys telling his visitors about them. In a real sense, he is the museum.

Moving towards the other extreme we have the Museum of Modern Art in New York, which reported the following staff in June 1973:

Office of the Director	3
Curatorial and Program Departments	
Painting and Sculpture	17
Drawings	5
Prints and Illustrated Books	6
Architecture and Design	10
Photography	4
Film	19
Exhibition Program	3
International Program	7
Registration	15
Conservation	8
Publications	11
Bookstores	10
Graphics	4
Rights and Reproductions	5
Photographic Laboratory	3
Library	9
Education	3
Membership	10
Public Information	9
Lobby/Admissions	10
Development and Corporate Relations	3
Finance	21
Data Processing	5
Administration	4
Personnel	2
Building Operations	19
Workshops	9
Purchasing/Services	8
Mail Room	6
Warehouse	9
Special Events	2
Restaurants	3
Penthouse	18
Garden Restaurant	18
Staff Lounge	1
Security	8
Guards	48
Checkroom Attendants	3

The Museum of Modern Art is by no means one of the largest museums in the world: there are several which employ ten times this number of people, and more. But its staff list gives a fair idea of the range of specialists which a museum of any size reckons to employ nowadays, and of the kind of budget which is required to pay for them. The list corresponds fairly closely to the pattern of 'posts usual in a museum of some size', which Dr Grace Morley described recently in a work[1] primarily intended for museums in South-East Asia. Her list shows the full panoply of Chief Chemist, 'assisted by assistant chemist, metal conservator, restorer, etc.'; Curator (Keeper) of Education, 'assisted by lecturers, guides, projectionist, etc.'; Curator (Keeper) of Presentation (Display), 'assisted by draughtsmen, installation technicians, cabinet makers, skilled mechanics, metal workers, etc.'; Administrative Officer, or Business Manager, 'assisted by accountants, stenotypists, and clerks, etc.'

This is a perfectly accurate description of the way in which things are organised in a large, well-financed, solidly-established museum. The implication is presumably that every museum, large or small, should, in the interests of efficiency, get as close to this pattern as it can. There is reason to wonder, however, if this is necessarily the wisest or the most constructive approach. Anyone who attempts to run a parish church as if it were a cathedral is likely to be doomed either to never-ending frustration and disappointment, or to a life of fantasy, and one's personal observation would suggest that both situations are fairly common.

WHAT IS A 'MUSEUM PROFESSIONAL'?

It can be argued, of course, that any public institution must always set its sights high in order to receive any funds at all, since it can be sure that no matter what the level at which estimates are set, pruning is certain. From this point of view, staffing will always be inadequate, no matter how large the annual budget is. But common sense will show that, no matter what the current economic climate may be, a museum in a town of 50,000 people is extremely unlikely to be as large or as well funded as one in a town of 500,000 or five million. The small-town museum must inevitably expect to have a considerable amount of doubling-up of jobs, with the director being the curator as well, and quite probably looking after the accounts in his spare moments. Geology, natural history, science and technology may all have to be in the charge of one person, and to have a single specialist responsible full-time for registration, special events, publications, corporate relations and all the other activities specified in the Museum of Modern Art's staff list would seem, to most of the world's museums, an impossible dream or, just possibly, a nightmare to be avoided.

In these circumstances, which are not unlike those to be found in teaching, it can reasonably be doubted if there is such a thing as the 'museum profession'. As the Director of what might fairly be claimed to be the best Department of Museum Studies in the world, Raymond Singleton, of Leicester, has said,[2] the Museums Association in Britain is 'an incoherent body; incoherent as individuals and incoherent as institutions'. Museum activities, he points out – and he is not, of course, referring only to Britain – are a curious and fascinating mixture, 'a mixture of concern with the physical care of objects, the academic knowledge which surrounds them, the information which can be extracted from them, the presentation and exhibition of these various objects, each demanding differences of treatment, both in display and in general preservation; concern with the educational value of the objects, and their aesthetic value; concern with a multitude of types of visitors and users, each with different needs.' This is complicated enough, but when we add the necessity for the individual curators to be part administrator, part communicator, part scientist, part box-office manager and many other things, as well as a scholar in his own field, we can understand why so many people find it, in Mr Singleton's excellent words, 'So difficult to recognise a genuine profession at the heart of all this', and why some curators 'tend to take refuge in their work as scholars in their own special fields and prefer not to look too closely at their other responsibilities to the community'.

Yet Mr Singleton is surely right in saying that museum professionals cannot, so to speak, abdicate into scholarship and that the essence of a true museum profession lies in acknowledging and accepting its role as an instrument of social progress. 'This', he believes,

is the key to the situation. This is the common ground, the one factor which unites and integrates all museums, whatever their size and function, into a single body, with a special unique contribution to make to the life of the community. And it is only when we give deep and careful thought to the needs of the community and to our potentiality for filling those needs that we see our work in perspective and realise that it is providing a public service, not

specifically as archaeologists or art historians, not as naturalists or numismatists, but as museum men and women, that we become a profession.

If Mr Singleton's opinion is well founded, two consequences follow:

1. The person who has not given adequate thought to the purpose of museums, including his own, has forfeited the right to be called a truly professional curator.
2. The museum training course which is not based on questioning, analysing and discussing everything that is done in museums is a poor course, the existence of which it is difficult to justify.

Mr Singleton is fortunate, perhaps, in working where he does. The Museums Association in Britain is a unique organisation. No other body in the world does so much for the education and training of its members, by its examinations, by its tutoring system, by its meetings and, above all, by the all-embracing nature of its membership. Its publications reflect this, not least in the lists of appointments and vacancies which regularly occupy several pages of its monthly *Bulletin*. These lists, which include both important and comparatively humble posts, in both large and small museums, are an extremely useful way of welding museum people together and of encouraging them to think of themselves as a single professional body. Once again, this is at present a uniquely British phenomenon, but one which other countries might well consider developing for themselves and in their own way.

REQUIREMENTS FOR PROFESSIONAL POSTS

One of the most valuable functions of having a system of publicly advertising vacancies for posts is that it encourages, if not compels, the employing authority to think carefully about its requirements and about the conditions it is offering. Advertisements are, too, an excellent way of improving the public image of a museum and of telling the general public, as well as prospective applicants, what the current concept of professional standards is.

In the autumn of 1975 the British Museum, for example, was advertising in the national press for a person to take responsibility for its Educational

Service. The salary offered – £7560 to £9160 – probably came as a surprise to many of those who saw this large advertisement in the course of reading their daily paper and may have caused them to revise their previous idea of museum work as an underpaid, unattractive profession.

The broad aim of the Head of the Educational Service [said the advertisement, which was, incidentally, of equal size to those for important industrial posts] will be to enable adults and older children to benefit from an organised approach to, and interpretation of, the objects in the collections. To achieve this the successful candidate will need considerable innovatory skills and should, ideally, have flexibility of approach, a sensitivity to artefacts, and some interest in archaeology.

The Service is well furnished with the necessary equipment and facilities, and direct lectures can be supplemented by various techniques such as the use of publications. One of the special responsibilities of the post will be the planning and initiation of suitable material for such publications. Close liaison with educational bodies will be involved.

Candidates should normally be at least 30 and must have an honours degree, a postgraduate degree, or an equivalent qualification, in a field relevant to the Museum.

A similarly impressive advertisement, from a Government Department – the Department of the Environment – was aimed at attracting a Restorer of Paintings. 'This London-based post', it announced,

is in the Conservation Section which deal with the restoration and preservation of mural and ceiling decorations and easel pictures in the care of the Department.

Candidates, aged at least 28, must have at least 7 years' experience of modern techniques in the examination, conservation, cleaning and restoration of paintings, painted murals and ceilings. They should normally hold a relevant diploma or other qualification awarded by a recognised College of Art.

In the provinces, the Lincolnshire Museum Service required a Keeper of Display Services. The advertisement emphasised the need for a qualified and experienced person or, in other words,

a professional. 'The Keeper', it specified, 'will be responsible for the display of the permanent collections, for establishing a circulating exhibition service, and for the implementation of interpretative schemes in historic buildings within the County. The post offers considerable scope for initiative and flair for a person interested in the presentation of museum collections.'

It is good for the morale of people employed in museums to see their field of work publicised in this way and to observe their kind of activity standing in the advertisement columns side by side with demands for scientists, industrial executives and other prestigious and well-paid people. And, once the system exists and is publicly making demands for 'a person who has recently completed a formal course of training', 'a professional qualification in the conservation of paintings' or 'successful completion of a postgraduate course in museum studies', suitable courses have to be available. Over the years, the Museums Association has both created the market for properly trained people and done its best to make sure that the market is supplied. This is the situation one would wish to see developing everywhere, but the evidence suggests that there is as yet considerable progress to be made towards it. The majority of the museum training courses which are available at the present time are not producing professionals in the sense in which Mr Singleton uses the term, and in the way in which ICOM would like to see the task carried out.

PROFESSIONAL TRAINING

In 1971, Miss Oddon, now of the ICOM Training Unit, and at that time working at the UNESCO Training Centre for Museum Technicians at Jos, in Nigeria, prepared an important and comprehensive document which surveyed the facilities which existed throughout the world for the professional training of museum personnel, and made recommendations for the kind of syllabus which should be followed. The situation has not greatly changed since the preparation of her report, which was issued in June 1972.[3]

In the introduction to her report, Miss Oddon noted that ICOM, through its International Committee for Professional Training, regarded the museum profession as 'a science, an art

and a craft, which can be related to a dozen or more different disciplines, and which can be treated at University level as well as at a technical level'.

The syllabus presented by Miss Oddon had been first prepared by the ICOM Training Unit and then discussed and revised in co-operation with a working party of the ICOM International Committee for Professional Training, which met in June 1971. The final syllabus was then presented to the Committee during the 9th ICOM Conference in Grenoble in September 1971, and approved. It was designed as a basic programme for both theoretical training (museology) and practical training (museography), and it was intended to be adaptable to various teaching levels and basic disciplines.

'We have agreed', says the Report, 'that the basic or core disciplines, such as History of Art, Archaeology, History, Ethnology, Natural or Exact Science, Technology, should be studied either before professional training in museology is undertaken, or simultaneously with it at the university level. The same provision should apply to the courses in chemistry and technology which are specially designed for museum curators, restorers and preparators.' Even so, it continues, 'the main disciplines in the academic fields must be considered in relation to their museological implications in every complete training syllabus', and it refers particularly to the way in which this has been done in the course organised by the Department of Museum Studies at the University of Leicester.

'Knowledge of the environment,' it stresses, 'both natural and human, is indispensable and the relevant teaching should constitute a pre-requisite to any curriculum in the field of museography', and also, it might usefully have added, to the field of museology. What, however, does this diplomatic phrase, 'knowledge of the environment', mean? What should it mean? It could be best translated, perhaps, as 'sensitive awareness of the world in which we live', and this could be expanded into 'understanding of today's political and social problems and determination to make one's professional work relevant to these problems'. This is exactly the same as Raymond Singleton's insistence that museum professionals are entitled to the name 'professional' only in so far as they acknowledge their social responsibility.

'It is imperative', says the ICOM Report, 'that professional and/or vocational training in museology at all and any level should include practical work in a museum or a laboratory.' This, one might think, was obvious, but the sad fact is that many courses which apparently exist in order to train future curators and other museological and museographical professionals are almost wholly theoretical. Their students are neither required nor encouraged to carry out practical work in museums and their teaching-bodies often include nobody at all with such experience. The blind are, in a very real sense, leading the blind.

In one South American country, those who complete the national course in museology are immediately recruited into the Civil Service, from which privileged and remote position they control the activities of the lesser beings who actually run museums. It is not surprising, therefore, that the course they follow is entirely theoretical and academic.

ICOM is not in a position, and it may never be, to set up what would be, in effect, an accreditation system for museum courses, not to organise any kind of inspection routine. It has to depend on the information it receives from its members and, although it may sometimes suspect that such information is not altogether what it seems and that a certain amount of interpretation or reading between the lines is necessary, it must assume that its informants are not deliberately setting out to mislead. *Professional Training of Museum Personnel in the World* makes this point with extreme delicacy and tact. 'It is not always possible', it says, 'to evaluate the character of the course, because of the ambiguities of our professional terminology; neither could we in every case discriminate between museology and museography, nor know for sure if a university qualification means a museological degree, or only "credits" attached to some academic discipline.' Some courses, in other words, are a good deal better than others, but ICOM cannot, for obvious reasons, allow itself to be placed in the position of an arbitrator. It can, even so, offer certain tests and principles which will help potential customers to discriminate.

Museological training is not, of course, something which can be done and finished with in a year's course. There is no field in which opportunities

and situations change faster than in museum work, and there is consequently an ever-present need to keep oneself up to date, by attending conferences and short courses and by reading. Unfortunately, the present position with regard to these possibilities is far from satisfactory. Two features are particularly in need of improvement:

(*a*) Those who attend international conferences, and often national conferences as well, are almost invariably directors of museums or very senior members of their staff. Younger men and women, who are often considerable experts in their field, rarely have the chance to take part in these conferences and to make their views and knowledge more widely known. The full potential of the occasion is consequently not realised.

(*b*) Many of the museum-aldermen who attend such conferences with great regularity have obviously not had a new idea for a very long time and, although they may speak with the authority of their office, their contributions to the proceedings are often neither as creative nor as relevant as those of their younger colleagues would be.

These failings are especially noticeable when there are political difficulties in getting delegates to international meetings. The very senior and long-established figures are given the necessary visa and travel funds, while less exalted people who would have more to give to the conference and who would gain more from it are held back.

To some extent, this problem can be overcome by international exchanges of museum staff – of which there are at present far too few – and by more efficient methods of producing and circulating periodicals and other specialist literature. Here again, the barrier tends to be that in many museums without a proper library organisation the latest issue of *Museum* or whatever the international journal may be is delivered to the Director's room and never leaves it. One hears, in the course of one's travels, all too many complaints of this kind. There are evidently directors who have not yet realised that the continuing education of their staff is the most important of all their responsibilities.

Returning, however, to the matter of

ICOM'S Common Basic Syllabus for Professional Museum Training, it will be noticed from the details given in Appendix 5.1 at the end of this chapter that it is divided into twelve sections, each of which can be completed by a bibliography suited to the language and attainments of the particular group of students. There is no point in including books or articles which students are unlikely to read, either because they are unobtainable or because they are written in a language the students cannot understand.

The syllabus first places museum work firmly and unmistakably in its philosophical, cultural and legal context and then concentrates, in considerable detail, on the practical problems involved in running a museum. The acquisition, recording, care and presentation of collections are dealt with in a systematic manner and the syllabus devotes a good deal of attention to the many aspects of the museum's responsibility to the public. A final section surveys the various ways in which the museum can ensure that its collections are as fully used as possible.

The syllabus is what it sets out to be, a basic syllabus. It can be expanded and adapted to meet the requirements of particular countries or groups of students, but, whatever the length and level of the course which is based on it, it guarantees, in the hands of competent teachers, that every student will be given an opportunity to understand the aims of museum work and to see how different specialities dovetail into one another. It assumes that students will be involved in a wide range of practical work during the course and that they will complete their studies with a good general grasp of what modern museums are all about, as well as a knowledge of how to adapt their own particular academic experience to a museum context.

All potential recruits to the museum service who have a university qualification should be asked the following key question: 'Do you consider yourself a zoologist (art historian, physicist, geologist) first and a museum man second, or a museum man first and a zoologist second?' Those who put zoologist first should be regarded with considerable suspicion and, whenever possible, not appointed to the post. In some countries academic ambitions can be a considerable problem for those responsible for the staffing of museums. Many African museums, for example, find it extremely difficult to discover com-

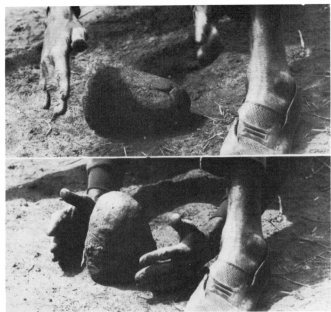

Reconstruction of the fortified wall of the ancient city of Kano, Nigeria, under the UNESCO–UNDP Regional Training Centre for the Preservation of the Cultural and National Heritage at Jos, Nigeria. These are photographs of the site at Jos where an open-air Museum of Traditional Architecture (MOTNA) is being prepared as part of the activities of the Jos Centre. The work is directed by Dr Dmochowski, a Polish architect who has studied traditional architecture in tropical Africa for over twenty years. Various stages in the reconstruction of ancient fortified wall.

(above left) *Moulding the bricks, which are made of clay and chopped grass.*

(above right) *Detail of the moulding process.*

(below left) *Pile of prepared bricks set out in the sun to dry.*

(below right) *Construction of the wall.*

(above left) *Alternating layers of brick and earth.*

(above right) *Close-up of completed wall before plastering. The shape of the bricks and the way in which they are laid defy all European notions of brickwork. What has in fact been constructed is not so much a brick wall, as an earth wall, using prefabricated components.*

(below) *Reconstitution of wall. Final layer of fine earth applied by hand by specialists from the Kano area. Such specialists are becoming more and more difficult to find.*

petent scientists who are willing to undertake museum work and to train for it. The prestige of a university or technical college post is felt to be so much greater than employment in a museum that suitable recruits do not come forward or, if they do, they are very likely to regard their stay at the museum as only temporary, until they can find something more suited to their talents and ambitions.

For this reason, the ICOM decision to put, in the basic syllabus, the research functions of museums before their responsibilities to the general public was probably not wise, since, although this may not have been intended to indicate an order of priority, the arrangement could well encourage wrong thoughts. In the year 1977 one has to say bluntly and on all possible occasions that the scholarly and research aspects of museum work are *not* the most important. They are, if one is compelled to make a decision of this kind, considerably less important than the responsibility of the museum to the community as a whole, and it is sheer snobbery to pretend otherwise. Much unnecessary and frustrating conservatism in museums is caused by people who have failed to obtain some kind of academic post and who either make it constantly clear that they regard museum work as very much a second best or who attempt to transform at least their own department of the museum into a kind of sub-university. If people of this kind are not weeded out during their period of professional training, they can do a great deal of harm to the atmosphere and motivation of the museum. They are not, unfortunately, as rare as one might hope.

The Department of Museum Studies at Leicester tries to deal with this problem in three ways, first by accepting for its course only those students who already have some museum experience, secondly by making sure that the members of its staff are enthusiasts who have modern and progressive ideas about museums, and thirdly by compelling students to think of their particular speciality in its human and social context. Two extracts from the Leicester syllabus, one for the History of Science and the other for Natural History, will illustrate how this is done.

History of Science

a. The evolution of scientific thought and the advance of technology in the west, from their beginnings in ancient Greece to the establishment of classical mechanics in the seventeenth century.
b. The development of chemistry and historical sciences, to the middle of the nineteenth century.
c. The philosophical components of the development of science. The mutual relations between scientific, social and economic progress, and the changing intellectual attitudes of European society.
d. The principal advances in the major sciences.
e. The beginnings of modern science, and the application of new scientific theories to industrial techniques.
f. The contribution made by scientific societies and journals.
g. The economic, social and technical factors involved in mechanisation; sources of power; raw materials; the preparation of chemicals and the fabrication of metals.
h. Methods of transport, and the influences of economic factors and technical progress on their lines of development.
i. The museum applications of the history of science.

Natural History

a. Historical studies in Zoology and Botany.
b. Taxonomy, in relation to identification.
c. Type specimens, and their care.
d. Ecological studies in Zoology and Botany.
e. Economic applications.
f. Organisation of field-work.
g. Techniques of collection and preservation.
h. Nature conservation.
i. Recording of information.
j. Preparation of exhibits.
k. Museum applications.

Leicester makes it clear to its students that most museum employment involves, and should involve, work which has nothing directly to do with the academic disciplines in which they were originally trained. This does not necessarily mean, of course, that on joining the staff of a museum a zoologist has to forswear zoology for ever, as a monk gives up worldly pleasures once he enters the monastery. Any museum which fails to make full use of the special talents and knowledge of its employees is very foolish. What it does mean is that the museum profession today demands a wide range of skills on the part of everyone working in it and that the person who clings to narrow specialisations of an academic kind is not likely to progress very far or indeed to be very happy.

Museology courses do not have a monopoly of encouraging this necessary breadth of vision. Acquiring it is a continuous process and a good museum, with a proper social orientation, will automatically help its staff to acquire it. To illustrate the importance of this, we may consider what has been happening at one of the most important art museums in Latin America, the Museum of Fine Art in Rio de Janeiro.

Until 1970, the Museum was an exceedingly conventional art gallery, with very little to excite or inspire the people who came to visit it. In that year, however, it was fortunate enough to obtain the services of a very forceful and imaginative woman as Director, and she began immediately to haul and push the Museum into the modern world. Some of the changes she made were of a very practical nature. When she came to the Museum, it was still obligatory for visitors to wear slippers, as if they were entering a mosque. The floors do not appear to have suffered since she abolished this rule and she is now in the first stages of putting slippers on the floor, so to speak, instead of on the feet of visitors, by carpeting the galleries in a restful dark green. This forms part of her policy of making the museum an oasis of relaxation, colour and peace in a city plagued with noise, tension and pollution. People, including museologists, need to be educated in this respect, she says, and she regards the creation of the right atmosphere in the museum as of supreme importance. This is a reflection of her conviction that the well-being of people is much more important than the well-being of museum objects, a point of view which a great many art historians, inside and outside museums, would regard as heresy of the most dangerous and pernicious kind.

She has plenty of professional help. The members of the staff are remarkably enthusiastic and nearly all young. They have, without exception, attended the city's museology course and they make it clear, if pressed, that they do not think it helped them a great deal. Real learning, they say, started when they came to work in the

Museum. The Director is trying to push this learning process further and further back, so that the Museum is not required, in effect, to carry out remedial work on behalf of able and intelligent people who have been stifled and corrupted by the academic machine. Undergraduates in their last year at the university are now coming to help in the Museum and great efforts are being made to forge creative links between the Museum and the schools. A kindergarten party who visited the Museum in 1974 said the modern art they saw there was just like what they themselves did at school. The Museum staff regarded this as a very worthwhile testimonial to their philosophy and their efforts.

Contemporary Brazilian artists are given subsidies to make it easier for them to work while they are making a reputation and they are allowed to give exhibitions in the Museum. In the near future there will be studios in the Museum building, together with a club for artists. The effect of this new policy is to make the Museum a place in which artists and members of the general public are more likely to feel at home than art historians. It has become, in other words, what it certainly never was before, a dynamic, socially-conscious institution. This does not mean that the Director has broken off all communication with academics. On the contrary, she feels that their knowledge is a necessary part of the background to her work. But, and this is the important point, it is now part of the background, not, as previously, of the foreground.

One could summarise the Museum's philosophy by means of a diagram:

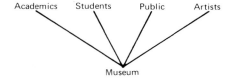

Academics   Students   Public   Artists

Museum

Or one might say that the Museum is a public company in which each of these four groups of people holds equal shares. This point of view will be made even clearer during the next few years, when the Director hopes to be able to implement her vision of an art museum which would be away from its present

city-centre site and grandiose Victorian building, and would be set in a complex including sports facilities, a theatre and a library. The art museum, in other words, would become the core and the creative impulse of a broadly-based cultural centre.

In academic circles, the process of change is notoriously slow, but it cannot be many years before the revolutionary and obviously successful concepts of the Museum of Fine Art and other innovatory museums in Brazil begin to change the emphasis and approach of the museological course which is available to Brazilian students. It would be unfair to say that the changes at the Museum of Fine Art have been solely due to the appearance of an unusually energetic and imaginative new Director, important as this has undoubtedly been. If the Museum and Brazilian society had not been ripe for such changes, the best of Directors would have achieved very little. What this particular Director did was to point the Museum's nose in the right direction and then push it hard and continuously until it began to understand what was required of it. In other South American countries she would undoubtedly have found the process a great deal more difficult and frustrating. One must, however, accept that good museological theory is useless without skilful museum politics to implement it. Museums do not live by museology alone. All changes need strong personalities to bring them about and really talented, forceful, persuasive people are as rare in the museum field as any other. In this sense, the Museum of Fine Art is not typical, either of South America or of Museums of Fine Art, any more than its Director is typical. But this book is about new ideas, and new ideas are not produced by typical people.

The list given in Appendix 5.2 gives some idea of the range and interest of the training courses which are available at the present time. In ten years' time such a list will undoubtedly look very different. One can be certain that

(a) the pattern of museological and museographical courses is going to change a good deal during the next ten years, to meet new concepts of what a museum is and what it should be trying to do, and of the financial and other facilities which are likely to be available for the purpose;

(b) museums will increasingly be competing for well-educated people, and such people are always in short supply, especially in the developing countries.

Three points should be emphasised in connection with the courses provided in North American universities, examples of which are given in Appendix 5.2. The first is that, in most cases, students are given a diploma which entitles them to put AM, or Master of Arts, after their name. The second is that the History of Art is too well catered for, by comparison with other subjects – this fact is often concealed by the fact that what is officially described as 'multidisciplinary' or 'inter-disciplinary' courses often make much better provision for Art History students than for any others. The third point, also not evident from the syllabuses, is that a high proportion of the students on museum courses are women, many of whom are likely to spend only a short time working in museums. This explains a paradox which might otherwise be found puzzling – that, turning out considerable numbers of museum graduates each year as they do, the American museum-schools have apparently only produced a total of 10,000-11,000 professionals actually working in museums at the present time, to meet the needs of more than 8000 museums.

A number of universities give credits in museology which count towards a degree. This is particularly common in the United States, where the Universities of New Mexico, Illinois, Ohio, Iowa, Idaho and Arizona all provide this kind of opportunity. So, too, does the George Washington University in Washington DC, and the History Department of the University of Delaware, in conjunction with the Hagley Foundation and Winterthur Museum. The University of Paris has two general courses in museology, in different sections of the University, which give credits towards a postgraduate degree.

Courses of a different type are available at many centres throughout the world for training museum personnel whose work is of a mainly technical nature. At Jos, in Nigeria, museum technicians from African countries are taught in both French and English at a centre organised and supported by UNESCO. The eight-month course here pays particular attention to the needs of the ethnographical and archaeological museums, both of which are of great importance in Africa. At Mainz, in the German Federal Republic, the Römisch-Germanisches Museum trains conservators specialising in history and archaeology, also in an eight-month course, and courses of a similar length are available at several universities and colleges in the United States, among them the Department of Anthropology at the University of Missouri and Huntingdon College, Alabama.

APPRENTICE-TYPE TRAINING

The courses listed in Appendix 5.2 give a fair impression of the kind of training opportunities which exist at the present time outside particular museums. They do not reflect the apprentice-type training which is available at most large museums throughout the world and which is of very variable quality, partly because not all experts have the gift of reaching young people and partly because what a boy or girl is able to learn depends on the standard of the museum. In-service training is always liable to this kind of criticism, and also to the accusation that the museum is more interested in the student's labour than in his education. One should bear in mind, however, that apprenticeship is the traditional way of learning skills and that it is foolish to abandon a system which has produced excellent results over such a long period and in so many regions of the world. The developing countries are used to this method of passing on techniques from one generation of craftsmen to another. Properly handled, it is a cheap, efficient, interesting and humane way of going about the business. Learning by watching, imitating and doing what someone who is a master at his work is performing easily and almost unconsciously, is an unbeatable way of acquiring a skill, but it may need to be supplemented by a course for four reasons:

1. Because, for one reason or another, there is a need for more young craftsmen than the old system can provide.
2. Because completely new skills have to be developed.
3. Because a new kind of job may involve more than one skill.
4. Because, in order to function in a fully effective way, a craftsman may have to learn to work in a non-traditional context.

The UNESCO Centre at Jos, in Nigeria, exists to meet these four demands. If the existing training facilities had provided an ample supply of museum people of the quality required, Jos need never have been set up. No apprenticeship can be better than the establishment in which it takes place, but it would be quite wrong to suppose that the best training is always and necessarily to be found in the larger museum.

It is interesting, and sad, to note in this connection that experience in a large national museum can be a disadvantage to people who apply for posts in smaller provincial museums. This has happened in recent years, for example, to men and women who have begun their museum career in the British Museum and who, for various reasons, have become anxious to leave London. They have found, usually to their suprise, that provincial museums are all too likely to regard them as narrow, academic specialists, corrupted by the British Museum's scholarly atmosphere, out of touch with modern museological trends and ignorant of the needs and wishes of the general public. They have become, so to speak, the prisoners of the big-museum system. They cannot escape, much as they might wish to.

A first-class museum training may mean two quite different things:

(a) that the student has the advantage of being in daily contact with acknowledged experts, possibly of world renown, and of being able to work with the most up-to-date equipment and techniques;

(b) that the atmosphere and organisation of the museum are such that the student has a chance to try his hand at many things and to acquire a good knowledge of what museum work as a whole is about.

Ideally, (b) should precede (a), and all students should experience both (a) and (b), but how many people are, in fact, so fortunate? It is, alas, not true that a first-class course in museology and museography allows a person to transform a poor job in a frustrating museum into something much more satisfying and worthwhile. On the contrary, a good course is very likely to make a student realise how unsatisfactory his normal working conditions are. In a rich country, such as France or the

United States, this may simply lead to a change of job, but in the developing countries such a move is much more difficult and in these circumstances a study-trip abroad not infrequently makes for discontent and unhappiness.

CONSERVATION COURSES

This appears to be particularly true of students who attend courses on the conservation of paintings and other art objects, much less true of those who specialise in ethnography, archaeology and technology, which are fields in which imagination, resourcefulness and adaptability count for at least as much as sheer expertise. Unfortunately, as the list of courses given above makes clear and has already been stressed in a previous section, art courses of one kind and another are much more numerous than courses in other subjects. Both nationally and on a world scale, provision is absurdly unbalanced at the present time and, in the interests of both the advanced and the developing countries, one would hope to see the position change considerably and radically during the next ten years. This can only happen if a much wider definition of 'cultural property' becomes generally accepted, a process which has a good deal further to go in some countries than in others.

It is, of course, essential that training, especially in conservation, is based on an up-to-date knowledge, but one must not underestimate the difficulties involved in this. The speed of both technological and philosophical change has become very great and, with the best will in the world, it is far from easy for departments of museology to keep themselves fully in touch with new developments. Two examples will illustrate this. Until comparatively recently – the mid-nineteenth century is a reasonable date – artists took great care in the preparation of their paints. As research increasingly makes clear, the painters of former generations attached the greatest importance to this and an understanding of their techniques is essential for the effective conservation of their work. How many conservationists, however, are in possession of this information, and how many serious blunders are committed in good faith and with a clear conscience as a result of such ignorance? A second problem arises from the use by modern artists of a range of materials which were completely unknown to previous generations and whose properties and durability are only gradually becoming understood. The habit of concentrating, in conservation courses, on the treatment and care of older works leaves the average museum expert ill-equipped to deal with many of the paintings and sculptures produced in his own century. The old-master obsession dies hard.

It seems very probable that proper conservation of all types of cultural property and proper training for those who wish to undertake this work can be achieved only by means of a carefully thought-out national plan. The *ad hoc* and piecemeal situation which is normal throughout the Western world, and which is illustrated by the examples given earlier, leads to three major forms of inefficiency:

1. A poor use of scarce expertise, both for training and for carrying out skilled work.
2. The over-development of courses in fashionable and financially attractive subjects and the neglect of poor-relation subjects.
3. Financial waste.

These shortcomings are now fairly generally realised, and most countries have attempted to introduce some degree of co-operation and co-ordination into the methods of training conservation staff and of getting the necessary work done. In a socialist country, with elaborate and highly-centralised planning machinery, it is not at all difficult to achieve, at least on paper, a system which avoids waste, overlapping and gaps and which makes full use of skilled resources, but, as well-informed observers can see for themselves, theory and practice are not always the same. In all industrialised countries, no matter what their political complexion, it is far from easy to persuade intelligent boys and girls to take up conservation work, which they are very likely to feel is lacking in glamour and prestige, and which will bring them a smaller income than they can get in other fields. A visit to most conservation workshops and sites will show all too clearly that a high proportion of the workers are elderly. When they retire or die, it is going to be exceedingly difficult to find adequate replacements for them. One can go further and say, withh certainty, that much of the restoration work which was carried out all over Europe during the 1940s and 1950s to repair wartime

damage would be impossible to carry out today. The skilled people required are simply not there to do it. The old one have gone and better-paid work elsewhere has cut off the supply of young people to succeed them.

A NATIONAL CONSERVATION SYSTEM

With these criticisms in mind, it is useful to examine the organisation and aims of the most complete national system so far to be found anywhere in the world, especially so far as the training and use of skilled personnel is concerned. This is the network of centres known collectively as the Ateliers for the Conservation of Cultural Property, in Poland. Known in Poland by the initials PKZ (Pracownie Konserwacji Zabytków), this State-owned company is entrusted with 'the restoration and conservation of all kinds of cultural property and historic monuments in the country', an aim which it is not as yet in a position entirely to fulfil.

PKZ has a supervisory and planning board and twenty-three divisions responsible to it.

1. Departments of Historical Documentation.
2. Scientific Research Laboratories.
3. Archaeological Conservation Departments.
4. Photographic Studios.
5. Design Offices (General).
6. Design Offices for Historic Parks and Gardens.
7. Managements of Working Groups.
8. Ateliers of Painting Conservation.
9. Ateliers of Sculpture Conservation.
10. Ateliers of Decorative Art Conservation.
11. Ateliers of Stained Glass Preservation.
12. Ateliers of Textile Conservation.
13. Ateliers of Metalwork (Ferrous) Restoration.
14. Ateliers of Furniture Restoration.
15. Ateliers of Conservation of Graphic Art and Old Books.
16. Centre of Information for Conservators.
17. Atelier for Preservation of Ancient Organs.
18. Export Office.
19. Department of Ancient Style Pottery.
20. Stonework Department.
21. Photogrammetric Atelier.
22. Artistic Furniture Manufacturing Department.
23. Department for the Restoration of Non-Ferrous Metalwork.

These departments, in their headquarters and branches, are well distributed over the country. There are, for example, Archaeological Conservation Ateliers in Warsaw, Cracow, Poznań, Szczecin, Kielce and Lublin, and Scientific Research Laboratories in Warsaw, Toruń and Szczecin. The Atelier for the Conservation of Ancient Organs is at Cracow and the Department of Ancient Style Pottery is at Kadyny.

The organisation manufactures as well as restores. It has workshops for making reproduction furniture and owns its own brickworks and potteries for the production of hand-made bricks and tiles of all types and for terra-cotta work. PKZ carries out conservation contracts abroad. In recent years these have included stone sculptures in the Netherlands; the Isar Town Gate in Munich; the restoration of the Old Town buildings at Stralsund; the conservation of the temple of Queen Hatshepsut, near Luxor; and the rebuilding of the fifteenth-century mausoleum, mosque and monastery of Ameer Qurgumas, near Cairo. Since its formation in 1951, PKZ has developed into a very large and efficient business and a considerable earner of foreign currency.

It employs many thousands of highly-skilled people. The Design Offices, for example, have more than 400 architects and technicians, and the Ateliers of Painting Conservation have 200 expert full-time restorers. To maintain the quality and numbers of its staff, PKZ has a very large training programme, which embraces nearly all its employees, from the directors downwards. It has close links with the universities. The Technical University in Warsaw runs special conservation courses for architects and civil engineers and the Copernicus University at Toruń trains both graduate conservators and building technicians. Within the organisation of PKZ itself a number of highly-skilled and experienced master-craftsmen are responsible for passing on their vanishing skills to apprentices and every year dozens of the Company's employees are sent to study new methods abroad. Conferences and seminars are held regularly in order to give conservation staff from all over Poland an opportunity to exchange information on techniques. The Board of PKZ is undoubtedly correct in claiming that its enterprise is unique, and there is no doubt that other countries can learn a great deal from it. In acknowledging this, one must remember the real nature of PKZ's innovations and pioneering. Faced with the huge scale of conservation problems and with the frightening shortage of skilled craftsmen, all countries have been forced to develop some kind of co-operative organisation, with or without Government help. In France, for instance, there is the Mobilier National, with its workshops and training facilities in Paris for the repair and conservation of old fabrics, and, also in Paris, a special department at the Bibliothèque Nationale which deals with the conservation of manuscripts, printed books and photographs. Britain has its centre, on the London outskirts, where cabinet-makers and upholsterers can learn the special techniques of restoring antique furniture, using items from houses open to the public as training material; the Smithsonian Institution, in Washington, has its own full-time millwright, whose services are available to American owners of windmills and watermills which are in need of care and attention; and, in a number of Western European countries, the cathedral works departments carry out restoration on contract for churches within their diocese.

To be successful, any centralised conservation department requires:

1. A guaranteed, month-by-month and year-by-year flow of work, so that its skilled staff can be given the security of permanent employment and so that an adequate number of recruits can be attracted and trained.
2. The ability to pay wages and salaries at a level which will make it unnecessary for staff to seek more remunerative work in other fields.

The Poles, it will be noticed, have tried to meet these two conditions by seeking out every possible market for their employees' skills. They make and sell high-quality reproduction furniture, both at home and abroad; they produce old-type bricks, tiles and pottery; they

carry out surveys and restoration contracts abroad. What is more difficult, however – and none of the socialist countries has so far solved this problem with much greater success that the capitalist countries – is to match the kind of wages which are offered to skilled workmen in the general construction industry, where this type of person seems to be in perpetually short supply. In both the German Democratic Republic and Czechoslovakia, for example, the State departments responsible for the restoration of historic buildings have experienced great difficulties in finding the skilled labour they need and in persuading boys to train for the work, and the cause is simply money. If the Poles have overcome this problem, as they claim to have done, they can be proud to be the first country in the world, with the possible exception of China, to do so.

SOME CURRENT SHORTCOMINGS IN CONSERVATION

All restoration work is, by modern standards, exceedingly expensive. At St Paul's Cathedral, in London, where the stonework has suffered a great deal from atmospheric pollution, a team of about twenty skilled masons and carvers has been recruited and held together during the past twenty years. In 1975 it was acknowledged to be the best team working on any cathedral in the country; in 1976 there were no carvers and only four or five masons, although the architect in charge has estimated he could have used the whole of his original team continuously for the next thirty years. The Cathedral simply does not have the money to pay them.

To a greater or lesser extent, the St Paul's situation is being repeated throughout the world, irrespective of the way in which a country's economy is organised. It is, of course, made greatly worse by inflation, and by the need of both governments and private organisations to devote their scarce funds to what they conceive to be productive purposes. Beauty is not, in the political and economic sense, productive, whatever its effect on the morale and well-being of the population may be, and it is an inevitable casualty of an inflationary situation. More seriously, perhaps, if conservation and restoration projects are not continued with or if they are greatly slowed down, the opportunities for training the next

generation of skilled craftsmen are lost, and this is exactly what is happening throughout the world. Nothing less than a thoroughgoing plan, on the Polish model, seems to have any chance of preventing the situation from deteriorating even further.

But, and the point has to be made, PKZ has its gaps and its imperfections. These arise from the narrowness of the definition of 'cultural property' on which its work rests. These sectors of 'cultural property' do not, at the present time, meet with its attention.

1. *Technological material of all kinds.* PKZ does not concern itself either with conserving old machines, scientific instruments or tools, or with the preservation of technical drawings.
2. *Industrial archaeology.* Old factories, mills, bridges, railway stations, canal installations and so on come within its province only if they can be shown to have some aesthetic importance, or, in other words, if the art historian puts his seal of approval on them.
3. *Ethnographical material.* PKZ has the authority to look after this only if it can be brought under one of its approved headings, such as Textiles or Decorative Arts. Many items of great ethnographical significance must necessarily escape its attention. Toys and kitchen equipment are cases in point.
4. *Agricultural material*, and items connected with food processing.
5. *Musical instruments*, with the single exception of ancient organs.

One can easily think of other absentees from the PKZ list, although fully entitled to the label 'cultural property'. It may be true that museums and other organisations are taking care of these items and training people in the necessary skills – the National Technical Museum and the Polish Academy of Sciences have a joint responsibility for recording and safeguarding industrial and technical monuments, for example – but to mention this is to miss the point. If one is to experience the full advantages of scale in an organisation such as PKZ, it must be truly all-embracing. It would seem foolish, for instance, that PKZ's large and splendidly equipped design offices, laboratories and photogrammetry services should not be available for the benefit of old mills and iron-foundries as much as for palaces, churches and medieval town centres. If there is to be a special Atelier for the Preservation of Ancient Organs, then why stop at organs? If a staff of experts is maintained in order to look after tapestries, ecclesiastical vestments and valuable upholstery fabrics, why should their knowledge not be equally available for old uniforms and peasant costumes? Do PKZ's woodworkers and metal restorers have nothing to contribute to the conservation of farm implements?

In practice, of course, mutual help and advice must take place. Experts have a way of knowing one another, even if there is no official encouragement for doing so. All that is being emphasised here is that, with both money and skilled human resources as short as they seem certain to be for the foreseeable future, the old parochialism and dividing lines between the staff, funds, technical equipment and training facilities of individual institutions and Government departments will have to go. They are a luxury the world can no longer afford, if indeed it ever could.

OFFICERS AND OTHER RANKS

Another kind of barrier, that which divides officers and other ranks in museum work, unfortunately shows few signs of crumbling, and in the years ahead urgent and serious attention will have to be given to it. Two courses which were recently held in Britain illustrate the problem clearly.

The first covered such practical matters as security, attendants' duties, first-aid and accident prevention, fire and fire prevention, care and handling of collections and cleaning. This was obviously a course for other ranks, who were not supposed to be concerned in any way with the aims of the museum, with interpretation and presentation or with all the other problems which make the lives of the professionals interesting and worthwhile. Attendants spend the whole of their working week among museum collections, but they are not required or expected to take any interest in them. Their job is to clean, move and prevent thefts, fires and accidents. Anything more than that is the exclusive concern of the officers.

The officers' course was very different. Entitled *Museums and Interpretative Techniques*, its aim was 'to discuss how a better understanding and usage of interpretative techniques by museum staff could improve and heighten awareness and enjoyment of their environment by the public'. There were

> an introduction to the subject, a number of short papers by experts in relevant fields, e.g. a director of a museums service, an education officer, a designer and an audio visual specialist, and visits in small working groups to sites of particular interest in the locality. The sites included an agricultural museum complex, a field centre and nature reserve, a small town and Canterbury Cathedral. The intention of these visits is to evaluate present methods of interpretation and to discuss ways in which these could be improved.

In their different ways, both of these courses were no doubt valuable and there is not the slightest intention of decrying them. But the cast-iron division between them indicates a serious weakness in the present selection and training of museum staff, a weakness which is present in every country in the world, although it is undoubtedly more marked in some museums than in others. If museologists insist, as they now do, that the public must be actively involved in what museums are trying to do, it is clearly ridiculous to exclude from the process those members of the museum staff who spend their whole time in direct contact with the public, watching them, listening to them and answering their questions. Such people, one would have thought, are all-important allies in a museum's task of understanding the habits and wishes of its visitors. They see most of the game and, suitably encouraged and instructed, they have a valuable contribution to make in the difficult struggle to achieve more satisfactory communication. But to achieve this, they must be treated as partners in a common enterprise, not as coolies. They must be given a clear idea of what the museum is trying to do.

There is a strong case for obliging all new recruits to the museum profession to spend a period in the ranks or on the shop-floor, according to the metaphor one chooses to adopt. Future curators would benefit enormously from a few months as a gallery attendant or at the sales counter of the museum shop or bookstall, just as a spell as hospital orderlies or nurses would do future doctors no harm. And museum administrators should always be on the look-out for technicians, clerical staff, or 'permanent' attendants who show a strong enough interest in museum work to be worth training for duties on the curatorial side. The museum world as it now stands contains far too many dull and uninterested people with the right academic qualifications and practically nothing else, and far too many intelligent, lively-minded people who find themselves labelled for ever as 'technicians' or 'attendants', with a brick wall between them and any promotion to more interesting and more responsible work. Some way must be found of breaking through these crippling conventions, and the developing countries, where institutions are still in a relatively fluid state, have a splendid opportunity to work out ways of doing so. Museum work, like teaching, is a field in which enthusiasm and an instinct for experiment count for a good deal more than diplomas. If diplomas are felt to be essential, then ways must be found of helping a much wider range of people to acquire them.

APPENDIX 5.1

The ICOM Basic Syllabus for Museum Training

1. An introduction to museology

This aims to place museum work firmly and unmistakably in its social context, and covers:

(a) The general concepts of museology and museography;
(b) The history of museums and collections, with special reference to those of the country in which the course is being held;
(c) The role and importance of museums in the modern world;
(d) Museums and the national heritage;
(e) Museums and research;
(f) The public and its needs;
(g) General programming;
(h) The various types of museum, with a study of present trends;
(i) The legislation affecting museums: a world survey;
(j) Co-operation between museums on the national level;
(k) Co-operation between museums on the international level.

2. Organisation, operation and management of museums

(a) The legal status and administrative authorities of museums;
(b) Management problems;
(c) Budgeting and financial resources;
(d) Selection and training of personnel;
(e) Maintenance of premises and equipment;
(f) Security;
(g) Public relations;
(h) Statistics.

3. Architecture, layout, equipment

(a) History of museum buildings;
(b) Location;
(c) Space and design;
(d) Building and layout to suit the type of museum;
(e) Building and layout to suit the particular climate;
(f) Adaptation and use of old and probably historic buildings.
(g) Air conditioning;
(h) Lighting;
(i) Safety;
(j) Movement of staff, visitors and material into and around the buildings;
(k) Layout and furnishing in different museum departments, to suit their own special requirements;
(l) Audio-visual equipment.

4. Collections: origin, related records, set-up and movement

(a) General principles of acquisition;
(b) Ethics of acquisition;
(c) Acquisition policy;
(d) Problems of acquisition, including terms and conditions, forgeries, replicas, reproductions.

5. Methods of acquisition

(a) Collection in the field, i.e. from original sites or from the places where the objects were used;
(b) Purchase;
(c) Donations and bequests;
(d) Loans and deposits;
(e) Exchanges.

6. Natural parks and their geological and organic properties

7. Data and documents related to collection items

(a) Terminology used to describe objects;
(b) Identification of items at the time of acquisition;
(c) Registration: the numbering and marking of items;
(d) Cataloguing and classification;
(e) Files related to collections;
(f) Checks on items registered but not at present in the museum;
(g) Audio-visual collection;
(h) The museum library;
(i) Information on the collections for the use of the public;
(j) Reception, transport and storage of collection;
(k) Collections designed primarily for research purposes.

8. Scientific activities and research in museums

(a) General principles of museum research;
(b) Museum research departments;
(c) Links between museums and outside scientific institutions, including universities;
(d) Museums and fieldwork;
(e) Museum reports and publications.

9. Preservation and care of collections

(a) The general principles, aims and limitations of preservation;
(b) Physical, chemical and biological factors influencing the condition of museum items;
(c) The establishment and operation of workshops and laboratories;
(d) Conservation techniques;
(e) Workshops for the preparation of casts, models and dioramas;
(f) Records of conservation treatment.

10. Presentation: exhibitions

(a) General theory of communication;
(b) Principles and techniques of presentation;
(c) The types of exhibition;
(d) Graphic aids;
(e) Evaluation of the success of exhibitions.

11. The public

(*a*) General principles underlying the planning and use of the museum as a public facility;

(*b*) Educational and cultural responsibility of the museum staff;

(*c*) Knowledge of the community served by the museum;

(*d*) Studying the behaviour of visitors;

(*e*) Organisation of the facilities and services available to the public;

(*f*) The range of facilities for the public;

(*g*) Statistics relating to museum visitors.

12. Cultural and educational activities of the museum

(*a*) Public relations;

(*b*) Friends of the Museum;

(*c*) Educational activities;

(*d*) The role and training of the museum's educational staff;

(*e*) Special exhibitions and programmes for children and adults;

(*f*) Publicity;

(*g*) The museum's extra-mural work;

(*h*) Museums and creative activities.

APPENDIX 5.2

Illustrative List of Training Courses in Museum Work

A University centres granting diplomas in museology and museography

EUROPE

Brno, Czechoslovakia. Course run by the School of Museology at the University. Two-year, multi-disciplinary. Museology. 'Multi-disciplinary', or, as it is sometimes called, 'interdisciplinary', means that the course provides museological training for people who have previously studied a wide range of academic subjects and who wish to learn how their special subject can be handled in a museum.

This statement needs to be interpreted with considerable caution, however, and not only as regards Brno, of course. Museological students usually have to be slotted into the ordinary courses of the university, so far as work in their special subjects is concerned, and it is not infrequently the case that a student's first choice of subject cannot be met. 'Multi-disciplinary' does not, in other words, mean 'omni-disciplinary'.

Leicester, England. Course run by the Department of Museum Studies at the University. One-year, multi-disciplinary. Museology and museography.

Manchester, England. Course run by the Department of Art History at the University. One-year, multi-disciplinary, but with a special emphasis on the fine and decorative arts.

NORTH AMERICA

Ann Arbor, Michigan. Course run jointly by the University of Michigan Museum of Art and the Rackham School of Graduate Studies. Two-year, multi-disciplinary. Museology and museography. One of the two years is spent in what the Americans call 'internship., i.e. working in the Museum. American universities are peculiarly well suited to this practice, since so many of them have a university museum of considerable size and quality.

Boulder, Colorado. Course run by the University of Colorado Museum. Three multi-disciplinary courses, lasting from one to two and a half years. Museology and museography.

Cleveland, Ohio. Course run jointly by Case Western University and the Cleveland Museum of Art. Two years, History of Art. One of the two years is spent as an intern. Museology and museography.

Cooperstown, New York. Course run jointly by the State University College at Oneonta and the New York State Historical Association. Three years, History, Anthropology, Ethnography, Conservation. Museology and museography.

Detroit, Michigan. Course run jointly by Wayne State University and Detroit Institute of Art. Two years, History of Art. Museology and museography.

Milwaukee, Wisconsin. Course run jointly by the University of Wisconsin and Milwaukee Public Museum. One year, Anthropology and Ethnography. Museology and museography.

Minneapolis, Minnesota. Course run by the Art History Department of the University of Minnesota. Two years, History of Art. Museology and museography.

Toronto, Canada. Course run jointly by the University of Toronto and the Royal Ontario Museum. Fifteen to twenty months, multi-disciplinary. Museology and museography.

SOUTH AMERICA

Buenos Aires, Argentina. Course run by the University School of Museology. Four years, Art and History. Museology. Linked with a course in museography at La Plata.

ASIA

Baroda, India. Course run by the University of Baroda's Department of Museology, in co-operation with two local museums. Two years, multi-disciplinary. Museology and museography.

Benares, India. Course run by Benares Hindu University. Two years, Archaeology and History of Art. Museology and museography.

Calcutta, India. Course run jointly by the University of Calcutta and the Asutash Museum of Indian Art. Two years, multi-disciplinary. Museology and museography.

Tokyo, Japan. Course run by the Department of Museology of St Paul's University. One year, multi-disciplinary. Museology and museography.

B Specialised training in conservation

EUROPE

Frankfurt-am-Main. Senckenberg Museum of Natural Sciences and Research Institute. Two courses, each lasting two years, for people working or intending to work in science museums:

(a) for technical assistants, leading to the State Diploma;

(*b*) for preparators, leading to the Museum Diploma.

Rome. The International Centre for the Study of the Preservation and Restoration of Cultural Property. Two courses are organised:

(*a*) in collaboration with the Faculty of Architecture at the University of Rome – a six-month course, intended primarily for graduate specialists, in the conservation and restoration of historic monuments and sites;

(*b*) in collaboration with the Central Institute of Restoration in Rome – a six-month course in the examination and conservation of mural paintings.

Stuttgart. Course organised jointly by the State Academy of the Visual Arts and the Institute for the Technology of Painting. A three-year course, with particular emphasis on the restoration of mural paintings and wood-carvings.

Vienna. Academy of the Visual Arts. A five-year course in conservation, leading to the Diploma of the Higher School (Meisterschule) of Conservation and Technology.

NORTH AMERICA

Los Angeles. University of California. Two terms (approximately six months), giving credits towards a university degree. Conservation and restoration of works of art.

New York. Conservation Centre of the Institute of Fine Arts at New York University. A four-year course, leading to the MA degree in the History of Art and the Diploma in Conservation.

SOUTH AMERICA

Mexico. Latin-American Regional Centre for the Conservation and Restoration of Cultural Property. A two-year course in conservation, leading to either a certificate or diploma, depending on the level of the student's work. The course is supported by UNESCO.

ASIA

Katmandu, Nepal. Laboratory and conservation centre in course of formation, with the support of UNESCO.

New Delhi, India. National Museum. Central laboratory and regional training centre in course of formation, with the support of UNESCO.

6 Museum Management

Museums all over the world are short of money to an extent which must cause observers to wonder if museums, like the writing and publishing of poetry, are still viable institutions. Since museum management is concerned at least as much with making sure that museums exist within their budget as with providing the public with an attractive service, the question 'Can society afford the kind of museum that museum professionals want to run?' is worth putting and answering. It amounts to asking if today's museum managers, the administrators and curators, are setting themselves an impossible task.

The country in which the financial problem has recently become most acute and most clearly realised is the United States and an examination of how that country has been trying to deal with its difficulties should throw light on what developments are likely to be elsewhere.

The nineteenth-century founding fathers of many of America's principal museums certainly had profound faith that if they contributed their substance toward the birth of these temples of the muses, succeeding generations would continue their support and expansion. They had no doubt that they were building for posterity. In the twentieth century, governmental bodies which assumed all or part of the support of a number of privately-founded museums had the same high-minded optimism – the taxpayers would always continue their support, since now these museums were *publicly* owned. They belonged to the taxpayers. Why, then, in this third quarter of the twentieth century is America's huge family of

museums in such financial difficulties? What is the nature and cause of their sickness?

The museum malady in America is certainly not one of visitors or supporters. The former crowd through the doors in unprecedented numbers; annual museum attendance in the United States exceeds the country's total population, and some museums frequently find that at any one time they have more visitors inside the building than they can really handle. Museum memberships double and triple, volunteers and trustees give unlimited hours of free time which the benefiting museum could not possibly purchase. Why should there be a problem?

The answer can only be that museums have been over-ambitious. They have attempted too much. To service the public with the educational programmes and changing exhibitions it has come to regard as its right, the professional staff has been constantly expanded. To exhibit even more works of art, more ethnographical and scientific displays, permanently and temporarily, more and more expensive space has had to be added to the museum buildings with the resulting burden of more guards, technicians and maintenance men. Inflation has been the last straw. The gap between income and expenditure has widened each year, and without the discovery of some miraculous new source of revenue cutbacks in staff and facilities have become inevitable. Their extent and their drastic nature often make them appear more like amputations than reducing diets. Museums have been mutilated, rather than slimmed down. In circumstances such as these, American museums have naturally been asked what form of financial support is the best insurance

against further crippling cutbacks or even bankruptcy and closure? Throughout the formative years of American museums there have been two fundamentally-opposed schools of thought:

1. The advocates of private support, whose warning has always been: 'Keep the museum out of the hands of politicians!'
2. The public support protagonists who confidently predicted that tax support would be a solid guarantee of continuing existence, since it would rise automatically along with increasing financial needs.

Both schools are as right or wrong as they have ever been and are capable of giving only limited guidance to the guardians of tomorrow's museum. Museums with very adequate private endowments, such as Toledo, Cleveland and Kansas City, are in a relatively good financial position and have generally kept away from public support, except for membership. But museums which try to struggle along on an endowment income which is inadequate to meet the increased cost of maintenance are in trouble. Museums which relied on the proverbial inevitability and elasticity of taxes, mostly municipal, have sadly discovered that many citizens are taking their property and therefore their liability to tax away from the city and out to the suburbs. 'Old' cities, such as New York, have become increasingly vulnerable to this kind of movement and are becoming steadily bankrupt as a result. Federally supported museums in the United States, such as the Smithsonian, do not as yet face the same problem. But many of their European counterparts do, as evidenced by the curtailed opening hours of a number of Italian museums. Even with central government support, income does not keep pace with inflation.

The support history of the Detroit Institute of Arts illustrates the shifting foundations on which an American museum rests. It was founded in 1885 with $100,000 of contributions from slightly over 2000 citizens, forty of hom gave $1000 each. By 1893 private support was proving inadequate and the City of Detroit made its first maintenance contribution of $5000, which was derived from liquor taxes. Public support of this private museum increased in the early twentieth century until legislation was instituted to determine whether public funds could be used in Michigan to support a private institu-

tion. The course decision was 'No', and as a result it was clear that the only salvation of the museum was to make it an official City department, under the new municipal charter of 1919. The Board of Trustees turned over the building and collections to the City, retaining only the endowment funds, which were to be used for the benefit of the new Detroit Institute of Arts, successor to the original Detroit Museum of Art. The City built a new museum in the 1920s and allocated generous purchase funds which the Director, Dr William Valentiner, used to buy many of the collection's major masterpieces.

The great economic depression brought about an entirely new situation. In the early 1930s the Museum

was virtually closed down and most of the staff were laid off. Private support then came to the rescue and maintained the nucleus of the professional staff until the City struggled back to some kind of financial stability in the late '30s and was in a position to resume its maintenance of the Museum, but not to provide money for purchases. Since the Second World War support has been divided roughly 50:50 between public and private sources. Now a major crisis again looms. The shrinking City tax base has necessitated a 5 per cent cut in the 1975–6 budget. In January 1975 eleven employees of the Museum were laid off the City payroll, five of them curators, but were taken on a month later, funds having been obtained from the Federal Government.[1]

Detroit Institute of Arts, USA. The results of private generosity: Gallery 244.

Shortly afterwards, the Mayor of the City of Detroit directed that the Institute should make a 25 per cent cut in its budget by dismissing staff. As a result, the galleries were closed during July until the laid-off attendants could be re-engaged with Federal funds. Even then, it was possible to open only 40 per cent of the galleries, on a five-day week basis. How long this situation is likely to continue, it is impossible, at the time of writing, to say.

The Detroit situation is a microcosm of what happens in the United States as a whole. The Institute gets its money where and how it can. Of its 198 employees, only 47 per cent are on the City payroll: 23 per cent are paid by the Founders Society (the Museum's private affiliate); 17 per cent by the Federal Government; 5 per cent by the State of Michigan; and the remaining 8 per cent by a private theatre arts organisation. In addition, there is support for particular projects from the National Endowment for the Arts and from various local foundations. There are well-informed people who believe this is what the typical American museum's support for the future will be – a patchwork quilt of contributions from a variety of sources, with the total sum available still falling far short of what is required to maintain the museum's programme.

The January/February 1975 issue of the American periodical *Museum News* gives a cross-section of the feast-and-famine situation which exists at the present time. 'The push–pull of recession–inflation', it reports, 'is having a variety of effects on the museum field. The confusion is illustrated by some museums undertaking major, community-supported expansion while others are forced into cutbacks and closings.'

The Parkersburg (West Virginia) Art Center began a building fund drive in June. By mid-November, it was just $35,000 short of its $335,000 goal; city and county governments gave $75,000 in revenue-sharing money. Just two weeks after announcing a million dollar building-endowment fund drive, the Newport Harbor (California) Art Museum was half-way to its goal. Two major monetary gifts pushed

Detroit Institute of Arts. Foundation work for an addition to the Museum's investment in bricks and mortar.

the fund over the $400,000 mark. The two-acre site for that museum was donated by the Irvine Company.

In Mesa County, Colorado, citizens decided in a vote of more than three to one to make the Historical Museum and Institute of Western Colorado a fully county-supported facility. Beginning this month, the museum will be a department of the county government, and residents may be taxed up to one mill for its support. According to officials of the nine-year-old accredited museum, the change assures its future.

The Charleston (South Carolina) Museum was given overwhelming support in its campaign to raise $6 million for the construction of a new museum facility. Charleston County residents voted six to one to authorize the sale of $4 million in bonds; in the same election, Charleston city voters – who will be taxed twice for the museum – approved a $2 million bond issue by a three to one vote. This was the museum's first attempt to have the bond issues approved and only the second time in history that voters there have approved a joint bond program.

The New York Cultural Center, citing 'rising operating costs' that 'make it no longer realistic … to rely upon the generosity of the limited number of individuals who have been our mainstay', will terminate its operations this year. All the major exhibitions scheduled for the 1975 season will be concentrated in the six-month time span between now and June, when the center will close. The center's financial statement sets the land, building and improvements value at $7.16 million.

After 55 years of operation, the College of the Dayton (Ohio) Art Institute will close after commencement exercises in May. The trustees said they were compelled to make the change because of the declining student enrollment and competition with new, less expensive arts colleges in the immediate area. The art museum itself will not be affected by the decision.

In October, the Winnipeg Art Gallery announced a major austerity program that involves the dropping of 19 staff positions and scheduled exhibitions as well as cutting the museum's hours by 26 hours per week. The total cutback of approximately $180,000 accounts for 15 per

cent of the gallery's projected expenditures of $1.1 million in the current fiscal year. Provincial, municipal, corporate and other support was $200,000 short of the minimum operating level for the gallery.

It will be seen from the *Museum News* report that the success stories are largely connected with physical expansion and the failures with maintenance. Enthusiastic public and private generosity usually accompanies the construction of a new building or the addition of a wing to an existing one. But, when the increased square footage becomes too burdensome to maintain, similar support is notably missing, and the museum is on its own. An example of this unfortunate situation is the Pasadena (California) Art Museum, with a beautiful new building and distinguished contemporary collection in a fairly wealthy community. Mortgage payments could not be met and a private individual, Mr Norton Simon, had to come to the rescue with a gift of $800,000 to save the museum from bankruptcy. The Museum's programme of work had to be drastically curtailed and the public was deprived of access to the galleries during the period of reorganisation.

To anyone working in a museum in a developing country, the financial problems of a large American museum are likely to appear more than a little unreal. What the Detroit Institute of Arts considers dire poverty would seem like unimaginable affluence to Calcutta or Cairo. One should, even so, think very carefully about the money problems of the world's major museums, as a warning against dreams of grandeur and as a reminder that, to be secure, every museum has to be relevant within its own society at the present time and in the immediate future. It is useless and highly dangerous for an American museum to be relevant to yesterday's America. What matters – the only thing that matters – is whether it fits sensibly into today's America; and exactly the same criterion applies to museums in Switzerland, Czechoslovakia or any other country.

ADMISSION CHARGES AS A SOURCE OF INCOME

It is often asked, and not only, of course, in America, why museums, with their increasing attractiveness to the public, should not find it possible

to pay their way with admission charges. The suggestion is, unfortunately, not realistic. Using the Detroit Institute of Arts as an example, the combined public–private budget of $4,000,000 with roughly 1,000,000 visitors a year means that it costs $4 for the Museum to provide each visitor with the facilities he or she receives. A $4 admission fee is out of the question. If it were instituted, the attendance would certainly drop, thereby sending the cost per visitor even higher. After experimenting for two years with a compulsory admission charge, the Institute has returned to its previous system of asking visitors to pay what they can afford, $1 being suggested for adults, and 50 cents for children, as a suitable amount. This produces only $50,000 in revenue annually, about 1 per cent of the total operating budget.

Other art museums now have similar admission policies. One of the most heavily endowed in the United States, the Metropolitan Museum of Art, was forced into collecting from its visitors, if it was not to lose its sizeable subsidy from the City of New York, which paid for the Museum's attendants. Some payment for admission is mandatory, but the amount is optional and it can be as little as one cent. The annual revenue from admissions is about $900,000, which is $7\frac{1}{2}$ per cent of the Museum's total income. This admission income comes from $2\frac{1}{2}$ million visitors, in a city which has a considerable tourist influx.

The admission charge for a special exhibition further illustrates the inadequacy of the box office as a way of making ends meet. Despite international scholarly collaboration to assemble what can fairly be claimed to be distinguished exhibitions of masterpieces from public and private collections, with wide publicity, such efforts seldom pay for themselves. Often the gap between income and expenditure is considerable. Admission fees admittedly go up each year, but costs, notably insurance, rise even faster. Federal underwriting of insurance for major loan exhibitions in the United States is being seriously discussed at the present time. Meanwhile, the financing of most major exhibitions is a mélange of money from all possible sources: operating budget, endowments, private contributors, admissions, Federal grants, State grants, municipal grants, private foundations, publications sales, and so on.

WAYS OF REMAINING SOLVENT AND THRIVING

Directors and boards throughout the United States are not unnaturally asked what the answer is to the appallingly difficult problem of museum financing. A favoured few museums – and they are very few – have little or no problem. These are the well-endowed private museums, the prestigious national museums and those institutions whose endowment income plus admission receipts cover costs. But for the great majority of museums hobbling along on insecure financial footing there is no simple answer. It is unthinkable, or one would hope it is unthinkable, that those with important collections and considerable attendance would be allowed to close their doors; some public or pri-

Income

Endowment funds	608,015
Museum Common Fund	498,879
Museum investments	19,485
Membership	113,795
Art School	299,069
Concert tickets	57,080
Government grants	53,430
Other	117,767
	$1,767,520

Expenditure

Administrative	476,701
Building maintenance	290,999
Library	47,323
Maintenance, art collections	148,828
Art school	492,453
Music Department	193,188
Exhibitions	59,903
Other	75,902
	$1,785,247

vate rescuer, or a combination of the two, will appear at the last moment. But the problems of survival are sufficiently real that in partnership situations, where both public and private funds

support a museum and ownership of the collection is in the public sector, museum trustees privately express apprehension that if the situation gets sufficiently desperate the politicians might insist on selling objects from the collection in order to pay maintenance costs and keep the galleries open.

The Toledo Museum of Art's balance sheet for the year ending 31 August 1975 (above) illustrates the difficulties in which even a well-endowed, energetically-managed museum can find itself at the present time. Expenditure is not meeting income.

North America contains well over a third of the world's museums. Many of them are small and far from rich, and to a small-town museum in Ohio or Tennessee the world of the Detroit Institute of Arts seems as exotic and far away as it does to a small-town museum in Egypt or Brazil. Yet, even so, there is much to be learnt from the American picture, provided one takes the trouble to translate it into one's own national terms. Certain problems exist everywhere and all solutions are worth considering.

In the present very unsettled state of the world economy, these recommendations have been made to American museums as a whole.

1. Attempt to obtain a combination of public and private support in order that either one or the other can keep the museum afloat in times of financial adversity. Such a partnership also helps to enlist the support of all sections of the

Sotheby & Company, London. Sale of a painting by Turner for £85,000, on 16 July 1975. Publicised as 'a world record for an English watercolour'.

community and helps to refute such criticisms as 'the museum is just a rich people's plaything' or 'we support the museum with our taxes – we shouldn't have to contribute'.

2. If your museum is not accredited by the American Association of Museums, make every effort to achieve this. Accreditation is a prerequisite of grants, besides establishing your museum as an institution which meets minimum professional and managerial standards.

3. Pursue every possible means of support – public and private. Look into your museum's eligibility for all types of grants from tax funds at all levels – city, State and Federal. Investigate grants from any private foundations. Cultivate the wealthy private donor. Get professional advice on fund-raising and membership solicitation. Have a corporate giving programme which includes annual contributions from local business and industrial firms. Publicise your programme and activities by every possible means.

4. Exchange ideas on financing with other museums. Urge your museums association at both a national and a regional level to hold seminars on sources of museum support as well as publicise new ideas which have proved effective. Work towards the same dissemination of fiscal ideas that exists in the areas of art history and conservation.

5. Follow a sound fiscal policy, especially when it comes to expansion of programme or physical property. Are there really enough funds assured to sustain the expansion, especially with the inevitable rise in costs? Will the temporary satisfaction and publicity in an expansion move be more than offset by the embarrassment when a new programme has to be cancelled or a new area inadequately maintained? Even if you are proudly giving birth to a new museum, should it really be brought into this world if it cannot be adequately fed, clothed and housed? The theory which in the past has aided the population explosion in museums – an inadequate museum is better than no museum at all – certainly warr-

ants re-examination by tomorrow's museum directors, administrators and trustees.

This is the crux of the matter. A hard, dispassionate look at the world situation might well suggest that museums have for some time been attempting the impossible and that the true nature of the museum crisis is not being realised. As a result of the steady accumulation of artifacts of all kinds, desultory and haphazard as this may be, there is simply too much of everything. Today is becoming impossibly cluttered up with the remains of yesterday. Each generation adds to the mountain of books, pictures, photographs, recordings, clothes, furniture and objects of all kinds. It is impossible to store it all, let alone conserve it, and to make an intelligent and manageable selection demands almost superhuman powers. If the relics of the recent past – and what happened in America or Bulgaria or Sweden in the 1940s merits equal attention with the manifestations of the 1840s or 1740s – are to be given anything like adequate museum treatment, the demand for both money and space is certain to be insatiable. It cannot be right for an art museum or an ethnographical museum to attempt to solve its problems by announcing that it will do this by admitting nothing later than, say, 1850 to its collections, or for a science museum to banish history altogether and to concentrate wholly on the present. But, faced with such an overwhelming burden of material, what is a museum to do but make some kind of arbitrary choice, hoping against hope that a home may be found elsewhere for what it cannot take itself? The problem is worldwide has no connection with political or economic systems. Museums in the United States are more likely to publicise their dilemma than museums in the Soviet Union. The Americans believe, rightly or wrongly, that it is beneficial to air both private and public problems as much and as often as possible, whereas the Russian style is to regard problems as failures and confessions of weakness, to be kept strictly within the inner family circle.

Although the matter would never be discussed in such terms, war greatly eases the accumulation-burden of those countries which suffer badly from destruction. For this reason, and because it has produced so much more of everything during the past century, the United States faces more severe

museum problems than the Soviet Union, Poland, Yugoslavia or even the German Federal Republic. The private and public stocks of possessions in America have not been thinned out by bombing and battles, and they have been continuously augmented by the country's great wealth, which has allowed and encouraged it to buy in all kinds of interesting and valuable material from overseas. Other countries have exported even their surplus buildings to America, windmills from Denmark and the Netherlands, London Bridge, Wren churches and Tudor manor houses from England. The museum administrators have good reason to panic.

What this amounts to inescapably is a ruthless, but constructive look at what might usefully be called the museum process. The museums which continue to be viable and successful during the next quarter of a century are likely to be those with a management that has identified and faced up to three crucial questions:

1. What are we really trying to do?
2. What do we need in the way of staff and equipment in order to allow us to do this?
3. What is the minimum amount of money we need if we are to fulfil our purpose and how are we going to get it?

A great many museums, perhaps the majority, do not know what they are trying to do. They exist, so to speak, because they exist and because there has so far been just enough money to stop them from closing. They are there for much the same reason as Nottingham has a theatre, Milan an opera house, and Chicago a symphony orchestra – because museums, theatres, opera houses and symphony orchestras are reckoned to be symbols of the Good City. These amenities may well be, in one sense, desirable, but they are becoming almost impossibly expensive to run and, at that point when some kind of large public subsidy is inevitable, the orchestra, museum, opera house or even school has to be in a position to justify its existence. If it cannot do this, it deserves to sink and almost certainly will.

All decisions involving public funds are ultimately political decisions. Those who govern their use and who decide to allocate dollars, roubles or yen to particular purposes have come to the conclusion that less trouble will be caused or more votes won if the money is placed here rather than there. Museums, libraries and opera houses are unfortunately not in the same category as sewers, power-stations and crematoria, which have to be financed somehow if society is to be kept functioning and in a reasonable state of health. From this point of view, no country 'needs' museums to the extent that it 'needs' drains and hospitals. The prime task of any museum administrator is to convince first himself, then the general public, and then the potential sources of finance that museums in general and his own in particular are worth supporting. This task is as central and ever-present in the socialist countries as it is in the United States, especially when the museum is of a new type or when it wants to go about its work in a non-traditional way.

A very good example of this is the museum and demonstration mine at the Alte Elisabeth pit at Freiberg, in the German Democratic Republic. This ancient silver mine, which was in production from medieval times until after the Second World War, has preserved a remarkable series of technical installations, covering several centuries. It also has the pithead chapel which was used by the miners before going down the pit and after emerging from it after the shift. In 1972, a group of local enthusiasts, mostly connected with the Mining Academy, drew up a plan to convert the surface installations and part of the underground galleries into a public museum. This required, of course, considerable expenditure, and the battle to obtain the necessary funds, even in a country which constantly emphasises the importance of understanding the history of labour and technology, was in every way as difficult as a similar struggle would have been in the United States or Belgium. Eventually the basic finance was forthcoming, on the strict understanding that the museum would be nursed only for the first three years. After that, it was to be on its own, a situation which the Americans would understand entirely.

Much of the difficulty in which museums in the relatively wealthy countries find themselves at the present time is psychological quite as well as financial. They have to adjust themselves to the change from the fat years, the period in which money was comparatively easy to get, to the lean years, in which every penny has to be fought for. Many of them still delude themselves that their difficulties are temporary, and that the good times, 'normalcy', are certain to come back again.

At this point, it seems useful to return to one of the clearest-minded and most hard-headed men in the museum world, Mr Alfred Waldis, the founder and director of the Swiss Transport Museum, in Lucerne. Mr Waldis, it will be recalled, believes that the amount of public money which is likely to be available to support museums in the future is likely to be as limited as the supply of wealthy private individuals. Museums, in other words, have got to find some means of paying their own way. Those who fail to do so will simply disappear.

The budget which has been achieved at the Swiss Transport Museum would seem both miraculous and impossible in the United States. On the income side, his budget, in 1974, was:

Entrance fees	70%
Membership (Friends of the Museum)	15%
Restaurant and rental of offices in the museum building to other bodies	15%

This totals approximately 3 million francs, or $1,230,000. The entrance fee was, at that time, 5 francs for adults,

Freiberg, GDR. The Alte Elisabeth pit, conserved to display traditional silver-mining techniques in their historic setting.

2.50 francs for children or, in American terms, something like $2 and $1. It has since gone up slightly, as has the number of visitors. In 1975, the Swiss Transport Museum attracted more than 600,000 people, which is more than 10 per cent of the population of Switzerland. This may well be the highest proportion achieved by any country in the world and, equally important, the Swiss Transport Museum may have the highest annual return on its investment of any museum in the world. If that is a criterion of good management, this is a very well-managed museum. How is it done?

To begin with, Mr Waldis was responsible only to the members of the Museum Association. He raised all the money needed for the building (500,000 francs of this was a loan from the Swiss Federal Railways pension fund, on which the Museum, like any other borrower, pays $7\frac{1}{2}$ per cent interest), built the Museum, planned the exhibits. 'I have made it all myself,' he says, 'I am a dictator. It is the only way.'

This may well be true. The whole establishment undoubtedly revolves around the Director. Staffing is cut to the bone. There is nobody to whom he can delegate authority in his absence, and, as a result, he finds it extremely difficult to be away from Lucerne, if only for a couple of days. He is the Museum. All the ideas, the planning and the control stem from him. There is a very small office staff; a designer, who works to a tight brief; a model-maker; and a technician. The assistants in the galleries are all pensioners, who do the job for a small salary as a way of supplementing their pensions. They are benign and helpful, but they have no special or detailed knowledge of the collections.

The Swiss Transport Museum balances its books by cutting staff and overheads to the limit. This is how it achieves what a large American museum would regard as impossible, making entrance fees cover 70 per cent of the expenditure. The Director freely admits that he needs more staff, especially if the educational side of the Museum is to be expanded, but, since the money is not available at present and never will be, unless by some miracle a grant should become available from the Federal or Cantonal government, that is that. By keeping a firm and direct hand on the way the Museum is run, the Director is able to hold unswervingly to his belief that the idea of a museum, its philosophy, is far more important than the size and permanence of its collections. A good museum, in his opinion, is one which is always changing, one in which there is no difference between a museum and an exhibition. In his own case, the idea which the museum exists to serve is the importance of transport at all periods of history and the need for transport to constantly adapt itself to new opportunities and techniques. Since the Swiss Transport Museum exists only in order to illustrate this central theme, there is no need for it to be a mere repository and no need, therefore, for it to outgrow its strength or resources. It can hold and display only what happens to suit its present purpose. If it requires exhibits dealing with space travel, it has so far been able to borrow them where it pleases. It does not have to give them a permanent home and bankrupt itself in order to do so. On the other hand, there is always bound to be the nagging question as to whether the material one may need to use one day is in fact being preserved elsewhere. One can only be really sure about the items which are under one's own roof, a realisation which drives many museums on to collect everything possible, in the hope that it may all be useful one day.

The most significant aspect of what might be called the Waldis approach at the Swiss Transport Museum is that it shows clear evidence of understanding the four fundamental problems affecting museums today. These are:

1. That the museum must look and feel modern in order to compete with the other attractions which tempt the purse of the public.
2. That every possible attempt must be made to limit the museum's growth.
3. That every square metre of the museum plant must be efficiently and productively used.
4. That the bill for wages and salaries must be kept as low as possible.

Of these four items, the last is perhaps the most critical.

MUSEUMS AS A LABOUR-INTENSIVE INDUSTRY

The basic reason for the troubles being experienced by museums, especially large museums, in the United States and other advanced countries is that they are attempting to run a labour-intensive industry in a high-wage economy. Museums, like palaces and country houses, grew up and developed when wages and salaries were low, and it is very probable that they would never have originated under any other conditions. There is no essential difference between the present position of the management of the Louvre or the Detroit Institute of Arts and the owner of a large mansion, who wishes to continue to live in it and keep it in good working order. So long as they persist in relying on a large supply of labour, their position is hopeless. They cannot win. If they wish to survive, the recipe has to be:

(*a*) to reduce the size of the buildings and the estate to manageable proportions;
(*b*) to install every possible labour-saving device;
(*c*) as a result of (*a*) and (*b*), to cut down the staff bill to a practicable amount.

This does not, of course, mean that the day of the fully automatic museum has arrived. What it does mean is that, in museums as in all other types of modern organisation, employees should be treated as the expensive commodities which they now are and that the organisation of the museum should be based on this central fact. Some people are, of course, more expensive than others. There is nothing at all immoral in the Swiss Transport Museum's practice of using pensioners as gallery attendants and in paying them less because they are pensioners. On the contrary, it is an entirely sensible and socially constructive thing to do, since the pensioners are saved from rotting in idleness and boredom and the Museum is helping them to lead a much more comfortable life than would otherwise be possible. The job is entirely suited to elderly people and there is something frankly ridiculous in employing men in the prime of life to carry out duties of this kind. A sensible use of pensioners in museum work could reduce the wage-bill very considerably, but Switzerland is an unusually sensible and practical country and in many other parts of the world both the trade unions and the professional organisations would no doubt require a good deal of education before they agreed to such a step.

It is also possible to argue that

museums are paying much more than they need to for at least some of their technical staff. During the boom years after the Second World War, when skilled labour of any kind was exceedingly difficult to find, the Royal Scottish Museum in Edinburgh hit on the very sensible and praiseworthy idea of recruiting qualified and experienced men with physical or psychological disabilities which made it difficult for them to undertake ordinary industrial employment. The quiet conditions and unhurried pace of behind-the-scenes museum work were ideally suited to the needs of this kind of man, and the Museum is entirely satisfied with the experiment. What it is, in fact, doing is to provide sheltered employment for people who would otherwise, in all probability, be a charge to the community and public funds, and there seems to be no reason at all why this should not entitle this or any other museum to some kind of Government subsidy, which would reduce their wage-bill. Since society appears to be producing more and more of this type of casualty – the skilled toolmaker who loses a leg or arm in a road accident, the welder who has broken down under the speed and noise of the factory environment, the draughtsman who has developed a neurosis which prevents him from working in a room full of other people – it could be that museums will come to be seen as excellent places for these newly-handicapped people to work, to the advantage of everybody.

It is also possible to suggest that during the fat years of the 1950s and 1960s the museum public has been spoon-fed to a quite unnecessary extent. Under the great financial pressure which they have been experiencing recently, museum management is beginning to take a hard look at the cost-benefit of its existing educational and public relations departments, both of which are expensive in terms of skilled manpower. No properly ruthless analysis has yet been made of the real value of what museums are accustomed to call their educational programmes. It has been assumed that gallery lectures, guided tours for school parties, film shows, activity centres and all the rest are a good thing and that one can never have enough of them. Every large museum has, at some time during the past twenty years, publicly regretted that its funds do not allow it to expand its educational work. But is there, in fact, any solid evidence that either children or adults learn more by being taken in hand by members of the museum staff and formally instructed about the riches the museum has to offer? Might they not, in fact, do just as well, or possibly better, if they were encouraged to go round the museum in the old-fashioned way, with nothing but their curiosity and the labels to guide them? No education worth anything at all is achieved without a great deal of personal effort and it could well be that many museums have been ignoring this truth at their peril.

It would seem a safe prophecy that the next ten years are likely to see a considerable extension of self-guiding techniques, partly in the form of walk-round orientation centres, partly in press-button and slide-tape explanations, and partly in free pick-up leaflets. The self-service element will grow in museums exactly as it has in food stores, and for much the same reasons. The essence of self-service is that it shifts the expense of providing service from the shop to the customers. If the museum cannot afford to pay assistants, the visitor will have to look after the matter of service for himself. A large part of the expense of the enterprise is then transferred from the providing body to the consumer, which seems entirely reasonable.

It is interesting to examine the annual budget of a large museum today and to try to imagine what the picture will be in ten years' time. The accounts of the Deutsches Museum in Munich will do very well for the purpose.

The Museum's 1973 report showed that of every 13 marks that were spent for all purposes, 11 went on salaries, wages and social insurance contributions. All the other items were so modest by comparison that anyone looking at the balance sheet could be forgiven for concluding that the main function of the Deutsches Museum was to employ as many people as possible. There is nothing untypical about this particular budget. The proportions of expenditure are exactly the same for the British Museum, the Nordiska Museum in Stockholm, and the Museo del Popolo in Rome. The conclusion is inescapable that museums are among the most labour-intensive establishments in the world, second only to schools and universities, which have financial problems of a similar size and which have equally failed to develop techniques of self-help for their customers.

A cautious forecast for the year 1983 might be that, by then, the Deutsches Museum and its peers will have cut the wages and salaries proportion of its expenditure from the equivalent of 11 marks in every 13 to 8. If it has not managed to do this, its financial situation is likely to be very serious indeed. The income side of the same Museum's accounts shows how remarkable the achievement of the Swiss Transport Museum has been. In Lucerne, 70 per cent of the annual income comes from entrance fees: in Munich it is almost exactly 10 per cent. The bulk of the funds of the Deutsches Museum comes from three sources:

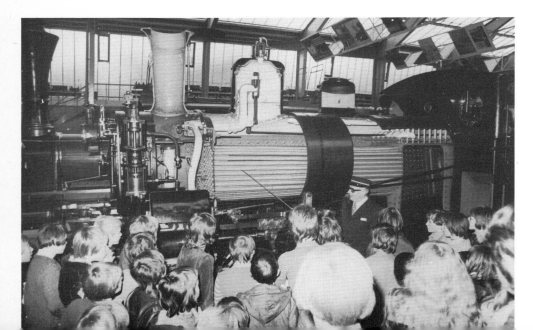

Swiss Transport Museum, Lucerne. Pensioner employed as gallery attendant explains the working of a steam locomotive to schoolchildren.

(*a*) Income from its own very substantial investments.

(*b*) Annual grants from major industrial concerns.

(*c*) Grants from public authorities in cash and kind. The City of Munich, for example, pays the Museum's electricity and telephone bills.

One could express this differently by saying that the financial stability of the Museum is directly dependent on the prosperity of German industry. If Daimler-Benz, AEG, Bayer and Agfa-Gevaert should happen to find themselves in financial trouble, which at present seems somewhat unlikely, the Deutsches Museum would go down with them.

The Deutsches Museum, like the Museum of Science and Industry in Chicago, has been bound into the nation's industrial, commercial and political fabric with extraordinary skill. The pattern of its administration is something of a museum classic. This, in addition to the Museum's own full-time administrative staff, is at two levels, in the normal German fashion, a supervisory board and an advisory board.

The supervisory board contains nominated members from the Länder; the Cities of Berlin, Bremen, Hamburg and Munich; the various Federal ministries; the principal Academies of Science; industrial and professional associations, together with representatives of leading industrial firms. The advisory board, which is also very large, is similarly composed of people from industry, banks, the technical press and the universities. If one looks carefully at the membership of these two boards, it is difficult to think of an organisation of any importance within the industrial, commercial or scientific fields which does not send its representative to the annual meetings of the Deutsches Museum. Attendance at these board meetings is, one should emphasise, a the expense of the organisation in question, not of the Deutsches Museum.

The contribution which German industry makes to the Deutsches Museum does not stop at its annual donation and

at the presence of many of its most distinguished figures on the Museum's governing bodies. Each year there are valuable and important gifts of both old and modern technical equipment, as well as loans of items for special exhibitions. The firm of Carl Zeiss pays for the supervision and operation of the Planetarium, Siemens looks after the repair and maintenance of the Museum's communication section and a number of other industrial concerns give similar help. Gifts of materials, furnishings and working equipment of all kinds are frequent, and all the principal publishers provide the Museum library with free copies of any new books which come within its field. The Deutsches Museum has good reason to count itself among the world's most fortunate and best-provided museums.

But, and the point cannot be emphasised too strongly, even the Deutsches Museum is vulnerable to economic depressions and to changes in the political atmosphere. Its tactics to date have been to make sure that the people who run Germany industry feel that the Deutsches Museum is 'their' museum, and that they have an almost automatic and instinctive duty to finance it. So far, this policy has worked extremely well, but there are certain indications that a somewhat broader basis of support may be needed in the future. It is not outside the bounds of possibility that within the

next ten years the Federal Republic will show more socialistic tendencies than it does at the present time, that a museum of science and technology will be expected to display rather more awareness of the social and human aspects of technical change, and that a considerably larger part of the Museum's income will be derived from public funds, that is, from taxation. It would therefore seem prudent to prepare for this possibility by including one or two trade union representatives on the Museum's boards, together with various specialists whose interests are sociological instead of purely technical. At the moment, one could perhaps be forgiven for saying that the composition of both boards looks rather too much like yesterday's Germany for safety. The same comment could, of course, be made with equal force of the boards of trustees for most American museums. If museums are to be forced to depend more and more on public funds, no harm would be done by making their policy-making and governing bodies look a little more like the community as a whole, rather than merely the upper, more prosperous and more conservative sections of it. A very important part of museum management, perhaps the most important, consists of being sensitive to political, social and economic changes, preferably before they happen.

An important part of the industrial base of the finances of the Deutsches Museum, Munich: the Stuttgart headquarters of Daimler-Benz.

THE COST-BENEFIT MUSEUM

What is quite certain already is that the days when a museum need pay no attention to the views of the general public have gone for ever, and that the museum of the future is going to involve its visitors in its planning to an extent which is so far hardly realised. 'Our' museum, in other words, is likely to belong much more to the Anacostia than to the Deutsches Museum and Louvre end of the spectrum.

Riksutställningar, Stockholm, Sweden. 'Looking at Animals – Fantasy and Research'. The work of the Swedish school of animal painters during the past two hundred years and its influence on the view we have of ourselves and of our environment.

This probably means both a change of balance in the staffing of museums and a differently assorted parcel of talents at the top. The ability to understand what visitors want to see and know is rapidly becoming at least as important as the arts of fund-raising and display, and deserves to be recognised in the pattern of management. We may be moving into a phase during which those who are responsible for running museums should be spending much of their time mixing with people whose work and interests have nothing directly to do with museums at all. At times of rapid and far-reaching change, to suffer from parochialism and inbreeding are grievous and crippling handicaps.

There is, fortunately, no need to regard the individual museum as a self-contained unit. Many museum administrators are coming to think of their work in co-operative and regional terms, realising that it is both intellectually and financially stupid to try to solve all their problems individually and for themselves. The organisation which, more than any other, has pointed the way in which museums have got to go, if they are to continue to exist at all, is Riksutställningar, Swedish Travelling Exhibitions. Ten years ago its philosophy and its methods were considered revolutionary and futuristic: today they are accepted as reasonable and normal. If this present survey of trends within museology and museography is to be summarised in anything like a coherent and meaningful way, one can hardly do better than attempt to digest what Riksutställningar has discovered since it was set up in 1965.

One can perhaps do this without undue misrepresentation or disortion under four headings, each corresponding to a need:

1. To make the best possible use of the available talent and money.
2. To interest a much wider public in what museums are trying to do.
3. To think all the time of the social implications of what one is attempting.
4. To use every possible method of discovering how the public is responding to what one is offering them.

Certain characteristics of the confirmed and habitual museum-goer are now

known, and they have been described earlier in the present work. Such a person is energetic and extraverted above the average. He goes more frequently to concerts, theatres, libraries, cinemas, restaurants and sporting events. He is better educated, and more likely to be young and either unmarried or with children of school age. All this is known to an extent to which it was not known ten years ago, and there is no point in particular museums going over the same ground again.

What is also known is that people who live at a considerable distance from the large centres of population in which museums are usually situated will rarely visit a museum and that, if what one might call museum-contact is to be made with them, the museum has to go to the customer and not vice versa. It is realised, too, that the preparation and presentation of travelling exhibitions is a highly skilled business, which demands a new kind of museologist.

Cynically, one could say that Riksutställningar has done no more than apply ordinary commercial principles. Given the innate conservatism of the museum world, however, this is a very considerable achievement, which demands both acknowledgement and gratitude. It is therefore fitting to end this survey of bright museum ideas around the world with these words from Riksutställningar's sociological consultant, Mr Göran Nylöf:[2]

> To get to know one's visitors, their wishes, opinions and interests, must inevitably make the work of the exhibition designer easier. If one tries to present material to an anonymous mass of people, without receiving in return any information about the degree of success one is achieving, one's efforts and one's message are unlikely to meet with rewarding results. Consequently, it seems natural and reasonable to try to establish contact with the visitor.

This is what the author of the present book has been trying to emphasise. It is the most up-to-date, most succinct definition of the art and the science of museology. Establishing contact with the visitor is half the problem. The other half consists of attracting the visitor in the first place, and the proportion of people who are persuaded to ender the door of a museum even once a year is still far too low.

Notes

Introduction

1. 'Some problems in museum education', in *Museums and Education*, ed. Eric Larrabee, Washington, 1968, p. 79.
2. Musée Royal, Mariemont, Belgium; Museo del Prado, Madrid; Musées d'Archéologie et des Arts Décoratifs, Liège; Ethnographical Museum, Antwerp.
3. Notably Bernice P. Bishop Museum, Honolulu; National Science Museum, Tokyo.
4. *Museums in Search of a Usable Future*, 1970, pp. 203–4.
5. *Exploration of the Ways, Means and Value of Museum Communication with the Viewing Public*, Museum of the City of New York, 1969, p. 3.
6. *The Voices of Silence*, 1954, pp. 13–14.
7. London (1851, 1862, 1871); Paris (1867, 1878, 1889); Antwerp (1869); St Petersburg (1870); Moscow (1872); Vienna (1873); Philadelphia (1876); Chicago (1893).
8. *The Museum and Popular Culture*, 1939, p. 10.
9. T. C. Worsnop, of the Department of Science and Art, South Kensington, later to become the Victoria and Albert Museum, in *Journal of the Bath and West Society*, 1873, pp. 37–8.
10. 'Design standards in museum exhibits', *Curator*, 1/1958, p. 29.
11. *The Museum: its History and its Tasks in Education*, 1949, pp. xxiii-xiv.
12. *Changing Museums: their Use and Misuse*, 1967, p. ix.
13. 'The role of museums of history and folklore in a changing world', *Curator*, vol. 6 no. 2 (1963).
14. Dr A. A. Y. Kyerematen: *Ghana National Cultural Centre: Building for Future Generations*, Kumasi, 1970.
15. 'The museum as a cultural centre', vol. 23 no. 4 (1970–1).
16. A report on the Round Table is to be found in *Museum*, vol. 25 no. 3 (1973).

Chapter 1 The Museum's Resources

1. *Musée des civilisations nègres, Dakar*, UNESCO working paper, 1975.
2. *Museum*, vol. 22 no. 2 (1966).
3. See his article, 'Salvaging ethnology', in *Museum*, vol. 23 no. 3 (1970–1).
4. The gap is being at least partly filled by UNESCO's *General History of Africa*, which is now in preparation, but in full recognition of the fact that the individual African countries will all in time want to write their own histories, both as a source of confidence and as a proof of national maturity. Each of the eight volumes is edited by an African. The first two have already appeared and the complete series is expected to be available by 1981. The *General History* will appear, to begin with, in an English and a French version. About a year after the main edition is published, a popular but complete edition, aimed at the general public, is being brought out. At the same time, it is planned to translate each volume into various other languages, including abridged editions in a number of African languages.
5. In Baxi and Dwivedi, *Modern Museum: Organisation and Practice in India*, 1973, pp. 20–1.
6. *Norfolk Carnegie Project: Proposals for a Scheme of Regional Interpretation for the County of Norfolk*, 1975.
7. J. Geraint Jenkins, 'The collection of ethnological material', *Museums Journal*, vol. 74 no. 1 (June 1974) p. 7.
8. *Libraries, Museums and Art Galleries: A Report of the Advisory Council on Education in Scotland*, 1951, p. 91.
9. J. Geraint Jenkins, op. cit.
10. Described by Baxi and Dwivedi on pp. 24–5 of *Modern Museum* . . .
11. 'The ethics of museum acquisitions', *Museum*, vol. 26 no. 1 (1974).
12. Its results were reported in *Museum*, vol. 26 no. 1 (1974).
13. Ibid. Dr Eric Westbrook, Director of the Ministry for the Arts, Melbourne, has made three practical suggestions, in his address to UNESCO's 1976 Tokyo seminar on the Adaptation of Museums in Asia to the Needs of the Modern World:

    1. that museums known to be receiving illicitly acquired material should be barred from representation at international conferences and exhibitions;
    2. that museums should agree not to buy from a black list of dealers known to be handling illicit material;
    3. that, since most private collectors are notoriously vain, no objects from a 'blacked' private collection should be borrowed for temporary exhibitions.

14. In a conversation with the present author, 12 November 1974.
15. In the same conversation.
16. *Final Report of Committee of Experts on the Risks incurred by Works of Art and Other Cultural Property* (Brussels: 19-22 November 1973). This has been amplified by another UNESCO report, of the *Committee of Experts on Insurance and other Forms of Coverage of Risks of Works of Art* (1974), which noted that the costs of insurance had become cripplingly high and recommended that 'UNESCO urges other governments to provide programmes by indemnity and guarantee for loans of valuable works of art for major international exhibitions'. It is the normal practice of governments not to insure their own property. The British Government extends the practice of non-insurance to the works of art which it borrows, but all the national museums and galleries, the British Council and the Arts Council are allowed to offer indemnities for works of art which they borrow for exhibitions.
17. *Étude préliminaire sur les aspects techniques, juridiques et administratifs de l'échange d'objets et spécimens originaux entre institutions de différents pays.*

Chapter 2 Conservation

1. *Conservation in Museums and Galleries: a Survey of Facilities in the United Kingdom*, United Kingdom Group, International Institute for Conservation of Historic and Artistic Works, 1974.
2. In *Museum Work*, published by the Department of Fine Arts in Commemoration of the National Museum, Bangkok, 1974.
3. These are set out in *Control of the Museum Environment: A Basic Summary*, 1967.
4. Reported in *Conservation in Museums and Galleries: A Survey of Facilities in the United Kingdom*, 1974.
5. The problem and the solutions to it are discussed in great detail, with special reference to paper and to printed material, in Dr Françoise Flieder's book, *La Conservation des documents graphiques*, Paris: Éditions Eyrolles, for ICOM, 1969. Dr Flieder is a scientist working in Paris at the Museum of Natural History.
6. For details of the control of lighting in museums, see *La Lumière et la protection des objets et specimens exposés dans les musées et galeries d'art*, sponsored by ICOM and published by L'Association Française de l'Éclairage. See also R. Feller's article in *Museum*, vol. 17 no. 2 (1964).
7. Universités de Paris 1 et 4: *Cours de Muséologie Contemporaine*, 'Aspects communs à la conservation des biens muséaux mobiliers et immobiliers', 1975.

Chapter 3 Museum Buildings

1. 'Planning a museum building', in Baxi and Dwivedi, *Modern Museum...*, 1973.
2. 'Thoughts on museum architecture', *Museum Work*, Bangkok, 1974.
3. See Adelhart Zippelius, *Handbuch der Europäischen Freilichtmuseen*, Bonn, 1974.
4. *The Directory of Museums*, London, 1975.
5. On this, see *Museum*, vol. 24 no. 2 (1972).
6. On this, see Masao Ishizawa, 'Report on developments in Japan', in *Report of the Round Table Conference on Modernisation of Museum Activities in Asia*, Tokyo, 1973.
7. At a UNESCO seminar on the *Adaptation of Museums in Asia to the Needs of the Modern World*. The Regional Seminar on the *Adaptation of Museums to the Needs of the Modern World*, held at Bangui in 1976, made recommendations to UNESCO on ways of meeting the special needs of African museums.

Chapter 4 The Museum and its Visitors

1. The proceedings of the seminar were published by Museum in 1969.
2. January 1972.
3. Described in *Museum*, vol. 23 no. 1 (1970–1).
4. The basis of such an exhibition is indicated, although not with an orientation centre in mind, by Philip Hendy and A. S. Lucas in their extremely interesting article, 'The ground in pictures', *Museum*, vol. 21 no. 4 (1968).
5. It was reprinted in *Curator*, vol. 6 no. 2 (1963).
6. *Proceedings of the National Museums Symposium*, National Museums of Ceylon Publications, 1967.
7. Published for the Countryside Commission, 1975.
8. 'Children and art', *Museums, Imagination and Education*, UNESCO, 1973. Victor D'Amico's philosophy of museum exhibitions is explained, with colour illustrations, in the November 1969 issue of the British periodical *The Connoisseur*.
9. For some not altogether clear reason, an Italian edition of the *Guide* has now appeared. Mr Sassoon was replaced as Curator in 1976, in accordance with the Government's policy of progressive Africanisation.
10. For example, the splendidly designed and printed *L'Art populaire en Wallonie*, with its 921 illustrations and 564 pages, sold by the Museum of Walloon Life at Liège, at 1,956 francs. Books such as this are assuredly destined to become collectors' pieces and, regrettable as this is, the likelihood of the Museum being able to produce them in 1985 is remote.
11. *Museum*. vol. 24 no. 4 (1972).
12. At Grenoble, a university town, there were 6322 visitors in two and a half days.
13. *Museum*, vol. 26 no. 2 (1974).
14. Peter Cannon-Brookes, 'The loan of works of art for exhibition', vol. 71 no. 3 (December 1971).
15. 'Television and the museum', *Museums, Imagination and Education*, UNESCO, 1973.
16. Robert E. Dierbeck, 'Television and the museum', no. 2 (1958).
17. See the paper presented by R. K. Dell, of the National Museum of New Zealand, at the 1976 UNESCO seminar in Tokyo, *The Adaptation of Museums in Asia to the Needs of the Modern World*.
18. *Museum News*, May 1972.
19. 'Museum audience research', *Museum News*, October 1961.
20. The system is described in Kenneth Barton, 'Recording attendances at Portsmouth City Museums', *Museums Journal*, vol. 73 no. 4 (March 1974).
21. On this, see A. J. N. Arber, 'A survey of visitors to the Rouault Exhibition at Manchester City Art Gallery', *Museums Journal*, vol. 75 no. 1 (June 1975), and P. Vervey, 'Report on Georges Rouault Exhibition', *Arts Council Bulletin*, 1974.
22. Arber, op. cit.
23. 'The Metropolitan Museum and its public: highlights of the Yankelovich survey', *The Metropolitan Museum of Art Report*, 1973–4.
24. This confirms W. J. Withrow's findings, 'Practical implications of the Toronto study', *Museum*, vol. 22 no. 3/4 (1969), that 'there is no relation between occupation, education and the results of an art appreciation survey'.
25. It is described by Brian McWilliams and Joyce Hopwood in 'The public of Norwich Castle Museum, 1971–72', *Museums Journal*, vol. 72 no. 4 (March 1973).
26. In the introduction to his report on the surveys undertaken at the Ulster Museum, published in the *Museums Journal*, vol. 68 nos. 1 and 2 (June and September 1968).
27. 'The Belfast public and the Ulster Museum', *Museums Journal*, vol. 70 no. 4 (March 1971).
28. Very similar views are expressed by W. E. Washburn in his article, 'The museum's responsibility in adult education', *Curator*, vol. 7 no. 1 (1964).
29. 'Museum function or policy: a comment on the public of the Ulster Museum', *Museums Journal*, vol. 68 no. 4 (March 1969).
30. The experiments are described by Herbert Goldhammer, 'Über die systematische Entwicklung von differenzierten Formen und Methoden der Bildungs- and Erziehungsarbeit im Kunstmuseum', *Neue Museumskunde*, vol. 14 no. 3, 1971.
31. 'Reflections on MUSE', *Museum News*, May 1972.
32. Published as *L'Amour de l'art: les musées et leur public*, 1966.
33. Its findings were summarised in the journal which sponsored it, the *Illustrated London News*, April 1974.

Chapter 5   Selection and Training of Personnel

1. 'Museum organisation', in *Museum Work*, Bangkok, 1974.
2. *Museums Journal*, vol. 71 no. 3 (December 1971). Dr Eric Westbrook reinforces Mr. Singleton's argument by saying that the successful curator 'must have a firm streak of practical ability. He or she must not be so lost in the subtleties of a discipline that the understanding and attitudes of the non-scholar are not understood. A good museum officer must live in the real world which the great number of his fellow-citizens inhabit.'
3. Under the title *Professional Training of Museum Personnel in the World*. During the 1976 Plenary session in Paris, ICOM's International Committee on the Training of Personnel set up a working party to review and extend ICOM's Basic Syllabus for Professional Museum Training, adopted at the Ninth ICOM Conference.

Chapter 6   Museum Management

1. The size of the Federal Government's support of museums is not widely realised. The 1975–6 budget for its Arts Endowment has allocated $6,905,000 for spending on museums. This figure represents 10.6 per cent of the total budget for the arts.
2. *Some notes on the evaluation of exhibitions*, published by Riksutställningar, 1974.

Publications likely to be helpful

A PERIODICALS AND SERIES

Runs of any of these have a way of turning up in the most improbable libraries and museums, largely, one suspects, as a result of exchange systems or of campaigns of cultural propaganda. The present author has seen examples of them in places where it seemed most unlikely that there would be anyone capable of reading the language in question, but where further investigation revealed one's error. The developing African countries, for example, have sent many students to universities in Central and Eastern Europe, with the result that it is now not too difficult to find professional members of museum staffs in, say, Accra or Lagos who can cope easily with Czech, Hungarian or Russian.

To list the periodicals which follow is not, therefore, merely a proof of the author's erudition. All one is doing is to recommend potentially useful working tools.

Periodicals

APOM Informaçoes, quarterly bulletin of the Portuguese Association of Museums, Lisbon: Museu Nacional de Arte Antiga, Rua das Janelas Verdas.

Art and Archaeology Technical Abstracts (formerly IIC Abstracts), New York: New York University Conservation Center, Institute of Fine Arts, 1 East 78th Street, New York.

Biblioteka muzealnictwa i ochrony zabytków, Warszawa: Ośrodek Dokumentacji Zabytków, Ul. Senatorska 13/15.

Bilten-informatica museologica, Zagreb: Muzejski Dokumentacioni Centar, Mesnička ul. 5.

Bulletin van de Koninklijke Nederlandse Oudheidkundige Bond, & Nieuws-Bulletin, Voorburg: Balen van Andelplein; and Amsterdam: 31 Korte Hoogstraat.

ICOM Education, (formerly *Museums' Annual*), published by ICOM's international Committee for Education and Cultural Action.

Curator, New York: The American Museum of Natural History, Central Park West at 79th Street.

ICOM News, Paris: ICOM, 1 rue Miollis, 15e.

ICOMOS Bulletin, Paris: ICOMOS, published at Begijnhof, Leuven, Belgium.

Information. Mitteilungsblatt des Verbandes der Museen der Schweiz, Zürich: Schweizerische Landesmuseum, Postfach 8023.

Journal of Indian Museums, New Delhi: Museum Association of India, c/o National Museum, Janpath.

Kalori, Journal of the Museum Association of Australia, Melbourne: Science Museum of Victoria, Swanston Street 304-328.

Metodický list, Praha: Muzeologický Kabinet při Národním Muzeu, Mála Strana, Ul. Lužického semináře 13.

Mitteilungsblatt der Museen Oesterreichs, Wien: Verband Oesterreichischer Geschichtsvereine, Burgring 5.

Monumentum, Paris: ICOMOS, published at 95 Groot Begijnhof, Leuven, Belgium.

Musées et collections publiques de France, Paris: Association générale des conservateurs des collections publiques de France, Palais du Louvre.

Musei e gallerie d'Italia, Roma: Associazione nazionale dei musei italiani, 49 Piazza San Marco.

Museum, Paris: UNESCO, 7 place de Fontenoy, 7e.

Museum News, Washington DC: The American Association of Museums, 2233 Wisconsin Avenue N.W.

Museums Calendar, London: The Museums Association, 87 Charlotte Street, W1P 2BX.

Museums Journal, London: The Museums Association, 87 Charlotte Street, W1P 2BX.

Museumskunde, Berlin: Deutscher Museumsbund, Ägyptisches Museum, Schlosstr. 70, Berlin-Charlottenburg, GFR.

Museumsnytt, Oslo: Norske Kunst og Kulturhistoriske Museer & Norske Naturhistoriske Museers Landsforbund, St Olavsgate 1.

Muzealnictwo, Poznań: Osrodek Dokumentacji zabytków, c/o Muzeum narodowe, 9 Marcinkowskiego Avenue.

Muzejní a vlastivědná práce, Praha: Museologický Kabinet, Mála Strana, Ul. Lužického semináře 13.

Muzeologické sešity, Brno: Katedra muzeologie filosofické fakulty UJEP, Moravske Muzeum, nám. 25, února 8.

Muzeologija, Zagreb: Muzejski Dokumentacioni Centar, Mesnička ul. 5.

Múzeum: Metodický, študijný a informačný materiál, Bratislava: Muzeologicky Kabinet při Slovenskom Národnom Muzeu v Bratislave, Vajanskeho nábr. 13.

Neue Museumskunde, Berlin: Rat für Museumswesen, Müggelseedamm 200, Berlin 1162, GDR.

Der Präparator: Präparationstechniken für Naturwissenschaften Museum, Medizin, Kultur- und Kunstgeschichte. Bochum: Vereiningung der Präparatoren und Dermoplastiker Deutschlands, Postfach 1404, 463 Bochum, GFR.

Revista muzeelor, Bucuresti: Comitetul de Stat pentru cultura si arťa, Calea Victoriei 120, Sect. 1.

SAMAB, Bulletin of the South African Museums Association, Cape Town: South African Museums Association, PO Box 61.

Schule und Museum, Berlin: Museum für Deutsche Geschichte, Arbeitsgruppe Museumspädagogik, Unter den Linden 2, Berlin 108, GDR.

Smithsonian Institution Information, Systems, Innovations, Washington DC 20560.

Studies in Conservation, The Journal of the International Institute for the Conservation of Historic and Artistic Works, London: IIC, 608 Grand Buildings, Trafalgar Square.

Studies in Museology, Baroda: Department of Museology, MS University of Baroda, India.

Series

Handbooks for Museum Curators, London: The Museums Association

History News Technical Leaflets, Nashville, Tennessee: American Association for State and Local History.

Information Sheets, London: The Museums Association.

Instructions for Collectors, London: British Museum, Natural History.

Musées et monuments, Paris: UNESCO.

Muzejní Práce, Praha: Muzeologický Kabinet.

Politiques culturelles: études et documents, Paris: UNESCO.

Technical Papers, Ottawa: Canadian Museums Association.

Travaux et documents muséographiques, Paris: ICOM.

Travaux et Publications, Paris: ICOM; and Roma: International Centre for the Study of the Preservation and the Restoration of Cultural Property.

B BIBLIOGRAPHIES

Art and Archaeology Technical Abstracts (formerly IIC Abstracts), New York: New York University Conservation Center, Institution of Fine Arts, 1 East 78th Street, New York.

Borhegyi, Stephan F. de, Dodson, Elba A., and Hanson, Irene A., *Bibliography of Museums and Museum Work, 1900–61*, Milwaukee: Milwaukee Public Museum, 1961.

Borhegyi, Stephan F. de., *Chronological Bibliography of Museum Visitor Surveys*, Milwaukee: Milwaukee Public Museum, 1966.

International Museum Bibliography, Paris: ICOM; and Praha: Muzeologický Kabinet.

Rath, Frederick L., Jr, and O'Connell, Merrilyn Rogers, *Guide to Historic Preservation, Historical Agencies and Museum Practices: a Selective Bibliography*, Cooperstown, New York: New York State Historical Association, 1970.

Vyberová bibliografia zahraničnej muzeologickej literatúry, Praha and Bratislava: Muzeologický Kabinet.

C BOOKS AND ARTICLES

The literature of museology and museography is enormous and most of it now has a quaintly old-fashioned look about it. The pedigree of ideas is, of course, fascinating, but recent technical and philosophical changes have been so far-reaching that one can say, with little fear of exaggeration, that any book or article about museums which was written and published before 1960 is now virtually obsolete, although the process of obsolescence has been more rapid in some countries than in others.

In drawing up the list which follows, two principles have been followed:

(*a*) Each book or article mentioned should still, despite the process of time, have something important and relevant to say to the reader.

(*b*) The balance of contemporary need and opinion throughout the world should be fairly represented, despite the fact that the items listed cover works published in a very small selection of the world's languages.

It is, in fact, a basic list, which can be extended at will by consulting the bibliographies given above, under B. Many of the books mentioned have, in any case, their own special bibliographies.

The major museum periodicals, and especially *ICOM News*, report new publications promptly, and the number of additional books and articles which appear each year suggests that the creativity of the museum profession is not yet exhausted.

1. *General Works on Museology and Museography*

Adam, T. R., *The Museum and Popular Culture*, American Association for Adult Education, 1939.

Alexander, Edward P., 'The regional museum as a cultural centre', *Museum*, vol. 23 no. 4 (1970–1).

Assogba, Romain-Philippe, 'Revolution and the conservation of a national heritage'. *Museum*, vol. 28 no. 4 (1976).

Baxi, Smita J., and Dwivedi, Vinod P., *Modern Museum Organisation and Practice in India*, New Delhi: Abhinav Publications, 1973.

Bazin, Germain, *The Museum Age*, New York: Universe Books, 1967. Published in French as *Le Temps des musées*, Liège and Brussels: Desoer, 1967.

Benoît, Luc, *Musées et muséologie*, Paris: Presses Universitaires de France, 1960.

Cameron, Duncan F. (ed.), *Are Art Galleries Obsolete?* Proceedings of a seminar organised by the Art Gallery of Toronto; Toronto: Peter Martin Associates, 1969.

Finlay, Ian, *Priceless Heritage: the Future of Museums*, London: Faber, 1977.

Greenaway, Frank, *et al.*, *Science Museums in Developing Countries*, Paris: ICOM, 1962.

Harrison, M., *Changing Museums: their Use and Misuse*, London: Longmans, 1967.

Hudson, Kenneth, *A Social History of Museums*, London: Macmillan, 1975.

Hudson, Kenneth, and Nicholls, Ann, *The Directory of Museums*, London: Macmillan, 1975.

ICOM, *The Problems of Museums in Countries Undergoing Rapid Change*, Symposium organised by ICOM, Neuchâtel, 1962; Paris;: ICOM, 1964.

ICOM, *The Protection of Cultural Property: Handbook of National Legislations*, Paris: ICOM, 1974.

Jelinek, Jan, 'The modern, living museum', *Museum*, vol. 27 no. 2 (1975).

Kyerematen, A. A. Y., *Ghana National Cultural Centre: Building for Future Generations*, Kumasi, 1970.

Malraux, André, *The Voices of Silence*, London: 1954.

'The museum as a cultural centre', *Museum*, vol. 23 no. 4 (1970–1).

Myles, Kwasi, 'Museum development in African countries', *Museum*, vol. 28 no. 4 (1976).

Potts, Peter H., 'The role of museums of history and folklore in a changing world', *Curator*, vol. 6 no. 2 (1963).

Ripley, Dillon, *The Sacred Grove*, New York: Simon & Schuster, 1969.

Rivière, G. H., *Musée des civilisations nègres*, *Dakar*, UNESCO, 1975.

UNESCO, International symposium on museums in the contemporary world, *Final Report*, Paris: UNESCO, 1970.

de Varine-Bohan, Hugues, 'The modern museum: requirements and problems of a new approach', *Museum*, vol. 28 no. 3 (1976).

Wittlin, Alma S., *Museums in Search of a Usable Future*, Cambridge, Mass.: MIT Press, 1970.

2. *Museum Buildings*

American Society of Heating, Refrigerating and Air-Conditioning Engineers, *ASHRAE Guide and Data Book*, vol. I: *Fundamentals and Equipment*, 1964–5; vol. II: *Applications*, 1966–7; New York: ASHRAE.

Belcher, M., *Wall Coverings*, London: The Museums Association, 1972.

Belcher, M., *Floor Coverings*, London: The Museums Association, 1973.

Bell, James, A. M., *Museum and Gallery Building: a Guide to Briefing and Design Procedure*, London: The Museums Association, 1972.

Brawne, Michael, *The New Museum: Architecture and Display*, New York: F. A. Praeger, 1966.

Celestino, Antonio, 'The Carmelite monastery in Salvador, Bahia', *Museum*, vol. 27 no. 3 (1975).

Coleman, Laurence Vail, *Museum Buildings: a Planning Study*, vol. 1, Washington: The American Association of Museums, 1950.

Doe, G., 'Notes on museum and art gallery lighting in the tropics', *Studies in Conservation*, vol. 19 no. 2 (1965).

Felice, Ezio Bruno de, *Luce-Musei*, Rome: De Luca, 1966.

Fry, Maxwell, and Drew, Jane, *Tropical Architecture*, London: Batsford, 1964.

Hopkinson, R. G., Petherbridge, P., and Longmore, J., *Daylighting*, London: Heinemann, 1966.

Illuminating Engineering Society, *Lighting of Art Galleries and Museums*, London: Illuminated Engineering Society, 1971.

Jørgensen, Bent, 'From Pole to Pole: new exhibition hall at the Copenhagen Zoological Museum', *Museum*, vol. 27 no. 3 (1975).

Lehmbruck, Manfred, 'Museum architecture', *Museum*, Paris: UNESCO, vol. 26 no. 3/4 (1974).

Lorentz, Stanislaw, 'Nieborów', *Museum*, vol. 27 no 3 (1975).

Passarelli, Lucio, 'The new wing of the Vatican Museums', *Museum*, vol. 28 no. 2 (1976).

Thomson, Garry (ed.), Contributions to the London Conference on *Museum Climatology*, 18–23 September 1967, published by the International Institute for Conservation of Historic and Artistic Works.

UNESCO, 'Contemporary architecture and museums', special issue of *Museum*, vol. 9 no. 2 (1956); Paris: UNESCO.

UNESCO, 'Museum architecture: projects and recent achievement', special issue of *Museum*, vol. 17 no. 3 (1964); Paris: UNESCO.

3. *Management, Finance, Security*

Allen, D. A., *et al.*, Administration, in the series *Handbooks for Museum Curators*, London: The Museums Association, 1960.

Final Report of Committee of Experts on the Risks incurred by Works of Art and Other Cultural Property, Paris: UNESCO, 1974.

Foramitti, Hans, *Mesures de sécurité et d'urgence pour la protection des biens culturels*, Rome: Centre for the Protection of Cultural Property, 1972.

Goy, F., and Varine-Bohan, H. de, *Étude préliminaire sur les aspects techniques, juridiques et administratifs de l'échange d'objets et spécimens originaux entre institutions de différents pays*, Paris: UNESCO, 1975.

Guthe, Carl E., *So You Want a Good Museum: a Guide to the Management of Small Museums*, Washington: The American Association of Museums, 1973.

Howard, Robert, 'Museums in a period of inflation', *Museums Journal*, vol. 75 no. 3 (December 1975).

Keck, Cardine K., *et al.*, *A Primer on Museum Security*, Cooperstown: The New York State Historical Association, 1966.

4. *Staffing and Training*

American Association of Museums, *Museum Studies: A Curriculum Guide for Universities and Museums*, Washington: American Association of Museums, 1973.

American Association of Museums, *Museum Training Courses in the United States and Canada*, Washington: American Association of Museums, 1971.

Association of Art Museum Directors,

Professional Practices in Art Museums, New York: Association of Art Museum Directors, 1971.

Gibbs-Smith, Charles H., *The Art of Observation: a Booklet for Museum Wardens*, London: Victoria and Albert Museum, 1971.

ICOM, *Papers Concerning Professional Training*, London: Evelyn, Adams & Mackay, for ICOM, 1968.

ICOM, *Training of Museum Personnel*, London: Hugh Evelyn, for ICOM, 1970.

Nair, S. M., 'A pioneer museum training program in India', *Curator*, vol. 13 no. 2 (1970).

5. *Acquisition, Recording, Cataloguing*

Bostick, William A., 'The ethics of museum acquisitions', *Museum*, vol. 26 no. 1 (1974).

Dudley, Dorothy H., and Bezold Wilkinson, Irma, *Museum Registration Methods*, Washington: The American Association of Museums, 1968.

Higgs, J. W. Y., *Folk Life Collection and Classification*, in the series *Handbooks for Museum Curators*, London: The Museums Association, 1963.

ICOM, 'Meeting of experts to study the ethical rules governing museum acquisition', Conclusions, *ICOM News*, vol. 23 no. 2 (1970).

Jeannot-Vignes, Bernard, 'Collecting material for an ethnographical exhibition: an experiment conducted by the "Ecomuseum" of the Urban Community of Le Creusot–Montceau-les-Mines', *Museum*, vol. 28 no. 3 (1976).

Jenkins, J. Geraint, 'The collection of ethnographical material', *Museums Journal*, vol. 74 no. 1 (June 1974).

Libraries, Museums and Art Galleries: a Report of the Advisory Council on Education in Scotland, 1951.

Myles, Kwasi Addai, 'A museum for an African community: an experiment in acquisition at the Ghana National Museum', *Museum*, vol. 28 no. 3 (1976).

Nunoo, Richard B., 'Salvaging ethnology', *Museum*, vol. 23 no. 3 (1970–71).

Ripolli-Perelló, Eduardo and Greco, Enrique Sanmarti, 'Ampurias: a history of the site, the excavations and the museum', *Museum*, vol. 28 no 2 (1976).

Schneider, Mary Jane, *Cataloguing and Care of Collections for Small Museums*, Columbia: Museum of Anthropology, 1971.

UNESCO, *Convention on the Means of*

Prohibiting and Preventing the Illicit Import, Export and Transfer of Ownership of Cultural Property, Paris, UNESCO, 1970.

UNESCO, *Index of National Legislation on the Protection of Cultural Heritage*, Paris: UNESCO, 1969.

UNESCO, *Recommendations on International Principles Applicable to Archaeological Excavations*, Paris: UNESCO, 1957.

6. *Conservation, Restoration, Storage*

Agrawal, O. P., *Museum Work*, Bangkok: Department of Fine Arts in Commemoration of the National Museum, 1974.

Alderson, William T., 'The objectives of historic site preservation', *Museum*, vol. 27 no 3 (1975).

Allen, Jim, 'Port Arthur Site Museum, Australia: its preservation and historical perspectives', *Museum*, vol. 28 no. 2 (1976).

Berner, A. *Preservation and Restoration of Musical Instruments. Provisional Recommendations*, London: Evelyn, Adams & Mackay, for ICOM, 1967.

Boustead, W., *The Conservation of Works of Art in Tropical and Subtropical Zones*, Rome: Rome Centre Publication no. 3, 1960.

Clapp, Anne F., *Curatorial Care of Works of Art on Paper*, rev. ed., Oberlin: The Intermuseum Laboratory, 1973.

Conservation in Museums and Galleries: a Survey of Facilities in the United Kingdom, United Kingdom Group, International Institute for the Conservation of Historic and Artistic Works, 1974.

Control of the Museum Environment: a Basic Summary, International Institute for Conservation of Historic and Artistic Works, 1967.

Coremans, P., 'Preservation of the cultural heritage in tropical Africa', *Museum*, vol. 18 no. 3 (1965).

Cunha, G. M. and D. G., *Conservation of Library Materials*, 2nd ed., Metuchen: Scarecrow Press, 1971.

Dowman, Elizabeth A., *Conservation in Field Archaeology*, London: Methuen, 1970.

Feller, Robert L., 'Control of deteriorating effects of light upon museum objects', *Museum*, vol. 17 no. 2 (1964).

Feller, Robert L., *et al.*, *On Picture Varnishes and Their Solvents*, rev. ed., Cleveland: Case Western Reserve University Press, 1971.

Flieder, Françoise, *La Conservation des documents graphiques*, Paris: published for ICOM and Rome Centre by Eyrolles, 1969.

Gettens, Rutherford, J., and Stout, George L., *Painting Materials*, New York, 1947.

Glover, Jean M., *Textiles: their Care and Protection in Museums*, London: The Museums Association, 1973.

Groupe français, 'Éclairage des œuvres d'art', *La Lumière et la protection des objets et spécimens exposés dans les musées et galeries d'art*, Paris: Association française d'éclairage, 1971.

Hendy, Philip, and Lucas, A. S., 'The ground in pictures', *Museum*, vol. 21 no. 4 (1968).

ICOM, *Problems of Conservation in Museums*, London: Allen & Unwin, for ICOM, 1969, French edition, Paris: Eyrolles, 1969.

Jenkins, Jean (ed.), *Ethnic Musical Instruments: Identification and Conservation*, London: Hugh Evelyn, for ICOM, 1970.

Kathpalia, Yash Pal, *Conservation and Restoration of Archive Material*, Paris: UNESCO, 1974.

Keck, Caroline, *A Handbook on the Care of Paintings for Historical Agencies and Small Museums*, Cooperstown: American Association for State and Local History, 1965.

Kelly, Francis, *Art Restoration*, Newton Abbot: David & Charles, 1971.

Leene, Jentina E., *Textile Conservation*, London: Butterworth, 1972.

Leigh, David *et al.*, *First Aid for Finds: a Practical Guide for Archaeologists*, Southampton: RESCUE, and Department of Archaeology, University of Southampton, 1972.

Mayer, Ralph, *The Artist's Handbook of Materials and Techniques*, 3rd ed., London: Faber, 1973.

Mora, Pablo, *Causes of Deterioration of Mural Paintings*, Rome: International Centre for Conservation, 1974.

Mühlethaler, Bruno, *Kleines Handbuch der Konservierungstechnik*, Bern and Stuttgart: Paul Haupt, 1967.

Plenderleith, H. H., and Werner, A. E. A., *The Conservation of Antiquities and Works of Art*, 2nd ed., London: Oxford University Press, 1972.

Plenderleith, H. J., *Preservation of Documentary Material in the Pacific Area: A Practical Guide*, Canberra: Australian Government Publishing Service, for the Australian Advisory Committee for UNESCO, 1972.

Price, Marjorie and Marko, Ksynia

'The storage of museum textiles in Switzerland, West Germany and Holland', *Museums Journal*, vol. 76 no. 1 (June 1976).

Rühemann, Helmut, *The Cleaning of Paintings: Problems and Potentialities*, London: Faber, 1968.

Stansfield, G., *The Storage of Museum Collections*, 2nd ed., London: The Museums Association, 1974.

Stolow, Nathan, *Controlled Environment for Works of Art in Transit*, London: Butterworth, for the International Centre for the Study of the Conservation of Cultural Property, 1966.

Thomson, Garry, *Conservation and Museum Lighting*, 2nd ed., London: The Museums Association, 1974.

Thomson, Garry (ed.), *Recent Advances in Conservation*, London, 1963.

UNESCO, *The Conservation of Cultural Property, with Special Reference to Tropical Conditions*, Paris: UNESCO, 1968.

Waterer, John W., *A Guide to the Conservation and Restoration of Objects made wholly or partly of Leather*, London: Bell, 1972.

7. *Presentation and Display*

The Audio-Visual Equipment Directory, 18th ed., Fairfax, Virginia: National Audio-Visual Association, 1972.

Belcher, m., *et al.*, *Silk Screen Printing*, London: The Museums Association, 1973.

Beneš, Josef, 'Audio-visual media in museums', *Museum*, vol. 28 no. 2 (1976).

Buck Anne, *Costume*, in the series *Handbooks for Museum Curators*, London: The Museums Association, 1958.

Butler, Patricia M., *Temporary Exhibitions*, London: The Museums Association, 1970.

Cordingly, David, *Methods of Lettering for Museums*, 2nd ed., London: The Museums Association, 1975.

Cranstone, B. A. L., *Ethnography*, in the series *Handbooks for Museum Curators*, London: The Museums Association, 1958.

Franks, J. W., *A Guide to Herbarium Practice*, in the series *Handbooks for Museum Curators*, London: The Museums Association, 1958.

Hall, Pauline, *Display: the Vehicle for the Museum's Message*, 2nd ed., Ottawa: Canadian Museums Association, 1971.

Harding, E. G., *The Mounting of Prints and Drawings*, London: The Museums Association, 1972.

McLuhan, Marshall, *Exploration of the Ways, Means and Value of Museum Communication with the Viewing Public*, New York: Museum of the City of New York, 1969.

'Museums and interpretive techniques: an interim report', *Museums Journal*, vol. 75 no. 2 (September 1975).

Neal, Arminta, *Help! for the Small Museum: A Handbook of Exhibit Ideas and Methods*, 2nd ed., Boulder, Colorado: Pruett Press, 1969.

Norgate, Martin, *Linked Tape and Slide Audio-Visual Displays*, London: The Museums Association, 1973.

Norgate, Martin, 'Tape and slide scripting', *Museums Journal*, vol. 74, no. 4 (March 1975).

Pennyfather, Keith, *Interpretative Media and Facilities*, London: The Countryside Commission, 1975.

Rivière, Georges Henri, and Visser, Herman F. E., 'Museum showcases', special issue of *Museum*, vol. 12 no. 1 (1960); Paris: UNESCO.

UNESCO, 'Models in museums of science and technology', special issue of *Museum*, vol. 23 no. 4 (1970–1); Paris: UNESCO.

Warren, Jefferson T., *Exhibit Methods*, New York: Sterling Publishing Co., 1973.

Witteborg, Lothar P., 'Design standards in museum exhibits', *Curator*, 1/1958.

8. *The Educational Work of Museums*

Alexander, Eugenie, *Museums and How to Use Them*, London: Batsford, 1974.

Condit, Louise, 'Children and art', *Museums, Imagination and Education*, Paris: UNESCO, 1973.

Dierbeck, Robert E., 'Television and the museum', *Curator*, 2/1958.

Engström, K., and Johnels, A. G., *Natural History Museums and the Community*, Oslo: University Press, 1973.

Friedländer, Renate, *Mein Museumsbuch*, Köln: Kölner Museen, 1974.

Gazeau, Marie-Thérèse, *L'Enfant et le musée*, Paris: Les Editions Ouvrières, 1974.

Gibbs-Smith, Charles H., *The Arranging of Lectures*, 2nd ed., London: The Museums Association, 1974.

Group for Educational Services in Museums, *Museum Education Services*, 3rd ed., London: The Museums Association, 1975.

Harvey, E. D., and Friedberg, B., *A*

Museum for the People: a Report of Proceedings at the Seminar of Neighbourhood Museums, New York: Arno Press, 1971.

Hezekiah, Lloyd, 'Reflections on MUSE', *Museum News*, May 1972.

Larrabee, Eric (ed.), *Museums and Education*, Washington: Smithsonian Institution Press, 1968.

Larrauri, Iker, 'The school museum programme in Mexico', *Museum*, vol. 27, no. 2 (1975).

Museum und Schule in der Deutscher Demokratischen Republik, Berlin: Zentral Fachstelle für Museen, 1966.

Oliver, Ruth Norton, *Museums and the Environment: a Handbook for Education*, New York: Arkville Press, for the American Association of Museums, 1971.

Olofsson, Ulla Kedding, 'Temporary and travelling exhibitions', *Museums, Imagination and Education*, Paris: UNESCO, 1973.

Ordóñez, Coral, 'The Casa del Museo, Mexico City: an experiment in bringing the museum to the people', *Museum*, vol. 27 no. 2 (1975).

Osten, Gert von der, *Museum für eine Gesellschaft für Morgen*, Köln: Wienand Verlag, 1971.

Osten, von der Gert, *et al.*, *Unterricht im Museum*, 2nd ed., Köln: Kölner Museen, 1974.

Pirlot, Constant, *Musées, film, télévision*, Liège: Soledi, for ICOM, 1972.

Read, John, 'Television and the museum', *Museums, Imagination and Education*, Paris: UNESCO, 1973.

Rebetez, Pierre, *How to Visit a Museum*, Strasbourg: Council of Europe, Council for Cultural Co-operation, 1970.

UNESCO, 'Museums and education', special issue of *Museum*, vol. 21 no. 1 (1968).

Washburn, W. E., 'The museum's responsibility in adult education', *Curator*, vol. 7 no. 1 (1964).

Wittlin, Alma S., *The Museum: its History and its Tasks in Education*, London: Routledge and Kegan Paul, 1949.

Young, Rachel M. R., *Museum Enquiries*, London: The Museums Association, 1972.

Zetterberg, Hans L., *Museums and Adult Education*, London: Evelyn, Adams & Mackay, for ICOM, 1968.

9. *Research*

ICOM, *Museums and Research*, München: Deutsches Museum, for ICOM, 1970.

Neustupný, Jiří, *Museums and Research*, Prague: National Museum, 1968.

10. *Public Relations and Market Research*

Arber, A. J. N., 'A survey of visitors to the Rouault Exhibition at Manchester City Art Gallery', *Museums Journal*, vol. 75 no. 1 (June 1975).

Arnell, Ulla, *et al.*, *Going to Exhibitions*. Stockholm: Riksutställningar, 1976.

Barton, Kenneth, 'Recording attendances at Portsmouth City Museums', *Museums Journal*, vol. 73 no. 4 (1974).

Bourdieu, Pierre, and Darbel, Alain, *L'Amour et l'art: les musées et leur public*, Paris, 1966.

Cameron, Duncan E., and Abbey, D. S., 'Museum audience research', *Museum News* (October 1961).

Digby, Peter Wingfield, *Visitors to Three London Museums*, London: HMSO, 1974.

Dixon, Brian, *et al.*, *The Museum and the Canadian Public*, Toronto: Culturcan Publications for Arts and Culture Branch, Department of the Secretary of State, Government of Canada, 1974.

Doughty, Philip S., 'Surveys at the Ulster Museum', *Museums Journal*, vol. 88 nos. 1 and 2 (June and September 1968).

Erwin, David G., 'The Belfast public and the Ulster Museum', *Museums Journal*, vol. 70 no. 4 (March 1971).

Goldhammer, Herbert, 'Über die systematische Entwicklung von differenzierten Formen und Methoden der Bildungs- und Erziehungsarbeit im Kunstmuseum', *Neue Museumskunde*, vol. 14 no. 3 (1971).

McWilliams, Brian, and Hopwood, Joyce, 'The public of Norwich Castle Museum, 1971–72', *Museums Journal*, vol. 72 no 4 (March 1973).

'The Metropolitan Museum and its public: highlights of the Yankelovich survey', New York: *The Metropolitan Museum of Art Report*, 1973–4.

'Public Relations', papers from the 1964 Museums Association Conference, London: *Museums Journal*, vol. 64 no. 3 (December 1964).

Sizer, C. A., 'Museum function or policy: a comment on the public of the Ulster Museum', *Museums Journal*, vol. 68 no. 4 (March 1969).

Vervey, P., 'Report on Georges Rouault Exhibition', London: *Arts Council Bulletin*, 1974.

Withrow, W. J., 'Practical implications of the Toronto study', *Museum*, vol. 22 no. 3/4 (1969).

Glossary

In all languages, the way in which members of the museum profession attempt to communicate with one another, both in speaking and in writing, has been seriously contaminated in recent years by the terminology which is current in the pseudo-sciences of psychology and sociology. Museologists are becoming increasingly familiar with such statements as:

Too many exhibits, or an imbalance between exhibits and labels, might well have caused conceptual discontinuity and prevented the transfer to the long-term memory of stimuli derived from the exhibit.

And

From a series of pilot tests conducted to establish a hierarchy of criteria using the physical properties of minerals and rocks and an indication of conscious and subconscious perceptions, tactile experience was found to rank very highly.

Exhibits are no longer exhibits, but 'series of learning stations'; a modern curator does not try to make his collections interesting and intelligible, but 'plans a sequence of learning experiences'; teachers go round museums with 'customised worksheets' to tell them how much their pupils are getting out of the visit.

This kind of language will eventually, no doubt, work its way through the museum system and be flushed away to join the linguistic absurdities of previous generations. Meanwhile, however, it forms a considerable barrier to understanding, especially internationally, and one can do no more than try to interpret whatever meaning may lie behind this inbred terminology. Some of the items in the glossary which follows have this aim in mind. The remainder represent an attempt to introduce a little more agreement and genuine comprehension into a situation which has lately shown signs of getting out of control.

It should be emphasised that, although this particular glossary includes only English terms, an equally long and discouraging list could be compiled in French, German, Russian or any other of the world's major languages.

Accession. Until recently, this could be used only as a noun. One referred to a museum's accessions, meaning the additions it made to its collections. Nowadays, however, American museums accession objects and the process is known as accessioning, an innovation which displeases older people, but is accepted as normal by most of those under thirty.

Air-conditioned. If one says that a room or a building is air-conditioned, one means, or should mean, that the temperature, humidity and cleanliness of the air are all exactly as one would have them and under constant control. Not infrequently, however, 'air-conditioned' is found to imply something much less complete and thoroughgoing than this, and becomes almost a synonym for 'artificially ventilated'. It is well to insist on a precise definition of what is being offered.

Antiquities. There seems no good reason why this useful word should not mean remains, relics or monuments of antiquity in a general sense, with no restriction as to period or region of the world. It is often used parochially, however, to refer exclusively to the antiquities of Greece, Rome and the Middle East.

Applied art. This very vague, but much-used, term means 'art put to some practical use' or 'art which embellishes everyday objects'. It is frequently and inevitably a near-synonym for 'decorative art' and 'industrial art'. An advertisement in the *Museums Journal*, in 1972, invited applications for the post of 'Keeper of Decorative Arts' in the Leicester Museum Service, and went on to say, among other details, that 'the successful candidate will be responsible for all the important applied art collections'.

Artefact or *Artifact.* Literally, 'skilfully made', but often used by those members of the museum world with little or no knowledge of Latin to signify any man-made object, however crude or primitive it may be.

Bygones. A useful word, too simple and Saxon for the more scientifically-minded professionals, who tend to mistrust words without Greek or Latin roots, but now showing signs of a revival. It is a generic term for objects once in everyday use and has overtones of affection or nostalgia for the articles in question, which may account for the unwillingness of some people to use it.

Catalogue raisonné. A catalogue containing detailed descriptions and assessments of the items mentioned in it, a catalogue characterised by scholarly length and depth. An accepted English equivalent for this rather snobbish and off-putting term is badly needed. 'Full catalogue' or 'catalogue in depth' might meet the situation.

Cataloguing. The process of compiling a full methodical description of an accession to a museum collection and adding it to the museum's information system.

Ceramics. Archaeologists and craftsmen tend to speak of 'pottery', but museum people seem to prefer the more upstage word 'ceramics'. The range of meaning varies. To some curators and scholars it appears to cover any object made of baked clay, to others pottery, porcelain and tiles, to others again pottery and porcelain, but not tiles. For this reason, to say that a museum's collection includes 'ceramics' can be misleading, and there is need for more uniformity and agreement in the matter.

Children's museum. The main difficulty here is to know when a child ceases to be a child. In America, but not, as yet, elsewhere in the English-speaking world, there are 'junior museums', which cater mainly for teenagers, and 'children's museums', which have a younger age-group in mind. Nowadays a children's museum is usually one which plans and presents its collections and organises its activities in ways which seem likely to appeal to children, but the term can also be applied, with perfect propriety, to museums which contain material, such as toys or dolls, which children enjoy seeing, but which can also give great pleasure to adults.

Circulation pattern. A somewhat pompous term, indicating the route which visitors are observed to choose as they move from floor to floor and gallery to gallery, the extent to which they linger at particular points, and those parts of the museum which receive larger or smaller numbers of people. Many of the large museums have prepared circulation charts, which closely resemble the traffic-flow diagrams used by highway engineers and the police.

Colonial. A difficult word, to be used with great tact and discrimination. Used objectively, the 'colonial period' means the years during which a particular country was ruled by a foreign power. By extension, 'colonial' describes what was made or took place during that period. One therefore speaks of 'colonial art' in Brazil or Mexico, and 'colonial architecture' or 'colonial furniture' in the United States. For many people in America, especially in the North, however, 'colonial' also implies 'hand-made, beautifully designed, of high quality, belonging to the pre-factory age', much as 'Georgian' does in Britain. Over much of the rest of

the world, however, it has a pejorative flavour, recalling the bad old days of oppression and exploitation by foreigners.

Communication/Communicator. This is one of the new in-words, and not only, of course, among museologists. It is widely used, but often without adding markedly to understanding or enlightenment. Since, however, there is now a new museum sub-profession, communicator, some effort to find a real concept behind the word seems desirable. The task is far from easy.

A book, a painting or a play may, in the old-fashioned sense of the word, communicate, it may have something to say which catches the attention and appeals to the mind or the senses. This is not the same, however, as Communication, with a capital C. Beethoven and Rembrandt may have communicated with many millions of people, but they do not Communicate. They are not Communicators. To deserve this title, one must have:

(*a*) used approved psychological and sociological techniques to determine the characteristics and needs of the audience;

(*b*) decided what it is that has to be Communicated;

(*c*) worked out a form of presentation which will ensure that Communication takes place;

(*d*) arranged appropriate tests to discover if Communication has taken place.

Conservation. Conservation, not to be confused with Preservation (q.v.), involves treating buildings or museum objects in such a way as to improve their condition and lengthen their life. This has now become a profession, or sub-profession, in its own right, and relies on scientific knowledge and equipment which did not, for the most part, exist a quarter of a century ago.

Costumes. This word may mean either (*a*) yesterday's clothing, irrespective of social status, or (*b*) the clothing once worn by socially superior people. Most museums seem to find 'clothes' or 'clothing' rather low. Collections of costumes sound more prestigious and valuable than collections of clothes. The most useful distinction, which shows some signs of becoming adopted, is to keep 'costumes' for ceremonial or exceptionally elegant clothes.

Country park. It is not always easy to distinguish a country park from a national park or a wildlife park, and perhaps there is no great point in trying. If there is a genuine difference, it is probably that the country park is on a smaller scale than a national park and that its emphasis is on domestication and man-controlled nature, rather than on nature-in-the-wild.

Crafts. Strictly speaking, 'craft' refers to the skill, not to the products of that skill. Basket-making is a craft, a basket is a craft-product. In ordinary usage, however, the distinction between the two has become blurred, so that many people will, for example, speak of a 'craft shop' in a way that suggests that they go into the shop in order to buy crafts. There is no need at all, however, for museums to imitate this particular manifestation of illiteracy. Some museums, it may be noted, claim to illustrate 'crafts' and others 'handicrafts'. It does not appear possible to draw a sharp dividing line between the two words, although it has been suggested that 'crafts' implies a rather higher degree of artistic quality, smaller-sized products and less elaborate equipment than 'handicrafts'. This appears doubtful. What seems more likely is that 'craft' is more attractive, especially to journalists, because it is shorter than 'handicraft', and that 'craft' and 'craftsmen' are a much more practical pair of words than 'handicraft' and 'handicraftsman'.

Curate/Curating. Curators and the curatorial function have been with us for a long time, but the verb 'to curate' and the noun 'curating' are recent innovations, thought up in the United States and now increasingly widely used. At one time it was normal to say 'I am a curator at the City Museum, Manchester', but now there is a serious chance, unless a determined and successful counter-attack is launched, of 'I curate the City Museum, Manchester' or 'I go in for curating at the City Museum, Manchester'. One has not yet reached the point, however, of 'I keep the British Museum'.

Customised. Customised is an American word, meaning 'made to suit the requirements of a particular customer'. It has recently entered the museum field, in such compounds as 'customised worksheets', which are nothing more remarkable than 'specially prepared'. There is nothing that 'customised' can do that 'specially prepared' cannot do equally efficiently and a great deal more elegantly. The bluff of 'customised' should be called immediately and its use avoided by all decent people.

Decorative arts. 'Applied arts' and 'decorative arts' have become almost interchangeable terms, although there are those who insist that there is a difference, in that the decorative arts are supposed to place a rather smaller emphasis on the usefulness of the object in question. This is difficult to support. Is a vase, for instance, to be regarded as an example of decorative art and a bed-coverlet of applied art? What form of art is a frivolous hat?

Designer. This is a comparatively new profession. The pre-1945 museum world had no designers, in the sense of people who had overall responsibility for the arrangement and appearance of an exhibit, a gallery or a complete museum. What causes problems, however, and makes it difficult to arrive at a satisfactory definition of 'designer' is that the extent of a designer's responsibility varies a great deal from project to project and employer to employer. In some cases he is a mere cook, hired to prepare a meal to a menu and set of recipes strictly laid down by those who pay him, but in others he himself plans the meal from the sketchiest instructions and information. Broadly speaking, the independent designer is likely to demand and get more responsibility and freedom than the designer on the staff of a museum, and sometimes the difference is so great that one has good reason to wonder if the two kinds of person belong to the same profession. What can be said with confidence, however, is that the successful designer, the good designer, is someone who understands what the museum, at its best, is trying to do and who is, in the true sense of the term, a creative artist who has breathed his own spirit into the material which has been given to him. The person who does no more than give evidence of expertise as a visual technician is not a designer.

Documentation. There is no essential difference between documentation and cataloguing. Both are concerned with accumulating, selecting and recording the information which exists about each item in a museum collection. The distinction, where it exists, is one of scope and detail. A catalogue entry consists of a summary of what is known and observable about an object, together with the circumstances of its acquisition and its history since it entered the museum. The documentation relating to the object would contain the catalogue entry, but might also include what could be described as context material – articles, notes and pictures about typology, materials, sale prices and so on, which would set the particular item in its place among comparable and related material.

Educational programme/department. Any museum is, in the broad sense, educational. Without any deliberate attempt on the part of its management and staff, it can and no doubt often does allow its visitors to acquire fresh information, become interested in new subjects, reshape their values, change their order of priorities – all the things which education is supposed to do. An educational programme or department represents a conscious, organised attempt to do with the help of specialist staff what is otherwise left to chance. It is usually, but not exclusively, concerned with providing special facilities for schoolchildren. In many museums, in fact, 'educational department' is synonymous with 'schools department'.

Environment. A much-beloved word nowadays. It means, when it means anything, the environment in which human beings live and work, which is the equivalent of the earth and its atmosphere and everything on the earth. More commonly, it is used in a number of more restricted senses – urban areas, the countryside, the air we breathe. A study of the use which is made of this superficially attractive, 'concerned', word suggests that one should try very hard not to use it by itself, since without the help of other, limiting words it is likely to mean very little. To speak of 'the urban environment' or 'a child's home environment' is useful; 'the Minister of the Environment' and 'environmental problems' sound impressive, but mean practically nothing.

Ethnography, ethnology. These two words are very commonly confused, and perhaps it is now too late to restore the original distinction between them. Ethnology is the study of cultures and of their physical manifestations, in the form of clothing, tools, music, crafts and so on. Ethnography could be defined as applied ethnology, the description and presentation of the ethnological material. Museums are concerned with both ethnology and ethnography, but the person who attempts to communicate his knowledge to the public is more likely to be an ethnographer than an ethnologist.

Exploratory situation. A new museum jargon phrase. It means, briefly, a planned combination of museum activity and museum display by which the visitor is encouraged and helped to discover information for himself.

Fine Art(s). A fundamentally absurd phrase, which one is still unfortunately compelled to use. It means works of art which have only their beauty to recommend them. Fine Art items are essentially useless items, to be appreciated only through the eye. But the definition is not foolproof, since one can never be absolutely sure that a Ming vase would not be used for umbrellas or a Rembrandt and its frame as a tea-tray. Most things have possible uses, however perverted and unlikely they may be. The criterion is presumably the artist's original intention. One has to ask, 'Would the creator of the Ming vase have expected his masterpiece to be used as a useful household article, or as an object of contemplation?' The object of contemplation is Fine Art, the useful household article is Applied Art.

Folk Art. The various forms of painting, carving and ornamental crafts carried out by the common people in their spare time. 'Popular art', a literal translation from the French which sounds odd and misplaced in English, has become barely usable since the universal acceptance of Pop Art as a recognised genre. To find Popular Art in one's local museum of ethnography and Pop Art in the Museum of Contemporary Art in the next street is to confuse both curators and the public unreasonably. So, for all its cosy, patronising, folksy overtones, Folk Art apparently has to stay, until something more satisfactory turns up.

Folklore. The traditional beliefs, legends and customs of the common people. A museum cannot, strictly speaking, contain folklore, although it can find ways of illustrating and reflecting it, by means of collections of artifacts. What has happened over the years is that 'folklore' has come to be used as an abbreviation of 'the tangible evidence of folklore'. It is impossible to draw a line between folklore on the one hand and ethnology and ethnography on the other. One shades off into the other. In general, however, ethnography and ethnology are considered to be more systematic and 'scientific' than folklore and have a higher reputation in the museum profession.

Furniture, furnishings. The two words are not used with any great precision but, broadly speaking, museums use the label 'furniture' for objects one sits at or on, or lies on, or keeps one's possessions in, and furnishings for everything else in the house, except for another vague category, 'domestic equipment', the use of which is mostly confined to the kitchen and outhouses. 'Domestic equipment' or its synonym, 'household equipment', are the housewife's working tools.

Graphics/graphic communications. In the language of designers and display artists, graphics are usually two-dimensional messages, as distinct from the three-dimensional objects which they describe and which represent the bulk of a museum's stock-in-trade. They may consist of drawings, photographs, typography or hand-written lettering. Some museums and writers on museum topics have chosen, for some reason, to narrow the meaning of graphics to 'messages in letters and figures'. This habit seems to offer no particular gain.

Heritage. A much-used, trendy, emotion-loaded word of the 1970s. One wonders how previous generations got along without it. Phrases such as 'safeguarding our heritage', 'conserving our heritage' and 'creating an awareness of our heritage' are to be found in every museum journal and heard at every museum conference. The definition appears to be 'objects of cultural importance which have been handed down from the past'. The countryside and the coast are not normally included under the heading 'national heritage' or 'European heritage', although exactly why it is difficult to say. One would suspect that this appallingly hard-worked word

will have been worn out and discarded well before the end of the 1980s.

Historical archaeologist. This very curious profession was invented in the United States and appears, as yet, to be little found outside that country. If one meets an historical archaeologist and asks him to define himself, the most frequent reply is that he is a person who has graduated in historical archaeology in order to qualify himself to work in that field, which does not help a great deal. In fact he is an archaeologist who specialises in the historical period, that is, the period covered by written records. This is a peculiarly American concept, not relevant to many other countries. There are, for example, written records of the history of Rome, but an archaeologist specialising in Roman material would not describe himself as an historical archaeologist. We are therefore obliged to define the term at present as meaning 'archaeologist concerned with American sites of the sixteenth to twentieth centuries', although no doubt another ten years will see the extension of the profession to other countries and continents.

Historic(al) sites. A loosely-used term, depending on what one means by a site. At what point does an historic building become a site? Is it always a site or does it become one only when it is in a ruinous condition or down to the foundations? One asks, not because the distinction is of any great importance, but because the existence of booklets listing 'Historic buildings and sites' and 'Historic monuments and sites' suggests that to some people at least there is a significant difference. The matter is further complicated by the fact that a complex of buildings and installations is often described as a site. The public expectation seems to be, however, that a site is where something used to be, rather than where something now is, and the most sensible practice would therefore be to follow common usage in the matter.

House-museum. The Great Man's former home, or, at least, a house in which he once stayed, and in which the visitor can see a collection of his possessions and, if he was an artist, musician or writer, of his works. Sometimes, unfortunately, the name is all, and the contents of the house

may have no direct connection with the man whose name it bears. This smacks of dishonesty and can cause disappointment and frustration to people who have been misled by the museum's title.

Indexing. Recording the bare details of an object added to the museum's collection, in order that it can be quickly and accurately identified and located. A step taken prior to cataloguing and designed to meet a different set of requirements.

Industrial art. A nineteenth-century term, meaning applied art produced by machinery or on a mass-production basis. A wide range of metalware, pottery, glass and textiles received the accolade of 'industrial art' as a reward for being better designed and better-looking than the average. Nowadays, with most things made by machinery, the phrase is of little value as a description of contemporary products, but it is still helpful in connection with earlier material.

Information point. A desk within the public area of a museum at which visitors' queries can be answered.

Interpretation centre/interpreter. Interpretation is what, in the opinion of many museologists, sorts out the progressive museums from the rest. It is not, however, easy to say what interpretation is, although one can describe a number of museum departments which call themselves interpretation centres or visitor centres and attempt to discover some key factor which they have in common. Their aim appears to be to prepare the visitor for coming to grips with the museum proper, by giving him guidelines through the collections and sufficient background material to allow him to see the particular museum in its context. The interpretation centre has to assume that visitors come knowing nothing, and the development of techniques aimed at partially filling this vacuum demands great tact and skill. An interpretation centre, one might say, makes it less likely that a visitor will blunder round the museum in a fog of ignorance and prejudice.

Learning station. A unit in a planned series of exhibits which are designed to present a coherent theme or body of information.

Living museum. This term is used in two senses: a museum in which there is a good deal of participation (q.v.) on the part of visitors, and a museum in which some or all of the exhibits are actually alive. It seems preferable and sensible to confine oneself to the second usage.

National museum. This has different meanings in different countries. It may mean that the museum in question is financed by the State, or, like the Swiss Transport Museum, that it is a country's main or only effort in this particular direction, or that it is the central mother-museum, controlling the activities of provincial museums in the same field. The term has to be interpreted within its national context.

National park. An area protected from building development and from the requirements of the armed forces, which has been designated for preservation because of its amenities or historical importance. The early national parks were all, in effect, nature reserves and most of them are still that, but in recent years the concept has been widened, as at Ironbridge, in England, to include industrial and transport sites. There seems to be no reason to object to this.

Natural history. This, in its various translations, originally meant the systematic study of all natural objects, whether animal, vegetable or mineral. More recently, it has tended to become restricted to the study of living creatures and to acquire something of a popular and non-scientific flavour. When an institution describes itself as a museum of natural history, or says it has natural history collections, it is not always possible to decide exactly what is meant.

Natural science(s). At one time the natural sciences were concerned, briefly and simply, with the study of nature and its phenomena. Now the term is often reserved for those sciences, principally chemistry and physics, which do not involve the study of living matter, although a wider and equally current definition includes the biological sciences as well.

Open-air museum. Following the original example, Skansen, an open-air museum still means, for the most part, a collection of rural houses, farmhouses, churches, workshops and mills which have been brought together from different parts of the country and re-erected on the museum site. There are, however, a number of other kinds of museum, ranging from industrial archaeology

sites to sculpture-parks, which seem to deserve the title 'open-air'. In future, they will probably be called 'outdoor museums', leaving 'open-air' for something closer to the Skansen type.

Palaeontology. The scientific study of fossil animals and plants. The key words are 'scientific study'. Many museums, however bad, contain fossils, but what they engage in and offer cannot reasonably be described as palaeontology.

Participation. Active museum visiting. Participation may take many forms: pressing buttons to make models work and charts come alive; speaking on special museum telephones or television circuits; looking at one's face in a mirror to decide one's anthropological type, and so on. It can also mean taking part in workshop activities, demonstrations or performances organised by the museum.

Peasant. The word is not used, either in Britain or America, except in a derogatory sense, to describe any of the present inhabitants of those countries. In the English-speaking world farming families, no matter how small their scale of operations, do not enjoy being called peasants. It has to be farmer, however flattering this description may sometimes be.

Pioneer. Much used in the United States, Canada, Australia, South Africa and New Zealand, as a synonym for 'first-generation white settlers' in an area. Non-white immigrants are, for some reason, rarely referred to as 'settlers'. Negro and Chinese people are consequently not represented, except in a subsidiary role, in American and Canadian pioneer museums.

Preservation. Protecting objects from deliberate or accidental destruction. Until the establishment of conservation as a professional activity, 'preservation', in most people's minds, included some element of treatment against further decay, but nowadays the two words have different and fairly precise definitions. The conservationist is not concerned with acquisition, ownership and legal protection; the preservationist is. Conservation makes preservation possible, and vice versa.

Regional museum. The difficulty is to find an English word which corresponds to the German *Heimatmuseum*. A *Heimatmuseum*, easily trans-

latable into most languages other than English, means, roughly, 'museum of the area in which I live', but the word has a patriotic and cosy element which the translation misses. It is both a Little-Grey-Home-in-the-West museum and a Fatherland or Motherland museum. 'Regional museum', by contrast, is administrative, non-emotional, cold.

Resource-centre. An American term, now partly assimilated into British English. It means a room, department or building which houses museum objects and a range of audio-visual material likely to be helpful to teachers.

Retrieval. The process of extracting the information one needs from the places in which this information is stored – a computer, a printed catalogue or a book. One does not dig out information any more, one retrieves it.

Sign-posting. Making sure that visitors find what they are looking for in a museum and that they understand what they are looking at once they have found it. A dynamic form of labelling.

Simulation. The modern preferred word for replica or reconstruction.

Site-museum. A museum set up on an historic site, in order to protect, display and explain what has been found there.

Stimulus exhibition. A museum exhibit which aims more at arousing visitors' curiosity and initiative than at providing them with information.

Structured interview. An interview, designed for gathering information about the characteristics and opinions of museum visitors, which keeps replies within a tightly-prescribed framework and uses one stage of the interview to help the next.

Study collections. A collection maintained specifically for students and with no pretensions to attractiveness or glamour.

Supportive services. The services, such as public relations, visitor research and library facilities, which make it easier for museum staffs to do their job adequately.

Travelling exhibition. Identical with a circulating exhibition. A display which has been planned and constructed to give people living at a distance from a particular museum the benefits of its collections and expertise.

Visitation. A dreadful, totally illiterate American innovation, to be absolutely barred. The Visitation of the Holy Ghost to the Virgin Mary, or the visitation of a diocese by its bishop, is correct and in order. The visitation of museums, meaning the number and kinds of people who visit museums, is a nonsensical barbarism.

Visitor centre. See Interpretation centre.

Volunteers. People who carry out museum duties without payment, and for the satisfaction of helping the museum and the community.

Workers' movement. Many museums in the socialist countries announce that they have collections illustrating 'the workers' movement'. This is a general, unscientific term, describing the forces and activities which led to the establishment of the present régime. 'Workers' movement', like 'revolutionary movement', looks strange in English, but it is difficult to think of a substitute.

Worksheet. A prepared paper on which visitors, particularly schoolchildren, can note the information they obtain from museum exhibits and their reactions to it. Other types of worksheet allow teachers to 'structure' the way in which they present museum collections to their pupils.

Picture Credits

All the pictures reproduced in this book are by permission of the Museum mentioned in the caption, with the following exceptions.

Index

Note: Throughout the text and therefore here in the Index, foreign names have been anglicised, except where a translation would have been intolerably clumsy, as in the case of Römisch-Germanisches Museum, or where the original name is so well known and so much part of the life of the country in question as to make an English version unnecessary or absurd. The Deutsches Museum in Munich and the Bibliothèque Nationale in Paris, for example, were felt to be of this order.